Changes in Western
European Banking

Changes in Western European Banking

EDWARD P. M. GARDENER

University College of North Wales

and

PHILIP MOLYNEUX

University College of North Wales

London
UNWIN HYMAN
Boston   Sydney   Wellington

Published by the Academic Division of
Unwin Hyman Ltd
15/17 Broadwick Street, London W1V 1FP, UK

Unwin Hyman Inc.
955 Massachusetts Avenue, Cambridge , MA 02139, USA

Allen & Unwin (Australia) Ltd
8 Napier Street, North Sydney, NSW 2060, Australia

Allen & Unwin (New Zealand) Ltd
in association with the Port Nicholson Press Ltd
Compusales Building, 75 Ghuznee Street, Wellington 1, New Zealand

First published in 1990

British Library Cataloguing in Publication Data

Changes in Western European banking. – (Studies in financial
  institutions and markets).
  1. European Community countries. Banking
  I. Gardener, Edward P. M. II. Molyneux, Philip III.
  Series
  332.1094

ISBN 0–04–445220–9

Library of Congress Cataloging in Publication Data
Gardener, Edward P. M.
    Changes in Western European banking / by Edward P. M. Gardener
  and Philip Molyneux.
    p. cm. – (Studies in financial institutions and markets : 6)
  Includes bibliographical references.
  ISBN 0–04–445220–9
  1. Banks and banking – Europe. 2. Europe 1992. 1. Molyneux,
  Philip. II. Title. III. Series.
  HG2974.G37 1990
  332.1′094–dc20
                                                                    90–34538
                                                                       CIP

Typeset in 9 on 11 point Times by Computape (Pickering) Ltd, North Yorkshire
and printed in Great Britain by Cambridge University Press

Contents

	Page
List of tables	xiii
List of figures	xvi
Preface	xvii
Chapter one Introduction	1
Background	1
General perspective	1
Before the revolution	1
The new era	2
Changes in Western European banking	3
Analysing change	5
Towards the year 2000	5
A methodological backcloth	6
An integrative framework	7
Concluding Remarks	7
Chapter two Current trends in banking and financial systems	9
Introduction	9
Real and financial developments: stimulants of banking change	9
Economic and related sectoral trends	9
Financial systems and the macroeconomy	12
Banking regulatory and policy trends	14
European institutions and international influences	16
Perspectives of European banking systems	19
A short history of banking in Europe	19
Structural differences between European banking systems	20
European banking compared to US and Japanese banking	23
Conclusion	24

Chapter three   Structure and performance   28

Introduction   28
Structure and competition   28
  Historical and evolutionary perspective   28
  The structure and performance relationship   29
  Rules and regulations affecting structure   30
  Competition and competitors   30
Size, concentration and performance characteristics   32
  Size and concentration   32
  Performance and ownership characteristics of the largest banks   34
  Competitive pressures in the run-up to 1992   36
  Structural trends and balance sheet effects   37
Conclusion   39

Chapter four   Monetary regulation, 1992 and supervision   42

Introduction   42
Monetary policy in Europe   42
  The monetary environment   42
  Historical overview   43
  Monetary aggregates and contemporary monetary policy   47
  Financial innovation and monetary policy   49
  European Monetary System and the European Central Bank   50
Banking supervision and 1992   52
  The EC environment   52
  Banking supervision and convergence   53
  European convergence   58
  Investment and securities business   59
Conclusion   60

Chapter five   Changes in balance sheet structure   64

Introduction   64
Changes in balance sheet structures and income statements   64
  Historical overview   64
  Changes in balance sheet and income statement structures of all Euro-
  pean banks   68
  Changes in balance sheet and income statement structures of large
  European commercial banks   71
  Changes in balance sheet and income statement structures of European
  savings banks   73
Developments in asset and liability management and OBS finance   73
  Objectives and methods of asset and liability management   73

CONTENTS

Off-balance sheet activities of European banks 76
Growth in off-balance sheet activities 77
Comparative capital adequacy, profits and PERs 78
Conclusion 81

Chapter six Retail banking 83

Introduction 83
A perspective of retail banking 84
  Historical context 84
  European trends: demand factors 85
  European trends: supply factors 89
Market environment 93
  Products and services 93
  Competition 98
  Technology 102
  Balance sheet implications 106
Conclusion 107

Chapter seven Corporate banking 110

Introduction 110
A perspective of corporate banking 110
  Historical context 110
  European trends 113
  Relations with industry 114
Market environment 117
  Products and services 117
  Selected country comparisons 118
  Competition 119
  The securitization challenge 122
  Technology 124
Conclusion 126

Chapter eight International banking and foreign banks 128

Introduction 128
The internationalization phenomenon 128
  Historical perspective 128
  Modern international banking 130
  Internationalization and globalization 131
International and multinational banking 133
  Foreign banks and Europe 133

CONTENTS

Nationality structure of international banking and the expansion of
networks   135
Products and services   137
Innovation and fragility   140
Conclusion   141

Chapter nine Financial centres   143
Introduction   143
Major European centres   143
The history, role and development of major European centres   143
London   146
Frankfurt and Paris   150
Switzerland, Luxembourg and Amsterdam   153
Other financial centres and 1992   157
Other European financial centres   157
Copenhagen   157
Stockholm   158
Brussels   160
Milan   160
Madrid   161
Smaller financial centres   162
Why host an international financial centre?   162
General implications of 1992   163
Conclusion   164

Chapter ten Securities markets and business   167

Introduction   167
Capital markets   167
Historical perspective and the economic role of stock exchanges   167
A comparative overview   168
Exchange reforms   170
Securities business   173
New issues and trading   173
Rise of the Euroequity   174
Securitization developments   176
Risk-management products   181
Conclusion   183

Chapter eleven Investment banking   185

Introduction   185
Industrial structure and competition   185
Definitions   185

Historical background	187
Modern evolution and structure	189
Products and services	192
Market environment	192
Capital raising	194
Advisory, mergers and acquisitions	196
Brokerage, trading and investment management	199
Conclusion	202

Chapter twelve Banking strategy and 1992	204

Introduction	204
Strategic management challenges	204
Investment banking strategy after the crash	204
Strategic marketing orientation	207
The build-up to 1992	208
Towards 1992 and beyond	214
Organizational design as strategy	214
The size issue	215
Beyond economies of scale	216
Conclusion	218

Statistical and country appendix	221

Austria	222
Belgium	226
Denmark	230
Finland	235
France	239
Greece	243
Republic of Ireland	247
Italy	251
Luxembourg	255
Netherlands	258
Norway	262
Portugal	265
Spain	268
Sweden	272
Switzerland	276
United Kingdom	280
West Germany	285

Glossary	290

Index	294

List of tables

2.1	Growth of GDP at constant market prices	10
2.2	Average annual growth rates	10
2.3	Net savings per capita as a proportion of net disposable income per capita at constant prices	12
2.4	Economic dimensions of the financial services sector, 1985	13
2.5	Summary of sector ownership of European banking institutions, 1988	21
2.6	Change in market shares of European banks by ownership category, 1983–8	22
3.1	Deposit bank assets as a percentage of GNP	32
3.2	Market concentration and size of banking sectors in Europe, 1988	33
3.3	Statistical summary of the ownership of top banks in the EC, 1987	35
3.4	Gross income as a multiple of operating expenses for commercial banks	38
4.1	Principal policy planning indicators in the early 1980s	45
4.2	Basle transitional arrangements	56
4.3	BIS proposals: some sample estimates, 1988	57
5.1	Percentage of bank liabilities remunerated on money market terms	65
5.2	Demand deposits as a percentage of total bank liabilities	66
5.3	Changes in balance sheet, income statement and other accounting items for all European banks between 1982 and 1986	69
5.4	Extreme values of European banks' balance sheet items, 1986	70
5.5	Changes in balance sheet, income statement and other items for large European banks, 1982–6	72
5.6	Changes in balance sheet, income statement and other items for European savings banks, 1982–6	74
5.7	Banks' off-balance-sheet items	77
5.8	Banking rates of return and capital adequacy in selected countries	79
5.9	Comparative profitability and capital ratios for *The Banker* Top 300 banks in Europe, 1987	80
5.10	Market characteristics of European banks	81
6.1	Spread of banking habit and wage payment methods	87

6.2 Household financial wealth, debt and lend-back ratios, 1981 and 1986   88

6.3 Commercial banks, mutual and postal institutions, market shares, 1986   90

6.4 UK high-interest chequing accounts   94

6.5 Plastic cards, end-1986   96

6.6 Retail banking products expected to be offered by new entrants in selected European countries   100

6.7 Percentage differences in prices of standard retail financial products compared with the average of the four lowest national prices   101

6.8 Overview of payment systems and services in EC member states, 1986   103

6.9 ATMs in the European Community, United States and Japan, January 1987   104

7.1 Debt/equity ratios of the non-financial corporate sector   112

7.2 Funds raised by domestic non-financial borrowers   113

7.3 Lending to industry by the banking sector   115

7.4 The extent to which different European financial institutions are significant in providing business loans   120

7.5 Corporate banking products offered by new entrants in selected European countries   121

7.6 Competitive strengths and weaknesses in European corporate banking   123

8.1 Euromarket financial activities   132

8.2 Average size of 'international' banks in London   132

8.3 Foreign banks in selected European countries   134

8.4 International bank assets, by nationality of banks   135

8.5 Gross earnings margins of banks   137

8.6 The currency composition of reporting banks' cross-border positions   138

9.1 Economies of scale and financial centres   145

9.2 UK banking sector deposits, 1988   146

9.3 External position of banks in individual banking centres, end-1988   149

9.4 How Frankfurt compares with other stock exchanges   152

10.1 European stock market performance   169

10.2 Market value of securities listed on the ISE   170

10.3 International equities   175

10.4 Top lead and co-lead managers: international equities, 1987   177

10.5 Global commercial paper market   178

11.1 Selected indicators of primary Eurobond concentration   192

11.2 Management buy-outs and buy-ins in Europe, 1980–87   198

11.3 Growth of cross-border portfolio investment: pension and tax-exempt funds   200

11.4 Top 15 International ERISA fund managers   201

LIST OF TABLES

12.1	Top lead managers of Eurobond new issues	206
12.2	Planning issues: country comparisons	206
12.3	Recent merger and acquisition activity in key European markets	209
A1.1	Austrian banking system: institutional and sector breakdown by assets	223
A1.2	Sector ownership 1983–8: Austrian banking system	224
A1.3	Top five Austrian banks, 1988	225
A2.1	Belgian banking system: institutional and sector breakdown by assets	227
A2.2	Sector ownership 1982–8: Belgian banking system	228
A2.3	Top five Belgian banks, 1988	229
A3.1	Danish banking system: institutional and sector breakdown by deposits	231
A3.2	Danish banking system: institutional and sector breakdown by advances	232
A3.3	Sector ownership 1983–8: Danish banking system	233
A3.4	Top five Danish banks, 1988	234
A4.1	Finnish banking system: institutional and sector breakdown by assets	236
A4.2	Sector ownership 1982–8: Finnish banking system	237
A4.3	Top five Finnish banks, 1988	238
A5.1	French banking system: institutional and sector breakdown by assets	240
A5.2	Sector ownership 1983–8: French banking system	241
A5.3	Top five French banks, 1988	242
A6.1	Greek banking system: institutional and sector breakdown by bank credits	244
A6.2	Sector ownership 1983–8: Greek banking system	245
A6.3	Top five Greek banks, 1988	246
A7.1	Ireland's banking system: institutional and sector breakdown by assets	248
A7.2	Sector ownership 1983–8: Irish banking system	249
A7.3	Top two Irish banks, 1988	250
A8.1	Italian banking system: institutional and sector breakdown by assets	252
A8.2	Sector ownership 1983–8: Italian banking system	253
A8.3	Top five Italian banks, 1988	254
A9.1	Luxembourg banking system: institutions	255
A9.2	Top five Luxembourg banks, 1988	257
A10.1	Netherlands banking system: institutional and sector breakdown by assets	259
A10.2	Sector ownership 1983–8: Netherlands banking system	260
A10.3	Top five Netherlands banks, 1988	261
A11.1	Norwegian banking system: institutional and sector breakdown by assets	263
A11.2	Sector ownership 1983–8: Norwegian banking system	264

A11.3 Top five Norwegian banks, 1988 264
A12.1 Portuguese banking system: institutional and sector breakdown by assets 266
A12.2 Sector ownership 1988: Portuguese banking system 266
A12.3 Top five Portuguese banks, 1988 267
A13.1 Spanish banking system: institutional and sector breakdown by assets 269
A13.2 Sector ownership 1985–8: Spanish banking system 270
A13.3 Top five Spanish banks, 1988 271
A14.1 Swedish banking system: institutional and sector breakdown by assets 273
A14.2 Sector ownership 1983–8: Swedish banking system 274
A14.3 Top five Swedish banks, 1988 275
A15.1 Swiss banking system: institutional and sector breakdown by assets 277
A15.2 Sector ownership 1983–8: Swiss banking system 278
A15.3 Top five Swiss banks, 1988 279
A16.1 United Kingdom banking system: institutional and sector breakdown by assets 281
A16.2 Sector ownership 1983–8: United Kingdom banking system 283
A16.3 Top five UK banks, 1988 284
A17.1 West German banking system: institutional and sector breakdown by assets 286
A17.2 Sector ownership 1983–8: West German banking system 288
A17.3 Top five West German banks, 1988 289

Preface

The idea for this book arose out of research undertaken by the authors within the Institute of European Finance (IEF) at the University College of North Wales, Bangor. We were struck by the lack of a systematic, functional study of the key European banking sectors within a single volume. There are many excellent directories and textbooks that document the banking and financial systems in individual countries. However, these are invariably institutional and primarily descriptive in their orientation. Some are also soporific because of the inevitable style in which they have to be written.

We certainly do not dispute the need for this kind of institutional knowledge. The present textbook also contains a Statistical and Country Appendix that embodies in summary form this kind of documentation. Our primary focus in the main part of this book, however, is on changes in Western European banking from a functional perspective: the two key words are 'changes' and 'functional'. Let us focus first of all on the word 'change'. Our concern throughout this book is primarily with current trends and developments, rather than a simple documentation of the *status quo*. In this approach we have used the relevant historical context as a backdrop, but we have drawn additionally on a wide variety of contemporary sources.

Our choice of sources material has been eclectic. We have used extensively the impressive resources of the Information Centre (and its staff) at the Institute of European Finance. Our own research within the Institute has allowed us access to materials and other sources not normally available to academic researchers. Many bankers in the City and throughout Western Europe contributed views and suggestions. We were also able to draw on the friendly contacts that have been established through the 'European Club of Banking Professors', the 'Wolpertinger Club'. This is a kind of informal society that meets once a year in a different European venue; it has proved a fruitful channel for important applied research in European banking.

The second of the key words that differentiates this volume is 'functional'. We have identified key areas of banking activity or areas of concern to banks, and focused on these rather than simply documenting institutions and markets. Many authors have set out to do this in a comparative banking text, but we found few who have been outstandingly successful. In writing this textbook we discovered the reason! Researching and writing this book was not easy. We certainly do not claim to have produced the final volume in this research effort, but we believe it is at least a useful step forward.

At a methodological level this book is concerned primarily with documenting and analysing changes in a particular industry, West European banking. Like the work of the early industrial economists, this is the essential first step towards any kind of unified theory of banking or a coherent treatment of the industrial economics of banking. The study of comparative banking is an important field of study for students of banking and finance because banking theories and policies are shaped to a significant extent by the specific institutional and market environment of different banking systems. There are various commonalities, but these do not run through all banking systems. Informed study and knowledge of particular systems are necessary 'methodological toolkits' of banking and finance students.

One important distinguishing feature of different banking systems, for example, has been regulation. Regulation in all its forms has been a key factor in shaping evolution, development and policies in banking. Deregulatory trends (like that of 1992) and supervisory harmonization developments (like the new – July 1988 – Basle, or BIS capital adequacy rules) herald in part a renewed surge towards a more integrated banking system within Europe. One ugly label for this kind of process is globalization. For present purposes it helps to vindicate further the logic of our functional approach within this book. A functional approach is a convenient and logical way of focusing on developing common threads in main banking sectors and related areas of concern.

The book is divided into two main parts. The first part comprises twelve chapters that cover the most important sectors of activity – like retail, corporate, international and investment banking – and related functional areas – such as structure and performance, regulation, changes in balance sheet structure, financial centres and securities markets. Chapter 12 concludes by examining the broader bank strategy and management implications of changes in European banking.

The second part of the book is a Statistical and Country Appendix, containing 17 country sections (Appendices 1–17) in which each country is analysed in a systematic and structured way. Individual country appendices are complemented by a (largely) common series of supporting tables. This section reflects more of the standard approach towards comparative banking, although we have sought to retain our primary emphasis on change. Nevertheless, we believe it is important that the reader is able to draw on this kind of material in order to help set parts of the first section into context. Banking researchers may also find useful some of the material and sources documented in the second section.

Although the book is unavoidably a little technical in places (like Chapter 4 on regulation and supervision), it is intended for a wide audience. Students and researchers in banking, finance, economics and management should find the book useful. European bankers and bankers in non-European countries should also find that it provides a broad perspective of major changes under way today in European banking. We believe that it will appeal to a wide audience. The growing importance of financial sectors in the economies of important European countries is one sign of the so-called post-industrialized phase through which many countries are now evolving. Banking and finance impinge daily on a growing number of activities in society.

Several acknowledgements are in order. We are grateful to all the bankers in London and abroad who contributed material and answered many questions. We are grateful to Professor Jack Revell who encouraged us to write the book; it will be clear that we have drawn extensively on his publications and suggestions. Professor Alan

Winters read and commented on Chapter 2. Jon Teppett and David Michael Lloyd-Williams (Research Officers in the Institute of European Finance) helped in the compilation of some of the tables; Simon Adamson of IBCA Banking Analysis was also very helpful. Karen Hickson, Helen Treece and Linda Jeavons typed and re-typed many drafts; Lesley Prendergast proof-read many of the corrections on various drafts. Christine Owen (Information Officer in the Institute of European Finance) played her usual efficient role in directing and controlling many stages of the 'book project'.

Finally we must thank our respective families. Phil Molyneux thanks Delyth, his wife, for her encouragement and support whilst writing and researching this text. He also thanks his daughters, Lois and Rhiannon, who taught him that sleepless nights are one of the great joys of fatherhood. Ted Gardener thanks his wife, Ann-Christine, and his children, Michael, Emma, John and Peter, for their usual forbearance with projects of this kind. Any errors or omissions are assumed, of course, by the authors.

Institute of European Finance
School of Accounting, Banking and Economics
University of Wales, Bangor
November 1989

Edward P. M. Gardener
Philip Molyneux

Chapter one

Introduction

Background

Since the late 1960s, world banking and financial systems have been living through a period of marked change. The expression 'financial revolution' has been coined to describe the scale and nature of these changes. Traditional methods of banking and finance are being replaced increasingly by new techniques. Globalization trends are rendering traditional national sovereignty in financial systems an anachronism. Globalization refers to the expansion of the Euromarkets on an international scale and the use of swaps to arbitrage international rate differences. It is also used more generally to refer to the growing integration of world capital and financial markets: the so-called 'global village' concept. In this environment many banks have adopted a corresponding global outlook in their strategies as they expand abroad and penetrate international and foreign markets.

Within this financial environment, European banks and banking systems are altering at a rapid pace. These changes are not uniform, but there are often important common elements. The industrial structure of European banking and European bank strategies are now in a fundamental process of realignment and adaptation. Banks, other financial institutions and financial systems across the globe are involved generally in a major restructuring process. Within this process there are increasing pressures for banks to be proactive rather than merely reactive to change. Banks need to anticipate new developments and plan accordingly. Our concern here is with analysing these developments within West European banking in a systematic and structured manner. A useful starting point is the construction of a general perspective of change in European banking.

General perspective

Before the revolution

The nineteenth century was a period of considerable changes and new developments in world banking. For most of the twentieth century, however, banking and financial systems settled into stable, well-ordered patterns. Most banking and financial systems became highly structured within the confines of their own national boundaries: financial institutions and markets specialized in well-defined areas and activities. Banking systems were also highly specific to each country, and individual governments exercised a significant degree of independent control over their own

1

systems. These two principles of specialization and national control of banking systems by individual countries influenced banking developments for most of the twentieth century.

During this period a pattern emerged whereby banking and financial systems were shaped strongly by the history, conventions and institutions of individual countries. It is in this sense that banking systems evolved as country-specific. Multinational banking declined sharply during this period compared with the nineteenth century. Change – a prominent feature of nineteenth-century banking – was not a noteworthy feature of twentieth-century banking, especially from the 1930s up to the 1960s. Even in the 1960s, Sayers (1967, p. 16), a distinguished banking academic, was able to observe:

> the banking business of the world is organized in the main on national lines, and in the present century this has become more rather than less true .... banking organization does not easily straddle national frontiers.

The new era altered this pattern of stability; change and growing interdependence became the order of the day.

The new era
From the 1960s, banking competition began to intensify. Structural deregulation policies – liberalizing financial institutions and enabling markets to compete more freely – were pursued by many leading governments. Technology began to exert a bigger impact on banking, and high rates of financial innovation became the norm. These developments were not spontaneous; they resulted from the interplay of many factors.

Developments in the real economy prompted many changes (see Chapter 2). They stimulated demands for new kinds of financial services: syndicated lending and the rise of Eurobonds are just two examples. World trade grew rapidly. Multinational and international banking revived as banks followed their large corporate customers abroad. The Euromarkets grew at a remarkable pace in response to the need for a less regulated, international financial market. Financial markets became more integrated internationally.

Structural deregulation has been both a policy response and a stimulus of change in banking and financial systems. New kinds of banking emerged that challenged contemporary regulatory systems. Wholesale banking and liability management developed rapidly in the 1960s and 1970s. Capital market products, treasury and off-balance sheet (OBS) banking became features of the 1980s.

Inflation and high nominal rates of interest in the late 1960s and 1970s increased the economic impact of traditional regulations on banks. High rates of interest increased the prospective returns from innovating around existing restrictions. Intensifying competition from new and old banking competitors further increased these pressures to innovate. Technology also began to lower the corresponding costs of innovating behaviour by banks and other operators. These economic forces, combined with a growing commitment by many governments toward monetarist policies and market solutions, helped to produce an environment of marked structural deregulation.

The barriers between traditionally separate financial institutions and markets began to erode in many countries. New instruments and techniques were developed to integrate financial markets across the globe: swaps are an important example. Domestic financial markets began to coalesce in some countries as new instruments, like money market funds (MMFs), spanned historically segmented financial markets. Computing and information technology spawned novel fund-raising and risk-management techniques. New innovations and financial engineering possibilities moved swiftly from the realms of theory to market reality.

Alongside structural deregulation trends, there has been growing supervisory re-regulation (increased prudential monitoring of financial institutions by the authorities) in many European countries and within the international banking system. Domestic supervisory systems have had to adapt in order to cope with the new kinds of risk exposure that characterized the financial revolution. Traditional supervisory methods have been found lacking in many cases. At the same time, there has been increasing international co-operation in order to protect the resilience of the international financial system. In this general context, convergence of bank capital adequacy regulations has become an important policy objective in Europe and within the international banking system.

Changes in Western European banking

Many of the broader developments in international banking and finance have a direct relevance to European banking. Indeed, they are characteristic of a completely new environment in European banking and finance. Some of the most important of these changes are summarized below:

- traditional barriers have broken down between historically segmented financial institutions (despecialization) and markets (interpenetration or coalescing of markets).
- global conditions (compared with national conditions) have exerted a much greater influence on the structure and operations of banking systems (globalization). The rise of the Eurocurrency and Eurobond markets in the 1960s marked the beginnings of this process.
- rapid banking and finance sector growth has been experienced in many European countries.
- increased concentration has occurred within leading sectors of European banking. A trend towards smaller numbers of larger institutions (through mergers, acquisitions, etc.) has emerged in many leading banking sectors.
- there has been a marked trend towards the formation of all-purpose financial groups in many important European banking sectors. These 'financial supermarkets' (universal banks or conglomerates), or FSMs, have developed in many European countries (like Germany and Switzerland) for some time.
- recently there has been an increasing tendency to form inter-country and inter-institutional links within the all-purpose financial groups that have developed.
- many countries have adopted deregulation (liberalization) policies in order to make their financial institutions and markets more open to equal, or 'level playing fields', competition. Taxation and other regulatory systems that affect banking have also changed.

3

- structural deregulation policies have been pursued in different ways and at different paces in various sectors of European banking. This has affected policy issues like reciprocity and national treatment. Monetary control systems have become more market-orientated.
- supervisory re-regulation has been a noteworthy trend in most European countries. Capital adequacy and associated risk regulation have been important policy issues in this respect.
- banks have faced new competitors, and new forms of competition have developed.
- technology has already had a significant impact on European banking in areas like competition, new products and payments systems.
- new kinds of payments systems and associated payments services have developed in different countries.
- a high rate of financial innovation has been a marked feature of many sectors of European banking. It has been evidenced in new techniques, novel financial instruments and new process innovations in banking. Various banking and financial sectors in Europe have exhibited different patterns of financial innovation.
- retail customers have become more sophisticated in their banking needs.
- banking has become more international and banks have expanded into foreign banking systems.
- corporate banking has become much more sophisticated and competitive in many key market segments. There has been an increasing tendency for some important and traditional credit flows to by-pass the banking system (securitization, or the market-based intermediation of debt). One aspect has been the growth of commercial paper (CP) markets in many European countries. Another, more general aspect has been the much greater emphasis given to investment banking and the role of banks in capital markets.
- there has been a marked growth in off-balance sheet (OBS) business in banking associated with securitization trends. This has led to a new emphasis on treasury activities in banking and new kinds of financial technology in banking balance-sheet management.
- many of the changes in European banking reflect corresponding important changes in real areas like industrial investment, production and social demography. In the industrial sectors, for example, many European banks are emphasizing more strongly the provision of venture capital. In the retail market bank customers are living longer and they have more to spend, and they are becoming increasingly more sophisticated in their financial needs.
- in strategic management a much greater emphasis and organizational priority is being given to a planning and marketing. Banks are being driven increasingly by the pressures of the market.

These are just a few of the multiplicity of changes that are now under way in European banking. Many of these are intensifying and a number have only just begun to affect significantly the structure and operations of European banking. Some of these important changes originated in the United States, but their applications in Europe are often quite different because of markedly different banking systems,

4

laws and regulation, and history.

Despite international and global developments, many key sectors of European banking are still shaped by a collection of factors that are unique to the individual countries. As a result, wider global developments affect different banking sectors in different ways. All-purpose banking, for example, is the norm in some important European countries. In others a high degree of specialization and institutional segmentation still exists. These differences and the corresponding developments that are under way in these sectors are a product both of history and of the contemporary financial environment.

Analysing change

Towards the year 2000

Banking changes associated with technology are expected to increase significantly in Europe during the next decade; this is particularly evident in retail banking. The retail banking revolution in Europe up until recently has not been primarily technology-driven, but this is now altering. With the marked slowdown worldwide in rates of real economic growth, technology looks set to continue the revolution in retail banking that was fuelled initially by high growth rates and rapidly rising standards of living.

In so-called bank-orientated systems (like Germany, France and Japan) there has been a corresponding historic bias towards the corporate sector: bank orientation refers to systems where banks and similar financial intermediaries dominate in credit intermediation. The resultant gaps in the financial systems of these countries allowed the savings banks and credit co-operatives to develop rapidly. Specialist mutual institutions also developed to provide long-term mortgage loans. There has been less scope for these other specialist institutions, except for those concentrating on mortgage finance, to develop in more market-orientated systems (where market-based credit intermediation is comparatively more important), like those of the United States and United Kingdom.

Banks now face a growing array of competitors in all segments of their business activity. In retail banking, these include building societies, savings banks (who challenge banks within some countries in various segments of corporate banking), postal giros, credit co-operatives, insurance companies, retailers and foreign bank and non-bank financial institutions (like Merrill Lynch and American Express).

In wholesale banking, similar competitive pressures exist. Securitization trends have shifted the focus in credit intermediation away from banks into the money and capital markets. The growth in ECP (Euro-commercial paper) and domestic CP markets represents further significant changes in European banking. The securitization phenomenon is characteristic of a generalized movement towards a greater market orientation, a greater comparative emphasis on market-based (as opposed to institution-based) intermediation in financial systems. The rise in importance of the corporate treasury function – exemplified by the formation of 'in-house banks' within the treasury divisions of companies like BP and Volvo – is indicative of continuing fundamental changes in traditional sectors of bank corporate activity.

5

Although the pace of change in the UK banking sector has been matched in other countries, like the United States, Canada and Australia, historically it has not been so evident in other Continental European countries, but this is now changing. Recent developments have forced European banks to develop appropriate strategies in response to the new environment. Planning has become a more professional activity and one with a higher organizational profile. Marketing is becoming a more critical banking function as changes in customer requirements increasingly shape bank strategies. It is widely accepted that successful product and service development, together with subsequent marketing, will be critical elements of bank profitability up to the year 2000.

A methodological backcloth
It is against this background that a strong case exists for some appropriate model of change. We need ideally to be able to measure and analyse banking developments in a systematic manner. Our approach will be characterized by a close examination of the banking industry, supported by comparative statistics and supplemented by relevant historical analysis. This methodological approach is similar in many respects to the early studies in industrial economics.

Changes in banking and financial systems are notoriously difficult to measure and analyse. It is invariably complex and often meaningless, for example, to attempt a separation of cause and effect. An involved interplay of many factors usually precipitates new banking and financial developments. Real and financial factors interact in complex ways that are still not fully understood.

One general explanation of institutional change lies in institutionalist economic theory: the theory of historical change expounded by Thorstein Veblen and his followers. Luckett (1981) argues that this institutionalist approach may be more appropriate than attempting to explain historical change using neo-classical economic theory. He suggests that conventional economics, using the econometric method, requires that the institutional structure of society be held constant. This produces a kind of logical paradox, because these institutional changes themselves constitute the basis of economic history.

It is not our intention to preach institutionalist economic theory, but rather to argue the need for some careful analysis of modern history and the wider social factors that characterize banking developments. We have already emphasized that contemporary changes did not suddenly appear: they are often the product of broader political, historical and social events. Even those changes that have apparently emanated from the financial system itself cannot be divorced completely from wider factors. Converting this eclectic view of change into a systematic model is difficult.

A number of more specific, but still general models exist to describe changes in banking and financial systems. In the early 1970s, for example, Revell (1973) used a 'logical, historical order' model to chart the evolution of financial systems. Revell's model was for an era before the modern 1980s securitization movement. A more recent model in this same vein is the Rybczynski (1985) model: change is analysed in the context of a generalized movement from bank-orientated through to market-orientated and strongly market-orientated financial systems.

An integrative framework

The preceding models typify at one level the methodological approach adopted in this book: a careful analysis of the banking industry and the historical dynamics of change. We do not claim to have done full justice to the latter, and this book is not an historical treatise. However, we have attempted to set the most important changes in the main European banking sectors within some historical context. This reflects our belief that seeking explanations for current banking phenomena and changes cannot be isolated from the historical, evolutionary process that is typically unique to individual countries.

Our objective is to identify the most important changes common to all West European banking systems and those changes that are specific to individual countries or sectors. This book is predicated on a detailed study of every West European banking system and sector, but it is not our purpose to document this level of detail in the main text. A statistical overview of all Western European banking systems is available in the Statistical Appendix. Summary select data on the quantitative elements of change are also included in this Appendix.

Highly summarized, balance sheet, sectoral income statement and risk indicator data will be used in various relevant places within the text to support the analysis. Wherever possible, we have attempted to standardize these data. We have not hesitated to use and (where possible) develop established data sources provided by organizations such as the OECD and the BIS. We believe that the data and source material provided in the main text and appendix should make this book a useful reference source for both academic researchers and banking practitioners.

Concluding remarks

A final noteworthy characteristic of the book is the study and comparison of the role of banks in the wider financial services industry (FSI). Even the term 'bank' is now misleading in many respects, because the traditional barriers between markets and institutions have eroded. Is a building society a bank? Is that part of a banking group providing insurance services a 'non-bank'? Many bankers prefer to describe themselves as financial services firms (FSFs). We shall adopt this term, which is itself an indicator of the fundamental changes that are sweeping through the European banking industry.

This is a good time to sit back for a while and attempt to take stock of changes in West European banking. The October 1987 crash in the world's financial markets has provided us all with food for thought. For a while at least, there is a renewed emphasis on more traditional aspects and techniques of commercial banking. Sound banking and effective risk management are being re-emphasized. The pace of financial innovation has slowed down from the heady surges experienced during many of the years up to 1987. Nevertheless, further banking changes are likely to be an inescapable part of society's move into the so-called post-industrialized society.

References

Luckett, David G. (1981), 'The future of banking in the United States: an application of institutionalist economic theory', *Nebraska Journal of Economics and Business*, vol. 120, no. 2, (August), pp. 25–36.

Revell, J. R. S. (1973), *The British Financial System* (London: Macmillan).

Rybczynski, T. (1985), 'Financial systems, risk and public policy', *Royal Bank of Scotland Review*, vol. 16, no. 4 (November), pp. 576–602.

Sayers, R. S. (1967), *Modern Banking*, 7th edition (Oxford: Clarendon Press).

Chapter two

Current trends in banking and financial systems

Introduction

The aim of this chapter is to identify the major trends that have affected European, as well as worldwide, banking and financial systems during the past two decades. The chapter will be divided into two main sections: the first dealing with the most important real and financial trends that have helped to stimulate change in European banking markets, and the second concerned with a pan-European perspective of banking systems. Many of the banking and related environmental developments identified in this chapter will be taken up later in greater detail.

Real and financial developments: stimulants of banking change

Economic and related sectoral trends
The economic environment of Western Europe has undergone considerable change since the early 1970s. High and volatile rates of inflation experienced in many countries during the early 1970s, together with increased budget deficits and balance-of-payments disequilibria, stimulated European banks to reassess their attitudes towards risk and uncertainty. These factors, coupled with the increased volatility of interest and exchange rates, were clear indicators that the overall macroeconomic environment had become much more uncertain. An OECD (1985) study pointed out that probably the most important 'hangover' from the inflation experienced during the 1970s has been to introduce much greater uncertainty into business and household expectations, be they concerned with prices, market outlets, exchange rates or interest rates.

The high and more volatile rates of inflation and interest, resulting mainly from the agency of changed economic policy, during the 1970s were major contributory forces leading up to the recession years of the late 1970s and early 1980s. The structural slowdown of economic growth and the deep-seated disequilibria of the period strongly affected the size, direction and variability of both domestic and international financial flows. This slowdown is witnessed in Table 2.1, which provides a summary of annual real GDP growth rates for a variety of European countries. The average annual GDP growth for many countries has been lower during the 1980s than in the second half of the 1970s. Only Spain and the United Kingdom experienced higher GDP growth in the 1980s.

9

Table 2.1 Growth of GDP at constant market prices (% per annum).

	1975–80	1980–88[a]
Belgium	3.0	1.0
Denmark	2.5	2.0
Germany	3.4	1.5
Greece	4.4	0.7
Spain	2.0	2.3
France	3.3	1.3
Ireland	4.6	1.6
Italy	3.9	2.1
Luxembourg	2.5	2.3
Netherlands	2.6	1.1
Portugal	5.4	2.0
United Kingdom	1.7	2.3
EC	3.0	1.8
United States	3.3	2.6
Japan	4.9	3.5

Source: Estimated from Eurostat (1987).
Note: a 1988 is an estimate.

Table 2.2 Average annual growth rates (%).

	Real net savings per capita		Real net disposable income per capita	
	1976–80	1981–6	1976–80	1981–6
Belgium	−8.4	31.6	10.8	11.4
Denmark	−15.6	52.1	10.9	17.2
Germany	8.6	24.4	15.4	13.6
Greece	11.1	−6.4	18.0	0.3
Spain	8.7	21.1	27.7	9.1
France	10.8	12.6	20.3	11.0
Ireland	−7.3	11.3	27.7	8.8
Italy	22.7	17.4	26.3	16.4
Luxembourg	21.5	22.0	18.5	19.0
Holland	6.2	14.8	12.9	8.9
Portugal	27.7	16.9	25.1	7.5
United Kingdom	25.7	3.8	42.4	4.1
EC	12.3	16.2	21.8	10.9
United States	24.4	28.8	26.0	11.7
Japan	27.6	28.9	29.4	26.4

Source: Eurostat Review (1977–86), Tables 2.1.49, 2.1.50, 2.1.69, 2.1.70, pp. 57 and 64.
Note: Real figures are calculated by using GDP and purchasing power parity deflations as at 1980.

Throughout Europe the household sector has remained the major surplus sector, although the size of these surpluses has fallen relative to national income. Conversely, although the corporate sector has traditionally been the most important deficit sector in almost all European countries since the 1960s, it now competes with the government sector for the major debtor status. The increased debtor status of the public sector has been primarily a result of increased government spending throughout the 1970s and 1980s, although there has been a reversal of the overall trend in some European countries, most noticeably in the United Kingdom.

It is also the case that debt-to-income ratios of the corporate, household and public sectors have risen in the major economies during recent years. The rapid growth of personal sector debt in various European countries has had important policy implications for controlling the money supply. The BIS (1987) notes that the overall growth in sectoral debt since the mid-1970s has aroused concern in many quarters. For the public sector debt, concern focuses on the possibility of 'crowding out', whereas growth in private sector debt raises questions about increased default rates. Davis (1986) finds that the non-financial private sector's portfolio behaviour has become more unstable since the 1960s and he suggests that many of these changes are contemporaneous with innovation and regulation.

There have also been dramatic changes in per capita disposable income and savings ratios in many European countries. Table 2.2 illustrates this point. Nearly all the countries experienced positive annual growth in real net disposable income and net savings per capita between 1976 and 1986. If one views the twelve countries that make up the European Community it can be seen that the growth rates of real net disposable income[1] increased, on average, nearly 11 per cent per annum between 1981 and 1986, whereas the real net savings figures increased by as much as 16.2 per cent per annum.

Table 2.3 illustrates how these developments have influenced savings ratios, and it is clear that between 1976 and 1986 for most countries savings as a proportion of disposable income have fallen. Nevertheless, this is somewhat misleading because if we consider the real saving ratios during the 1980s, only in Greece, France, Italy and the United Kingdom did the ratio decline. In all other countries in Europe the real savings ratio actually increased. Stevenson (1986) has pointed out that household financial assets are growing faster than liabilities in the major European economies, and this trend, together with the increasingly more sophisticated demands of the retail bank customer and the transformation in individuals' attitudes towards debt, have been important forces generating change in retail banking markets throughout Europe.

The financial assets of the corporate sector have increased in the major European countries since 1975 and in recent years UK firms have consistently run net financial surpluses. In countries such as France, the United Kingdom and the Benelux countries corporate liabilities tend to be dominated by changes in the valuation of equities. As with the personal sector, the gap between corporate financial assets and liabilities has widened over the last decade.

In the international economic arena, the increased scale and volatility of capital flows across countries, coupled with widescale financial liberalization, has encouraged the integration of international financial markets (Pecchioli, 1983). The OPEC surpluses generated in the post-1973 era have been replaced by surplus international

11

Table 2.3 Net savings per capita as a proportion of net disposable income per capita at constant prices (%).

	1976	1980	1986
Belgium	14.76	9.37	9.52
Denmark	12.02	6.61	9.15
Germany	13.09	11.56	12.78
Greece	18.51	17.72	8.68
Spain	13.76	11.55	11.80
France	12.72	12.05	8.79
Ireland	12.36	5.53	8.62
Italy	13.47	14.20	12.49
Luxembourg	30.80	31.44	43.01
Holland	16.17	11.66	15.05
Portugal	8.38	21.59	21.77
United Kingdom	8.35	7.15	4.76
EC	12.73	11.25	10.56
United States	7.56	6.73	2.81
Japan	23.03	21.06	21.42

Source: Estimated from Eurostat (1986).

capital flows mainly emanating from Western European and Japanese savers. The United States has changed its position within twenty-five years from being the largest creditor nation to the largest debtor nation. The US household sector surplus in 1986 was the lowest percentage of GDP since 1963.

The major methods of international finance have also changed. Rapid economic growth and an even faster rate of expansion of world trade in the late 1960s and early 1970s ensured a continuous demand for funds from the corporate sector as well as many governments and public corporations that had embarked on large investment programmes in both developed and less developed countries. The recycling of funds for balance-of-payments finance as well as the increased management of foreign-exchange reserves also helped to increase international lending activity. Between 1976 and 1986 real activity in the major financial markets has expanded at a faster rate than real output in the major industrialized countries.

In general, the macroeconomic climate experienced by European banks throughout the 1970s and 1980s has been of a much more volatile nature than that characterized by the economic environment of the 1950s and 1960s. The increased variability of almost all macroeconomic variables – interest rates, exchange rates, budget deficits and surpluses – has produced a much more uncertain environment.

Financial systems and the macroeconomy
The financial services sector is becoming more important to the macroeconomies of individual European countries. A recent EC study (*European Economy*, 1988a) noted that the financial services sector contributed 6.5 per cent of total value added and accounted for around 3 per cent of total employment within member countries. A summary of the size characteristics of various financial services sectors in European countries is provided in Table 2.4. In terms of total employment, Germany, France and the United Kingdom have by far the largest amount of workers in the financial sector: estimates range from around 600 000 for France to 800 000 for Germany (all

Table 2.4 Economic dimensions of the financial services sector 1985[a]

	Gross value added as a % of GDP[b]	Employment as a % of total employment[c]	Compensation of employees as a % of total for the economy
Belgium	5.7	3.8	6.3
Germany	5.4	3.0	4.4
Spain	6.4	2.8	6.7
France	4.3	2.8	3.8
Italy	4.9	1.8	5.6
Luxembourg[d]	14.9	5.7	12.2
Netherlands	5.2	3.7	4.9
United Kingdom	11.8	3.7	8.5
EC 8[e]	6.4	2.9	6.2

	Insurance premiums[f]	% of GDP Bank loans[g]	Stock market capitalisation[h]
Belgium	3.9	142[i]	92
Germany	6.6	139	89
Spain	2.5	99	69
France	4.3	93	85
Italy	2.2	96	75
Luxembourg	3.1	6,916	11,125
Netherlands	6.1	130	165
United Kingdom	8.1	208	149
EC 8[j]	5.2	142	116

Source: European Economy (1988a, p.87)
Notes: a Defined in the narrow sense as credit and insurance institutions.
b Including net interest payments.
c Employees in employment plus the self-employed.
d 1982.
e This aggregate accounted for 95% of total Community GDP in 1985.
f Average 1978–84.
g 1984.
h End-1985.
i 1982.
j Weighted average.

references to post Second World War Germany are to West Germany, unless otherwise stated or obvious), and the United Kingdom lies somewhere in between. In most European countries, banking and finance appears to contribute around two-thirds of the employment of the financial services sector, with insurance making up the remainder. Two extremes seem to be the United Kingdom and Luxembourg. In the United Kingdom the split is nearer fifty-fifty, whereas the employment contribution made by the insurance sector in Luxembourg is around 8 per cent. Employment in the banking and finance sector has increased in all European economies since the late 1970s, with the growth rates experienced in Germany, Netherlands, the United Kingdom and Luxembourg being the highest[2].

The value added figure provides some indication, together with the compensation of employees data, as to the relative importance of the financial sector. Table 2.4 clearly shows that gross value added as a percentage of GDP (at market prices) is roughly the same for most of the countries listed, the two major exceptions being the United Kingdom and Luxembourg, where value added amounts to 11.8 and 14.9 per cent of GDP respectively. In terms of compensation of employees, these two countries also stand out.

It seems unusual that two such markedly different financial systems should exhibit similar characteristics. One justification that could be put forward to explain these similarities relates to the comparative advantage of trade in financial services. A recent article by Arndt (1988) examined cross-border bank credit flows of twenty countries from which he identified five main categories:

● industrial countries with relatively small cross-border bank credit flows (United States, Japan, Germany, Italy and Spain).
● industrial countries with more substantial but moderate cross-border bank credit flows (France, Netherlands and Austria).
● industrial countries and newly industrialized countries (NICs) with very large cross-border bank credit flows (United Kingdom, Belgium-Luxembourg, Switzerland, Singapore).
● booking or reporting centres (Bahamas, Cayman Islands).
● oil exporters with surplus petro-dollars (Saudi Arabia, United Arab Emirates).

Arndt suggests that countries in the first two categories have been responsible for bank lending abroad in the same proportion relative to the size of their financial systems, whereas those in the other three categories have, 'in one way or another', specialized in international bank lending[3]. It could well be that this 'specialization' explains why countries such as the United Kingdom and Luxembourg exhibit markedly higher value added and compensation of employees figures than other European countries.

Banking regulatory and policy trends
Most European governments confined their macroeconomic policy attention towards dampening down inflationary pressures and expectations during the late 1970s and early 1980s. In addition, they also began to aim at reducing market supply-side constraints, thus placing greater emphasis on the allocative powers of the market. Throughout Europe there has been a noticeable rise of market-based methods of economic, financial and monetary control (see Chapter 4). The 1980s have witnessed a liberalization of worldwide financial markets as well as liberalization in the traditional banking arena.

Worldwide financial liberalization has been characterized *inter alia* by widespread capital market reforms, governments encouraging equity participation, privatization programmes and the dismantling of the traditional barriers between commercial banking and the securities markets. Liberalization in traditional banking markets has been evident through policies directed at increasing price competition as well as changing official attitudes towards the type of business activities in which banks and non-bank financial institutions can engage.

Regulators are finding it increasingly difficult to identify the relevant regulatees (those who are regulated). As the traditional barriers that used to segment financial business undertaken in different currencies and countries break down, so do those characteristics which used to differentiate financial and non-financial institutions. The blurring of distinctions between financial institutions is most noticeable in those countries which attempt (or have attempted) to apply a 'rigid compartmentalization of financial institutions' (Pecchioli, 1987, p. 65), as, for example, in the case of France, Italy and Spain. This process of change is also at work where banks are already allowed to operate as multi-purpose or universal financial organizations. The blurring of distinctions between financial institutions is usually referred to as the universalization of banking business, after the universal banking structures found in Germany, Switzerland and the Benelux countries. Even in those countries which were already perceived to have universal banking systems there has been a noticeable shift of emphasis towards capital market activities.

In countries like France, where there had been a distinct legal separation between banking and securities business, new laws (see *Economist*, 1986a, 1986b and *Euromoney*, 1988) have enabled banks to participate more actively in capital markets business. Restrictions on security underwriting are now 'virtually non-existent' (Pecchioli, 1987, p. 58) in European countries, and in the great majority of countries securities business is regarded as an important element of commercial banking. Another example of the decline in traditional demarcation lines in banking relates to the separation of short-, medium- and long-term business. Up until the early 1970s, banking business in France, Italy and Spain was clearly segmented, with different institutions doing the various types of term business. This distinction has almost disappeared in France and Spain.

Throughout the major European economies, 'it is possible to discern a long-term trend towards a regulatory framework which allows more effective competition between the various participants in the financial services industry' (OECD, 1985, pp. 21). Nevertheless, a concomitant policy reaction to the liberalization of both financial and banking markets has been the supervisory re-regulatory response (see Chapter 4). There has been a general increase in the supervision of financial markets and institutions. The recent international co-ordination of banking supervision and the increased concern of regulators with systemic risk have heightened both regulators' and regulatees' attitudes towards the solvency, liquidity and profitability of financial institutions. As financial institutions continue to undertake a wider range of activities, there is an associated need for co-ordination between banking and financial market supervisors, especially as:

> . . . the problem of systemic risk in capital markets may require tighter supervision of market makers' capital and liquidity whether market-making is undertaken as part of a banking conglomerate or not (BIS, 1987, p. 87).

In particular, there is still considerable confusion as to which should bear ultimate regulatory responsibility if a bank fails, due to its capital markets business.

As European macroeconomic policy attention in the late 1970s and early 1980s concentrated on dampening inflation and price expectations through tight monetary policy methods, experience throughout the 1980s has now convinced policymakers that even the largest countries must take their exchange rates into consideration when

15

formulating monetary policy. The link between exchange rates and monetary policy has become increasingly evident through explicit and implicit exchange-rate targeting. In the area of exchange-rate co-ordination, the European Monetary System (EMS) has been relatively effective at stabilizing member countries' exchange-rate parities. The widespread adoption by governments of co-ordinated exchange-rate intervention on a large scale has been an important feature of recent macroeconomic policymaking. The Plaza Agreement[4] of September 1985 and the Louvre Accord, confirmed by the Group of Seven in September 1987[5], were both directed at the problems associated with current account imbalances and stabilizing exchange-rate parities.

International co-ordination has since the early 1980s been dominated by the problems associated with the geographical pattern of payments imbalances between the industrialized countries and the indebtedness of developing countries. There is no doubt that the next few years will experience an ever-increasing movement towards the internationalization of regulatory frameworks. Nowhere will this be more apparent than in Europe where the EC governments aim to complete an internal market in financial services by 1992. The intentions – as set out in the 1985 EC White Paper on Completing the Internal Market (Commission of the European Communities, 1985) – are to eliminate all restrictions on capital flows[6] and create an internal market in financial services by 1992. The 'Horizon 1992' objectives will exact a strong influence on policymaking throughout Europe over the coming years; later chapters will explore various aspects of these proposals.

European institutions and international influences
Various institutions and international organizations have had a significant influence on moulding the financial and economic characteristics of European countries over the last thirty years. The establishment of the European Community and the EMS warrants a special mention. The signing of the Treaty of Rome in 1957, establishing the Community, was a watershed in the development of pan-European economic and monetary unification. The common market came into being on 1 January 1958 with six member countries: Belgium, France, Germany, Italy, Luxembourg and the Netherlands. It was this group that established the foundations for the ultimate goal of a unified internal market.

Under the Treaty of Rome the internal market was viewed as one which allowed 'free movement of goods, persons and services'. Throughout the 1960s, however, greater emphasis appeared to be placed on the real sector and intra-industry trade in general, and it was not until the late 1960s that European monetary integration was discussed in substantial detail. The establishment of the Committee of Governors of the Central Banks of the Member States of the European Communities in 1964, however, added a fillip towards these discussions. The most important factor influencing the move towards integration at the end of the 1960s was what various commentators, like Tsoukalis (1977) and Ypersele and Koeune (1984), have referred to as the 'cumulative logic of integration'. That is, the natural consequence of a common market in real goods calls for some form of monetary/financial integration, because the integration of markets makes economies more interdependent. In addition, the idea that EC countries could collectively lessen the adverse impact of external shocks by means of monetary integration was a further important factor supported by proponents of integration.

16

In early 1968 the Prime Minister of Luxembourg, Pierre Werner, issued a plan containing proposals for fixing exchange rates between Community currencies, a European unit of account and a European Monetary Fund. This led to a flurry of activity which resulted in a series of 'plans' on the co-ordination of economic policies and monetary co-operation within the Community. The Barre Plan (named after Raymond Barre, then the EC Commission's vice-president), submitted to the Council of EC Ministers on 12 February 1969, conspired to reawaken interest in monetary integration by proposing, among other things, that the Community should introduce a system for short-term monetary support as well as examining ways to eliminate fluctuation margins between European currencies. Other plans followed[7] and these formed the basis for examination by the Werner Group and the Werner Report, published in May 1970, which proposed that economic and monetary union should be achieved within ten years (i.e. by 1980). A second Werner Report, published in October 1970, reiterated the same points as the first, but introduced some minor qualifications (see Coffey and Presley, 1971, pp. 49–56).

At the beginning of 1973, Denmark, Ireland and the United Kingdom joined the European Community, but 'the progress towards economic and monetary union amounted to little over the period 1973 to 1977' (Ypersele and Koeune, 1984, p. 43). At the meeting of the European Council on 6–7 July 1978, the heads of state and government of the member countries decided to create a European Monetary System, whose main operational principles were defined later that year. The EMS had two main concerns: firstly, to stabilize exchange rates via an exchange-rate mechanism and, secondly, thereby to improve monetary integration and thus increase prospects for economic progress[8]. Members of the EMS included Belgium, Luxembourg, Denmark, Germany, France, Ireland, Italy and the Netherlands. Technically speaking, the United Kingdom has been in the EMS since its inception but does not participate in the Exchange Rate Mechanism (ERM). Greece joined the European Community in 1981 and Portugal and Spain entered in 1986, but only Spain (in June 1989) has subsequently joined the ERM of the EMS.

Although the EMS was introduced as an exchange-rate regime, an intervention system of central banks and a credit and settlement arrangement between central banks and governments, the system does have important implications for commercial banking. It provides a framework which affects:

> ... phenomena and attitudes in several markets in which commercial banks are active, viz the foreign exchange markets, the loan and deposits markets, the bond markets. The EMS bears on the relations between banks and public authorities. It means official interference in some financial markets, which the bankers usually dislike, but it also promises official backing and support for some financial activities and innovations, which the bankers usually like and request (Abraham *et al.*, 1984, p. 7).

De Boissieu (1988) provides a detailed analysis of financial liberalization and the evolution of the EMS.

When talking about the EMS one must include the ECU (European Currency Unit). The ECU is at the heart of the operations of the EMS, and is used to determine central rates in the exchange-rate mechanism as well as as a means of settlement between EMS monetary authorities. The increased official usage of ECUs has led to a widespread literature (Moss, 1984; Micossi, 1985; Jager and de Jong, 1988) on developing its private usage as well as proposing that the ECU become an International Currency. By the end of 1989 progress towards a European Monetary Union (EMU) was gathering pace and the concept of such a union includes the establishment of a European central banking system together with a much wider role for the ECU. The main features of the proposed union as outlined in the Delors Report are discussed in Chapter 4, which will also discuss the renewed emphasis towards a single European financial market associated with 'Horizon 1992', thus completing the European internal market.

Another organization that is increasing in importance in relation to European banking matters is the Bank for International Settlements (BIS). Based in Basle, Switzerland, this organization is the central bankers' central bank. It has for some time monitored international banking and financial business by obtaining data which banks in different countries report to it[9]. The collapses of Bankhaus I. D. Herstatt and Franklin National Bank in 1974 led to the establishment of the Committee on Banking Regulation and Supervisory Practices (better known nowadays as the Basle Committee, but formerly the Cooke Committee and initially the Blunden Committee), under the auspices of the BIS. The principal objective of this committee was to establish detailed supervisory practices to ensure that the foreign operations of banks could not escape the supervisory net.

The Cooke Committee[10] endorsed a concordat on international bank supervisory co-operation in 1975 which indicated the relevant supervisory responsibilities of parent and host country supervisors. During 1978 the Governors of the BIS endorsed the Cooke Committee proposals that banks' capital adequacy should be monitored entirely on a consolidated basis. Nevertheless, the collapse of Banco Ambrosiano Holdings in 1982 indicated certain failings of the supervisory framework and this led to a revised version of the 1975 concordat. In 1986 the Cooke Committee published a further document (BIS, 1986) concerned with the prudential features associated with off-balance sheet exposures.

The harmonization of international capital adequacy standards took a further step forward in December 1987 after the BIS outlined proposals to unify capital requirements for banks in the industrialized world. Of these, the European element refers to banks in Belgium, France, Italy, Luxembourg, Netherlands, Sweden, the United Kingdom, West Germany and Switzerland. The role of the BIS as a co-ordinator and standard-setter for bank supervisors will undoubtedly continue as capital adequacy continues to be one of the most important issues facing European banks today. Chapter 4 will examine this policy area in greater detail.

Finally, a brief note should be made about another prominent international organization that influences European banking and which has an important role to play in the world financial system. The International Monetary Fund's (IMF) main aim is to promote an international monetary system in which payments adjustment fosters international prosperity. Its objectives are to improve exchange-rate stability, to manage international liquidity and to deal effectively with debt restructuring programmes. Although the IMF provided the forum and staff input for the Plaza and Louvre agreements, and has increasingly stressed the need for structural reform in both developed and less developed countries, it appears to have little influence in the surplus countries (Hains, 1988). Nevertheless, its role as a multilateral lending institution, and the principal co-ordinator of Third World debt, together with the World Bank group, will influence the problems associated with Third World debt and this affects the provisioning responses of European banks.

Perspectives of European banking systems

A short history of banking in Europe

The historical development of European countries' banking and financial systems has been moulded by a wide range of diverse socio-economic, political and geographical factors. Nevertheless, it is possible to identify various broad banking trends that have been experienced in many of the industrialized European countries since the seventeenth century.

During the seventeenth and eighteenth centuries all European banking systems were unit-based. Banks were predominantly small private institutions that specialized in serving the needs of local markets. A small proportion of these banks were engaged in financing international trade and these tended to be based in the main financial centres. Revell (1987, pp. 17–18) identified that by the first half of the nineteenth century banking systems were characterized by two main banking groups; those based in large towns financing both domestic and international trade and those groups dispersed throughout the country financing local industry, which was predominantly agricultural. Kindleberger (1984, pp. 73) argues that, even by this stage, in many cases banking business was no more than an additional activity undertaken by goldsmiths, merchants, notaries, industrialists and tax farmers.

As the Industrial Revolution gained momentum it encouraged the establishment of new, large, joint-stock banks based in metropolitan areas. These banks competed with the unit banks which were country-based as well as with a whole range of (mainly) newly-established mutual bodies such as savings banks, building societies, co-operatives, agricultural credit associations and the like. The private country banks gradually declined in numbers, partially because the larger metropolitan joint-stock banks acquired them, and also as a result of the desire of the larger banks to establish substantial branch networks. As industry began to spread to new areas and also became more concentrated, banks increased their geographical coverage through branching and also grew in size so as to provide the funds required by their large industrial customers. In the last quarter of the nineteenth century nationwide branch networks were created by the large banks in most European countries.

Kindleberger (1984) identified the nineteenth century as also witnessing the rise of 'single financial centres', such as London and Paris, which tended to dominate national finance. The same process was at work in countries like Germany and Italy where 'political unification came later'. It was in these centres that groups of dominant or 'core banks' were based:

> Between about 1880 and 1920 there appeared in all countries a recognisable group of dominant or 'core' banks, recognised both by the authorities and by the general public. They were referred to popularly as the Big Three, the Big Five, or whatever the number may have been (Revell, 1987, pp. 21).

19

As the branch networks of the larger banks became dominant at the turn of the century, there were two main factors that restricted their growth. Firstly, there had been a trend in various Continental European countries, like France, for the local and regional banks to create groups that could compete effectively with the larger national banks in their own region. Secondly, political factors in various countries sought to encourage (protect) competition between regional and national banks. In those countries with Federal governments, like Germany and Switzerland, regional institutions will play a more important role. It is still the case that in countries such as France, Italy and Spain banks are registered at a local, regional and national level. In addition, branching restrictions that remained in many European countries up until the 1960s also helped to preserve the status of various regional and local institutions.

Throughout the nineteenth and early twentieth centuries the relationship between banking and commerce differed substantially from country to country (see also Chapter 7). In the United Kingdom banks mainly financed trade, and most industrial finance came via the capital markets or from internal funding. Occasionally UK banks undertook industrial lending but only on a short-term basis. In contrast, Continental banks fostered much closer relations with industry. Kindleberger (1984) notes that industrial banking began in Belgium in the second quarter of the nineteenth century. Banks in Germany, Austria, Sweden and, up until the 1930s, in Italy formed the closest links with industry. The twentieth century has witnessed the polarization of many of these trends. Banking markets have become more concentrated through amalgamations and takeovers, links with industry have been consolidated, sectoral ownership has continued to change and universal-type banking is becoming the 'norm' rather than the exception.

Structural differences between European banking systems

The study of structural development in European banking markets involves an examination of the changes in the size, numbers and comparative significance of banks and other financial institutions within a financial system as well as embracing those institutional changes which alter the ways in which financial services are demanded, used, developed and delivered. Although every European banking system has its distinguishing features, there are various characteristics that help to distinguish Continental banking systems from those based on the British model[11]. Revell (1987) identifies five common elements of Continental banking systems:

- the presence of various special credit institutions which are usually publicly owned and provide funds for various sectors such as industry, agriculture and property.
- the increased importance of savings banks, co-operative (popular) banks and co-operative credit associations, together with their central institutions.
- a long history of commercial banks' participation in the ownership and management of industrial enterprises, 'relics of which still linger on'.
- the importance in many European countries of banks and other institutions which are organized on a local or regional basis, 'usually reflecting the prevalence of small enterprises in both industry and agriculture'.
- and a degree of similarity between the new banking laws that were enacted in many countries following the crisis during the early 1930s.

20

Sometimes a distinction is made between the role that commercial banks in different countries play in financing industry. Some commentators (Frazer and Vittas, 1982; Rybczynski, 1984) distinguish between bank-based systems, such as those found in Germany, France, the Netherlands and Sweden, and market-based systems such as those found in the United Kingdom (and the United States). In the former group of countries, commercial banks have traditionally been strongly orientated towards the corporate sector, and this has provided opportunities for public sector and mutual institutions to adopt a more significant role within the banking system, through concentrating their business on the retail customer and small to medium corporate clients.

Frazer and Vittas (1984) explain that commercial banks in Germany, the Netherlands and Sweden made a concerted effort to improve their standing in the retail banking market from the late 1950s onwards. They also found that during the 1960s similar developments took place in Northern and Central European banking systems. This they have termed as the 'start of the retail banking revolution'. Changes in the competitive environment for retail banking took longer to emerge in Southern Europe (because of regulatory constraints and low standards of living) and in the United Kingdom (where there was less incentive for the clearing banks to move into retail banking business).

With regard to the sectoral ownership of banking institutions in various European countries, it can be seen from Table 2.5 that private domestic sector banks accounted for more than 50 per cent of total banking sector assets only in Denmark, Finland, Ireland, the Netherlands, Spain, Sweden and Switzerland in 1988[12]. On the other

Table 2.5 Summary of sector ownership of European banking institutions, 1988 (% of aggregate total assets).

Country	Private	Public (Central & local government)	Mutual	Foreign
Austria	0.4	43.8	55.8	-
Belgium	37.0	16.8	11.0	35.2
Denmark[a]	69.5	1.3	29.2	-
Finland	44.5	10.5	44.2	0.8
France	24.2	42.2	20.2	13.5
Germany	32.0	49.5	16.7	1.8[c]
Greece[b]	11.0	83.7	-	5.3
Ireland	61.7	4.0	12.9	21.4
Italy	12.3	67.9	16.8	3.0
Netherlands	61.2	8.1	17.7	13.0
Norway	41.2	19.9	38.9	-
Portugal	6.8	87.1	1.9	4.2
Spain	49.0	2.3	37.7	11.0
Sweden	52.9	19.3	24.9	2.9
Switzerland	53.4	19.6	15.8	11.2
United Kingdom	31.8	1.0	14.0	53.3

Source: Statistical Appendix
Notes: a Figures for percentage of total deposits.
     b Figures for percentage of total credit.
     c Branches of foreign banks.

Table 2.6 Change[a] in market shares of European banks by ownership category 1983–8 (%).

Country	Private	Public	Mutual	Foreign
Austria	−1.2	−0.2	1.4	–
Belgium[b]	1.5	−5.2	2.4	1.3
Denmark[c]	−0.1	−1.0	1.1	–
Finland[b]	1.0	−1.3	1.0	−0.6
France	19.7	−20.3	−2.7	3.4
Germany	0.9	0.4	0.7	−2.0[e]
Greece[c]	2.9	−5.1	–	2.2
Ireland	6.0	−0.2	0.7	−6.5
Italy	−9.1	7.5	1.2	0.4
Netherlands	2.5	1.0	−5.8	2.3
Norway	5.9	−11.6	5.7	–
Spain	−4.3	−5.6	6.2	3.7
Sweden	−1.6	0.7	−2.0	2.9
Switzerland[d]	2.0	−2.2	1.1	−0.8
United Kingdom	−1.4	0.0	0.8	0.7

Source: Statistical Appendix.
Notes: a Percentage share of total banking sector assets in 1988 minus percentage share of total banking sector assets in 1983.
    b 1982–8.
    c Change in market shares relate to total deposits (Denmark) and total credit (Greece).
    d 1985–8.
    e Foreign bank branches only.

hand, in 1988 public sector organizations[13] controlled over 70 per cent of banking sector assets in Austria and Greece and over 40 per cent in France (through the wholesale nationalization in 1981) and Germany. In Germany nearly 50 per cent of banking sector assets are controlled by public sector institutions, but they have a different significance from the same statistical phenomenon evident in France and Italy. Savings banks in Germany are under the control of local *Länder* governments. Their central institutions, the Girozentralen, are organized on a Federal basis and are very large international banks. Although they are in the public sector, these institutions cannot be regarded as nationalized institutions or under the direct control of the central government.

In Italy the central institutions of the savings banks, co-operative banks and rural banks are less important. The public sector in Italy is dominated by public law banks[14], national interest banks[15] and the savings banks. In Belgium the public sector consists of only three banks[16] which are controlled by central government. In Sweden there is only one state-owned commercial bank and the postal giro. Switzerland has a similar proportion of public sector banking institutions: these are the cantonal banks, which have been set up under cantonal law and occupy a similar position to savings banks in the German system. Finally, with regard to the public sector, Table 2.5 shows that it is relatively unimportant in Denmark, Ireland, the Netherlands and the United Kingdom.

The mutual sector[17] differs in importance and composition across European countries' banking systems, ranging from 11.0 per cent of banking sector assets in

Belgium to 38.9 per cent in Norway. In France (through Crédit Agricole) and the Netherlands (through Rabobank), the agricultural credit co-operatives dominate the mutual sector, although savings banks are relatively more important in France. In Denmark, Finland, Spain and Sweden, savings banks tend to dominate.

The relative importance of foreign banks also differs in European banking systems. It can be seen that foreign banks dominate in the UK banking system and also control a large proportion of banking sector assets in Belgium and Ireland. In Luxembourg, foreign banks account for somewhere around 90 per cent of the banking system's assets and most of their capital is held in currencies other than the Luxembourg franc (see OECD, 1987). Foreign bank penetration appears to be very low in Germany and Italy and other evidence suggests it is even lower in Denmark and Austria.

Table 2.6 illustrates the change in market shares by ownership category between 1983 and 1988. The public sector has declined in virtually all European banking markets, the notable exception being Italy where this sector increased its share by 7.5 per cent. The significant fall in the size of the public sector (and subsequent rise in the private sector) in France is attributable to the privatization of five large banks in 1986. Private sector banks' share of total banking sector assets has increased in the majority of European countries, the exceptions being Austria, Denmark, Italy, Spain, Sweden and the Netherlands. In all but Italy and Sweden, the private banks lost ground to the mutual institutions. In fact, the mutual institutions, contrary to popular belief, appear to have fared quite well in maintaining market shares throughout the 1980s. Table 2.6 also shows that foreign bank presence has increased in nearly all European banking markets, confirming the internationalization trend.

In terms of size, the German banking sector is the largest in Europe as measured by total assets. This is followed closely by the United Kingdom and then by France. The smallest banking systems include those of the Scandinavian countries, Belgium, Luxembourg, Greece and Portugal.

European banking compared to US and Japanese banking
One of the most noticeable differences between European banking systems and those of the United States and Japan is that in the latter two countries banking and securities institutions are separated by law, whereas in most European countries these activities can be undertaken within the same institution. It is also the case that if this institution happens to be a bank, it is subject to a uniform bank supervisory frame-work. In the United States, however, banking business is supervised by the Federal Reserve, the Federal Deposit Insurance Corporation and state authorities, and securities business is supervised by the Securities and Exchange Commission. In Japan, banking activities are regulated by the Bank of Japan, whilst securities business is supervised by the Securities Bureau of the Ministry of Finance. Dale (1987) argues that the separation of commercial and investment banking is more artificial in Japan than in the United States. Nevertheless, these mandatory divisions contrast markedly with the universal-type banking undertaken in Germany, Switzer-land, the Benelux countries and (to a lesser extent) the United Kingdom.

Similarities may be drawn between the Japanese and various European banking systems because of Japan's comparable size to the larger European nations. Probably the closest parallel system is that of Germany where banks form close links with industrial customers. The Zaibatsu groups that have dominated commercial activities in Japan for over 40 years often have large banks as their controlling elements. Similarly, in Germany the banks' controlling interests in industry are nurtured through cross-shareholdings and interlinking directorships. The sectoral ownership of the Japanese banking system is different, however, with the private sector (dominated by the 13 city and 60 or so regional banks) controlling around 50 per cent of banking sector assets. In addition, the mutual sector, through the credit co-operatives, controls around one-third of the banking system. The public sector, which dominates in Germany, is less influential in Japan because it consists of only one institution – the Postal Savings Bank. This bank, nevertheless, is the largest deposit-taking institution in the world and controlled around 18 per cent of the banking sector's total assets in 1987. The only other similarity to the German system is that foreign banks are relatively unimportant.

In contrast to the relatively concentrated European banking systems, the United States is characterized by a fragmented, unit-based banking system consisting of some 14,130 institutions at the end of 1986 (OECD, 1988). This has been brought about by the dual system of bank chartering and regulation and by various state branching laws. The state branch laws limit inter-state branching and some even restrict intra-state branching. Although these geographical restrictions can be circumvented (to a certain degree) through the establishment of reciprocal agreements, bank holding companies, and correspondent and chain banking activities, no US bank can be said to have a nationwide branch network. The US authorities recently set the legislative wheels in motion to dismantle branching restrictions by the early 1990s. In Europe every country apart from Italy had abandoned branch restrictions by 1988.

The introduction of a single banking licence in the European Community by 1992 may well have encouraged US legislation to break down the considerable barriers to branching still evident in the United States. In terms of banking structure, the large money-centre banks and the so-called super-regionals have tended to dominate the commercial banking scene over the last five years or so. The number of banking institutions in the United States and Japan has stayed constant since the early 1980s, although there has been a decline in the number of US savings and loans associations. This trend, however, has been counteracted by the associations converting to savings bank status. In terms of performance, OECD (1987) figures indicate that, although the average interest margins of commercial banks between 1980 and 1985 in the United States were amongst the highest (comparable with the United Kingdom and Italy), profitability was quite low (similar to the United Kingdom and France). Japanese banks' interest margins over this period, on the other hand, were quite low (only Switzerland and Luxembourg were lower) and so was their profitability. Despite these differences, both European and Japanese banks are now moving aggressively (back) into the US domestic market. Japanese banks have made major Californian acquisitions, whereas European banks have made mainly East coast purchases.

24

Conclusion

It is clear that the environment of European banking is complex and changing. Two major policy trends that have influenced significantly both the structure and strategies of European banks have been the dual forces of structural deregulation and supervisory re-regulation. The former had allowed banks to offer a broader range of products and services by dismantling certain demarcation lines between particular types of business. Banks in most European countries have been able for some time to participate freely in capital markets and investment banking business. On the other hand, the non-bank competitors have been allowed to offer banking-type services creating a major competitive threat, especially in retail banking markets. Financial and technological innovations have been the main underlying economic motives forcing these changes. Poised on the brink of 1992, European banking is now at a very important crossroads. Against the background of this broad overview, the following chapter will explore in greater detail some of its important structure and performance characteristics.

Notes

1. The figures used here relate to real net disposable income per capita. Real disposable income per household figures tend to provide similar outcomes for Germany, the United Kingdom, the United States and Japan, but provide much more favourable growth rates for countries such as France.
2. According to the Statistical Office of the European Communities, *Employment and Unemployment, 1987*, the rate of growth in employment in banking and finance between 1978 and 1985 for various EC countries was as follows: Belgium, 11 per cent; Germany, 15 per cent; France, 9 per cent; Luxembourg, 50 per cent; Netherlands, 15 per cent and the United Kingdom, 24 per cent.
3. Although there are various problems associated with this type of analysis, the pattern indicated by cross-border bank credit flows is 'probably as close as we can get towards identifying the major trade flows'.
4. The Plaza Agreement was made between the United States, Japan, Germany, the United Kingdom and France, and its aim was to lessen current account imbalances by an agreed change in parities.
5. The Louvre Accord, as confirmed by the Group of Seven, (United States, Japan, Germany, France, United Kingdom, Italy, Canada) aimed to stabilize the dollar vis-à-vis member currencies.
6. As at the beginning of 1990 capital movements are completely free in Denmark, France, Germany, Italy, the Netherlands and the United Kingdom and subject to the application of the two-tier exchange market in Belgium and Luxembourg. Apart from Spain and Portugal, the most recent members to the EC, only Greece and Ireland maintain restrictions.
7. The 'other' plans were, the Schiller Plan for Monetary, Economic and Financial Co-operation, the Second Barre Plan and various suggestions set out by M. Giscard d'Estaing for the creation of a European Reserve Fund.
8. Countries that are members of the EMS are entitled to take part in discussions on the functions and developments of the system, including the Exchange Rate Mechanism (ERM), and to attend conferences to alter central exchange rates, whether or not they are members of the ERM. All members of the EMS are allowed to join the ERM which obliges them to maintain their exchange rates within certain bands. Each ERM currency has a central rate of exchange against the other currencies in the mechanism. The European Currency Movement (ECU) is used as the *numéraire* where all participating currencies have an ECU-related central rate. Central rates are expressed as a certain quantity of

currency per ECU. Currencies are permitted to move up to 2.25 per cent above or below their central rate, although the lira and peseta have a wider margin of 6 per cent. Central banks agree to maintain the value of their currencies within these limits. If exchange rates cannot be maintained within these bands a realignment conference may be called to consider changes in central rates. Central rates can only be altered with the mutual agreement of the members of the mechanism. Since its inception the EMS has experienced eleven such realignments.

9. The BIS includes the Group of Ten (G10) countries (Belgium, Canada, France, Italy, Japan, Netherlands, Sweden, United Kingdom, United States and West Germany) as well as Luxembourg, Austria, Denmark, Finland, Ireland, Norway, Switzerland and Spain. It also covers various banks engaged in international business in the Bahamas, Cayman Islands, Hong Kong and Singapore, all offshore banking units in Bahrain, all offshore banks operating in the Netherlands Antilles and branches of US banks in Panama.

10. The members of the Cooke Committee consisted of representatives of the G10 countries and Luxembourg and Switzerland.

11. The distinction is made between those banking systems that follow the British model: Australia, Canada, Ireland, New Zealand and South Africa and those that have Continental banking system characteristics. The US banking system is viewed as a kind of hybrid.

12. See Statistical Appendix for detailed country breakdowns for 1983 and 1988.

13. Public sector institutions include nationalized commercial banks, postal giros and postal savings banks and specialized banks which deal mainly with export finance and long-term finance to industry.

14. Banca Nazionale del Lavoro, Banco di Sardegna, Istituto Bancario San Paolo di Torino, Monte dei Paschi di Siena, Banco di Napoli and Banco di Sicilia.

15. These comprise Banca Commerciale Italiana, Banco di Roma and Credito Italiano, which are state-owned but have a minority private sector shareholding.

16. The two largest public sector banks are Crédit Communal, which transacts business mainly with provincial and local authorities but has been increasing its general banking business, and Caisses Generales d'Epargne et de Retraite (CGER), the same as a post office or national savings bank, which was made into a public bank in 1980. The Office des Cheques Postaux (OCP) provides postal chequing facilities and is the third major public sector bank.

17. Mutual institutions include savings banks, building societies, co-operative banks, Raiffeisen credit co-operatives and credit unions, together with their central organizations.

References

Abraham, F. L. P., Abraham, Jean-Paul and Lacroix-Destree, Yvonne (1984), 'EMS, ECU and commercial banking', *Revue de la Banque*, vol. 48, no. 2, (February), pp. 5–35.

Arndt, H. W. (1988), 'Comparative advantage in trade in financial services', *Banca Nazionale del Lavoro*, no. 164, (March), pp. 61–77.

Bank for International Settlements (1986), *The Management of Banks' Off-Balance Sheet Exposures: A Supervisory Perspective*, Committee on Banking Regulations and Supervisory Practices (March), (Basle: BIS).

Bank for International Settlements (1987), *57th Annual Report* (Basle: BIS).

Bingham, T. R. G. (1985), 'Banking and monetary policy', *Trends in Banking Structures and Regulation in OECD Countries* (Paris: OECD).

de Boissieu, C. (1988), 'Financial liberalisation and the evolution of the EMS', *European Economy*, 36, (May), pp. 53–70.

Coffey, P. and J. R. Presley (1971), *European Monetary Integration* (London: Macmillan).

Commission of the European Communities (1985), *Completing the Internal Market*, White Paper from the Commission to the European Council, June (Brussels: EC).

Dale, R. (1987), 'Japan's 'Glass Steagall' Act', *Butterworths Journal of International Banking Law*, vol. 2, issue 3, pp. 1138–46.

Davis, E. P. (1986), 'Portfolio behaviour of the non-financial private sectors in the major economies', *BIS Economic Paper*, no. 17, (September).

Economist (1986a), 'Big Bang brief – the home teams', vol. 300, no. 7461, 30 August – (5 September), pp. 45–6.

Economist (1986b), 'Big Bang brief – the countdown to October 27th', vol. 300, no. 7457, (10 August – 16 August), pp. 50–1.

Euromoney (1988), 'Un tout petit boum', (January), pp. 95–9.

European Economy (1988a), 'The economics of 1992', no. 35, (March).

European Economy (1988b), 'Creation of a European financial area', no. 36, (May).

Eurostat, Data for Short-term Economic Analysis (Brussels: EC).

Eurostat Review (1977–86) (Brussels: EC).

Frazer, P. and D. Vittas (1984), *The Retail Banking Revolution* (London: Lafferty Publications).

Gordon, K. (1987) '1992 – Big Bang or little whimpers', *The Banker*, vol. 137, no. 740, (October), pp. 19–26.

Hains, Anthony (1988), 'Two plumbers work in brief', *Financial Times, World Banking Survey*, (18 May 1988), p. 3.

Jager, Henk and de Jong, Eelke (1988), 'The private ECU's potential impact on global and European exchange rate stability', *Banca Nazionale del Lavoro Quarterly Review*, no. 164, (March), pp. 33–60.

Kindleberger, C. P. (1984), *A Financial History of Western Europe* (London: Allen & Unwin).

Micossi, Stefano (1985), 'The intervention and financial mechanism of the EMS and the role of the ECU', *Banca Nazionale del Lavoro Quarterly Review*, no. 155, (December), pp. 327–45.

Moss, Frank (1984), 'The private use of the ECU: its implications for national monetary authorities in EEC member states', *Revue de la Banque*, vol. 48, no. 2, (February), pp. 41–64.

OECD (1985), *Trends in Banking in OECD Countries*, Committee on Financial Markets, Expert Group on Banking (Paris: OECD).

OECD (1987), *Bank Profitability, Financial Statements of Banks with Methodological Notes, 1980–84* (Paris: OECD).

OECD (1988), *Bank Profitability, Statistical Supplement, Financial Statement of Banks, 1982–86* (Paris: OECD).

Pecchioli, R. M. (1983), *The Internationalisation of Banking: Policy Issues* (Paris: OECD).

Pecchioli, R. M. (1987), *Prudential Supervision in Banking, Trends in Banking, Structure and Regulation in OECD Countries* (Paris: OECD).

Revell, J. R. S. (1987), *Mergers and the Role of Large Banks, IEF Research Monograph in Banking and Finance* no. 2 (Bangor: Institute of European Finance).

Rybczynski, T. M. (1984), 'The UK financial system in transition', *National Westminster Bank Quarterly Review*, (November), pp. 26–42.

Stevenson, M. (1986), 'A survey of international banking: the consumer is sovereign', *The Economist*, Special Survey (22 March), pp. 1–45.

Tsoukalis, Loukas (1977), *The Politics and Economics of European Monetary Integration* (London: Allen & Unwin).

Ypersele, Jacques van and Koeune, Jean-Claude (1984), *The European Monetary System* (Brussels: Commission of the European Communities).

Chapter three

Structure and performance

Introduction

The preceding chapter alluded to considerable differences in the structure and performance characteristics of various European banking markets. This chapter examines some of these major differences, and also identifies recent trends that have influenced the relationship between banking structure and performance. The first main section deals with market structure and competition, and the second part analyzes the size, concentration and performance characteristics of the various markets.

Structure and competition

Historical and evolutionary perspective

One general view (Rybczynski, 1984; 1988) of the modern evolution of banking and financial systems is to identify the broad stages of structural development in a kind of 'logical historical order'. From the bank-orientated stage, a system develops through the market-orientated stage to the so-called securitized phase. In the bank-orientated stage the majority of external funds raised by non-financial companies are obtained from the banking system in the form of loans. An exception to this is countries with universal banking systems, such as in Germany and the Benelux countries, where banks supply risk capital in some form of another. In the bank-orientated era the degree of risk an economy bears is primarily determined by the owners of the productive resources and the banks.

The next stage of development is known as the market-orientated phase. Here external funds obtained by non-financial firms are obtained primarily through the capital markets. These latter markets channel a growing proportion of savings of the personal sector, and non-bank institutions like life assurance companies, investment trusts and other portfolio-type institutions become more important. In the final securitized (or 'strongly market-orientated') phase the majority of external funds raised by non-financial firms are acquired through the capital and credit markets. During this period, non-bank institutions such as finance companies and building societies rely more on funds raised through the open credit markets. Depository institutions move an increasing proportion of assets off their balance sheets and trade in them. Securitization and the rapid development of sophisticated off-balance sheet (OBS) techniques are characteristic of this stage.

It is argued that as a financial system moves from the bank-orientated to the securitized stage the capacity of an economy to assume risk increases; it 'is also the active and indispensable ingredient of re-structuring all mature and de-industrialising economies if all its constituent parts (that is primary and secondary capital and credit markets, markets for corporate control and makets for venture capital) function effectively' (Rybczynski, 1988, p. 11). In Europe, only the United Kingdom has reached this securitized phase. Regulations have recently been passed in France, Italy and Spain that aim to move the respective financial systems towards more market-orientated systems. Germany's financial system is still heavily entrenched in the bank-orientated phase of development. Despite these very broad but important differences in the evolution of financial systems, all European countries have experienced marked structural developments during recent years.

The structure and performance relationship

The structure of any market is determined by a broad range of economic as well as non-economic factors. These non-economic factors include various geographical, legal, philosophical, political and social forces which mould the institutional character of banking markets over time. Consequently, European banking systems are characterized by a complex array of institutions, organizational forms and legal frameworks, all of which have contributed to the myriad forces that have created their different market structures.

The aforementioned background begs the question: 'Why does structure matter?'. Industrial economic theory suggests that there is a causal link between market structure and bank conduct and performance. More specifically it has been argued that, in concentrated markets, banks may earn collusive profits (Weiss, 1974; Heggestad and Mingo, 1977; Spellman, 1981; Rhoades, 1982). A substantial literature has burgeoned that is aimed at testing the theoretical SCP (structure-conduct-performance) relationship. It has been argued, however, that this literature contains too many inconsistencies and contradictions to provide a satisfactory description of the SCP relationship in banking (Gilbert, 1984; Osborne and Wendel, 1983). Contemporary approaches to the explanation of the link between market structure and performance have emphasized an alternative 'efficient structure' hypothesis. This postulates that an industry's structure arises as a result of superior operating efficiency by particular firms. As a result, a positive relationship between bank profits and structure can be attributed to gains made in market share by more efficient banks. Various studies undertaken on the US banking industry (Brozen, 1982; Smirlock, 1985; Evanoff and Fortier, 1988) suggest that firm-specific efficiency seems to be the dominant variable explaining bank profitability.

One of the major problems associated with the structure-performance literature is how to measure structure. Most of the studies use measures of concentration to proxy for market structure. Others consider measures that encapsulate the degree of openness of markets by considering exit and entry barriers. Overall, structural measures are extremely naive. They barely take account of the main forces that influence the institutional nature of banking markets, such as the regulatory framework, sector-ownership and so on. It seems indisputable, however, that the structure of a market influences the way in which banks operate in that market. With these points in mind, we can examine a number of important factors affecting banking structure in Europe.

29

Rules and regulations affecting structure

The legal and supervisory framework under which banks operate is one of the most important factors influencing the present and developing structure in European banking markets, although there has never been a uniform approach to banking law throughout Europe. Even though the banking laws enacted in most Continental European countries after the widespread banking crises of the 1930s were similar in nature (Revell, 1987), there is currently no legal consensus as to what constitutes 'banking business' and the permissible scope of banking activity. The banking laws of Austria, France and Germany[1] provide a detailed description of what constitutes banking business, whereas those of Belgium, Denmark, Ireland, Italy and the United Kingdom are very broadly defined. In contrast, the banking acts of Switzerland do not provide any precise definition of banking business[2]. This, however, does not necessarily mean that banking systems that have a detailed legalistic definition of 'banking business' are more restrictive: for example, the detailed and wide-ranging German banking laws actively promote banks to operate as universal-type institutions. The largest banks in the United Kingdom have now partially achieved universal bank status, despite a completely different legal framework.

Regulatory bodies can influence the size and structure of the banking sector through their control over access to the banking system via licensing. Compulsory bank licensing systems were introduced in Ireland (1971), the Netherlands (1979), the Unite Kingdom (1979) and France (1984)[3]. In these countries authorization procedures are usually based on the fulfilment of specific legal requirements where the supervisory authorities have a certain degree of administrative discretion. Licensing bodies have full discretionary authority in countries such as Greece, Norway, Portugal, Spain and Sweden (see Pecchioli, 1987, pp. 46–56 and OECD, 1984, for a detailed examination of licensing and branching regulations in OECD countries). In addition to the granting of licences, the regulatory authorities have the power to control the opening of new domestic branches by authorized institutions. In various European countries the opening of a new domestic branch requires either notification to the relevant supervisory authorities[4] or is subject to non-statutory requirements[5]. On the other hand, in Finland, Greece and Italy[6] prior authorization by the central bank is required. Since the 1960s, regulations have been modified significantly in only a handful of countries: most notably in France and Italy.

Competition and competitors

Over the last decade or so, three overriding competitive trends in European banking systems have been quite clear: competition has increased between commercial banks; competition has increased between financial institutions; and competition has increased in the market for financial services. This more competitive environment has encouraged banks and financial service firms (FSFs) of all kinds to broaden and improve the quality of their services and hence their customer bases. The general feeling is that European commercial banks will have to become more market-orientated (see Arthur Andersen, 1986) in their outlook if they are to consolidate their positions as the major FSFs in European countries.

In the area of retail banking, customers are becoming relatively older, wealthier and financially more sophisticated. As retail demands become more sophisticated, customer loyalty decreases. Retail customers are now demanding more services, better information, and most importantly value for money. As a result, banks have to be able to identify their markets. Through market segmentation, product differentiation and accurate packaging, banks are now beginning to offer services in designated 'target' markets—one-parent families, high net worth individuals, house buyers and the like. Maintaining a strong hold on the payments mechanism is a critical factor in preserving customer bases within the retail banking market.

Corporate customers will continue to demand highly specialist products and will expect to pay competitive, cost-based charges for them. As the demand for traditional corporate banking services from the largest of corporations declines with the securitization phenomenon, banks will increase their focus on the small to medium-sized corporate customer. Only the larger savings and mortgage institutions are likely to compete aggressively with the commercial banks for a portion of this market.

Commercial banks are likely to face a substantial competitive threat from three types of financial organization over the next decade or so. These are the savings and/or mortgage institutions, insurance companies and stockbrokers and financial intermediaries. Postal organization, retail and leasing/hire purchase companies will probably form the second line of attack[7]. The threat posed by these groups appears to vary throughout Europe. Mortgage institutions (especially as they can now choose to go public) are expected to make significant inroads in the United Kingdom, whereas insurance companies are more likely to have a greater impact in France and Germany. Stockbroking and other financial intermediaries will probably have a greater impact in Southern European countries. There is a general feeling that these competitors will emerge mainly from the domestic arena, and only in the case of stockbrokers and financial intermediaries will there be a significant potential foreign threat. This, of course, does not rule out the possibility of acquisition, takeover, stakeholding or the formation of joint ventures with foreign organizations.

Revell (1985) suggests that financial services will in the future be supplied by various types of corporate entity: conglomerates, specialists, agents and franchisers, groups and associations. Conglomeration is probably the most important of these trends applicable to European banking. It refers broadly to the provision of a range of financial services by a collection of FSFs under common ownership or control. The conglomeration movement is characterized by the desire of the larger European banks to maintain a global presence as well as to offer a universal range of bank products and services. At the present time only a few European countries – Germany, Luxembourg, Spain, Switzerland and the United Kingdom – do not apply specific restrictions on the interests of commercial banks in other corporate entitities, and as such it seems likely that conglomeration will be a more important phenomenon in these countries. This view has been supported by the large number of mergers and takeovers in the European financial services marketplace which have taken place since 1986, as reported by de Jonquières (1988).

The conglomerate trend will continue as long as larger institutions wish to expand their multi-product and geographical coverage and as long as the predators have sufficient excess capital to swallow their victims. Partnerships and cross-shareholdings in the financial services marketplace are now widely being used as either insurance policies against the threat of takeover or as a prelude to a possible full merger. The main impetus towards a conglomerate trend during the past decade has been the perceived growth in importance of investment banking and securities markets activities.

31

Size, concentration and performance characteristics

Size and concentration

Despite differences relating to establishment and branching, every banking system in Western Europe has a group of dominant or 'core banks' which are recognized by both the authorities and the general public[8]. In many European countries there has been a trend for local and regional based banks to form groups that could effectively compete against the national 'core' banks. Those countries with a large number of mutual and co-operative banks, such as Germany, Spain, Italy and France, tend to have a stronger regional focus than countries which have a small number of relatively large private banks. This seems to have little impact on the overall size of European banking markets.

If we take the size of individual economies into consideration the relative importance of bank assets in relation to gross national product can be analysed. Table 3.1 shows that deposit banks' assets as a percentage of GNP for almost all European countries have increased substantially between 1980 and 1986. This measure is sometimes used to gauge the degree of financial depth in an economy. If we accept this as an acceptable measure then it would be fair to say that the financial systems of Ireland, Spain, Portugal and Sweden hardly deepened between 1980 and 1986, whereas those of Belgium, Germany and the United Kingdom certainly did.

Table 3.2 illustrates the various structural characteristics of EC banking markets at the end of 1988. It shows that the German, UK and French banking systems are by

Table 3.1 Deposit bank assets as a percentage of GNP.

	1980	1981	1982	1983	1984	1985	1986
Austria[a]	139.3	148.0	152.4	160.4	167.4	169.7	175.6
Belgium	112.7	137.7	144.7	135.9	173.8	172.8	161.4
Denmark	51.7	52.9	53.7	60.1	70.4	84.2	87.1
Finland	55.6	57.1	63.3	68.2	74.9	76.9	87.8
France[b]	107.0	109.7	113.2	116.9	114.7	(80.5)	(79.6)
Germany	137.3	144.0	148.8	151.3	154.5	181.6	191.4
Greece	79.8	91.8	97.2	101.8	106.9	110.2	106.7
Ireland	110.7	110.2	85.1	90.5	95.0	94.0	105.9
Italy	116.9	113.5	113.7	116.8	116.7	115.2	–
Luxembourg	2080.4	2520.4	2543.1	2801.9	2783.0	2664.6	–
Netherlands	181.3	193.4	197.3	205.4	213.3	214.1	221.2
Norway	118.1	115.8	116.2	118.2	124.9	132.5	141.5
Portugal	80.6	91.5	97.0	94.0	88.0	–	–
Spain	120.2	113.2	120.5	122.9	128.7	127.9	123.4
Sweden	127.2	135.9	139.9	140.2	141.7	136.6	–
Switzerland	182.8	188.1	233.8	243.5	219.8	224.9	224.3
UK	101.4	130.1	147.0	157.9	185.8	165.5	186.1
USA	99.0	95.2	99.1	101.9	100.2	104.0	108.5
Japan	202.3	208.5	219.2	231.7	237.2	246.1	264.1

Source: Calculated from various editions of IMF, *International Financial Statistics*.

Notes: a The 1980–83 bank asset figures for Austria do not include claims on state and local government.

b French data are for bank assets as a percentage of GDP and figures for 1985 and 1986 understate the situation because they exclude claims on other banking institutions.

Table 3.2 Market concentration and size of banking sectors in Europe 1988.

Number of banks in market	Size of banking sector		Concentration % of total market			
		Assets ($bn)	Assets		Deposits	
			5-firm	3-firm	5-firm	3-firm
4465	Germany	1465.0	31.2	21.2	30.5	19.1
661	UK	1337.8	32.6	26.5	30.3	21.6
367	France	1012.6	63.0	42.3	65.2	45.5
980	Italy	529.2	55.1	35.2	68.5	41.6
349	Spain	332.3	34.7	21.9	38.8	24.3
81	Netherlands	272.3	–	71.3	–	83.9
86	Belgium	228.3	84.7	57.1	87.5	59.0
120	Luxembourg	198.1	22.4	16.7	–	16.5
216	Denmark	111.9	50.9	36.7	58.6	45.3
n/a	Greece	48.4	–	–	–	49.7
40	Portugal	43.3	–	49.7	–	49.6
43	Ireland	22.1	–	71.0	–	–

Source: Molyneux (1988)

General notes: a The market size figure for Greece is a deposits figure.

b Sources of information for banking sector size; OECD (1988) and various central bank publications.

c 3-firm and 5-firm concentration ratios calculated using data taken from the consolidated accounts published in *The Banker* 'Top 500'.

d The number of banks in France increases to around 6000 if mutual associations are included.

e Only 12 of the 120 Luxembourg banks are domestic institutions.

far the largest in the EC. Using total banking sector assets as a size measure, the Italian banking market is less than half the size of the French system and a third that of Germany. The largest non-EC banking market in Europe is that of Switzerland, which is around the same size as Spain. Other non-EC banking sectors, such as those in Scandinavia and Austria, are all smaller than the Belgian banking market.

The concentration measures show that, of the largest four banking sectors in Europe, Italy and France have the most concentrated markets. The market power of the main banks in Belgium, the Netherlands, Finland, Sweden, Switzerland and Portugal also seems to be significant. [Other studies undertaken by Molyneux (1988) and Revell (1987) confirm these findings.] It is interesting to note that, of the four largest banking markets, it is those in which regulations are currently most restrictive – France through nationalization and Italy through branching restrictions and central government ownership – which are the most concentrated. In fact, central government ownership of banking firms is also much more significant in France (around 50 per cent) and Italy (around 40 per cent) than in other larger banking sectors, although this trend is currently being reversed in France.

As already mentioned, it is a peculiar feature of banking markets that in almost every developed country a handful of large banks tend to emerge over time through either government encouragement or the workings of the market mechanism. The recent mergers between top banks in Spain has partially been encouraged by the realization that Spain's largest banks look small when viewed in a European context[9]. The newly merged Bilbao-Vizcaya bank will constitute around 20 per cent of Spain's 'banking market' (Metaxas-Vittas, 1988, p. 12). In October 1988 Banco Español de Crédito signed a merger agreement with Banco Central which would have created Spain's largest bank, but the deal fell through in February 1989.

The concentration of European banking markets has also been an important feature of structural change. Concentration is by no means a recent phenomenon, and many countries' banking systems have been dominated by a handful of large banks for at least half a century or so. The way we measure concentration is also important. If it is measured on a 'consolidated groups basis' then the Netherlands and France appear to be the most concentrated systems, whereas Germany and the United Kingdom appear to be the most dispersed (Revell, 1987, pp. 27). Other results (Baer and Mote, 1985) indicate that the French banking system has become twice as concentrated since the 1930s, whereas the degree of concentration in the German banking market has fallen by some 50 per cent.

From a general perspective, it is difficult to appraise accurately either the efficacy or extent of increased concentration within individual banking systems. It is also becoming much more difficult to measure concentration by contemporary measures, because of the blurring of demarcation lines between banking and other financial markets. It is clear, however, that there appears to be a current preference for larger size in many banks within different European countries. The desire to obtain economies of scale and scope appear to be the main driving force behind the trend towards larger-sized institutions, which is another reflection of the so-called conglomeration movement.

Performance and ownership characteristics of the largest banks

The relative performance of industrial countries' banking systems can be gauged by the distinguishing characteristics of the major banks that operate in these markets. It is also the case that the degree of change in market size, concentration and ownership resulting from major reforms, such as the 1992 proposals, will be determined primarily by the ability of the larger banks to discover and exploit new profitable opportunities within domestic and across country boundaries. An analysis of the major structure and performance characteristics of top banks operating in the EC (between 1985 and 1987) has been undertaken by Molyneux (1988). The most important findings are as follows:

- Top French banks are on average the largest in the EC, but employ considerably less staff than their UK counterparts.
- The major UK banks have the largest branch networks and employ considerably more staff than their counterparts in other EC countries. The labour-intensive nature of the UK payments system and the different production functions of UK banks compared with EC banks are usually cited as important causal factors in this differentiation.
- Comparing the relative performance figures for top banks in the bigger banking markets it can be stated that Italian and Spanish banks have the highest ROAs (return on assets) and the highest ROC (return on capital) ratios. Italian banks have quite small branch networks.
- The performance figures for the top 44 German, 33 Italian and 13 Spanish banks

34

are less dispersed than if we compare similar figures for the top 15 UK and 20 French banks.

- The biggest banks in Germany and France have markedly lower capital:assets ratios than banks in the UK, Spain and Italy. The top German banks have quite similar capital:assets ratios. Some of these points can be explained by the role of hidden reserves and attitudes to loan capital in Germany and the role of the state in France.

The above observations are consistent over time as illustrated in Molyneux (1988).

It has already been mentioned that an important feature distinguishing Continental European banking systems from British-based systems is that publicly controlled banks (whether by central or local government) are much more important in EC countries. Table 3.3 shows that out of the 162 EC banks listed in the 1987 *Banker* 'Top 500', 69 were privately owned and 67 publicly owned. The mean performance figures for the public banks are marginally worse than those for private banks, although it could be fair to say that both sectors exhibit remarkably similar characteristics, apart from the average number of employees. The average public bank employs half as many staff as the private banks. The reasons for this are not immediately clear, but it could be the case that central management costs and staffing levels of some public banks are hidden in government accounts.

Credit co-operatives found in this group tend to be larger than their public and private bank counterparts, and this is because they are central institutions representing thousands of small operations. The mutual institutions (savings banks) are the smallest category and tend to be much smaller in size, even though their ROA (return on assets) and ROC (return on capital) statistics are comparable with those of private

Table 3.3 Statistical summary of the ownership of top banks in the EC, 1987. Arithmetic means and standard deviations

No. of EC banks in *Bankers* Top 500		Assets $ m.	PTP	PTP/ Assets	PTP/ CAP	CAP/ Assets	NINT/ Assets	Employees
					%			
Private	69	37,601	207.2	0.77	16.36	4.81	3.01	15,948
		(1.15)	(1.61)	(0.89)	(0.80)	(0.48)	(0.59)	(1.36)
Public	67	31,133	158.9	0.61	14.30	3.70	2.14	7,261
(Central & local govt)		(1.09)	(1.43)	(1.1)	(0.66)	(0.54)	(0.60)	(1.48)
Co-operative	14	41,402	242.8	0.89	17.31	5.16	2.06	12,124
		(1.36)	(0.95)	(0.60)	(0.40)	(0.58)	(0.62)	(1.69)
Mutuals	12	10,421	77.5	0.81	14.78	6.14	3.99	4,419
		(0.50)	(0.64)	(0.46)	(0.52)	(0.39)	(0.29)	(0.56)

Source: Molyneux (1988).

Notes: a Classification after Revell (1987). Large German savings banks are controlled by local government organizations and therefore are classified as public rather than mutual organizations.

b Figures in parentheses are standard deviations/means.

c PTP = pre-tax profits, CAP = Capital, NINT = net interest income.

and public banks. It is interesting to note that, of the top 162 banks in the EC, 93 are not run for a commercial profit or to satisfy the requirements of private shareholders. These institutions cannot be acquired through hostile takeover. Even though various countries, such as Denmark and the UK, are establishing legislation which will enable mutual societies to convert to corporate status, there will not be a great deal of merger activity between these groups until widespread conversion from public to private ownership takes place. Many public, co-operative and mutual banks, however, operate in the same way as private banks and their ownership status does not preclude them from being aggressive acquirers of private banking institutions.

One could be so bold as to state that, of these top EC banks, 93 cannot be acquired and 25–27 are too large and nationally too important to allow any foreign predator to acquire them. This leaves about 42–44 large size banks that are potential acquisition targets; in fact, at least 25 of them are already controlled by other institutions or groups of institutions. In the run-up to 1992 the value of these particular banks will no doubt require a distinct market premium. The corollary of this is that, if widespread acquisitions take place, it will be mainly medium- and small-sized local and regional banks that become foreign-owned. The limited takeover opportunities available to large banks may encourage them to establish branch networks overseas, and there could be fierce competition and widespread growth in branch numbers where entry via takeover is naturally restricted. Limited takeover opportunities will also accelerate the current move of large banks to form joint ventures with other financial institutions in EC countries.

Competitive pressures in the run-up to 1992

The European banking system will change considerably in the next few years in response to the EC plan to create a single internal market by 1992. It is generally believed that a handful of large European multinational operators will emerge to fight off the challenge from the Americans and Japanese. Of the 14,000 or so banks in Western Europe the vast majority will have to 'settle for whatever pickings are available, either in products or regional specialisation. The minnows will be swallowed up by the bigger fry or scatter for shelter in bigger boutiques' (Jones, 1988, pp. 56).

Various large EC banks already own foreign branch networks, for example Deutsche Bank's purchase of Banca d'America e d'Italia in 1986. Deutsche has also purchased a Portuguese merchant bank, holds a 50 per cent stake in H. Alfred de Bory (a Dutch investment bank) and has increased its holding in Banco Comercial Transatlantico, a $1.7 billion Spanish bank. Recent moves by Deutsche Bank confirm its avowed interest in the French and UK market (see Chapter 12). Banks in Germany and the United Kingdom have already made clear their wider European interests by recently forging links with Spanish, Italian and French banks. In fact, many large European banks appear to be focusing their attention on the United Kingdom, Spain and Italy. The relatively high margins that can be earned in Spain and the considerable growth in consumer lending (mainly housing finance) experienced in recent years in the United Kingdom are also of noticeable interest to the large Swiss and German banks.

Cross-border acquisitions to date have involved large banks acquiring much smaller banks. Reciprocal equity stakes, for example, like that between the Royal

36

Bank of Scotland and Banco de Santander, have generally been taken by medium-sized banks, the proposed 25 per cent share swap between AMRO and Generale Bank in 1988 being the general exception. (The latter was expected to be a precursor for a full merger, but only 5 per cent of equity had been swapped by mid-1989 and plans for a full-scale merger were abandoned.) Recent alliances have also been formed by various Nordic banks in preparation for increased competition in the 1990s[10]. Mergers between large banks within countries have taken place in Spain, Denmark, the Netherlands and Norway, and a merger between two larger German Ländesbanken was recently (January 1989) proposed[11]. Smaller banks that do not have the resources to make acquisitions may form associations or banking clubs like the ones prevalent in Europe during the 1970s. Large banks may establish limited branch networks and various joint ventures because of restricted large-scale takeover opportunities. No widespread acquisitions of large banks is likely to take place in the run-up to 1992 (see also Chapter 12).

The authorities' desire to harmonize bank regulations and to bring about a 'level playing field' by the end of 1992, coupled with the above corporate restructuring, will no doubt lead to a more competitive banking environment. The increase in competitive pressures facing banks can be partly illustrated by the fact that, between 1986 and 1987, 80 per cent of EC banks experienced a fall in their ROA, 25 per cent of European banks reduced their staffing levels, and over two-thirds increased their capital:assets ratios.

Despite these pressures, European banks in total are still one of the most important and powerful forces in world banking. Revell (1988) shows that in the world's top 500 banks for 1987, Western European banks accounted for 42.5 per cent of total assets (36.2 per cent by EC banks), Japanese banks 32.9 per cent and US banks 12.9 per cent. The top 300 banks in Europe had around $7 trillion in assets and almost $300 billion in shareholders' equity. They made between $35 – $40 billion in pre-tax profits and employed more than two million people.

Structural trends and balance-sheet effects

Two recent reports (OECD, 1987 and 1988) indicate a number of important trends that have been occurring in European banking systems since the early 1980s. In the area of sectoral ownership, the number of mutual organizations appears to be declining in most countries, and this phenomenon is most marked in Scandinavian countries. The only major European country not to follow this trend is Germany, where there was a 59 per cent increase in the number of co-operative banks between 1982 and 1986. In fact, it appears that the number of banks in Northern Europe is declining whereas the opposite is the case for Southern Europe.

The number of bank branches in most countries has also increased over this period, with a greater than 10 per cent increase in Austria (11 per cent), Germany (12 per cent), the Netherlands (34 per cent) and Norway (13 per cent). The only European country in which the size of the branch networks fell dramatically was Switzerland (− 20 per cent), although declines occurred in Belgium (− 1.0 per cent), Denmark (− 3.8 per cent), France (− 1.3 per cent) and Sweden (− 2.0 per cent). The size of UK branch networks also fell during this period. Employment in the banking systems of European countries increased over the same period, the largest increases being in the Scandinavian countries, Greece, Luxembourg and, most surprisingly,

37

Table 3.4 Gross income as a multiple of operating expenses for commercial banks (1980–85 averages).

Country	Multiple
Luxembourg	3.33
Switzerland	1.78
Portugal	1.64
Sweden	1.60
Netherlands	1.56
Germany	1.53
Italy	1.52
Spain	1.52
France	1.47
United Kingdom	1.44
Finland	1.28
Belgium	1.20

Source: Adapted from *Retail Banker International*, 1987, p. 11.

Switzerland. Staff costs also appear to have risen more rapidly in these countries. On average, between 1982 and 1986 absolute bank staff costs in European countries rose by some 57 per cent (see OECD (1988) for further detailed breakdowns)[12]. Nevertheless, over the same period European banks' total assets grew at a greater rate and subsequently staff costs as a percentage of total assets fell by some 7 per cent (see Table 5.3).

An interesting trend identifiable from the OECD (1987) study was that, with regard to average interest margins of commercial banks, low interest margin countries tend to reflect the relative importance of wholesale banking compared to retail activities. European countries such as Luxembourg and Switzerland tended to have the lowest interest margins, whereas banks in Spain, Italy and the United Kingdom had the highest margins. High interest margins tend to be translated into high net income ratios[13], but if one considers operating expenses to gross income figures this provides a satisfactory measure for making international comparisons[14]. Table 3.4 shows that banks in Luxembourg and Switzerland appear to be the most profitable in Europe, whereas those in Belgium, Finland and the United Kingdom are the least profitable. Other measures of performance from the OECD study indicated that, in the two systems which had experienced widespread nationalization programmes (France and Portugal), ROA had fallen dramatically between 1980 and 1985, whereas the largest increases occurred in Germany and Switzerland. In general, ROA figures were higher for those countries which had experienced some form of structural deregulation.

As well as the above developments, there has also been a marked increase in the number of foreign banks and other financial institutions doing business in European markets (see Chapter 8). The internationalization of European banking has led to increases in:

● the importance of foreign assets and liabilities of domestic banks (Harrington, 1987)

- the number and type of foreign institutions operating in domestic banking market (BIS, 1986, p. 151).
- the assets of foreign banks operating in European banking markets (BIS, 1986, p. 152).

The outcome of these trends is that foreign banks will increasingly pose a threat to domestic banks in European banking markets for the large to medium-sized corporate customer and also for wealthy personal clients.

Although some commentators may disagree (Arthur Andersen, 1986), there appears to be a definite trend towards outsider penetration in these markets, especially when the incumbent domestic banks are perceived as lacking expertise. In Europe over the next ten years foreign banks are not expected to form the major competitive threat in retail banking markets, unless they are free to acquire organizations with large customer bases or able to obtain access to the market for wealthier customers. Nevertheless, Eurocurrency banking business will continue to displace domestic currency banking business in the balance sheets of many European banking sectors.

Conclusion

The structure of European banking markets has changed markedly over the last decade or so. The banking sector in almost all European countries has grown in size relative to gross national product. Restricted growth has been most common in Southern European countries such as Spain, Portugal and Italy. Banking markets have also become more concentrated, with public ownership still playing an important role in many financial systems. The number of bank branches and the level of employment in the banking sectors have increased in all the major European countries during the 1980s, despite the indication that this trend might have reversed in 1987. There has been a marked increase in the number of foreign operators doing business within Europe, and many non-bank financial institutions have sought to compete in markets that were once the sole preserve of banks. Despite these factors and the moves to harmonize structural deregulation and supervisory re-regulation, we can still identify substantial 'country-specific' characteristics relating to banking markets. For example, UK large banks tend to employ many more staff than their West German and French counterparts. Certain countries' banking systems are much more concentrated than others, and banks perform much better in some countries compared with others. It seems unlikely from historical experience and recent trends that the 1992 proposals will cause the structural and performance characteristics of banks and banking systems within EC countries to become rapidly more alike.

Notes

1. In 1978 a specific definition of 'banking activity' was introduced into Finnish legislation. It may be noted that a very detailed description is also enshrined in Japanese banking law and banks' allowable business powers are well documented by regulations in Canada and the United States.
2. However, in the case of the United Kingdom and other countries the central bank is

responsible for making sure that a bank's business is undertaken in such a manner that it does not jeopardize the position of depositors.

3. Also in Luxembourg (1981) and Portugal (1983).

4. In Austria, France, Germany, Spain, Sweden.

5. As in Belgium, Denmark and the Netherlands.

6. As well as Luxembourg, Norway and Portugal.

7. Other organizations like information technology and telecommunications specialists are not expected to diversify into the market for financial services over the next ten years.

8. For example, in the United Kingdom, Barclays, National Westminster, Midland, Lloyds; in France, Crédit Agricole, BNP, Crédit Lyonnais, Société Générale, Paribas; in Italy, Banca Nazionale del Lavoro, Istituto Bancario Sao Paolo, Monte dei Paschie die Siena; and in Germany, Deutsche Bank, Dresdner Bank, Commerzbank.

9. Banco de Bilbao failed to take over Banesto, but its merger with Banco de Vizcaya in early 1988 has created the largest Spanish bank. This will probably lead to more mergers among Spanish banks. The new group has stated that it will sell a large number of its duplicated (excess) branches so as to raise funds for overseas expansion. The new bank was the 28th largest bank in Europe, according to consolidated total assets at the end of 1988.

10. Kansallis-Osake-Pankki, Finland's biggest bank, has agreed with Sweden's sixth largest bank. Götabanken, to form a group. There has been a less formal alliance between Sweden's Skandinaviska Enskilda Banken, Norway's Bergen Bank, Denmark's Privatbanken and Union Bank of Finland since 1984, known as Scandinavian Banking Partners.

11. Westdeutsche and Hessische Landesbank. A merger would make it the second largest bank in Germany with assets of $137 billion.

12. Staff cost percentage increases for banks between 1982 and 1986 in European countries were: Austria (37 per cent), Belgium (30 per cent), Denmark (41 per cent), Finland (62 per cent), France (36 per cent), Germany (32 per cent), Greece (127 per cent), Italy (78 per cent), Netherlands (30 per cent), Luxembourg (61 per cent), Norway (66 per cent), Portugal (144 per cent), Spain (56 per cent), Sweden (58 per cent), Switzerland (41 per cent), and the United Kingdom (19 per cent between 1984 and 1986).

13. Net income ratio equals pre-tax profits as a percentage of assets.

14. This is because net income measures do not take into account the difficulties associated with bad debts, taxes, different countries' accounting policies, hidden reserves and profit-smoothing techniques.

References

Arthur Andersen (1986), *The Decade of Change: Banking in Europe – The Next Ten Years* (London: Lafferty Publications).

Baer, Herbert and Mote, Larry R. (1985), 'The effects of nationwide banking and concentration: the evidence from abroad', *Federal Reserve Bank of Chicago Economic Perspectives*, vol. 9, no. 1 (January/February) pp. 3–16.

Bank for International Settlements (1986), *56th Annual Report* (Basle: BIS).

The Banker, (1988), 'Top 500', vol. 138, no. 749, (July), pp. 56–151.

Brozen, Y. (1982), *Concentration, Mergers and Public Policy*, (New York: Macmillan).

Evanoff, D. D. and Fortier, D. L. (1988), 'Reevaluation of the structure-conduct-performance paradigm in banking', *Journal of Financial Services Research*, vol. 1, no. 3, (June), pp. 277–94.

Gilbert, R. A. (1984), 'Bank market structure and competition', *Journal of Money, Credit and Banking*, vol 16, (November), pp. 617–45.

Harrington, R. (1987), *Asset and Liability Management by Banks* (Paris: OECD).

Heggestad, A. A. and Mingo, J. J. (1977), 'The competitive condition of US banking markets and the impact of structural reform', *Journal of Finance*, vol. 32, no. 6, (June), pp. 649–61.

de Jonquieres, Guy (1988), 'The search for a flying start', Third in a series of five articles of the EEC 1992 completing the internal market proposals, *Financial Times*, (29 February), p. 5.

Jones, Colin (1988), 'On your marks, get set, go ...' *The Banker*, vol. 138, no. 752, (October), pp. 56–77.

Metaxas-Vittas, T. (1988), 'Spain: tremendous opportunities for further expansion', *Retail Banker International*, (16 May), pp. 9–12.

Molyneux, P. (1988), '1992 and its impact on local and regional banking markets', Paper given at the *Regional Studies Association Annual Conference*, November 1988.

Osborne, D. K. and Wendel, J. (1983), 'Research in structure, conduct and performance in banking 1964–79'. *Research Paper 83–003 College of Business Administration*, Oklahoma State University, (July).

OECD (1984), *International Trade in Services in Banking* (OECD: Paris).

OECD (1987), *Bank Profitability, Financial Statements of Banks, With Methodological Country Notes, 1980–84* (Paris: OECD).

OECD (1988), *Bank Profitability, Statistical Supplement, Financial Statement of Banks, 1982–86* (Paris: OECD).

Pecchioli, R. M. (1987) *Prudential Supervision in Banking. Trends in Banking, Structure and Regulation in OECD Countries* (Paris: OECD).

Revell, Jack (1985), 'New forms of competition and new competitors' *Revue de la Banque*, vol. 49, no. 2, (February), pp. 45–53.

Revell, Jack (1987), *Mergers and the Role of Large Banks, IEF Research Monograph* no. 2. (Bangor: Institute of European Finance).

Revell, Jack (1988), 'Bank preparations for 1992: Some clues and some queries, paper presented at the *European Association of University Teachers in Banking and Finance*, Paris (September).

Rhoades, S. (1982), 'Welfare loss, redistribution effect, and restriction of output due to monopoly', *Journal of Monetary Economics*, vol. 9, no. 3, pp. 375–87.

Rybczyski, T. M. (1984), 'The UK financial system in transition', *National Westminster Bank Quarterly Review*, (November), pp. 26–42.

Rybczynski, T. M. (1988), 'Financial systems and industrial restructuring', *National Westminster Banks Quarterly Review*, (November), pp. 3–13.

Smirlock, M. (1985), 'Evidence on the (non) relationship – between concentration and profitability in banking', *Journal of Money, Credit and Banking*, vol. 17, no. 2, (February), pp. 69–83.

Spellman, L. J. (1981), 'Commercial banks and the profits of savings and loan markets', *Journal of Bank Research*, vol. 12, (Spring), pp. 32–6.

Weiss, I. W. (1974), 'The concentration-profits relationship and antitrust'. In W. Goldschmid, M. M. Mann and J. F. Weston eds. *Industrial Concentration: The New Learning* (Boston: Little, Brown and Co.), pp. 184–233.

Chapter four

Monetary regulation, 1992 and supervision

Introduction

It is already clear that regulation of all kinds has intensified and continues to act as an important 'engine of change' in European banking. The first part of this chapter deals with monetary policy developments throughout Europe. It examines the most important instruments of monetary control that have been used by European central authorities throughout the 1970s and 1980s, including the significant role played by monetary aggregates during this period. Finally, this section illustrates how various financial innovations have reduced the effectiveness of traditional monetary policy practices as well as considering the future prospects for the European Monetary System and the proposed European Central Bank. The second part of the chapter focuses on the structural deregulation, or liberalization, moves associated with 1992 and the increasing importance of banking supervision throughout Europe.

Monetary policy in Europe

The monetary environment

The changes that have taken place in European banking and finance over the last two decades have had important implications for monetary policy. Changes in technology, competition, regulation and the economic environment have all played their part. New technology has substantially altered the relative costs of providing various services and has also created access into new areas of banking and reduced transactions costs. Increased competition coupled with supervisory deregulation has sought to break down demarcation lines between institutions and markets. This has helped stimulate important product and process innovations, and has led bank customers to be more aware of interest-rate differentials as well as levels.

The secular rise in inflation during the late 1960s and 1970s gave monetary policy a more important role in the formulation of domestic economic policies. The related increased volatility of interest rates encouraged depositors to minimize their holdings of non-interest-bearing money, and also fuelled the emergence of close money substitutes bearing market-related rates of interest. As a result, the definition of what constitutes a transactions balance has become increasingly blurred, as has the general definition of money itself.

The substantial growth of financial markets and instruments throughout the 1970s and 1980s, coupled with the securitization phenomenon, have also helped to increase the similarity between monetary and non-monetary financial assets. Many of the aforementioned developments have contributed to a gradual change in monetary policy formulation. Throughout Europe there has been a more systematic use of monetary and credit aggregates in policy formulation and these have been subject to both implicit and explicit targeting. The increased internationalization and inter-penetration of financial markets has also led monetary authorities to reassess their views concerning both internal and external objectives by directing policy so as to maintain the internal and external value of currency. Subsequently this has led to a change in policymakers' attitudes towards the policy role of interest rates and exchange rates. An explicit exchange-rate policy subsumes an implicit interest-rate policy if exchange rates are flexible and the demand for money is endogenous. Many European countries in recent years have sought to emphasize monetary policy objectives related to the internal and external value of their currency.

Despite all the above developments, the introduction of new types of monetary policy instruments throughout Europe has for the most part been gradual. All monetary authorities have utilized traditional policy instruments such as credit ceilings, reserve requirements, interest rates, central bank credit facilities, public sector borrowing and open-market-operations techniques to manage their monetary sectors.

Historical overview

Of all the European central banks only those of Switzerland and Germany are legally empowered with the final authority to conduct monetary policy. These two central banks have governors who are not directly appointed by the government. The Dutch central bank has a specific economic objective (price stability) included in its constitution, which provides it with very slight independence (although Eizenga (1987) argues that both the Deutsche Bundesbank and the Nederlandsche Bank have a similar degree of independence). All the other central banks are subservient to their governments in both the day-to-day management and longer-term formulation of monetary policy.

At the beginning of the 1960s monetary policy transmission was quite different from what it is today as Bingham (1985, pp. 41–2) points out:

> Even though banks are not responsible for more financial intermediation than now, the process of marketisation of banking and finance had not advanced very far, and many important monetary policy tools impinged on them directly. The authorities were in general unwilling to see large swings in interest rates because of concern about financial stability ... Interest rate controls were also more wide-spread than today.

During this period European central banks generally focused their attention on credit conditions, and especially bank credit conditions, mainly because it was believed that this sector was the most important source of credit. Emphasis tended to be placed on direct administrative controls aimed at regulating the quantity of credit rather than the price. Nowadays, emphasis focuses on indirect price controls through manipulating market rates.

Throughout the period from the middle of the 1970s, all European governments became preoccupied with money aggregates because of the failure of traditional monetary control in the early 1970s to stem accelerating inflation. 'Targeting' became a buzz-word in monetary circles. As the main objective of monetary policy is to influence either the quantity or price of credit available in an economy, regulators aimed to achieve their objectives by directing their policies on two so-called intermediate targets, interest rates or/and monetary aggregates (Bingham, 1985)[1]. Because the intermediate targets were (and still are) considered difficult to manipulate given the policy instruments available, regulators tended to focus on more easily managed 'operating targets' or 'intermediate indicators' which bore a stable and well-established relationship with the intermediate targets. For example, throughout the 1970s the main intermediate indicators of monetary policy in European countries were the monetary base[2] in Switzerland and Italy; short-term money market interest rates in the United Kingdom and Austria; and bank liquidity ratios in Germany, Netherlands and Spain. Table 4.1 illustrates these operating targets that were being used in the early 1980s.

Table 4.1 emphasizes the importance of broad money measures and exchange rates used in the policy planning process of European monetary authorities in the early 1980s. If a similar table were drawn up for the 1960s it would highlight three major differences. Firstly, policy planning indicators would appear to be more arbitrary as monetary authorities tended to emphasize 'vaguely defined "credit conditions"' (Bingham, 1985, p. 60). Secondly, there would be a much greater number of entries in the credit and interest columns and no column for monetary aggregates. Finally, exchange rates were not considered to be indicators as they were more or less fixed. During the 1970s and 1980s monetary authorities throughout Europe have elevated exchange rates and (in most cases) demoted interest rates from intermediate status. This is probably the most important change in monetary policy planning, even more so than the widespread use of monetary aggregates in the major European countries.

The aforementioned 'planning targets' or 'planning indicators' have been strongly influenced by the policy instruments available to the central banks, and these in turn are quite dependent on the financial structure of the economy. Traditional textbook, open-market operations – whereby the authorities intervene in the secondary government paper markets to influence aggregate liquidity – have taken place on a substantial scale only in the United Kingdom and Italy. At the other extreme the Spanish, Belgian and Austrian authorities rarely intervene in government paper markets. Various European countries have utilized repurchase arrangements[3] to adjust liquidity in the system and this technique has been most widespread in Germany from 1973 onwards.

A noticeable development, especially in the United Kingdom, has been the increased use of primary issues of government paper to influence liquidity[4]. Central banks have increasingly used debt management operations in the primary market to enable the non-monetary funding of the public sector borrowing requirements (PSBRs)[5]. Other main methods of market intervention undertaken by European central banks include intervention in private sector paper markets – most commonly in commercial bills – which occurs in France and the United Kingdom. Central banks

Table 4.1 Principal policy planning indicators in the early 1980s.

Country	Monetary base	Money		Exchange rate (reserves)	Credit		Bank	Interest rate
		Narrow	Broad		Total	Domestic		
Australia			X	O(–1983)				O
Austria				X				O
Belgium		X(1975–82)		X			O	
Canada								
Denmark				X			O	O[a]
Finland			X(1977–)	O	O			
France			X(1974–)	X				
Germany			X					
Greece				O		X		
Ireland				X		O		
Italy				O		O		
Japan			O					O
Luxembourg				X			O(72–5)	
Netherlands			O	X				
Norway				X			X	X[a]
Portugal				X	O	X	O	O
Spain			X(1973–)	X			O	O
Sweden								O
Switzerland	X(1979–)	X(1975–8)		O(X, 1978)[a]				O
Turkey	X(1978–)							O
United Kingdom		X(1981–[b])	X(1976–)	O				O
United States		X(1970–)	X(1983–)					O

Source: Bingham (1985 pp. 61–3)
Notes: The table depicts major prices and quantities used in policy planning, not instruments wielded by the monetary authorities. 'X' indicates a primary role, 'O' a secondary role. The dates given are indicative only because of the tendency to experiment informally before introducing new planning indicators.
a Real rates, in the United Kingdom both nominal and real interest rates since 1981.
b As measured by base money since 1984.

in Denmark, Germany, Ireland, Norway, Spain and Switzerland have also sought to influence domestic liquidity by issuing paper instruments. Finally, during the 1970s very few European banks sought to influence domestic monetary and liquidity conditions through activity in the foreign-exchange markets[6]. However, this position has reversed in the 1980s, and certainly the central banks of the largest EC countries would see foreign-exchange intervention (certainly post-Louvre Accord) as one of the most important methods of market intervention.

Other important instruments of monetary control are portfolio restrictions. Reserve requirements are the most widely used form of portfolio restriction and evolved predominantly as a supervisory rather than a monetary policy instrument. They have been used primarily for monetary policy purposes only in Germany and in Spain from the late 1970s onwards. One trend, however, that is quite noticeable is that reserve requirements have been extended in many European countries to include a broader range of financial institutions. For example, in Sweden reserve requirements were extended to all banking institutions in 1981, and Germany extended them to loan and savings banks in 1984.

One might expect that with the growth of markets in quasi-reserve instruments and the rapid increase in broad money measures during the 1980s, the reserve assets to broad money ratio would follow a long-term downward trend. This appears to be the case in Denmark, Germany, Norway and the United Kingdom. However, some countries like Finland, Greece, Italy and Sweden appear to be experiencing upward trends during the 1980s. In some European countries banks and other financial institutions are obliged to invest part of their assets in financial claims designated by the central authorities. This has been traditionally the case in Belgium, France, Italy, Norway, Portugal, Spain and Sweden, although a number of countries have sought from the early 1980s onwards to reduce the importance of these controls. This has been most noticeable in Italy and Norway. In Spain these requirements still appear onerous but are gradually being dismantled.

Controls on bank lending, or more formally credit restrictions, were widely used in Europe throughout the 1960s and 1970s. Most countries' central banks have at some time resorted to a form of direct control on lending either by establishing credit ceilings or by introducing schemes which impose progressively harsher penalties for expanding credit faster than a stipulated rate. Throughout the 1970s these ceilings were a central instrument of French monetary policy (*Economist*, 1978, p. 14) and they have also been widely used in Italy, the Netherlands, Norway, Portugal and Sweden[7]. They have never been used as a monetary policy tool in Germany. The major criticism of this type of control is that they distort the market and are easily circumvented. A common regulatory response to circumvention has been to extend the range of institutions to which they apply. During the 1980s there has been a marked tendency for central banks to reduce the role of credit ceilings on the grounds that this method of credit control is likely to stimulate new financial products and processes that circumvent regulation.

One area where there has been a substantial change in the implementation of monetary policy over the last two decades or so has been the relaxation of direct controls on interest rates. In the mid-1960s every European central bank had one form or another of direct interest-rate controls. These controls applied to retail and wholesale deposit rates as well as restrictions on lending and capital market rates (see

Bingham, 1985, pp. 129–33). Even though central banking authorities adopted a much more liberal stance on interest rates during the 1970s, bank rates remained regulated in most European countries. Even by the mid-1980s only in Denmark, Germany, Switzerland and the United Kingdom were interest rates no longer subject to substantial direct controls.

Central bank credit facilities[8], or 'accommodation' as they are sometimes known, have also been a widely used method adopted by European central banks to implement monetary policy. The general level of commercial bank indebtedness to the central authorities varies greatly from country to country. For example, during the 1970s it was relatively high in France and non-existent in Britain, mainly because in the United Kingdom the central bank lends indirectly through the discount market to the commercial banks. Long-term trends – illustrated in Bingham (1985) – suggest that there has been an increase in the relative importance of this type of control in Germany, the Netherlands and Norway, and a decline in Greece and Italy. The increase in securitization and the growth of financial markets, coupled with a greater use of asset and liability management by commercial banks, have been three major contributory forces which have helped to lessen the perceived discriminatory nature of various central bank credit facilities.

Monetary aggregates and contemporary monetary policy
During the 1970s the focus of monetary policy in most European countries broadened to include: a wider range of institutions falling under the scope of monetary policy; an increase in the number and the broadening of monetary aggregates; and longer planning time-periods. Monetary policy had traditionally focused predominantly on banks, but as a growing number of institutions sought to compete in traditional banking areas offering almost indistinguishable products and services most central banks decided to broaden the institutional coverage of monetary policymaking. By the late 1970s the majority of European countries had some form of published money targets. Policymakers viewed monetary aggregates as a more efficient (compared with manipulating interest rates) intermediate target of monetary policy in periods characterized by highly volatile inflationary expectations. The main problems associated with targeting these aggregates relate to defining and picking the 'right' aggregate and making sure there is a stable and predictable statistical relationship between the money aggregate and nominal income[9].

Switzerland, Germany and Spain have had official monetary aggregate targets longest, although countries such as Norway, Italy and the United Kingdom have used measures of domestic credit expansion since the 1960s. The Belgian authorities, on the other hand, have never formally used monetary aggregate targeting. All European central banks, apart from the Swiss, have focused on broad money measures. Switzerland has traditionally used a narrow money measure (M1 between 1975 and 1978) which over time has become even narrower (monetary base used from 1979 onwards). Some of these targets have meant much more than others. The Spanish targets during the 1970s meant little in practice, whereas the German ones, despite periodic overshooting, were strongly adhered to. The range and variety of monetary aggregates targeting used by the UK Conservative government in its Medium Term Financial Strategy (MTFS) in the early 1980s illustrated the prominence that these intermediate targets had achieved in the policy planning process.

The MTFS also illustrated the move by the UK authorities to introduce longer-term planning horizons by trying to influence longer-term price and therefore nominal expectations.

During the 1980s European central banks' conduct of monetary policy has been severely hampered by four major factors: the money-income relationship has been found to be unstable (Leigh Pemberton, 1986); fiscal imbalances have exacerbated monetary policy where policy has been constrained by domestic budget deficits as well as the financing requirements of other governments; exchange-rate variability; Third World debt and bank solvency. Despite these problems, monetary targeting techniques (multiple targeting, changing importance of different targets, etc.) have still been flexibly used predominantly for restrictive monetary policy purposes.

From the middle of the 1980s the exchange rate has played an increasingly important role in the formulation of monetary policy. A report by the Group of Ten central banks (BIS, 1986), noted that the higher degree of capital mobility that has accompanied developments in international financial markets implied that the effects of changes in domestic monetary policies are likely to be transmitted quickly to other countries through exchange-rate, interest-rate and capital-flow adjustments. Atkinson and Chouraqui (1987) argue that as far as European countries are concerned, the internal and external policy planning difficulties associated with monetary policy have been most acute in the United Kingdom[10]. They note that the problems associated with financial innovation, exchange-rate volatility and Third World debt have been 'somewhat less severe' in Continental European countries. In Germany the approach to monetary policy has, until recently, been less constrained than in the United Kingdom, and there has been strong adherence to pre-set targets in order to reduce inflation. Nevertheless, a large overrun on the money supply targets during 1986, together with strains on Deutschmark stability within the EMS, prompted the Deutsche Bundesbank to introduce new credit policy measures in January 1987 (de Meyer, 1987)[11] and re-emphasized the external constraint on domestic policymaking.

Atkinson and Couraqui (1987, p. 19) note that:

> Most other European countries, except the United Kingdom and Switzerland, have been constrained in their scope to be flexible by exchange rate commitments vis-a-vis the Deutschmark within the EMS or, in the case of Sweden, an exchange rate policy formulated in terms of a currency basket in which the Deutschmark has a large weight.

The Netherlands, for example, has two monetary policies. A 'narrow' policy which aims to stabilize the external value of the guilder and a broad policy that aims to stabilize the domestic price level (Kana, 1988). All European countries' monetary authorities now stipulate that the maintenance of a stable exchange rate is a critical aspect of monetary policy, together with the constraint imposed by the need to finance external deficits (for example see *European Economy* (1987) for the reports on Belgium and Denmark). Nominal exchange-rate targeting has been widely used by the smaller European countries prior to the Louvre Accord and thereafter by the larger countries, most noticeably the United Kingdom (Bank of England, 1987). During 1988 the United Kingdom switched from an implicit nominal exchange-rate targeting policy to an explicit short-term interest-rate policy[12].

Financial innovation and monetary policy

The process of innovation in European banking markets has been brought about by various broad trends which were identified earlier in Chapter 2. Some of these have had a significant effect on altering the relationship between monetary policy and the macroeconomy. One major factor has been the breaking down of market segmentation in various national markets, 'which has been driven by deregulation and increased competition, but also by the introduction of new products' (BIS, 1986, p. 243). The traditional focus of monetary policy has been sector-specific and has paid particular attention to bank deposits, or lending, rather than to the activities of a broader range of institutions (see Rose, 1986, p. 22)[13]. Various financial innovations, such as currency swaps, Euronote facilities and mortgage-backed securities, have provided a broader range of institutions with easier access to a wide range of close substitute forms of credit. For example, securitization has meant that larger credit flows have been intermediated using marketable instruments. As a result, credit-rationing techniques have become less effective policy tools; also the traditional constraints that at one time would have been imposed on a bank's balance sheet can now be circumvented by widespread OBS activities.

The increased use of interest-sensitive funding by institutions and the more sophisticated cash-management techniques used by depositors have led to greater interest-rate competition and sensitivity. In conjunction with these trends, the move towards greater variable-rate lending by institutions and the shortening of maturities on financial instruments have, amongst other things, made the money supply more responsive to interest-rate differentials (rather than the general level of interest rates) (as identified by Akhtar, 1983; BIS, 1986; Goodhart, 1986; Dini, 1986; and Podolski, 1986, to name just a few). On the demand side the level of transactions balances (narrow money) required to finance a given level of output is declining. As with the supply side, the demand for money, especially the broader aggregates, has also become less sensitive to changes in interest-rate levels. A stable demand for money function has also become increasingly difficult to estimate. The major upshot of these developments is that, because monetary authorities find it difficult to alter relative interest rates, and because interest rates on closely competing financial claims tend to change together relative to market rates, the effective role of interest rates in the monetary policy transmission mechanism has declined and probably will continue to do so.

Financial innovation has probably had the most visible effect on the use of money aggregates as an indicator of monetary policy. In the United Kingdom, for example, there have been various redefinitions of narrow money aggregates throughout the 1980s in order to maintain the stable money to nominal income relationship. Various redefinitions have also taken place in France as Metais (1987, p. 25) notes:

> In countries which implemented monetary policies relying on targeting monetary aggregates, financial innovations soon disturbed the significance of the aggregates and the stability of money demand functions: in particular, because new assets are now available which allow economic agents to reconcile two traditionally rather conflicting features of financial assets, high liquidity (moneyness) and high yield. Although the French experience with financial innovation is recent, the monetary authorities have already been confronted with the same problems as previously hit their US, Canadian or British counterparts.

European countries that continue to use the targeting of monetary aggregates as an indicator of policy will no doubt become increasingly sceptical about the operational usefulness of this method.

The internationalization of financial markets has increased capital mobility, which in turn has re-emphasized the role of exchange rates in domestic monetary policy. As the degree of international capital mobility rises, so does the relative importance of the exchange-rate mechanism at the expense of the interest-rate channel[14]. The European policymaking aspects of these developments have been discussed in the previous section, and they lead to the general conclusion that the brunt of monetary policy now falls increasingly on the external sector of the economy. An increase in international capital mobility has also resulted in frequent calls for wider and more effective policy co-ordination, as witnessed by the Plaza Agreement and the Louvre Accord. Overall, financial innovation has made the management of domestic monetary policy a much more complex process. It has weakened the role of interest rates as an effective tool of policy, decreased the willingness of the authorities to use rationing techniques (because they can be easily circumvented), and also put exchange-rate management to the forefront of monetary policymaking.

European Monetary System and the European Central Bank

The EMS was established in March 1979, its main aim being to provide 'a zone of monetary stability in Europe'. It followed a variety of other attempts to link the currencies of the European Community member states. All twelve national EC currencies are within the EMS but sterling, together with the Greek drachma and the Portuguese escudo, do not take part in the Exchange-Rate Mechanism (ERM) of the EMS. (The Spanish peseta entered the ERM in June 1989.) Historically the eight participating currencies were allowed fluctuation bands of 4.5 per cent within the ERM, apart from the Italian lira which is allowed a broader 12 per cent band. Since its inception there have been eleven realignments of central rates within the EMS, and the ECU-denominated central rate has declined relative to the Deutschmark and Dutch guilder and appreciated against other ERM currencies. Dicks (1989, p. 32) points out that '... the EMS has convincingly defied its critics who expected it to go the way of its predecessor the "snake"'.

One of the major reasons for the United Kingdom's reluctance to join the ERM has been the perceived lack of domestic policy independence which would follow from joining a fixed exchange-rate system. The theoretical support for this viewpoint stems from the famous Mundell-Fleming model which states that if capital is freely mobile, monetary policy independence is lost. Conversely, the critical constraint of a fixed exchange-rate system is that the monetary authorities are obliged to intervene when their exchange rate falls out of line relative to the currencies with which they wish to maintain a peg. Wyplosz (1988, p. 91) notes that this constraint does apply to the EMS system[15]. As a result one would expect that the cost associated with membership of a (quasi) fixed exchange-rate system would be the increased variability of domestic interest rates, although it has been found that the evidence to support this view is weak (Taylor and Artis, 1988, p. 24)[16]. Nevertheless, despite the success of the EMS in dampening nominal and real exchange-rate volatility, it has not succeeded in making the EMS currencies close substitutes for one another.

The EMS has been subject to various criticisms during recent years and most of these have concerned the role of the Deutschmark. The Deutschmark plays the dominant position in the technical operation of the system, even though the German authorities did not really want a reserve currency role for the Deutschmark. As a result the EMS has often been referred to as a 'Deutschmark Zone'. Small countries party to the EMS (such as Belgium, Denmark and the Netherlands) have their domestic fiscal and monetary policy largely dictated by the larger EMS countries, and in particular by Germany (see Steinherr and de Schrevel, 1988, p. 145). If the United Kingdom participated in the ERM it would lessen the dominance of the Deutschmark in the system.

It has also been suggested by Reynolds (1988) that the operation of the EMS has benefited from French and Italian capital controls as well as the wider margins utilized by Italy and the dual exchange-rate arrangements operated by Belgium and Luxembourg. A recent study undertaken by Macedo (1988) suggests that similar dual exchange-rate arrangements and minilateral agreements devices may be adopted by the newly integrating countries (Greece and Portugal) when they join the EMS. The failure of the United Kingdom and possibly the newer members to join the ERM will continue to be interpreted as a lack of commitment towards Europe, and the political pressures to join will undoubtedly mount in the run-up to 1992.

Despite the aforementioned problems, the EMS will have an increasingly important role to play in the post-1992 internal market era. Dicks suggests (1989, p. 38):

It will supplement the programme to harmonise fiscal and monetary policy and further remove artificial barriers to competition. In a truly unified market, where cross-border differences have been fully eliminated, there will be no place for currency realignments.

By the end of 1988 progress towards a European Monetary Union (EMU) was gathering momentum. The concept of a monetary union within the EC includes the establishment of a European central banking system together with a much expanded role for the ECU. A committee set up by the EC heads of state and government at Hannover in 1988, chaired by Jacques Delors the President of the European Commission, was commissioned by the European Council of Ministers 'to study and prepare concrete stages leading towards economic and monetary union'. The Delors Committee Report was published on 17 April 1989, and provides both a clear statement of what an economic and monetary union is and a progressive step-by-step approach to the final objective of such a union in the EC. The Report states that it would necessarily imply complete freedom of movement for goods, services and capital, as well as fixed exchange rates and a single currency, which implies a common monetary policy as well as greater independence of macroeconomic policy-making.

The Delors Report also notes that:

The responsibility for the single monetary policy would have to be vested in a new institution in which centralized and collective decisions would be taken on the supply of money and credit as well as on other instruments of monetary policy, including interest rates.

51

Centralized monetary policy operations will be co-ordinated through what has been termed a European System of Central Banks (ESCB) which will be run along the same lines as the German federal system. The ESCB will have two main parts: a newly constituted (and independent) European central bank and the existing national central banks. It will be the role of the latter to implement the monetary policy set by the ESCB, although independent policymaking decisions will be permitted when these do not have 'adverse repercussions on the cohesion and functioning of the economic and monetary union'. In principle, it appears that the Delors Report permits a certain degree of monetary policy independence but it is difficult to see how this will operate in practice.

The Report suggests that the new ESCB will have the responsibility for supervising capital and banking markets business throughout the EC member countries, as well as being able to implement detailed monetary policies. Concomitant with these developments is the aim to establish a single currency throughout the Community, presumably by extending the role of the ECU. The first syndicated ECU loans were issued in 1980 and by late 1987 the size of total ECU-denominated bank credits amounted to ECU 78 billion (£54 billion), ranking fifth behind the dollar, mark, yen and Swiss franc. There have also been substantial ECU bond issues[17] although private ECU use is uncommon. Advocates of the EMU hope that some day the ECU will be the main, if not the sole, legal tender within the Community whereas others believe that discussions about the ECU as a currency are 'a distraction' because achievement of a common currency is not feasible until much wider economic convergence has been established[18]. In any event, the Delors Report states that full European monetary union will only be achieved when there is: the irrevocable fixing of exchange rates, the creation of a common currency, set rules on macro and budgetary policy, and ESCB control of monetary and exchange-rate policy. This still seems a long way off, despite the hype about 1992.

Banking supervision and 1992

The EC environment

We saw earlier that the EC has taken a number of decisive steps towards achieving a single European market in 1992. The EC 1985 White Paper (Commission of the European Communities, 1985), enunciated clearly a renewed commitment to the original Treaty of Rome. A fundamental objective of the EC internal market proposals is to direct resources towards the greatest economic advantage within each member state and also within the Community as a whole. Substantial economic gains have been estimated from the completion of the internal market in the Cecchini study (Commission of the European Communities, 1988a). Up to one-third of the growth expected from the Single European Market during the first six years is likely to come directly or indirectly through the expansion of financial services. The 1985 White Paper's programme for the liberalization of financial services attempts to achieve greater progress towards a common market than all that has been achieved since the Treaty of Rome became effective in 1958. The general objective is that from 1 January 1993 Europe will be one internal market – an area without internal frontiers.

An important feature of the White Paper is the free movement of capital and services, which is seen as a necessary precursor to full economic and monetary union. Europe 1992 is fundamentally concerned with the release and stimulation of greater competition. The 1985 White Paper affirms that the economic system of the EC will be basically that of a market economy, and there has been a strong movement during recent years towards the greater liberalization of capital movements within the Community. Following the 1985 White Paper, the Commission made several firm proposals to liberalize completely all capital movements.

The Capital Movements Directive (Commission of the European Communities, 1988f) aims to remove all exchange controls and to permit the free movement of capital throughout the Community. A safeguard clause allows controls to be imposed in cases where 'exceptional' short-term capital flows would seriously disrupt exchange-rate and monetary policies. This directive extends the list of liberalized transactions (adopted in 1986) to all capital movements within the Community. Greece and Portugal may be allowed until the end of 1995 to comply.

Liberalizing capital is an important requirement for a single financial market. Another important requirement is to liberalize financial institutions so as to enable them to offer their services throughout the Community. The timetable in the 1985 White Paper clearly specified 1992 as the deadline for liberalizing trade and establishment in banking, insurance and securities markets. Two periods were identified for liberalization purposes: 1985–6 and 1987–92.

The Commission's approach towards attaining one single financial market with equivalent regulatory regimes is based on two principles: home country control and mutual recognition. 'Home country control' reflects a principle enshrined in the Basle Concordat: for an institution operating across national boundaries, responsibility for supervision rests with the supervisory authority of the country where the head office is located. Home country control is acceptable so long as there is 'mutual recognition' that the respective supervisory systems are equivalent. The Commission is to apply a broad approach – not strict reciprocity – towards mutual recognition.

Banking supervision and convergence
The First Banking Co-ordination Directive was adopted by the Council of Ministers in 1977, but it left a number of obstacles outstanding. For example, a bank wishing to establish a branch in another EC member state still had to obtain the authorization of the host country supervisor. In most member states branches also had to have separate earmarked capital as if they were new banks or subsidiaries.

The Second Banking Directive (1988), passed by the EC Council of Ministers on 15 December 1989, sets out to eliminate the remaining intra-EC barriers to freedom of establishment in the banking sector. It provides for full freedom of banking services across intra-EC boundaries. The main aim of this legislation is to harmonize laws and rules for credit institutions so that they can set up and operate freely across the Community subject to adequate supervision. The main provisions of the directive are as follows:

- minimum capital requirements for banks of ECUs 5 million, with special provisions for smaller banks;
- provision for monitoring and vetting of bodies that have substantial bank shareholdings;

- controls over banks' long-term participation in non-financial companies;
- principles for granting host countries the right to control bank liquidity;
- the establishment of a single banking 'passport' to permit activity anywhere within the EC, which is based on 'home country control' and 'mutual recognition'.

The principle of the single banking 'passport' is of particular importance. Once a credit institution is authorized to do banking business by its home supervisor (home country control) it will have a 'passport' to sell its products and services throughout the EC as long as there is prior harmonization of essential supervisory rules (mutual recognition). This principle is also enshrined in the EC Mortgage Credit Directive (1987) (which allows mortgage lenders authorized to lend in one country to lend in other EC countries without having to be authorized locally) and the Investment Services Directive (1988) (which liberalizes the provision of investment services within the EC). The Second Banking Directive (1988) does not harmonize the conduct of business standards, and banks that sell a variety of products – such as consumer lending, mortgages, savings – will still have to ensure that they can comply with local host-country consumer protection and other country-specific laws. On the other hand, countries are not allowed to make these 'public good' laws discriminate against foreign entrants, they have to be applicable to a class of institution. Difficulties have arisen relating to the proposed treatment of non-EC banks. The draft directives did not make it clear whether non-EC banks would benefit from the planned single market in financial services, even if they were licensed to operate in a Community country. The draft Second Banking Directive suggested that some form of 'reciprocal treatment' rule would be used. This caused serious concern, especially for US and Japanese banks. These were concerned that if a strict interpretation of the reciprocity clause were used, a US or Japanese bank wanting to establish in the United Kingdom, for example, could be prevented from doing so by, say, the Portuguese authorities, if Portuguese banks felt that they were not getting proper access to the US or Japanese markets.

Despite these fears, however, narrow and rigid reciprocity clauses were watered down by the time the final Second Banking Directive was agreed. This legislation now allows access to the EC on the basis of access (not necessarily equal) by EC banks to third-country markets. The Commission still retains the right to take retaliatory action against third countries which do not grant EC banks the same conditions enjoyed by their own domestic banks. An important point to note is that the list of permissible activities includes all forms of transactions in securities. A vital, reinforcing feature of the Second Banking Directive is the associated supervisory arrangements.

We have already emphasized that, alongside the kind of strong, structural deregulation moves associated with the completion of the internal market, there has been a corresponding re-regulation of banking supervision. It seems almost paradoxical that these twin regulatory trends exist, but they are often seen to be mutually reinforcing. There is some evidence, for example, that structural deregulation may give rise to periodic bouts of excessive risk-taking, under-pricing of risks and 'overshooting behaviour' as some financial institutions adapt their portfolios and strategies to the new environment: see, for example, Llewellyn (1986) and BIS (1986).

Supervision is one way of helping to contain the possible contagion potential of these developments. Other pressures and rationales for increased supervision and investor protection are bound up with the rise of consumerism.

Capital adequacy is a central element within all European bank supervisory systems. A recent major survey of bankers in Europe (Arthur Andersen, 1986, p. 43) confirmed that risk management will continue to be a major preoccupation of senior bank management throughout Europe. This same survey reported that many survey respondents felt that capital adequacy will be one of 'the most critical success factors for bank management in the 1990s'. Nevertheless, substantial differences exist in the capital-adequacy ratios of banks in different EC countries and internationally. Capital-adequacy ratios indirectly help to set profit targets for banks and this may impact on their competitiveness. A number of studies (such as Revell, 1980) have also confirmed the wide differences in bank profitability and operating costs throughout the EC.

Against this background of marked international differences, a strong convergence movement in capital adequacy has developed. Three different 'levels of convergence' may be said to affect European banks:

- international convergence;
- pan-European convergence;
- intra-(within) country convergence.

The latter is concerned with 'levelling the playing field' for different kinds of institution operating in a single country. De-compartmentalization and liberalization trends have also made inter-institutional convergence a growing issue at the international level. A good example is the contemporary need for convergence of capital adequacy between banks and securities houses.

International and pan-European convergence initiatives are inextricably linked. Indeed, no 'classification model' of the kind presented above can present a truly neat and clear picture of the complex process of convergence and supervisory re-regulation now in progress. Much of the modern impetus for convergence arose out of internationalization and globalization developments in international financial markets.

Competition is particularly intense in international banking and financial markets. These are also markets where banks from different countries and subject to different capitalization requirements compete fiercely. Intensifying competition which has accompanied worldwide structural deregulation trends has increased the need to economize on scarce bank capital resources. Convergence emerged as a key issue in the need to help level internationally the playing field on which banks compete. As a result, the important banking nations of the world have moved closer throughout the 1980s to a common approach towards capital measurement and an internationally agreed standard: see Cooke in Gardener (1990).

The Basle Committee's December 1987 proposals reflect the culmination of its important work in the international convergence of capital adequacy. The Committee was charged by the G-10 central bank governors to seek a common approach among its members towards measuring capital adequacy and the prescription of minimum capital standards. Table 4.2 summarizes the transitional arrangements for

Table 4.2 Basle transitional arrangements.

	Initial	End–1990	End–1992
1. Minimum standard	The level prevailing at end-1987	7.25%	8.0%
2. Measurement formula	Core elements plus 100%	Core elements plus 100% (3.625% plus 3.625%)	Core elements plus 100% (4% plus 4%)
3. Supplementary elements included in core	Maximum 25% of total core	Maximum 10% of total core (ie 0.36%)	None
4. Limit on general loan loss reserves in supplementary elements[a]	No limit	1.5 percentage points, or exceptionally up to 2.0 percentage points	1.25 percentage points, or exceptionally and temporarily up to 2.0 percentage points
5. Limit on term-subordinated debt in supplementary	No limit (at discretion)	No limit (at discretion)	Maximum of 50% of Tier 1
6. Deduction for goodwill	Deducted from Tier 1 (at discretion)	Deducted from Tier 1	Deducted from Tier 1

Source: Committee of Bank Regulations and Supervisory Practices (1988, Annex 4).
Note: a This limit would apply only in the event of no agreement being reached on a consistent basis for including unencumbered provisions or reserves in capital (see paragraphs 20 and 21).

the Basle proposals. Six months were set aside for consultations and a July 1988 paper summarized the agreed results of this process. The intention is that the proposals for measuring and appraising capital adequacy that are emerging from the work at Basle and Brussels should, in the words of the Bank of England (1988, p. 2), 'be in all important respects compatible if not identical'. In this respect the Basle proposals are particularly important. A general hope and intention of this initiative is that countries outside the G-10 and the EC will adopt similar systems. The Basle proposals are now driving the capital-adequacy systems in Europe.

The Basle proposals are that banks should target to have a minimum capital to risk assets ratio of 8 per cent by 1992. A risk-assets ratio approach is proposed, which comprises five categories of risk classes or 'risk weights'. Off-balance-sheet items are included within the formula. Capital is sub-divided into core capital (Tier 1) and supplementary capital (Tier 2). Tier 1 comprise equity and disclosed reserves. Tier 2 includes items like undisclosed reserves, revaluation reserves, general provisions, hybrid debt capital instruments and subordinated term debt. Rules are laid down on the inclusion of all these terms. Tier 2 is limited to 100 per cent of Tier 1 capital.

Seven EC countries are party to the Basle (or Basel or BIS) agreement on capital adequacy, but Denmark, Greece, Ireland, Portugal and Spain are not. Table 4.3 summarizes some rough estimates of how a sample of European banks look under the

Table 4.3 BIS proposals: some sample estimates, 1988.
Capital adequacy ratios as defined by the Cooke Committee and calculated by Merrill Lynch

Bank		Tier 1	Tier 2	Total
Barclays		5.2	3.8	9.0
Lloyds		4.8	4.8	9.6
Midland		7.0[a]	4.8[a]	11.8[a]
NatWest		6.1[a]	3.6[a]	9.8[a]
TSB		12.25	1.75–2.75	14–15[a]
BNP	- incl. sov. reserves	4.1	4.1	8.2
	- excl. sov. reserves	4.1	2.2	6.3
Crédit Lyonnais[b]	- incl. sov. reserves	3.7	3.7	7.4
	- excl. sov. reserves	3.7	2.5	6.2
Société Générale[b]	- incl. sov. reserves	4.2	4.2	8.4
	- excl. sov. reserves	4.2	2.3	6.5
Paribas	- incl. sov. reserves	7–8[a]	2.0[a]	9–10[a]
	- excl. sov. reserves	7–8[a]	0.5[a]	7.5–8.5[a]
Crédit Suisse		6.1	4.4	10.5
Swiss Bankcorp		5.6	5.6	11.2
Union Bank of Switzerland		6.1	6.1	12.2
Commerz Bank		4.1	2.3	6.4
Deutsche Bank		5.3[a]	5.3[a]	10.6
Dresdner Bank		4.3	2.4	6.7
Algemene Bank Nederland		5.0	3.8	8.8
Amsterdam-Rotterdam Bank		4.6	3.9	8.5
Allied Irish Bank		6.5	2.7	9.2
Bank of Ireland		6.9	2.6	9.5

Source: Keller (1989, p. 61).
Notes: a actual ratio.
    b assuming 75% of capital notes issues counts as Tier 1.

new Basle proposals. The British and Swiss banks appear well capitalized under the new rules. Nevertheless, these rules will not guarantee competitive equality for a number of reasons. A great deal of work, for example, still needs to be completed on fiscal and accounting harmonization.

A more fundamental problem, perhaps, is that the market may overrule any such supervisory scheme aimed at 'levelling the playing fields'. Substantial differences still exist between different national stock markets. As a result, banks in a country covered by the new Basle arrangements may still be able to raise capital more cheaply if investors within this country require a comparatively lower rate of return than in other countries (see, for example, Table 5.10). Japanese banks, for example, have a WACC (weighted average cost of capital) that is often less than half that of corresponding US and UK banks. Despite these practical problems, convergence of capital adequacy is seen to be one necessary condition for level playing fields. In Europe, there has also been substantial and strongly related progress in this area.

European convergence

Work at Brussels on the development and testing of capital adequacy ratios for banks and other credit institutions started in the late 1970s. The work at Brussels and Basle overlapped to some extent, but there were important differences. Seven of the important EC member countries were also members of the Basle Committee. But the work on capital adequacy at Brussels was designed to cover banks and all credit institutions within the EC, and to be legally binding in all EC members. The Basle proposals do not have the force of law.

During the 1980s a consensus emerged within Europe that convergence of capital adequacy was a desirable requirement. Before the Second Banking Directive's provisions for mutual recognition and home country control can take effect, a harmonized approach towards capital adequacy is necessary. European legislation will need to be in place for defining own funds and prescribing at least the general framework of a harmonized solvency ratio. Together with the Second Banking Directive, they comprise the framework for the European 'level playing field' in banking and financial services from 1992. Both these policy areas are now well-developed, and there have been some rather unique difficulties. One is the political consequences of giving the Commission an important influence over a key sector like banking. Another has been the parallel work on capital adequacy convergence at Basle, although in practice the two sets of proposals have been developed closely in tandem.

The Solvency Ratio Directive (1988), COM (88)/194, was formally passed by the EC Council of Ministers on 17 December 1989. Its objective is to harmonize solvency ratios for credit institutions within the EC. For obvious (convergency) reasons it will be similar to the Basle proposals, but there will be some differences. These differences will be minimized, but there is a basic problem in that the Basle proposals are geared towards international banks, while the EC focus is more on domestic activities. One reflection of this is that Denmark, West Germany and Greece will be given three years to meet the Solvency Ratio requirement of a 100 per cent weighting for mortgages on commercial property. Like the Basle proposals, the EC solvency ratio is based on a risk-asset approach.

Alongside the Solvency Ratio Directive, the Own Funds Directive was adopted in

April 1989. This aims to harmonize the definition of the capital of credit institutions. It defines the kinds of unconsolidated capital to be employed and the numerator (or capital adequacy base) for solvency ratios. These definitions are very similar to those developed by the Basle Committee.

Several other EC directives have a bearing on banking supervision in a new, post-1992 Europe. The Consolidated Supervision (1983) Directive, for example, was adopted at the end of 1986. Its objective is to ensure that credit institutions are supervised on a consolidated basis. The Large Exposures (1987) Directive adopted at the beginning of 1987 harmonizes credit exposure limits for banks. The Deposit Guarantee (1987) recommendation adopted in the same year sets out to ensure that EC depositors are covered by suitable deposit-insurance compensation schemes.

The EC's attitude towards non-member institutions will hinge on its attitude towards reciprocity. It is not yet clear which non-EC institutions will benefit from the planned single market in financial services, even if they were licensed to operate in an EC country. The EC will probably wish to negotiate some kind of bilateral agreement with non-EC financial institutions to require reciprocal treatment for EC institutions. We saw earlier that there have been recent fears that the EC (and some countries within it) favoured a strict, reciprocal and retrospective approach towards reciprocity. It now seems to be adopting a less strict, bilateral approach for the moment towards third countries. This is likely to remain, however, a very fluid policy area. The spectre of future protectionism has been fuelled in part by those commentators who have suggested that the economic benefits of 1992 must be retained by the EC.

Investment and securities business

The strong movement by banks into securities business and associated investment banking activities (see Chapter 11) has emphasized the importance of regulatory developments in this sector to European banking. A directive adopted in 1985, which entered into force in 1989, liberalized the activities of undertakings on collective investment in transferable securities (UCITS). It will allow UCITS authorized by individual member states to be sold throughout the Community. EC public policy will undoubtedly have an important impact on capital markets and related business trends. Measures like antitrust policies, taxation and the rules governing takeovers and associated transactions are important in this context. Investment banking institutions will also be affected directly by rulings on conduct of business, capital adequacy and securities taxation.

The 1988 Investment Services Directive covering securities business crystallised EC thinking on firms involved in investment banking markets. Its aim is to liberalize investment services throughout the Community. In many respects this directive closely mirrors the UK's 1986 Financial Services Act. Investment firms are specified as registered and conducting defined investment business in one of the EC member states. EC 'home' and 'host' countries are prescribed carefully. As in commercial banking, the single licence 'passport' principle applies to investment firms duly registered and supervised in an EC country. The directive applies to non-credit institutions, but there is some overlap with the Second Banking Directive where banks are active in securities business.

Authorities in all EC countries and the European Commission must be kept fully informed of all new authorizations, acquisitions and participations in existing firms.

Third-country securities firms may be authorized to do business in an EC country through subsidiaries. Under these circumstances they become effectively indigenous investment firms. Investment firms that are members of the stock exchanges in their own countries will be able to apply for full trading privileges on all EC stock, options and futures exchanges. However, there is an exemption to this rule where host countries do not allow credit institutions to hold membership in stock exchanges or other organized securities markets.

An important feature of the new European environment is that close collaboration is envisaged between the EC Commission, the authorities responsible for securities markets and institutions, and banking and insurance regulators. Increasing collaboration and convergence will be needed within Europe and globally to handle the new kinds of financial services supermarket (FSM) that is developing in Europe with the approach of 1992. These evolutionary changes in the industrial structure of the financial services industry will test continually the feasibility of regulatory targets and instruments associated with areas such as small investor protection, competitive equality and risk containment.

The new directive contains some controversial proposals and omissions. Some parties, for example, have criticized the inclusion of non-governmental, self-regulatory organizations in the proposed scheme. Investment advice, secondary market-making, taxation of investments and investment-related transactions, conduct of business rules and capital adequacy harmonization of investment firms are some of the controversial omissions. Progress in the field of taxation harmonization has been rather slow to date. Capital-adequacy convergence is a thorny issue that will have to be tackled.

Harmonization of conduct of business rules in investment services is already proving much more difficult than agreeing a common passport for securities business. These rules cover areas like new issues procedures, securities prospectuses, share registration, investor protection rules, investment management and mutual funds, transparency, insider trading and related activities. To date, the same kind of impetus has not existed in investment business as that of convergence of banking supervision. Converging these kinds of rules for investment firms will be one of the big challenges for Europe in the new, post-1992 environment. Globalization developments imply that, as with banking, the EC approach will have to be integrated more closely with wider international developments.

Conclusion

The significant growth of financial markets and instruments during the 1980s, coupled with the securitization phenomenon, has helped to increase the similarity between monetary and non-monetary financial assets, and this has contributed to a gradual change in monetary policy formulation. Monetary policy throughout Europe has become more market-based, and policy objectives increasingly focus on the internal and external values of currencies. Despite the various difficulties associated with the EMS and the proposed European Central Bank, there is little doubt that the former will play an increasingly important role in the post-1992 era and that European monetary policy co-ordination will become much more important. This will inevitably be at the expense of domestic monetary policy independence. Alongside monetary regulations, the structural deregulation moves associated with 1992 have opened up new opportunities and threats for European banks. The adoption of the Second Banking Directive and associated directives will create the largest and most open banking market in the world. It is clear that 1992 and related supervisory developments will be important forces for change in European banking.

Notes

1. This study provides a comprehensive analysis of banking and monetary policy developments for 24 OECD countries between 1960 and 1984.
2. Currency plus the banking system's total reserves.
3. A repurchase arrangement is when the authority buys (sells) a claim from the banks or other market operators on condition that it be sold (bought) back at a prearranged price on an agreed date. As a result the central bank can inject (absorb) liquidity easily and flexibly.
4. This device was first used in the United Kingdom in 1981.
5. This has also led to the widespread practice of 'overfunding' the PSBR.
6. Only Germany (from 1979 onwards), Ireland, Austria and Switzerland used foreign-exchange intervention as a main monetary instrument during the 1970s.
7. Credit ceilings were abandoned in the United Kingdom after Competition and Credit Control (CCC) in 1971; they had been in existence since 1964.
8. These include:

    a) credit extended at discount rate up to a certain quota: Austria, Belgium, Denmark, Finland, France up until 1971, Germany, the Netherlands, Norway, Portugal, Spain and Switzerland.
    b) additional credit extended at a higher cost: Austria 1979 onwards, Denmark, Finland, Germany, Norway, Sweden and Switzerland.
    c) credit extended at or near market rates: Finland, France, Ireland, the Netherlands, Norway, Spain, Switzerland and the United Kingdom.
    d) non-pecuniary sanctions for 'excess' borrowing; Norway 1979–83.
    e) privileged credit: Austria, Finland, France and Portugal.
9. The selection of intermediate targets such as monetary growth does not reflect the stance of monetary policy. Targeting monetary aggregates can be either restrictive (low targets) or expansionary (high targets).
10. The UK authorities recognized the important role the exchange rate played in monetary policy formulation from 1981 onwards. At this time it was considered that the strength of sterling indicated that the policy stance was much tighter than the growth in M3 had suggested.
11. In fact the excessive growth in the money supply was caused more by external factors than by domestic credit expansion.
12. Despite the importance placed on exchange-rate targeting by the UK authorities, the Governor of the Bank of England stated in the seventh Mais Lecture that the only effective instrument of UK monetary policy was the short-term rate of interest; funding and exchange-rate policies had limitations.
13. Rose notes that this view rests on three propositions. Firstly, the view that it was a change in the 'liabilities of the banks alone, as "money", that had a significant effect on prices and employment. Second, that the reaction of non-bank intermediaries would not frustrate traditional monetary policies. Third, that only banks, if they increase their lending, can create deposits . . .'
14. If there are floating exchange rates: (a) when capital is immobile, changes in monetary policy are transmitted to the economy primarily through changes in interest rates; (b) when capital is mobile internationally, changes in monetary policy have their effect on the economy through induced changes in interest rates and the exchange rate; (c) the relative

61

importance of the exchange rate channel is enhanced (at the expense of the interest-rate channel) as the degree of international capital mobility rises.

15. The authors also note that the simple Mundell-Fleming model re-emphasizes the import-ance of fiscal policy.

16. The authors 'found unequivocal evidence that the ERM has brought about a reduction in both the conditional and unconditional variance of exchange rate changes and, far from having purchased this reduction at the cost of increased interest rate volatility, there is also some evidence of a reduction in the volatility of interest rates from ERM members. We attribute this to the enhanced credibility of the exchange rate policies of these countries.'

17. The UK government issued ECU-denominated Treasury bills in 1988.

18. This commentator argues that (a) it is not necessary to develop the ECU as a parallel currency, (b) it would be difficult to develop the ECU as a currency in parallel with other national currencies, and (c) to develop as a genuine reserve currency it needs to have a well-functioning capital and money market.

References

Akhtar, M. A. (1983), 'Financial innovations and their implications for monetary policy: an international perspective', *Bank for International Settlements Economic Papers*, December, no. 9 (Basle: BIS).

Arthur Andersen & Co. (1986), *The Decade of Change: Banking in Europe – the Next Ten Years* (London: Lafferty Publications).

Atkinson, Paul and Chouraqui, Jean Claude (1987), The Formulation of Monetary Policy: A reassessment in the light of recent experience', *SUERF Papers on Monetary Policy and Financial Systems*, no. 1 (Tilburg: SUERF).

Bank for International Settlements (1986), *Recent Innovations in International Banking* (Basle: BIS).

Bank of England, Banking Supervision Division Explanatory Paper (1988), *Proposals for Internal Convergence of Capital Measurement and Capital Standards*, no. 1/88, (January) (London: Bank of England).

Bank of England (1987), 'The instruments of monetary policy', *Bank of England Quarterly Bulletin*, vol. 27, no. 3 (August), pp. 365–401.

Bingham, T. R. G. (1985), *Banking and Monetary Policy*, (Paris: OECD).

Cecchini, Paolo (1988), *The European Challenge in 1992: The Benefits of a Single Market* (Aldershot: Gower).

Commission of the European Communities (1983), *Consolidated Supervision Directive* (83)350.

Commission of the European Communities (1985), *Completing the Internal Market*, White Paper from the Commission to the European Council, (June).

Commission of the European Communities (1987a), *Large Exposures Directive*, (recommen-dations), (87)062.

Commission of the European Communities (1987b), *Mortgage Credit Directive* (amended proposal), COM (87)255.

Commission of the European Communities (1987c), *Deposit Guarantee Directive* (recommen-dation), (87)063.

Commission of the European Communities (1988a), *European Economy: The Economics of 1992*, March (Brussels: EC).

Commission of the European Communities (1988b), *Second Banking Directive*, (amended proposal), COM (88)715 (Brussels: EC).

Commission of the European Communities (1988c), *Solvency Ratio Directive* (proposal), COM (88)194.

Commission of the European Communities (1988d), *Investment Services Directive* (proposal), COM (87)778.

Commission of the European Communities (1988e), *UCITS Directive*, (85)611 and (88)220 Amendments.

Commission of the European Communities (1988f), *Capital Movements Directive*, (88)361.

Commission of the European Communities (1989), *Own Funds Directive*, (89)299.

Committee on Bank Regulations and Supervisory Practices (1987), *Proposals for International Convergence of Capital Measurement and Capital Standards* (Basle: BIS), (December).

Committee on Bank Regulations and Supervisory Practices (1988), *International Convergence of Capital Measurement and Capital Standards*, (Basle: BIS) (July).

Delors Report (1989), *Commitee for the Study of European and Monetary Union. Report on European and Monetary Union in the EC, 12 April*, (Brussels: EC).

Dicks, Geoffrey (1989), 'The European Monetary System', *The Treasurer*, vol. 11, no.1, pp. 32–8.

Dini, Lamberto (1986), 'Towards a European integrated financial market', *Banca Nazionale del 'Lavoro Quarterly Review*, no. 159, (December), pp. 377–90.

Economist (1978), 'Europe's economies. The structure and management of Europe's ten largest economies', Special Survey, pp. 1–16.

Eizenga, Wietze (1987). 'The Independence of the Deutsche Bundesbank and the Nederlandsche Bank with Regard to Monetary Policy; A comparative study', *SUERF Papers on Monetary Policy and Financial Systems*, no. 2 (Tilburg: SUERF).

European Economy (1987), 'The economic outlook for 1988', vol. 34, (July) (Brussels: EC).

Gardener, E.P.M. (ed.). (1990), *The Future of Financial Systems and Services* (London: Macmillan).

Goodhart, Charles (1986), 'Financial innovation and monetary control', *Oxford Review of Economic Policy*, vol. 12, no. 4, pp. 79–102.

Kana, Igor (1988), 'Dutch monetary policy, *ABN Economic Review*, (April) no. 126, pp. 2–7.

Keller, Paul (1989), 'Need capital, banks? here's how', *Euromoney*, (April), pp. 59–63.

Leigh-Pemberton, Robin (1986), 'Financial change and broad money', *Bank of England Quarterly Bulletin*, vol. 26, no. 4 (December), pp. 449–507.

Llewellyn, D. T. (1986) *The Regulation and Supervision of Financial Institutions* (London: The Chartered Institute of Bankers).

Loehnis, Andrew (1988), 'European currency and European central bank – A British view', *Bank of England Quarterly Bulletin*, vol. 28, no. 3, (August), pp. 350–55.

Macedo, Jorge Braga de (1988), 'Perspectives on financial liberalisation in the newly integrating countries (NICs) of the European Community (EC)', *European Economy*, no. 35, (May), pp. 149–61.

Metais, Joël (1987), 'Financial innovations and new patterns of financing in France', *IEF Research Papers in Banking and Finance*, RP 87/4 (Bangor: Institute of European Finance).

de Meyer, Carlo (1987) 'German Monetary Policy: walking on a tightrope', *ABN Economic Review*, (April), no. 120, pp. 2–6.

OECD (1987), *Bank Profitability, Financial Statements of Banks, with Methodological Country Notes, 1980–84* (Paris: OECD).

Official Journal of the European Communities (1988), 'Council Directive of 24 June 1988 for the implementation of Article 67 of the Treaty' (8 July), pp. 5–18.

Podolski, T. M. (1986) *Financial Innovations and the Money Supply*, (Oxford: Basil Blackwell).

Reynolds, George (1988) 'Capital liberalisation and strengthening the EMS – an Irish view', *Central Bank of Ireland Quarterly Bulletin*, (Summer), pp. 63–71.

Revell, J. R. S. (1980) *Costs and Margins in Banking* (Paris: OECD).

Revell, J. R. S. (1985), *Costs and Margins in Banking: Statistical Supplement* (Paris: OECD).

Rose, Harold (1986), 'Change in financial intermediation in the UK', *Oxford Review of Economic Policy*, vol. 2, no. 4, pp. 18–39.

Steinherr, Alfred and De Schrevel, Geoffrey (1988) 'Liberalisation of financial transactions in the community with particular reference to Belgium, Denmark and the Netherlands, *European Economy*, no. 36, (May), pp. 115–147.

Taylor, M. P. and Artis, M. J. (1988), 'What has the European Monetary System achieved?' *Bank of England Discussion Papers* no. 31, March 1988.

Thorn, Peter, Clarke, Tim, Krakowian, Sophia and Giese, Jurgen (1988) *German Banks Review* (London: Citicorp/Scrimgeour Rickers).

Wyplosz, Charles (1988), 'Capital flow liberalisation and the EMS: A French perspective', *European Economy*, no. 36, (May), p. 85–114.

Chapter five

Changes in balance sheet structure

Introduction

The structure of European banks' balance sheets and income statements has altered considerably over the last twenty years in response to a variety of trends, many of which have already been discussed in earlier chapters of this book. These factors, such as increased competition, the breakdown in demarcation lines between different types of business, technological and financial innovation, supervisory re-regulation, increased volatility of interest and exchange rates, the securitization movement, and so on, have all had some form of direct or indirect effect on the balance sheet characteristics of banking firms. These forces helped to change banks' attitudes towards asset and liability management; they have also forced banks to seek new sources of income.

Changes in balance sheet structures and income statements

Historical overview

Throughout the 1960s and early 1970s bank balance sheet growth was predominantly asset-driven, whereby liabilities were managed so that banks could acquire their desired asset portfolios (Harrington, 1987, p. 43). Over this period the demand for credit was high and banks increasingly needed to compete against a range of domestic and foreign banks as well as other non-bank institutions in order to obtain resources. The increasing demand for wholesale time deposits culminated in the rapid growth of both international and domestic interbank markets, which by the mid-1970s had developed into closer analogues of perfectly competitive markets. The growth and competitive nature of these markets led to the marginal cost of funds approximating the corresponding average cost. Funding costs also rose because banks increasingly obtained their assets by taking deposits from the interbank markets at competitive rates.

Another factor that also increased the use of interest-sensitive funds was the adoption by depositors of the practice known as cash management (Akhtar, 1983, pp. 8–11). High levels of inflation during the 1970s led businesses and households to demand interest-earning financial instruments, whilst at the same time encouraging them to economize on non-interest-bearing transactions balances. As a result of these

Table 5.1 Percentage of bank liabilities remunerated on money-market terms.

	End of period	1960	1980
France	Banking system	1	35
Ireland	All banks	1	34
Italy[a]	All deposit-taking institutions	17	29
Japan	All banks	9	13
	City banks	12	21
Luxembourg	All banks	10	81
Norway	Commercial banks	29	40
	Savings banks	4	10
Sweden	Commercial banks	5	38
United Kingdom[b]	All banks	12	86
United States[b]	All banks	4	22

Source: Harrington (1987, p. 44).
Notes: a 1961–81
      b 1962–82
The figures involve varying degrees of approximation and should be interpreted as showing orders of magnitude only. They are not directly comparable across countries.

factors, banks have had to hold an increasing proportion of their liabilities in a form that pays variable rates of interest, most notably at money market terms. Table 5.1 shows that between 1960 and 1980 all European banks substantially increased their percentage of (funding) liabilities remunerated at money market rates, the biggest increases being in countries where international banking is more important.

In addition to the increased competition in interbank markets, competitive forces also began to filter down to the retail banking market where a growing proportion of term deposits were being remunerated at higher rates, thereby increasing the cost of small deposits. This phenomenon of an increased funding base linked to market rates of interest is sometimes called 'marketization'. Throughout the 1970s and 1980s banks in most European countries have witnessed a substantial decline in the proportion of demand deposits in their balance sheets. Table 5.2 shows that the only (European) countries where this has not occurred are Italy and Denmark where demand deposits pay market rates of interest anyway[1]. As a result, banks have had to compete more aggressively for sources of funds in the interbank markets and this in turn has encouraged them to manage their liabilities more actively. Overall, the main characteristic of liability management has been that it tends to reduce the role played by conventional deposits whilst increasing the role of 'bought-in' funds in the funding activities of financial institutions. Consequently, banks have become increasingly aware of the need to replace maturing liabilities by taking new interbank deposits; they have also had to manage more closely the matching of their assets and liabilities, together with the corresponding risk exposures.

The use of non-traditional or interest-sensitive sources of funds – such as borrowings in various short-term markets – to fund loan demand and other activities developed rapidly in the early 1970s and utilized practices that were concurrently being developed in the Euromarkets. More recently liability management has received further impetus from the effects of high and volatile interest rates, innovations in banking technology, and, in various instances, from interest-rate deregulations. By the mid-1970s liability management began to evolve into more complex asset and liability management (see Kane, 1979; Goodhart, 1982; Harrington, 1987 for the historical development of bank liability management).

From the mid-1970s banks and other financial institutions have found it necessary to match (or manage more closely) their interest-sensitive liabilities by increasing the proportion of variable rate lending and by shortening the maturities on loan contracts as well as various other securities issues. In international banking markets, medium-term lending funded by short-term deposits was made possible by the extensive use of roll-over loans: the rate on these kinds of loans is set at a margin above a market rate, such as the London Inter-Bank Offered Rate (LIBOR), and adjusted at regular intervals, usually three or six months. This development increased the need to match more closely and manage interest-rate risk exposures in the balance sheet. It also had the advantage of separating to some extent interest-rate risk from liquidity risk, thereby enabling institutions to undertake maturity transformation without necessarily incurring excessive interest-rate risk.

Floating-rate lending has also become more important in domestic markets. In the United Kingdom, Finland and Sweden, bank lending has traditionally been at

Table 5.2 Demand deposits as a percentage of total bank liabilities.

	1960	1971	1984
Australia	39.3	25.2	16.9
Austria	20.5	13.7	4.6
Belgium[a]	43.5	18.4	5.4
Canada	27.9	30.0	13.8
Denmark	33.9	44.6	38.9
Finland	12.1	10.3	8.4
France	49.3	39.3	19.2
Germany	15.9	11.1	8.6
Greece	17.3	9.9	5.0
Iceland	15.7	16.8	13.9
Ireland	35.6	19.7	8.2[c]
Italy	40.1	48.9	41.5
Japan	25.6	25.6	17.9
Luxembourg[a]	-	10.3	0.9
Netherlands	33.9	24.0	11.4
New Zealand	85.4	61.8	25.0
Norway	41.0	21.2	16.0
Portugal	59.7	38.9	19.6
Spain	33.7	24.9	12.9
Sweden	10.6	9.9	6.4
Switzerland	23.1	18.6	12.0
Turkey	34.4	32.9	17.1
United Kingdom[b]	45.6	19.0	6.6
United States	51.7	34.2	18.3

Source: Harrington (1987, p. 45).

Notes: a The 1960 figure for Belgium is for the Belgian-Luxembourg economic union.

  b the 1960 figure is derived from the Bank of England Statistical Abstract No. 1 and is partially estimated.

  c 1982.

Bank liabilities are defined broadly, but differences of classification as between countries are unavoidable. Hence the figures are not directly comparable between countries.

variable rates of interest, whereas in Spain it was first introduced in the late 1970s mainly on loans to corporations. In most other European countries there has been growth in variable rate lending, especially to corporations. Only in Germany is there no strong evidence of such a trend, where terms of loans appear to vary with the interest-rate cycle; fixed-rate borrowing tends to increase when interest rates are low and vice versa. Harrington (1987, pp. 47–8) points out:

> The movement towards greater use of variable rate lending (in one form or another) indicated an important shift in bank behaviour. It was no longer the case that banks were largely asset-driven and primarily concerned with just where to find resources to finance lending ... Banks were moving progressively to the stage of asset and liability management: adjusting liabilities in accordance with potential assets but also adjusting assets in accordance with potential liabilities. More generally there was a growing realisation of how an increasingly variegated balance sheet at a time of volatile economic conditions added to the risks facing banks and made necessary new techniques of risk management.

The 1982 debt crisis provided a further impetus for banks to focus their attentions elsewhere in order to compensate for the lengthening maturity structure of their loan books as well as the decreasing value of their assets. This led to a broad reassessment of the nature of credit risks and credit standards, and also reduced banks' previous emphasis on balance-sheet growth 'at any cost'. It was a major fillip to the securitization phenomena. Securitization has implied a definite shift away from asset growth and liability management towards asset management (Gardener, 1986).

Two kinds of securitization have been important to the banking firm. The first involves the shift in international financial intermediation away from bank credit flows to capital market ones, important examples being the development of the floating rate note (FRN)[2] market and Euronote facilities like NIFs (note issuance facilities) and RUFs (revolving underwriting facilities). In effect, market-based intermediation is used increasingly instead of institution-based intermediation. This is a replacement kind of process whereby previously non-marketable bank assets (like Euroloans or syndicated loans) are replaced by marketable ones (like FRNs and Euronote facilities). These latter instruments are used by banks on both sides of the balance sheets. The advantage of these 'new' types of instrument is that they enable institutions to obtain medium- and long-term funds which are interest-matched; in various countries some types of FRNs also qualified as capital for supervisory purposes. As well as earning fee income from arranging NIFs and similar Euronote facilities, banks have also been able to generate additional income by giving guarantees to provide funds under specified contingent circumstances. These are OBS activities that produce income and portfolio risk for individual banks. Such 'back-up' facilities include items like standby letters of credit and various types of loan commitments.

The second, broad type of securitization involves the sale of assets currently held on banks' books: examples include mortgage-backed securities, asset swapping, sub-participations and transferable loan facilities (TLFs). This technique effectively transforms an illiquid asset into a marketable instrument, but it is currently not so well-developed in international banking markets because of the comparatively low trading volume and associated lack of secondary market liquidity. In the United States, however, this kind of securitization has grown rapidly (see also Chapter 10).

Securitization has implied for banks a definite shift away from asset growth and liability management towards asset management. It has also brought with it a substantial change in the role of the international banker. Instead of reliance on earning a margin through providing funds, the emphasis has shifted towards OBS fee income for the services associated with the managing and placing of debt instruments with investors. In many instances these new securitized facilities involved banks acting as underwriters. This, coupled with the increasing willingness of banks to make loans marketable and the increased trading of such instruments in secondary markets, has blurred the traditional distinctions between commercial and investment banking.

In addition, securitization has enabled banks to move and also transact a considerable amount of business off the balance sheet (OBS). The ready acceptance by banks during the 1980s to become involved in new forms of financial transaction is further witnessed by the substantial increase in the use of currency and interest-rate swaps, financial futures, options and forward-rate agreements. Over the last five years there has been a phenomenal growth in contingent liabilities and outstanding commitments that do not appear on traditional bank balance sheets. As a result, bank management has been pressured increasingly to introduce state-of-the-art information systems in order to monitor the risk exposures of actual and contingent balance-sheet positions.

Changes in balance sheet and income statement structures of all European banks[3]

During the 1980s European banks witnessed a market change in their interest income and interest expense profiles. Table 5.3, estimated from OECD (1987 and 1988), shows that for all types of European bank interest income fell as a percentage of average total assets. Levels of net interest income, however, were maintained by a similar fall in interest expenses. These figures do not suggest any tightening of margins, merely a reduction in interest-rate levels.

Despite the emphasis placed on the securitization phenomenon and the increasing search for fee and commission income, mean figures suggest that between 1982 and 1986 there has been only a marginal increase in non-interest income and this, coupled with a small increase in operating expenses, has resulted in a small decline in net income. If one investigates the income profiles of different types of banks in various countries one can see that the relative significance of non-interest income as a percentage of total assets varies considerably. In 1986 non-interest income as a percentage of total assets varied between a low of 0.17 per cent for Belgian savings banks to a high of 2.07 per cent for Finnish commercial banks.

Overall, non-interest income is more important to European commercial banks, with an average contribution to gross income of 27.9 per cent in 1986 compared to 18.9 per cent for savings banks and 14.7 per cent for credit co-operatives. The actual contribution of net interest income to gross income, nevertheless, has fallen for commercial banks from 29 per cent in 1982 to 27.9 per cent in 1986, but has risen for savings banks (17.8 per cent to 18.4 per cent) and credit co-operatives (11.0 per cent to 14.7 per cent) over the same period. The relatively small decline in net income

Table 5.3   Changes in balance sheet, income statement and other accounting items for all European banks between 1982 and 1986[a].

% of average total assets

	1982	1986	Difference between 1982 and 1986	% change
Income statement				
Interest income	11.4760	9.4680	−2.0080	−17.4974
Interest expenses	8.8610	6.9160	−1.9450	−21.9501
Net interest income	2.6010	2.5450	−0.0560	−2.1530
Non-interest income	0.9380	0.9430	0.0050	0.5330
Gross income	3.5390	3.4870	−0.0520	−1.4693
Operating expenses	2.3430	2.3550	0.0120	0.5122
Net income	1.1950	1.1260	−0.0690	−5.7741
Provisions (net)	0.6295	0.5558	−0.0737	−11.7077
Profit before tax	0.5663	0.5747	0.0084	1.4833
Income tax	0.1918	0.2350	0.0432	22.5235
Profit after tax	0.4039	0.3289	−0.0750	−18.5689
Distributed profit	0.1658	0.1785	0.0127	7.6598
Retained profit	0.2990	0.2147	−0.0843	−28.1940
Other items				
Staff costs	1.4440	1.3320	−0.1120	−7.7562
Provisions on loans[b]	0.5900	0.4522	−0.1378	−23.3559
Provisions on securities[b]	0.0900	0.0350	−0.0550	−61.1111
Balance sheet				
Assets				
Cash and balance with central bank	3.480	2.985	−0.4950	−14.224
Interbank deposits	20.560	22.600	2.0400	10.077
Loans	49.930	48.040	−1.8900	−3.785
Securities	15.110	16.050	0.9400	6.221
Other assets	10.200	10.850	0.6500	6.373
Liabilities				
Capital and reserves	4.203	4.329	0.1260	2.998
Borrowing from central bank[c]	1.559	4.100	2.5410	162.989
Interbank deposits[c]	24.670	24.280	−0.3900	−1.581
Non-bank deposits	57.810	53.680	−4.1300	−7.144
Bonds	4.400	5.920	1.5200	34.545
Other liabilities	9.050	10.980	1.9300	21.326

Sources: OECD (1987) and OECD (1988).

Notes: a All banks include the following: Austrian large banks and savings banks, Belgian banks, Danish commercial and savings banks, Finland all banks, France all banks, Germany all universal banks, Netherlands all commercial banks, Norway commercial banks and savings banks, Portuguese banks, Spain all banks, Sweden commercial and savings banks, Switzerland all banks, UK London and Scottish clearing banks. Definition and source of data from OECD (1987 and 1988). Estimated figures are all arithmetic means.

b There is a scarcity of data for these two categories. Provisions on loans means are calculated from data reported by Denmark, Finland, Germany, Italy, Norway, Spain and Sweden. Provisions on securities figures are calculated from Italy, Spain and Sweden data.

c The figures reported for the United Kingdom do not distinguish between interbank deposits, borrowing from the central bank and non-bank deposits. The data are all classified under non-bank deposits.

Table 5.4 Extreme values of European banks' balance-sheet items, 1986.
Percentages of balance sheet total

Item	Country (L = lowest H = highest)	Institution	Value	SD/ means
		Assets		
Cash and balances with central bank	L Belgium	Banks	0.2	
	H Greece	Large banks	14.8	1.0
Interbank deposits	L Finland	Commercial banks	1.1	
	H Germany	Regional institutions of CC	57.6	0.7
Loans	L Germany	Regional institutions of CC	18.3	
	H Switzerland	Loan associations and agricultural CC	80.3	0.3
Securities	L Switzerland	Loan associations (and agricultural CC)	0.7	
	H Belgium	Private savings banks	53.4	0.6
Other assets	L Norway	Savings banks	1.5	
	H Italy	Large commercial banks	49.2	0.9
		Liabilities		
Capital and reserves	L Sweden	Savings banks	1.3	
	H Switzerland	Other Swiss and foreign banks	11.0	0.5
Borrowing from central bank	L Italy	Savings banks	0.2	
	H Norway	Commercial banks	14.2	1.0
Interbank deposits	L Finland	Savings banks	0.0	
	H Sweden	Foreign banks	78.2	1.0
Non-bank deposits	L Sweden	Foreign banks	2.0	
	H Greece	Large banks	86.4	0.4
Bonds	L Sweden	Co-operative banks	0.4	
	H Germany	Regional giro institutions	45.2	1.2
Other liabilities	L Germany	Regional institutions of CC	2.0	
	H Finland	Co-operative banks	85.3	1.2

Source: OECD (1988).
Notes: CC = credit co-operatives.
SD/mean = standard deviation divided by the respective mean.

shown in Table 5.3 has been translated into a much greater fall in banks' retained profits because of the greater income-tax burden banks have had to suffer. The figures illustrate that the mean retained profits for all European banks amounted to 0.299 per cent of total assets in 1982; this fell to 0.2147 per cent by 1986.

Despite the general view that banks have found it difficult to reduce staffing costs, the average figures indicate that these costs have fallen as a percentage of total assets. One cannot say anything meaningful about banks' provisioning from the table because the figures are not representative: they refer only to a handful of banks.

On the assets side, banks have on average experienced an increase in their interbank deposits, compensated by a decrease in the proportion of loans on their books as well as a fall in cash balances with the central bank. On the liabilities side, a large fall in the proportion of non-bank deposits as well as a marginal fall in holdings of interbank deposits have been compensated for by a substantial increase in borrowing from the central bank, as well as increases in bonds and other types of liabilities. Surprisingly, capital and reserves have only increased marginally; in one sense this is merely a reflection of the aggregate nature of our analysis, and the following section shows that the capital to asset ratios for large banks have increased substantially. Non-bank deposits, however, still constitute more than 50 per cent of European banks' liabilities, which are more than double the size of interbank deposits.

Table 5.4 illustrates the extreme values of European banks' balance-sheet items for 1986. It can be seen that the liabilities of large banks in Greece are almost wholly composed of non-bank deposits, whereas those of Finnish co-operative banks are made up entirely of types of liabilities other than those listed. The OECD (1988) data from which these figures have been taken only report on foreign bank operations in a few countries, and it is not surprising to see Swedish foreign banks having their liabilities dominated by interbank deposits. This would be the case for foreign bank operations in all European countries. Extreme values on the asset side of the balance sheet highlight the diverse nature of various types of European banks, such as the regional institutions of the credit co-operatives in Germany and the loan associations and credit co-operatives in Switzerland. What is interesting to note is that the specialist and mutual banks appear more often in this table than the commercial banks, thus indicating less diversified balance-sheet structures.

Changes in balance sheet and income statement structures for large European commercial banks[4]

The above section analysed the average balance sheet and income statement structures for all European banks as reported in the OECD (1988) statistical survey. This provides us with a broad picture, but it tells us little about the relative changes that have affected large banks. Table 5.5 uses the OECD (1988) definition of large banks to show how the balance sheet and income statement positions of this category of banks altered between 1982 and 1986. What is most noticeable if we compare Table 5.5 with Table 5.4 is that the average interest income of large banks has fallen relatively much more than for all banks – and so have interest expenses. Relative net interest income has fallen and so has non-interest income. Nevertheless, operating expenses have also reduced (compared with an increase for all European banks): the implication is that large banks have found it easier to reduce expenses (especially non-staff costs) compared with other banks.

Large banks have traditionally higher profit before tax as a percentage of total assets ratios than other types of banks. The increase in profit before tax between 1982 and 1986 was also much higher than for the all-bank category. Table 5.5 also illustrates that distributed profits and retained profit ratios are higher for large banks; the increase in retained profits between 1982 and 1986 was also much greater than for the average of all European banks. The income statement shows quite clearly that large banks have been able to increase their profitability substantially during the

Table 5.5 Changes in balance sheet income statement and other items for large European banks[a], 1982–6.

% of average total assets

	1982	1986	Difference between 1982 and 1986	% change
Income statement				
Interest income	12.910	8.3860	− 4.5240	− 35.0426
Interest expenses	9.840	5.5500	− 4.2900	− 43.5976
Net interest income	3.069	2.8360	− 0.2330	− 7.5921
Non-interest income	1.236	1.1830	− 0.0530	− 4.2880
Gross income	4.307	4.0200	− 0.2870	− 6.6636
Operating expenses	2.893	2.6630	− 0.2300	− 7.9502
Net income	1.411	1.3560	− 0.0550	− 3.8979
Provisions (net)	0.766	0.5671	− 0.1989	− 25.9661
Profit before tax	0.649	0.7870	0.1380	21.2635
Income tax	0.231	0.3186	0.0872	37.6837
Profit after tax	0.419	0.4670	0.0480	11.4558
Distributed profit	0.206	0.2367	0.0307	14.9029
Retained profit	0.210	0.2883	0.0783	37.2857
Other items				
Staff costs	1.666	1.8140	0.1480	8.8836
Provisions on loans[b]	0.620	0.4000	− 0.2200	− 35.4839
Provisions on securities[b]	0.030	0.0400	0.0100	33.3333
Balance sheet				
Assets				
Cash and balance with central bank	3.74	3.281	− 0.4590	− 12.273
Interbank deposits	24.34	24.680	0.3400	1.397
Loans	45.64	43.840	− 1.8000	− 3.944
Securities	13.83	13.400	− 0.4300	− 3.109
Other assets	15.44	14.800	− 0.6400	− 4.145
Liabilities				
Capital and reserves	4.09	4.867	0.7740	18.910
Borrowing from central bank[c]	1.34	2.528	1.1880	88.657
Interbank deposits[c]	27.67	26.770	− 0.9000	− 3.253
Non-bank deposits	55.80	53.380	− 2.4200	− 4.337
Bonds	4.97	6.360	1.3900	27.968
Liabilities	11.17	11.550	0.3800	3.402

Source: OECD (1988).

Notes: a Large banks constitute the largest banks in the following countries: Austria (8), France (8), Germany (6), Italy (3), Spain (7), Switzerland (5), United Kingdom (5). Definition and source of data from OECD (1987) and OECD (1988). Estimated figures are arithmetic means. Missing values and rounding errors account for some totals not summing correctly.

Notes b and c from Table 5.3 also apply to this table.

1980s compared with other banks throughout Europe. This is even more apparent when compared with the savings banks sector, as illustrated in the following section.

There were various changes in the balance-sheet characteristics of large banks between 1982 and 1986. On the liabilities side, falls in interbank bank and non-bank deposits as a proportion of the total balance sheet have been compensated for by increases in borrowing from the central bank and a substantial increase in capital and reserves. On the assets side, there were few relative changes, and it can be noted that securities and other assets are traditionally more important investments for big banks than for other types of banks.

Changes in balance sheet and income statement structures of European savings banks
Table 5.6 illustrates the change in balance sheet and income statements of European savings banks between 1982 and 1986. As with all other European banks, the savings banks sector also experienced a fall in interest income, interest expenses and net interest income as a percentage of total assets, during the period between 1982 and 1986. The proportion of non-interest income, however, increased over the same period. The sector as a whole has witnessed a decline in pre-tax profits, whilst the income tax burden has increased (although the increase is not as great as for large banks), resulting in a marked decline in profitability overall. Operating costs as a percentage of total assets have stayed constant even though staffing costs have fallen.

The asset structure of European savings banks' balance sheets has hardly changed during the 1980s, although it is important to note that the loans and securities components are much more important for these types of institutions than for other types of European banks. Similarly, on the liabilities side non-bank deposits and bonds have greater significance in savings-bank balance sheets, despite the fact that the proportion of non-bank deposits has fallen since 1982. This decrease has been compensated for by increases in the relative importance of all other liability categories and most noticeably the substantial increase in central bank borrowings, interbank deposits and other liabilities.

Developments in asset and liability management and OBS finance

Objectives and methods of asset and liability management
Market developments and competitive pressures have forced European banks to adopt a more formal approach towards asset and liability management, and one result of this has been to increase the importance of banks' treasury departments. Treasury functions developed during the mid-1970s, initially managing the portfolios of short-term assets and later the management of both short-term assets and liabilities. The development and growth of new short-term markets from the mid-1970s onwards encouraged treasury units to trade in instruments from both sides of the balance sheet as well as increasing the proportion of transactions with non-bank clients.

The relative importance of European banks' treasury functions grew markedly during the 1980s as new short-term markets in instruments like FRNs, Euronotes, ECP, swaps, options, futures and various derivative markets developed. As these

Table 5.6 Changes in balance sheet, income statement and other items for European savings banks[a], 1982–6.

% of average total assets

	1982	1986	Difference between 1982 and 1986	% change
Income statement				
Interest income	9.9620	8.4260	− 1.5360	− 15.4186
Interest expenses	6.9210	5.5250	− 1.3960	− 20.1705
Net interest income	3.0400	2.9020	− 0.1380	− 4.5395
Non-interest income	0.7720	0.8260	0.0540	6.9948
Gross income	3.8120	3.7320	− 0.0800	− 2.0986
Operating expenses	2.6050	2.6100	0.0050	0.1919
Net income	1.2060	1.1180	− 0.0880	− 7.2968
Provisions (net)	0.5550	0.4936	− 0.0614	− 11.0631
Profit before tax	0.6540	0.6245	− 0.0295	− 4.5107
Income tax	0.2440	0.2673	0.0233	9.5492
Profit after tax	0.4320	0.3564	− 0.0756	− 17.5000
Distributed profit	0.1767	0.1414	− 0.0353	− 19.9774
Retained profit	0.4100	0.2590	− 0.1510	− 36.8293
Other items				
Staff costs	1.5360	1.4280	− 0.1080	− 7.0313
Provisions on loans[b]	0.4833	0.4250	− 0.0583	− 12.0629
Provisions on securities[b]	0.1750	0.0350	− 0.1400	− 80.0000
Balance sheet				
Assets				
Cash and balance with central bank	2.658	2.870	0.2120	7.976
Interbank deposits	12.290	12.340	0.0500	0.407
Loans	57.500	56.560	− 0.9400	− 1.635
Securities	18.670	18.670	0.0000	0.000
Other assets	8.870	9.550	0.6800	7.666
Liabilities				
Capital and reserves	4.201	4.465	0.2640	6.284
Borrowing from central bank[c]	0.661	2.690	2.0290	306.959
Interbank deposits[c]	6.720	9.020	2.3000	34.226
Non-bank deposits	73.540	67.210	− 6.3300	− 8.608
Bonds	9.050	10.100	1.0500	11.602
Liabilities	7.380	8.980	1.6000	21.680

Source: OECD (1988).

Notes: a European savings banks include those from: Austria, Belgium, Finland, Germany, Italy, Norway, Spain, Sweden and Switzerland (including the cantonal banks). Definition and sources of data from OECD (1987) and OECD (1988). Estimated figures are arithmetic means. Missing values and rounding errors account for some totals not summing correctly.

Notes b and c from Table 5.3 also apply to this table.

markets grew, banking dependence on them increased. The growth of these markets created a broader range of opportunities available to the treasury units through which they could generate arbitrage profits as well as take positions in anticipation of expected changes in interest and exchange rates. The treasury evolved as a dynamic profit centre. Nowadays the treasury function embraces the trading of short-term assets and liabilities as well as having to monitor continually the banks' positions, ' . . . with respect to earnings and to risks due to maturity gaps and interest rate or foreign currency exposures, the treasury department has to liaise with other departments of the bank, notably those concerned with credit and with retail banking' (Harrington, 1987, p. 16).

Throughout Europe the methods adopted by banks to make marginal adjustments to their balance-sheet structures through money-market operations have differed considerably. As we have already mentioned, the most important route has been through the interbank markets and this has been supplemented by the use of an ever-increasing array of money-market instruments. Wilson (1985, p. 60) points out, for example, that resort to the bill markets has been widely used in Spain; Eurocurrency market transactions have been most widely used by banks in Switzerland, the Netherlands and France (French banks have traditionally used these markets extensively through the use of swaps for liability management purposes); and raising large direct deposits from customers has been important in France, Germany, the Netherlands and Ireland. The growth in CD (certificate of deposit) markets has also encouraged banks in most European countries (especially in the United Kingdom) to transact business using these instruments in order to manage their short-term liability positions.

On the assets side of the balance sheet the most important development in recent years for almost all European banks has been the increase in term-lending at the expense of overdraft finance (see Chapter 7). Bill finance has also declined in most markets, apart from countries like France where the discountable paper markets are still large and Portugal where a large proportion of bank advances is in the form of discounted promissory notes.

A critical aspect of asset and liability management is risk management. Efficient asset and liability management procedures should make a bank better able to control and limit risks associated with maturity mismatching, interest-rate gaps, foreign-exchange exposures and so on. Risks that stem from mismatching relate to five main types.

- credit risk: the possibility of default by the counterparty.
- market or price risk: the possibility of a decline in the market value of a financial instrument because of changes in interest rates or exchange rates.
- settlement risk: the risk that arises when a bank pays out funds before it can be sure that it will receive the funds on the due date from the counterparty.
- liquidity risk: the possibility that a tradeable financial instrument may not realize quickly (whenever needed) its full market value.
- contingent risk: risks associated with the growth of banks' OBS activities.

Given the aforementioned risks inherent in banking, it is the aim of asset and liability management to manage these risk exposures so that they are kept within acceptable levels and at the same time help to generate income and maintain profitability. The control and evaluation of risks is undertaken through using various techniques like gap analyses, maturity profiles and interest-rate ladders (Gardener, 1987). Banks have also had to develop their own procedures to evaluate currency mismatching and contingent risk exposures.

It must be remembered that many of these 'balance-sheet management risks' are by no means independent of one another. For example, the risks associated with a mismatched interest-rate position are not only limited to losses involved from unanticipated interest-rate changes, but they may also be related to credit, settlement and liquidity risks. Any hedging activity always produces some credit exposure for at least one of the parties concerned. The difficulties associated with monitoring and evaluating the risk positions of banks are further compounded by the ever-changing nature of banking and financial markets which in turn strongly influences the dynamic nature of asset and liability management strategy. The growth of OBS instruments and related techniques has allowed banks to disaggregate some important risks and shift them on to other market participants. At the same time, however, banks have been able to assume apparent higher risks themselves in the search for more profit.

Off-balance-sheet activities of European banks

The phenomenal growth of OBS activities has been clearly identified from US empirical evidence (Chessen, 1986; Andrews and Sender, 1986). In the United States, the value of OBS activities reported to the regulators in June 1987 amounted to some $3.1 trillion compared with commercial banks' reported assets of $2.9 trillion. US banks' positions are easier to identify compared with European banks because they are obliged to declare some of their OBS liabilities to the Federal Deposit Insurance Corporation. Some US banks even break down their positions by category.

Nevertheless, despite the fact that banking commentators know that OBS commitments are very large and that they are growing rapidly, it is difficult to obtain precise evidence as to what commitments European banks have incurred. Table 5.7 shows various estimated banks' OBS items for 1985. It illustrates that for the main European banks estimated contingent commitments did not exceed 100 per cent of their total balance-sheet size. No other source revealing this type of information for European banks has been published since 1986 (sic *Euromoney*).

Other market sources of information[5] indicate that the 'invisible' balance-sheet positions of the UK, French, Swiss and some of the larger Scandinavian banks are quite substantial, although this evidence is difficult to equate with the scale of operations suggested in Table 5.7. It is understood that German banks' OBS exposure is usually 'modest' in relation to the on-balance sheet position. Information provided by IBCA Banking Credit Analysis Ltd in London also implies that the OBS commitments of Italian and Dutch banks are quite small but this might merely reflect the paucity of information available.

Swaps activities tend to be the major OBS component for banks in most European countries, and the largest banks appear to have a substantially greater proportion of their activities dedicated to floating-rate assets business. A breakdown of European banks' OBS exposures would reveal that interest-rate swaps generally constitute a larger proportion, usually accounting for around 60 to 70 per cent of total swaps business (foreign currency swaps making up the remainder). Similarly, interest-rate options and futures activities usually constitute a much larger part of total business compared with currency-related transactions. What is clear from the limited information we have available on European banks is that there has been a substantial growth in all these activities during the 1980s. Piecemeal evidence also reflects their considerable significance in balance-sheet terms as well as their bewildering array.

Growth in off-balance sheet activities

The growth in OBS activities has been substantial because in the early 1980s they incurred hardly any extra regulatory costs to the banks. European banks were not required to maintain capital or to hold reserve funds against such activities and risks. These transactions provided a way of retaining customers and market share in an

Table 5.7 Banks' off-balance-sheet items (US$ bn).

		OBS if known	Total assets 1985	Estimated OBS
1.	Citicorp	260.7	167.2	
2.	BankAmerica	197.4	114.8	
				150
3.	Chase Manhattan	132.9	87.7	*
4.	J.P. Morgan	121.2	67.6	
5.	Bankers Trust	114.0	48.1	
6.	Chemical Bank	112.6	54.3	
				100
7.	Manufacturers Hanover	95.0	74.4	
8.	Fuji Bank		142.1	
9.	Sumitomo Bank		135.4	
10.	Dai-Ichi Kangyo Bank		157.6	
11.	BNP		123.1	
12.	Mitsubishi Bank		132.9	
13.	Sanwa Bank		123.0	
				75
14.	NatWest		104.7	
15.	Crédit Lyonnais		111.4	
16.	Industrial Bank of Japan		102.7	
17.	Deutsche Bank		95.7	
18.	Barclays Bank		94.2	
19.	Société Générale		97.6	
20.	Paribas		72.9	
21.	Bank of Tokyo		69.1	
22.	Midland Bank		83.8	
23.	LTCB		78.8	
				50
24.	Tokai Bank		90.4	
25.	Dresdner Bank		76.4	
26.	Mitsui Bank		88.5	
27.	UBS		67.2	
28.	Lloyds Bank		63.2	
29.	SBC		61.6	
30.	Royal Bank of Canada		67.2	

Source: Euromoney (1986), p. 122.

environment of increased competition in mainstream lending markets. Nevertheless, the growth in these transactions reached such proportions by the mid-1980s that it began to stimulate growing supervisory concern in the United States, Europe and Japan. Regulators began to perceive that these activities were possibly pushing banks' overall risk positions towards unacceptable levels.

There are problems, however, in assessing the riskiness of these types of activities. The volume of OBS business alone is not a guide to their risk potentials for banks, and it seems likely that these activities are generally less risky in the aggregate compared with traditional banking business. The problem lies in the fact that it is difficult to assess the risks (and the returns) associated with many of these activities. In addition, risks (undesirable outcomes) associated with the OBS position have a corresponding low (perhaps still immeasurable) probability of occurrence, but an associated probable high (and untested) loss potential. Banks and regulators have to make informed assessments of the interrelated risks being run in all these new activities. Of course, bankers should be aware of individual risks and more importantly they should also be aware of the risks entailed by the size and composition of all activities (see BIS, 1986, pp. 192–3 for a table showing the main risks associated with OBS activities).

The risks involved in this type of OBS banking business are inherently no different from other banking risks, but there is concern that banks are not allocating sufficient capital to cover them. There is also increasing competitive pressure on European banks, because of narrowing gross margins, to assume more risk in an attempt to bolster earnings. The growth of OBS risk-taking by banks and the concomitant decrease in the transparency of banks' balance sheets have brought calls for increased capital backing, and a new, more dynamic approach to capital adequacy. This has resulted in a shift in emphasis away from simple balance-sheet capital ratios based on accounting data to more dynamic approaches, such as risk-adjusted return on capital (RAROC) and return on exposure (ROX) techniques. In this new and demanding environment, the quality of bank management will be an important factor. Management ability to assess and control these new and still largely unexperienced risks will continue to be crucial elements in the maintenance of the strategic position and European banks' longer-term survival capabilities.

Comparative capital adequacy, profits and PERs

Capital adequacy is related to a bank's corresponding risk exposure. *Ceteris paribus*, the higher a bank's risk exposure, the more capital is required – balance-sheet ratios have traditionally been used to relate capital to banking riskiness. Supervisors have increasingly required more capital backing during the 1980s as the perceived riskiness of banking business has increased, and capital adequacy is a central issue in most supervisory systems (see Chapter 4). Banks have generally attempted to operate close to these standards or to modify them. This action by European banks has not necessarily been directly targeted as direct regulatory avoidance but has been more generally the result of increasing competitive pressures.

The post-1982 supervisory demands for more capital in banking have been reflected in rises in (book value) capital ratios and developments of new types of debt, such as floating rate notes (FRNs), which have certain attributes of capital and provide banks with a wider choice in long-term funding. Assets such as perpetual

78

Table 5.8 Banking rates of return and capital adequacy in selected countries (%).

Country	Return on assets (av.)		Equity/assets	
	1983	1986	1983	1986
Belgium	0.30	0.38	2.34	2.51
France	0.10	0.22	1.78	2.20
Germany	0.51	0.46	3.07	3.57
Italy	0.48	0.69	3.48	4.41
Netherlands	0.21	0.31	2.82	3.37
Norway	0.81	0.49	4.33	3.98
Spain	0.76	0.89	5.97	5.88
Switzerland	0.41	0.50	5.74	6.26
United Kingdom	0.88	0.90	6.24	6.32
Japan	0.15	0.19	2.29	2.22
United States	0.63	0.73	4.62	5.24

Source: Adapted from Table 1 of *Real Banking Profitability*, IBCA Banking Analysis Limited, 1986.

FRNs, or 'purples', and other subordinated loans, however, cannot be viewed as exact substitutes for traditional risk-bearing capital. Banks will continually be faced by the need to increase capital through higher retentions or by issuing new equity. Table 5.8 depicts the changes in banking rates of return and capital adequacy (see also Table 4.3) in selected countries and the comparative low positions of the French (as well as Japanese) banks may be noted (Monro-Davis, 1987)[6]. The table shows that capital to asset ratios have increased in all the reported European banking markets apart from Norway and Spain (These figures are estimated for the largest banks in these countries and thus corroborate our findings in Table 5.5.). At the same time one must be cautious about any such comparisons. Different accounting, fiscal and regulatory systems can distort international banking comparisons.

A comparatively low capitalization by international standards is a problem for the French banks in the current phase of intensive deregulation in France. A higher capitalization is undoubtedly required for the banks to break their traditional strong links with the state. French bankers argue that their large interbank positions and substantial volumes of new equity (not included in Table 5.8) mask their real capital-adequacy positions. The data in Table 5.8 are highly aggregated[7], but they do show clear improvements in banking ROA and equity to asset ratios for most large European banks from 1983 onwards.

It is also interesting to note the differences that exist in bank capital ratios between different European countries. In 1986, for example, equity to asset ratios ranged from 6.32 per cent in the United Kingdom to lows of 2.51 per cent for Belgian and 2.20 per cent for French banks. These kinds of differences are not only confined to country comparisons. For example, equity to assets ratios for Italy's ten largest banks in 1987 ranged from 12.33 per cent (Istituto Mobiliare) to 1.69 per cent (Banco di Napoli). In the United Kingdom equity to assets ratios for the ten largest banks ranged between 2.41 per cent (Standard Chartered) and 13.20 (TSB) (*The Banker*, 1988). These kinds of divergences between individual banks are least characteristic in France and Germany where the respective ratios for the top banks are very similar.

Table 5.9 Comparative profitability and capital ratios for *The Banker* Top 300 banks in Europe (1987).

Country	Number of banks in top 300	Average pre-tax profits to assets (%)	Average capital to assets (%)
United Kingdom	25	0.23	6.18
Ireland	2	1.47	6.12
Netherlands	8	0.57	4.23
Belgium	10	0.40	2.44
Luxembourg	7	0.55	3.78
France	25	0.50	3.14
Liechtenstein	2	0.63	8.21
Switzerland	25	0.61	5.70
Portugal	6	0.54	3.35
Spain	20	1.21	5.70
Italy	51	0.86	5.02
Norway	5	−0.39	2.82
Finland	5	0.40	5.99
Sweden	7	1.35	5.35
Denmark	8	0.53	6.79
W. Germany	70	0.44	3.07
Austria	10	0.39	3.52
Hungary	2	3.39	5.33
Yugoslavia	6	2.81	4.08
Greece	3	0.33	2.13
Turkey	3	1.60	6.08

Source: Jones (1988, p. 56).
Note: These data are computed on the same basis as *The Banker* (July 1988), Top 500.

Banks are heterogeneous in their business mixes, risk exposures, profitability and capital. Table 5.9 (and see also Table 4.3) confirms this picture of banking heterogeneity throughout Europe.

Although the capital strength of European banks has been largely unimpaired by the high level of LDC debt provisioning during the late 1980s (especially in the United Kingdom), profitability and capital strength in European banking markets remain below the levels of the late 1970s. Capital levels are also generally considered to be low in relation to the risks now carried in banking portfolios. Margins have been pared through intensive competition and ROAs have correspondingly come under pressure. The deterioration in real profitability and capital strength has generally been slowing down until 1987, but it appears that this trend has been temporarily halted. Bank capital adequacy will continue to be increasingly under pressure as supervisory agencies continue to capture a larger portion of banks' OBS activities under their regulatory net.

Previous sections in this chapter highlighted the various balance-sheet and performance characteristics of European banks. The marked differences in these characteristic features are (to a certain degree) also reflected in banks' share price valuations. Although cross-country comparisons are notoriously difficult to make (because of different accounting conventions, earnings prospects, stock market ratings criteria and so on) a brief look at the price-to-earnings ratios (PERs) and yields for different banking markets illustrates some interesting features.

Table 5.10 shows that the range of PERs for UK and Danish banks are significantly lower and (in most cases) narrower than for banks operating in other European banking markets. This implies that they are cheaper on PER grounds and undervalued relative to their European counterparts. There are also substantial differences in PERs and yields in France, Germany, Italy and Spain, which possibly reflect more heterogeneous domestic banking markets. In addition, the high PER ranges for bank stocks in Germany, Norway, Italy and Switzerland are indicative of how well rated banks are in these countries. Despite the problems associated with interpreting these kind of data, they do suggest that prospects for earnings growth appear to be above average, especially in Northern Europe, although it is impossible to ascertain from the survey whether this can be directly related to balance-sheet management or any other causal factor.

Conclusion

The on- and off-balance sheet characteristics of West European banks have been subject to unprecedented changes in the last decade. Increased competition in mainstream banking business has continued to promote the use of non-traditional sources of funds, squeezed interest margins, and has also led to the reduction in the overall profitability of many banks. The substantial increase in the growth and depth of new financial markets, coupled with balance sheet capital constraints, have encouraged European banks to undertake more formal and complex asset and liability management, and the importance of banks' treasury functions has correspondingly burgeoned. The growth of OBS risk-taking by banks and the related decrease in the transparency of their balance sheets will continue to force them to adopt a more dynamic approach towards capital adequacy. Risk containment will undoubtedly remain a central aspect of capital-adequacy analysis and a major issue for European bankers. Securitization through asset sales may also be used increasingly by banks and other FSFs to increase their (real) capital-adequacy positions (see Chapter 10). Following chapters will focus more specifically on many of the related 'business aspects' of change that have been discussed in this chapter.

Table 5.10 Market characteristics of European banks (%).

Country	PER	Yields
Belgium	7.3 - 9.0	4.1 - 4.6
Denmark	4.8 - 5.6	3.4 - 4.7
Finland	9.7 - 12.0	4.0 - 4.1
France	5.2 - 16.3	2.1 - 7.0
Germany	10.7 - 21.7	2.4 - 3.8
Ireland	8.9 - 10.3	4.6 - 5.0
Italy	10.0 - 32.0	1.0 - 7.4
Netherlands	7.5 - 7.8	5.0 - 6.7
Norway	16.3 - 17.9	5.5 - 6.0
Spain	8.5 - 18.5	2.1 - 4.9
Switzerland	16.3 - 17.4	3.7 - 4.0
United Kingdom	4.5 - 6.8	5.2 - 8.5
Average	9.1 - 14.6	3.6 - 5.6

Source: Morgan Stanley (1989, p. 27).

Notes

1. In Italy relatively high rates of interest are paid on all types of demand deposit. In Denmark high rates are paid on demand deposits which have no chequing facility.
2. Floating rate notes (FRNs) had first been introduced in the mid-1970s but were not widely used until after 1982.
3. See note a to Table 5.3 for a definition of all European banks.
4. See note a to Table 5.5 for a definition of large European commercial banks.
5. Various aggregate data provided by IBCA Banking Credit Analysis Ltd in London.
6. Japanese banks have come in for particular criticism. It has been alleged that their comparatively low capitalization has enabled them to compete and price more aggressively than their competitors. Japanese bankers argue that their high volumes of hidden reserves should be included in any such capital-adequacy comparisons, but the general view has not been sympathetic to this defence.
7. For example, they do not reflect the substantial LDC debt reserves raised within the balance sheets of banks in countries such as the United Kingdom and the United States.

References

Akhtar, M. A. (1983), 'Financial innovations and their implications for monetary policy: an international perspective', *Bank for International Settlements Economic Papers*, December, no. 9 (Basle: BIS).

Andrews, Suzanna and Sender, Henry (1986), 'Off balance sheet risk: where is it leading the banks?', *Institutional Investor*, (January), pp. 111–20.

Bank for International Settlements (1986), *Recent Innovations in International Banking* (Basle: BIS).

Banker, The (1988), 'Top 500', July, vol. 138, no. 749, pp. 56–151.

Chessen, J. (1986), 'Off-balance sheet activity: a growing concern?', *Proceedings of a Conference on Bank Structure and Competition*, (Chicago: Federal Reserve Bank of Chicago).

Committee of London and Scottish Bankers (CLSB) Statistical Unit (1988), *Abstract of Banking Statistics*, vol 5, (May) (London: CLSB).

Euromoney (1986), 'Will the system tumble', (September), pp. 112–31.

Gardener, E. P. M. (1986), 'Securitisation and the banking firm', *IEF Research Papers in Banking and Finance*, RP 86/15 (Bangor: Institute of European Finance).

Gardener, E. P. M. (1987) (ed.), *Interest Rate Risk and Banks*, *IEF Research Monographs in Banking and Finance*, no. 4 (Bangor: Institute of European Finance).

Goodhart, C. A. E. (1982), 'Structural changes in the banking system and the determination of the money stock', Paper presented to the *Conference on Western European Priorities at the Centre for European Policy Studies*, Brussels, (December).

Harrington, R. (1987), *Asset and Liability Management by Banks* (Paris: OECD).

IBCA Banking Analysis Ltd (1986), *Real Banking Profitability* (London: IBCA Banking Analysis Ltd).

Jones, Colin (1988), 'On your marks, get set, go . . . ', Europe Top 300, *The Banker*, vol. 138, no. 752, (October), pp. 56–7.

Kane, E. J. (1979), 'The three faces of commercial bank liability management', in M. P. Dooley, H. M. Kaufman and R. E. Lombra (eds), *The Political Economy of Policy-Making* (Beverly Hills and London: Sage).

Monro-Davis, R. (1987), 'Capital ratios are only one step', *The Banker*, (May), pp. 55–9.

Morgan Stanley (1989) 'Kredietbank in a class of its own', *European Banking Commentary*, (March).

OECD (1987), *Bank Profitability, Financial Statements of Banks, with Methodological Country Notes, 1980–84* (Paris: OECD).

OECD (1988), *Bank Profitability, Statistical Supplement, Financial Statements of Banks, 1982–86* (Paris: OECD).

Wilson, J. S. G. (1985), 'How assets and liabilities are managed around the world', *The Banker*, vol. 135, no. 712, (June), pp. 54–62.

Chapter six

Retail banking

Introduction

Of the 14,000 or so banks operating in Europe the majority are heavily involved in retail banking business. Retail banking has traditionally been supply-led. Through their branch networks, retail bankers have locked in passive retail customers by providing an efficient payments system. In this process banks have benefited by obtaining cheap retail deposits, which were available to on-lend to corporate or retail customers. This traditional situation is rapidly changing. The day of the uninformed or financially unsophisticated retail customer are over. The increase in competition which has affected all European financial markets – a product of trends such as technological advancement, deregulation and socio-economic change – has encouraged retail banks to broaden and improve the quality of their services, and to extend their customer bases correspondingly.

The European banking system is rapidly becoming universal, with banks increasingly being allowed to offer a wider range of financial services and products. At present the German, Swiss and Benelux systems are more advanced in this respect compared with the recently deregulated UK system. France, Spain, Denmark and other Scandinavian countries are currently deregulating their financial services industries and this process is also being pursued rather more slowly in Italy. We saw earlier that the consequence of this is that demarcation lines between institutions and markets have become increasingly blurred. Two forms of 'structural diffusion' illustrate the aforementioned phenomena: 'institutional structural diffusion' and 'market structural diffusion'. The former relates to broadening product and service facilities offered by a wider range of institutions. The widening of the product bases of financial institutions, de-specialization, has resulted in a greater variety of FSFs doing business in a more competitive market environment. The latter form of diffusion refers to the blurring of distinctions between the terms and types of business undertaken in different financial markets. For example, some UK retail deposits now earn money-market rates and corporate banking products like caps and collars are being offered in some retail mortgage market segments. In this context retail and wholesale banking markets have become more integrated during recent years.

The future looks bright. A recent study by Arthur Andersen (1988) predicts that retail banking business will be 'phenomenal' in Europe during the 1990s mainly as a result of reduced domestic, product and international barriers. Retail markets for deposits, loans and other products are likely to remain national even after 1992, and despite the growth of universal banking niche players may have an opportunity to profit from their domestic markets[1].

A perspective of retail banking

Historical context

The first retail banking revolution, a term first coined by Frazer and Vittas (1982), began during the 1950s in continental European countries such as Germany, Sweden and the Netherlands. This 'revolution' was characterized by various forces, the most important being the change in the attitudes of commercial bankers towards retail banking as a result of the considerable increase in the economic well-being of consumers. As the personal sector became the dominant supplier of surplus funds in the economy, it was clear that providing services to less affluent consumers (white-collar and skilled blue-collar workers) would be profitable and also provide a relatively cheap source of funding for corporate sector advances.

The populations of these three countries experienced the largest increases in prosperity and affluence among European countries during the 1950s and early 1960s, and it was also there that commercial banks had traditionally maintained a weak position in retail banking. The retail banking revolution dates back to the period when commercial banks in these countries decided to undertake various campaigns in order to attract retail business away from the savings banks, credit co-operatives and postal organizations that had traditionally dominated this market. Vittas *et al.* (1988, p. 7) point out:

> Similar developments took place during the 1960s and early 1970s in other continental European countries, especially in Northern and Central Europe. A distinctive feature of the entry of commercial banks into retail banking over this period was the ability of mutual and postal institutions to hold onto their own ground and retain their firm grip on personal banking.

It was only in the Scandinavian countries where mutual institutions were relatively weak that commercial banks have been able to establish a dominant market presence. In the United Kingdom the clearing banks have traditionally played a more significant role than their European counterparts in retail banking business because of their tighter control over the payments system.

Throughout the 1960s and 1970s the forces of deregulation (not so important in Germany and the Netherlands), advances in electronic and plastic technology (most evident in France and Sweden), and the changing demography and financial position of customers caused European bankers to be faced with an increasing retailing challenge. Greater emphasis has been placed on market segmentation, packaging, product differentiation and the directing of retail services to 'target' markets, such as one-parent families, high net-worth individuals, house buyers and the like. Despite these moves towards a greater market orientation, however, banks have managed to maintain their traditional customer bases by continuing to provide an efficient payments mechanism. It has often been argued that if banks cannot maintain their dominance of the payments mechanism, the size of their customer bases will recede

(Smith, 1984). As a result, commercial banks have aimed to consolidate their positions in this area. Houghton (1988, p. 6) suggests that in the early 1980s retail banking, 'fell out of vogue ... because people saw a huge opportunity in the capital market ... Too many people chased after that vision and as a result lost focus on a very important marketplace.' Banks are once again focusing their attention on the retail and private banking sectors as profits have become increasingly squeezed and losses and risks mount in other sectors.

Retail banking markets are now witnessing a second revolution. Vittas *et al.* (1988) note that in most advanced countries since the mid-to-late 1980s a new era of competition has emerged. Commercial banks have realized that, although retail business has high operating costs, it is also a high margin business, and these margins can be preserved through efficient marketing and pricing policies. There has also been increased competition in the consumer lending market (including mortgage lending) from the mutual sector as well as from merchant and investment banks, finance houses and High Street retailers. This increased competition, coupled with developments in technology (especially new electronic delivery systems) and an increase in the financial wealth of European households, has helped stimulate the second retail banking revolution. A noticeable difference between the first and second 'revolution' is that the first was not technology-driven, whereas the second certainly is. The authors of the aforementioned study argue that the second retail revolution is characterized by the emergence of three large regional markets: North America, Europe and East Asia.

Although the consumer financial services industry is closely related to investment and international financial markets and despite the fact that there are a variety of important global payments systems, Vittas *et al.* (1988, p. 14) suggest that retail banking business '... is still a long way from becoming a unified global industry in the way corporate banking and finance has already become'. The third stage of the revolution will inevitably lead to a truly global market in retail financial services (Smart, 1988).

European trends: demand factors
Banking markets in Europe can be broadly classified into three main groups (Nicholson, 1988, p. 6):

● Northern countries, whose banking systems exhibit reasonable profitability and low competitive prices: United Kingdom, Germany, Netherlands, Denmark and Scandinavian countries in general.
● Middle countries, whose banking systems generally exhibit poor profitability due to low prices and high costs: France, Belgium, Italy and Ireland.
● Southern countries, with good profitability and high prices, but high costs due to inefficiency: Spain, Portugal and Greece.

Figure 6.1 shows product growth, value added and profitability in France for a range of banking products and services. Each circle represents a product or service and the size of the circle represents comparative 'value-added', which is defined here as the average net interest margin plus fees earned. The position of the circles is remarkably similar for most European countries, although the Northern group of countries tend

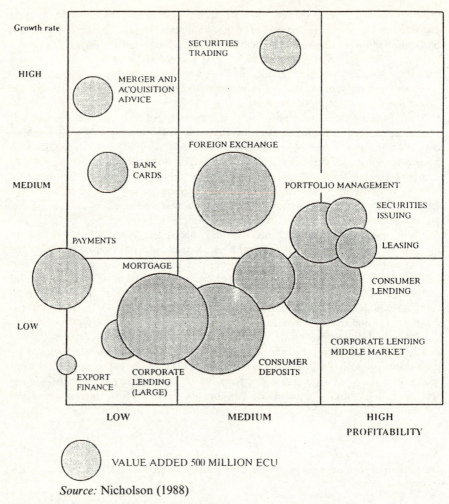

Growth rate

HIGH

SECURITIES TRADING

MERGER AND ACQUISITION ADVICE

MEDIUM

FOREIGN EXCHANGE

BANK CARDS

PORTFOLIO MANAGEMENT

SECURITIES ISSUING

PAYMENTS

LEASING

MORTGAGE

CONSUMER LENDING

LOW

CORPORATE LENDING MIDDLE MARKET

EXPORT FINANCE

CORPORATE LENDING (LARGE)

CONSUMER DEPOSITS

LOW   MEDIUM   HIGH

PROFITABILITY

VALUE ADDED 500 MILLION ECU

Source: Nicholson (1988)

Figure 6.1 Banking product profitability and growth in France 1987.

to exhibit higher profitability in local businesses (consumer lending and consumer deposits) while Southern countries exhibit higher profitability in almost all businesses.

Retail banking business obviously constitutes an important part of 'local banking business', and it is not surprising to see that the relatively profitable consumer lending of banks is compensated by the costly provision of a payments mechanism.

Probably one of the most important factors influencing the growth in importance of retail banking has been the increase in the number of adults who have chequing accounts and the decline in the proportion of the workforce paid in cash. In the late 1950s no European country had more than 30 per cent of its households holding chequing accounts. Table 6.1 illustrates that by the end of 1986 in Germany, the

Netherlands and Sweden virtually every adult held a chequing account and less than 5 per cent of the country's workforce was paid in cash. Of the European countries represented in the table the United Kingdom and Italy are the two countries where a large proportion of the workforce is still paid in cash. The concomitant growth of non-cash wage payment methods together with the spread of the banking habit in most European countries has broadened the consumer base and influenced the demand for additional consumer financial services.

In general, consumers have three main needs with regard to the provision of financial services. Firstly, they want to have the versatility to change their spending patterns independently of their income; secondly, they need to make payments; and finally they need services so they can insure against financial loss. The degree to which these requirements can be fulfilled depends entirely on the type of customer or group of customers being serviced. Over the last fifteen years, demographic factors have had a substantial effect on the demand for financial services. The age profiles of the largest OECD countries shows the proportion of the population under 24 years of age declining within every country. Stevenson (1986, p. 9) suggests:

> Amidst the general greying of the population, three groups stand out. The baby boomers born after the second world war, now 30 and 40 years old, are spending and borrowing to buy houses, raise children and enjoy a higher standard of living than their parents. Those a little older are saving and investing for a retirement ... Those over 65 – now close to 12 per cent of all Americans for instance – are selling their houses and stashing the proceeds in income producing investments.

These three groups have broadly different financial requirements on which commercial banks' retail segmentation strategy is based. Obviously age is not the only demographic feature that can influence demand. Marital status, family structure, occupation, ethnic origin and sex all have a bearing on the demand for retail services.

Households have also become wealthier. Real incomes per household have risen in most European countries since the mid-1970s and household financial assets are still

Table 6.1   Spread of banking habit and wage payment methods.

	Banking habit[a]	Cash payment[b]
Australia	less than 70%	majority
Canada	virtually 100%	less than 5%
France	90–100%	less than 15%
Germany	virtually 100%	less than 5%
Italy	less than 50%	majority
Japan	negligible[c]	less than 10%
Netherlands	virtually 100%	less than 5%
Sweden	virtually 100%	less than 5%
UK	about 65–70%	more than 30%
USA	over 80%	less than 5%

Source: Vittas *et al.* (1988, p. 50)
Notes: a Proportion of adults with a chequing account.
  b Proportion of workers paid in cash.
  c Personal chequing accounts are very rarely used.

Table 6.2 Household financial wealth, debt and lend-back ratios 1981 and 1986.

		Household wealth % of GNP				Household debt % of GNP			Lend-back ratios Loans as a % of deposits			
		Liquid assets	Market-able securities	Contrac-tual sav-ings	Total finan-cial assets	Consumer credit	Housing finance	Total house-hold debt	Commercial banks	Sav-ings banks	Other mutual insti-tutions	Total all insti-tutions
France	1986	48.9	35.9	27.9	112.7	3.1	19.8	22.9	54	22	54	50
	1981	58.9	19.4	7.9	85.6	2.5	20.2	22.7	54	-	68	54
Germany	1986	67.1	23.6	23.6	114.3	8.4	33.1	41.5	59	39	67	66
	1981	60.4	17.8	17.8	96.0	9.3	27.5	36.8	54	35	70	62
Italy	1986	88.9	62.4	17.2	168.5	2.7	6.7	9.4	11	11	11	11
	1981	74.3	19.6	6.0	99.8	2.4	5.0	7.4	8	11	9	9
Netherlands	1986	48.0	32.6	93.2	173.8	2.8	29.9	32.7	65	27	58	76
	1981	48.6	21.9	68.2	138.8	3.6	31.1	34.8	62	49	64	82
Sweden	1986	44.9	38.2	54.5	137.6	16.2	38.5	54.7	71	61	50	137
	1981	47.1	14.3	54.1	115.4	15.6	30.2	54.8	46	58	37	110
UK	1986	56.4	35.6	87.7	179.8	8.1	40.7	48.8	94	-	101	91
	1981	47.8	21.6	47.5	116.9	6.7	24.9	31.6	38	3	87	64
Japan	1986	108.3	41.4	44.4	194.1	11.2	19.4	30.7	21	27	16	30
	1981	99.0	18.0	30.6	147.6	5.6	18.5	24.1	18	17	18	26
USA	1986	70.7	75.7	47.8	194.2	21.8	38.8	60.6	43	59	65	89
	1981	62.2	50.7	33.8	146.7	14.6	34.4	49.0	51	46	85	91

Source: Vittas *et al.* (1988) Tables 3.3, 3.4 and 3.6
Note: The decline in the lend-bank ratio for US institutions is probably related to the secondary mortgage market. This is because banks and mortgage institutions still originate mortgage loans.

growing faster than liabilitites. Table 6.2 provides a summary of changes in the make-up of household wealth and debt between 1981 and 1986; it also illustrates various lend-back ratios for different financial institutions. The table confirms the view that household financial wealth is growing faster than household debt and also shows that most of the growth in wealth is in the form of marketable securities and contractual savings, rather than liquid assets. This is, no doubt, attributable to the widespread increase in worldwide stock market prices over this period. The proportion of household financial wealth held in marketable securities increased by at least 50 per cent in every country cited, apart from France. Contractual savings, on the other hand, more than doubled in France and Italy and almost doubled in the United Kingdom, although the starting-points for the former two countries were relatively low.

If we consider household debt, the 1980s illustrate that the bulk of the increase comes in the form of housing finance rather than consumer credit. Italy is noticeable for its very low level of household debt. Finally, the lend-back ratios illustrate what proportion of an institution's deposits is lent out. As would be expected, the country that has experienced the largest relative increase in household debt, the United Kingdom, has also experienced the largest increase in lend-back ratios. The lend-back ratios for Italian institutions are noticeably low and therefore offer substantial opportunities to various types of lending institutions after 1992.

In general, given the changing demography and financial position of customers, bankers are now being faced with a strong retailing challenge. Newman (1984) has argued that financial services are twenty years behind consumer goods in relation to retailing and marketing. Retail customers are no longer uninformed and retail demands are becoming more sophisticated and customer loyalty is decreasing (Frazer, 1985). Customers are demanding more services, better information, and most importantly, value for money. Traditional bankers have had to alter their cultural orientation more towards retailing and marketing.

European trends: supply factors
The supply of retail financial services in Europe has traditionally been dominated by institutions that have been able to establish nationwide (or at least substantial) branch networks: namely, commercial banks and mutual and postal institutions. In Germany, the United Kingdom and France, mutual and postal institutions dominate the market for retail deposits controlling around 70 per cent of the market. Table 6.3 illustrates this point.

In the Scandinavian countries the mutual and postal institutions have somewhere between 40 per cent (Norway) and 30 per cent (Sweden and Finland) of the retail deposit market. These proportions are similar for the Southern European countries such as Spain and Italy. The importance of the retail deposit-taking capability of these institutions is also reflected in their share of the household lending market. Only in Germany, the Netherlands and Spain do the mutual institutions control a significant portion of both the consumer credit and housing finance market.

Table 6.3 illustrates that certain groups of institutions tend to dominate various market segments. In Germany and France the savings banks are the most important retail deposit-takers, whereas the Dutch Rabobanks and UK building societies tend to dominate in both retail deposits and mortgage finance in their respective countries.

Table 6.3 Commercial banks, mutual and postal institutions, market shares, 1986 (%).

Country/ Bank	Retail deposits	Consumer credit	Housing finance	Household loans/ household deposits
France				
Crédit Agricole	15.7	8.1	21.2	62.3
Banques populaires	3.4	4.8	2.0	35.0
Credit Mutuel	5.6	6.0	4.7	43.3
Savings banks	24.3	1.8	–	...
Postal institutions	17.3	–	–	...
Commercial banks	22.2	43.3	20.8	54.0
Total	90.5	64.0[a]	58.7[b]	...
Germany				
Savings banks	41.8	33.1	22.3	38.9
Credit co-operatives	22.0	21.1	13.1	44.2
Building & loans assoc.	10.1	–	22.2	115.5
Postal institutions	3.5	–	–	...
Commercial banks	14.5	23.3	10.4	59.1
Total	91.9	77.5[c]	68.0[d]	...
Italy				
Savings banks	18.7	(e)	18.5	11.2
Co-operative popular banks	10.7	(e)	10.0	10.6
Postal institutions	9.5	(e)	–	...
Commercial banks	30.8	(e)	29.2	10.6
Total	69.7[f]	(e)	57.7[g]	...
Netherlands				
Rabobanks	38.1	15.7	36.0	68.3
Savings banks	15.7	4.1	5.8	27.3
Post Bank	19.8	11.6	9.6	37.3
Commercial banks	25.7	10.7	23.7	64.6
Total	99.3	42.1[h]	75.1[i]	...
Sweden				
Savings banks	27.5	35.8	2.4	61.1
Co-operative banks	5.9	6.1	0.5	49.5
Commercial banks	35.5	51.2	4.5	70.7
Total	68.9	93.1	7.4[j]	...
United Kingdom				
Building societies	57.3	–	75.8	100.8
National Savings	16.4	–	–	...
Commercial banks	26.2	77.5	16.8	93.6
Total	99.9	77.5[k]	92.6	...

Mutual institutions in Sweden concentrate on consumer credit and play virtually no part in the mortgage sector. Commercial banks dominate the consumer credit market in Sweden and the United Kingdom.

The range of FSFs in the retail banking market has widened considerably in recent years to include the following institutions: commercial banks, savings banks, co-operative and postal banks, housing finance specialists, finance companies, various specialist credit institutions, retailers, institutional investors and the government. Housing finance specialists dominate the mortgage market in the Netherlands and play an important role in France through the Caisses des Dépots and Crédit Foncier France. Specialist mortgage banks control nearly 20 per cent of the German mortgage markets. Finance companies also play an important role in the Netherlands and France, providing 52.9 per cent and 30.7 per cent, respectively, of consumer credit in 1986. Finance companies had over 10 per cent of the UK and German consumer credit markets in the same year. Retailing companies have predominantly entered the retail banking market by promoting storecards with credit facilities. Vittas *et al.* (1988 p. 29) observe:

> In both France and Italy, retailing groups, often associated with large manufac-turing concerns, have been a major force for innovation in the consumer financial services industry. In Germany, a number of retailers have recently grouped together to launch a new non-bank payment and credit card but it is too soon to judge how successful it will be. Kaufhof, a big department store, and Quelle, a mail order company, have made major inroads in the provision of consumer financial services.

The Quelle group has been providing standard bank services such as customer credits through its financial subsidiary, Norisbank, in order to increase its sale of goods. It currently offers savings accounts, known as Norisbank savings certificates. In general, Norisbank branches are located in Quelle department stores.

Pension funds, life insurance companies and various mutual fund companies play an important role in the investment of voluntary and enforced savings and therefore compete with other retail banking institutions in the personal savings market. Insurance companies are also active in the housing finance market. They

---

Source: Various tables from Vittas *et al.* (1988).

Notes: a Finance companies provided 30.7% of consumer credit in 1986.

b Caisse des Dépots (19.2%) and Crédit Foncier (21.8%), special credit and mortgage institutions, provided the bulk of the remaining housing finance.

c Finance companies (11.9%) and insurance companies (8.1%) are other medium-sized lenders to the consumer market.

d Mortgage banks accounted for 17.3% of the German mortgage market.

e Included with housing finance.

f Various Treasury instruments accounted for 20.3% of total retail deposits.

g Special credit institutions accounted for 29.7% of the Italian consumer credit market.

h Finance companies accounted for 52.9% of consumer credit in the Netherlands. Many of these are owned by banks.

i Insurance companies provided another 16%.

j Mortgage credit institutions provided 72.2% of the Netherlands housing finance in 1986.

k Finance houses provided 12.4% and retailers 7.5% of consumer credit.

provide around 16 per cent of housing finance in the Netherlands and more than 5 per cent in Germany. On the other hand, they account for only a small proportion of the consumer credit (no more than 2 per cent) in the main European retail banking markets. Mutual funds are also becoming more important since the remarkable success of Merrill Lynch's money market mutual funds and its famous Cash Management Account (CMA). France is home to Europe's largest mutual fund industry which amounted to $200 billion by the end of 1987, more than twice as large as its nearest rival, the United Kingdom. The funds markets in France and Italy have burgeoned in recent years, mainly as a result of fiscal advantages associated with the respective financial products. Mutual funds offering deposit-like facilities are beginning to appear in these countries. Finally, the government also plays an important role in various retail banking markets through the operation of national savings schemes and the issuance of various products usually with fiscal advantages[2]. This control is also exercised over various institutions through nationalization, as in France and Portugal, and through Federal control as in Germany and Switzerland.

Over the last decade there has been substantial growth in the range of financial institutions operating in a broad range of retail markets and a subsequent decline in business demarcation lines. The corporate characteristics of the suppliers of financial services have also changed. There is now a whole range of conglomerates, specialists, agents and franchisers, groups and associations that either undertake universal banking business or aim to fill niche markets. This trend exemplifies the applicability of the generic label FSF (Financial Services Firm), especially in retail financial services. Some have broadened their range of products and services by forming links with other organizations. For example, officials of Banco Santander (who agreed a reciprocal equity shareholding with the Royal Bank of Scotland in late 1988) suggested that one of the main advantages of the link-up was that the Spanish bank could benefit from the Scottish bank's successful experience in the UK credit card market[3].

Smaller retail financial intermediaries have been able to fulfil specialist roles in various ways, mainly as agents of outside groupings (Revell, 1985). The Bank of Scotland, one of the smaller UK clearing banks, has specialized in providing current account services for building societies and other organizations that were, prior to recent legislation, not able themselves to do so. Many commercial banks and mutual institutions throughout Europe act as agents for insurance companies by selling policies through their extensive branch networks. The Big Three banks in Germany (Deutsche, Dresdner, Commerzbank) all now employ agents to deal with their high net-worth retail customers (Bouveret, 1988). Agency and/or franchising agreements seem to be of particular interest to small and medium-sized institutions, because they offer the opportunity to provide well-known products and services in localized markets. Link-ups with other organizations 'may' reduce the vulnerability of small to medium-sized institutions from the threat of unfriendly acquisition. In the retail banking marketplace, the trend towards conglomeration and universal services provision may be counterbalanced to some extent by the increased formation of groupings and specializations within the financial system.

Market environment

Products and services

In retail banking deposit-taking is still the most important factor in maintaining an established customer base. As customers become more financially sophisticated they demand better facilities from their bank account. Smith (1984, p. 6) notes that customers generally want four things from their bank accounts: early and quick access to money, increased credit availability when necessary, money working for them at all times and reliable information about their financial position. Retail customers have become more reluctant to use accounts that offer zero or low rates of interest. Two trends are apparent: the first is for institutions to offer interest-bearing accounts that are very similar, and the second is that institutions aim to differentiate these accounts by offering a range of complementary, ancillary services. As with most financial services in recent years, there has been a move towards an increased service content and packaging in the provision of retail financial products.

Banks in most European countries – with the exception of Italy, the Netherlands, Spain, Sweden and the United Kingdom – offer zero or very low rates of interest on current accounts. The introduction of high-interest chequing accounts in the United Kingdom provides a typical example of how competitive pressures have forced the banks to develop such products. From the mid-1980s the UK clearing banks have offered some form of restricted, high-interest chequing account usually with a stipulated minimum balance of around £2,000 and a minimum value of cheques to be drawn on the account of approximately £200. Increased competition between the banks and building societies led Midland and Lloyds to introduce new accounts in January 1989 which were far less restrictive and also combined a whole range of complementary services (Hunter, 1989). Table 6.4 illustrates the main features of these new accounts and compares them with those offered by representative building societies. Other UK clearing banks have begun to offer similar products since 1989. Similar types of products are currently being planned to be introduced in most Continental European countries, although the French and German banks seem reluctant to develop such facilities.

There is no doubt that this trend towards an increased service and packaging content will continue in the provision of retail financial services throughout Europe. Banks are increasingly placing much greater emphasis on the customer relationship as a whole and concentrating on the cross-selling of services to specific market segments. To encourage the customer to use a broader range of services from the same institution, banks have utilized relationship-pricing techniques which offer customers preferential prices if they use a number of services. These pricing packages are generally 'free banking' facilities which are offered if balances are maintained at specific levels.

Other aspects of relationship pricing may include preferential rates on credit cards, consumer credit, mortgage finance and special deals on ancillary services. Banks have also widely used various differential pricing techniques aimed at encouraging the use of lower-cost transaction methods, such as those aimed at promoting the use of ATMs (automated teller machines) and plastic cards for cash delivery rather than traditional paper-based methods. Differential pricing has also been used to encourage a wider use of standing order and direct debit transactions.

Table 6.4 UK high-interest chequing accounts.

Account features	Midland Orchard	Lloyds Classic	Abbey National	Nationwide FlexAccount	Co-op Cheque and Save
Interest on balances	5% to £250 6% to £1,000 7.5% £1,000 +	4.5% to £500 6.5% £500 +	5% net all bals	2.75% to £100 4.25% to £500 5.5% £500 +	4.5% to £399 7% to £999 8% to £2,499 9% £2,500 +
Interest-free overdraft	no	£100	no	no	£200
Overdraft rates (APR)	23.1	22.4	auth. 19.5 unauth. 26.8	auth. 23.1 unauth. 34.4	29.8
Free in credit	yes	yes	yes	yes	yes
Overdraft charges	£5 monthly	£6 monthly	none	none	£18 quarterly
Cheque cards	£50	£50	£50 or £100	£50	£50
Other cards	Access ATM debit	Access ATM debit	ATM	Access ATM	Visa ATM
Extras	free life ins. on overdraft; composite statement	free life ins. on overdraft		homebanking	

Source: The Guardian 1989, 7 January p. 10.

Notes: Tiered interest means that interest is only paid on the band applicable.
£100 cheque guarantee card available with Orchard for £5 monthly fee.
Lloyds overdraft fee only when more than £100 overdrawn.
ATM = cash card.
Debit = payment card.
Composite statement = statement of all Midland accounts.

The problems associated with creating effective pricing policies in the future will be strongly influenced by the development of new products, such as universal accounts, which offer payment, deposit and credit facilities and also enable banks to build on their customer relationships. An emerging trend that is likely to have significant impact on the development of new deposit facilities is what Vittas *et al.* (1988, p. 66) refer to as the unitization of consumer banking. This relates to the linking of consumer credit and payment facilities to managed funds, like unit trusts, which provide consumers with the opportunity to earn capital market returns '... without running the risk of having to liquidate their holdings at inopportune times'. This trend has been bolstered by the success of the previously mentioned US money-market mutual funds – instruments which accumulate investments in relatively short-term, money-market instruments, pay a market rate of return and also provide chequing and payment services to customers. At present, however, only a few European institutions offer this type of product, although the market is expected to grow rapidly.

Bankers throughout Europe see consumer deposits remaining the major source of funds in the future. It is expected that even given the costs of providing an efficient payments and delivery system, consumer deposits will still rank as being a cheaper source of funds than 'bought-in' funds from the money markets (Arthur Andersen, 1986). Banks will have to compete in a more aggressive fashion if they are to maintain the bulk of this market. Emphasis on packaging, quality and relationship banking will be critical factors.

As in the market for funds, the consumer credit market is highly segmented. The availability, convenience and flexibility of services offered are important factors in influencing consumer demand. Instalment lending has traditionally been the forte of commercial banks in France, West Germany and Spain, whereas overdraft facilities are most widely used in the United Kingdom. It is estimated that both the consumer credit and mortgage markets will grow somewhere in the region of between 3 and 9 per cent in real terms over the next decade. An interesting feature of the European mortgage market is that it is one of the few retail banking markets that is serviced in many countries by specialist institutions (as in Denmark, Germany and Sweden) which traditionally use wholesale bond finance to fund their mortgage lending. The successful growth of specialist mortgage vehicles has been a recent phenomenon in the UK market[4] and is likely to continue throughout Europe with the growth in secondary mortgage markets and developments in mortgage-backed securities.

In addition to the traditional sources of consumer credit there has also been a rapid growth in the usage of plastic cards (especially credit cards) over the last twenty years. They have been the key to the new financial services environment – opening the door to ATMs, EFTPOS (electronic funds transfer at point of sale) and retailer credit. Table 6.5 illustrates the relative importance of various cards in different countries. It can be seen that there are considerable differences between European countries. Access and Visa dominate the UK bank-issued credit card market, whereas the rest of Europe can be split into countries like France, Italy and Spain where Visa is the major card, and countries where Eurocheques serve as the domestic chequing system, like Austria, Belgium, Germany, the Netherlands, Luxembourg and Switzerland. In the latter group, Visa has been essentially boycotted and the MasterCard-linked Eurocard has been promoted in the travel and entertainment

Table 6.5 Plastic cards, end-1986.

Thousands (up to the end of 1986)

Card		UK	France	Germany	Italy	Netherlands	Sweden	USA	Japan
Visa	Barclaycard	8,488	Carte Bleu	110	1,200	30	350	100,000	4,500
	Trustcard	2,540	8,600						
	Other	1,092							
MasterCard	Access	9,850	–	–	–	–	–	75,000	28,400
Eurocard		–	6,200	470	600	125	700	–	–
American Express		950	410	470	280	130	110	17,500	300
Diners Club		280	170	250	180	70	10	1,500	400
Retailers' cards		15,000	5,000	700[a]	600[a]	150	3,000[a]	360,000	35,000
Other				–	–	–	600[a,b]	146,000[c]	27,600[d]
Total		38,200	20,380	2,000	2,860	505	4,770	700,000	100,200

Source: Compiled from Vittas et al. (1988).
Notes: a Rough estimates.
b This represents Sparbanks Kort which is a combined credit, debit and ATM card.
c 130 million oil company cards, 3 million choice cards and 13 million Discover cards.
d 20 million Shinpan companies' cards, 7.6 million JCB cards and 4 million oil companies cards.

(T&E) segment of the market. As the Eurocard lacks many of the ancillary services provided by other T&E cards it has lost ground to American Express. MasterCard lags far behind Visa in Europe, both in terms of cards issued and retailer acceptance, mainly because of restrictions imposed by its links with Eurocard[5]. The Eurocheque/ Eurocard countries (excluding Belgium) have been some of the last countries in the developed world to introduce electronic payments sytems, mainly because in these countries the bulk of shop payments are made in cash, while virtually all other payments are through the bank giro system.

As competition has increased from retailers and Visa in these countries, banks have sought, especially in Germany, to make Eurocheque cards look more like credit cards. Deutsche Bank, in its rearguard action against US credit cards, announced in early 1988 that it was to introduce a Europlus card which would perform four main functions (see Nevans, 1988, p. 13): cheque guarantee card (like the Eurocard), delayed-debit card for teller and EFTPOS access, a delayed-debit card on the Eurocard model and (perhaps) a credit card. Moves to strengthen the position of the Eurocard were increased in April 1988 when a new agreement with MasterCard International gave up the latter's influence over card development in Europe. Later in October 1988 the European Accord for Bank Card Usage was signed by the major retailing banks, representing over 100 million card-holders. This lays down detailed commercial, technical and legal guidelines on card co-operation between banks, retailers and consumers. The accord sets the terms on which the two rival card systems, Visa and Eurocard/Eurocheque, will compete. At an official level the European Commission is completing a code of conduct which covers similar ground to the European accord.

Despite competition between the two aforementioned groups, retailer cards account for the bulk of plastic cards in circulation worldwide and also play an important role in European markets. These cards offer a much more limited service compared to bank credit cards; they increase customer loyalty by limiting credit to in-house purchases and subsequently aim to boost sales. Nevertheless, some retail organizations are now offering cash withdrawal facilities through ATM networks. This has major implications for European banks because if they lose control of the payments system they are in danger of losing the deposits that come with it. Banks in Europe will find it difficult to hold on to a dominant share of payments provision.

In the second retail banking revolution banks have had to broaden their range of services, maintain quality and price competitively to preserve their position in the market. Many banks throughout Europe have diversified into product areas like insurance broking, stockbroking, travel agencies, estate agencies and offering mutual fund facilities (a big success in France and Italy). The privatization programme in the United Kingdom provided the main impetus for retail banks to offer a broader range of collective investment schemes and direct investments in marketable securities to their customers. It has also encouraged new players to enter the market especially in the HNWI (high net-worth individual) segment. The major objective has been for banks to adopt an integrated approach which enables them to cross-sell products and services[6]. Banks will also continue to look for more fee-income based business and will continue to act as financial and business advisers across a wide range of activities. Many banks now offer retail advisory services in the areas of personal investment, life and pensions business as well as trust work.

Competition

Competition in retail banking markets has always been influenced by two conflicting forces. Firstly, the market for retail customers is localized. Consumers generally prefer convenient branch networks which they can easily reach from their home or place of work. Consumer choice is greater in those banking markets that have a few countrywide institutions together with a large range of autonomous local ones. Secondly, consumers require similar financial services and with developments in payments and delivery technologies retail products can potentially be offered in any country. As a result retail banking markets can therefore also be viewed as global (Frazer and Vittas, 1982).

Although the provision of retail financial services can transcend national boundaries, retail markets abroad are much more difficult to penetrate than capital markets, because of differences of habit and taste between customers in different countries, and legal and customary barriers which usually make it much more difficult to gather retail deposits. *De-novo* establishment of branch networks in the retail sector has not occurred in Europe. Establishment across borders is usually through some form of merger or acquisition strategy. The largest and most successful retail banking acquisition of this kind was probably Deutsche Bank's purchase of Banca d'America e d'Italia in 1986.

Another 1992-inspired retail banking alliance between the Royal Bank of Scotland and Banco Santander was agreed in November 1988. The major objective of these kinds of aforementioned strategies is for medium to large-size banks to establish a pan-European presence in anticipation of 1992. There is little indication, as yet, to suggest that this activity has had a substantial effect on the competitive environment in any European retail banking markets because domestic institutions still dominate retail banking business. Serious restrictions still exist in certain parts of the consumer banking market: for example, only the United Kingdom and Luxembourg offer free access to firms from other EC countries to their domestic mortgage market. At the other extreme, Denmark will not allow the establishment of any new specialist credit mortgage institutions, whether domestic or foreign (Kleinwort Grieveson Research, 1988, p. 20).

Traditionally, it has been the mutual and postal institutions in Europe that have posed the major competitive threat to the commercial banks. Savings and mortgage institutions have always been strong competitors to the banks, but their competitive strength has traditionally been nurtured by their narrowness of focus, which is now proving a disadvantage as their strong competitive position is currently being undermined. Metaxas-Vittas (1988, p. 13) argues that this is because of five main reasons:

- the rediscovery of retail banking by commercial banks;
- abolition of fiscal and regulatory advantages;
- increased competition, especially in the area of housing finance from secondary mortgage-market operators, insurance companies and institutional investors;
- increasing popularity of contractual savings and mutual funds linked with a decline in consumer liquidity preference;
- increased wealth and financial sophistication of consumers and an increase in their demands for more diversified services.

In recent years the mutual characteristics of many institutions have weakened as they have sought to widen their product as well as their funding bases. The major constraint on the expansion and diversification plans of mutuals has been their reliance on internally generated funds. This has prompted various institutions to convert to stockholder status so as to raise new equity finance. The United Kingdom has witnessed the public flotation of the TSB Group, and various savings banks in Norway and Denmark are considering raising new equity by issuing quasi-equity instruments with limited voting rights. Building societies in the UK can now opt for public limited status subject to shareholder approval. The pressures to convert from mutual to joint-stock status are 'very strong' in Scandinavian countries, although where savings banks and other mutuals have been allowed to undertake a broad range of commercial banking business for some time – for example, in Germany, the Benelux countries and Spain – the pressure will be less urgent. In these countries they have been able to compete effectively with commercial banks in their domestic markets.

Two major studies on the future developments in banking (Arthur Andersen 1986; Vittas *et al.* 1988) state categorically that two types of financial institution will pose the major competitive threat to commercial banks in the retail banking market over the next decade: mutual institutions and insurance companies. Table 6.6 illustrates the retail banking products and services that are expected to be offered by these and other competitors. It can be seen that savings and mortgage institutions, insurance companies, retailers and postal institutions (PTT) are expected to offer a broad range of retail products and services. Insurance institutions are expected to push hard and successfully into certain areas the banks have hitherto considered their province – unsecured lending and deposit facilities – in order to complement their range of investment products. Competition and over-capacity in insurance markets are forcing the major organizations to find different sources of income. Insurance institutions have branch networks in many European countries and already have expertise in the investment management and mortgage finance markets. With their significant capital resources, diversification into the banking sector is a natural extension of their business.

Retail organizations are rapidly extending their business into consumer banking markets. With a captive clientele, they have realized that a storecard improves customer loyalty, provides the opportunity for cross-selling other financial services and is also profitable. The French market has probably developed at the most rapid pace. French retailers have been allowed to deliver cash to their card-carrying customers, a facility that has angered French bankers (*Retail Banker International*, 1986). Retailers argue that they can provide consumer credit and other retail services at a lower cost than the banks. By the end of 1988 customers could obtain consumer credit, undertake securities transactions, purchase securities and unit trusts from a variety of UK high street chain stores. This trend will, no doubt, continue throughout Europe.

Increased competition in the retail banking sector will lead banks and other institutions to re-think their pricing strategies. Commercial banks have traditionally underpriced their deposit balances and offered payment services free of charge. As retail customers required convenient access to the branch network, the extension of their services was widely viewed as a form of non-price competition. The growing costs of supporting such networks, the increase in interest-bearing chequing accounts and the more sophisticated demands of consumers across Europe have led banks

Table 6.6 Retail banking products expected to be offered by new entrants in selected European countries.

Type of Institution	Deposit/savings accounts	Current accounts	Investment credit/ personal loans	Home mortgages	Credit/ debit cards	Electronic funds	Investment management
Savings and/or mortgage	B, F, FR, G, GR, I, IT, L, NL, S, UK	B, DK, F, G, GR, I, IT, L, NL, UK	B, DK, F, G, NL, GR, I, S, UK	B, F, G, GR, I, IT, L, NL, S, UK	B, F, G, I, NL, S, UK	B, F, NL, UK	IT
Insurance	B, DK, FR, G, NL, L, UK	IT	B, DK, F, UK	B, DK, F, G, I, L. UK			B, DK, G, GR, I, L, S, UK
Retailing	B, FR, G, L, NL, UK	B, G, L, NL	B, F, FR, G, I, L, NL, S, UK		B, DK, F, FR, G, I, L, NL, S, UK	B, FR, UK	
Stockbroking and financial intermediaries	DK, FR, L	DK, L					B, F, G, I, L, NL, S, UK
Hire Purchase/ Leasing	I	L	F, FR, I, L	IT	F		
PTT	B, DK, F, FR, I, L, NL, S, UK	B, DK, F, G, GR, I, L, NL, S, UK	G, GR, I, NL, S	NL, S	DK, I, L, NL, S, UK	DK, F, G, I, L, NL, S, UK	
Government institutions	B, F, I, S	B, G, I	B, L, S	F, I, L, S	B	B, I	
Trade unions	F, GR	F	F, GR, S	F	GR		

Source: Adapted from Arthur Andersen (1986, Diagram 2 series in country studies).
Note: In these countries the respondents to the Arthur Andersen survey estimated a likelihood exceeding 40%:

B   = Belgium   I   = Ireland   UK = United Kingdom
DK = Denmark   IT = Italy   F   = France
L   = Luxembourg   G   = Germany   NL = Netherlands
GR = Greece   S   = Spain

Table 6.7 Percentage differences in prices of standard retail financial products compared with the average of the four lowest national prices[a].

Name of standard banking service	Description of standard services	B	D	E	F	I	L	NL	UK
Consumer credit	Annual cost of consumer loan of 500 ECU. Excess interest rate over money market rates.	−41	136·	39	na	121·	−26	31	121
Credit cards	Annual cost assuming 500 ECU debit. Excess interest rate over money market rates.	79	60	26	−30	89	−12	43	16
Mortgages	Annual cost of home loan of 25,000 ECU. Excess interest rate over money market rates.	31	57	118·	78	−4	na	−6	−20
Travellers' cheques	Cost for a private consumer of purchasing 100 ECU worth of travellers' cheques	35	−7	30	39	22	−7	33	−7

Source: Cecchini (1988, Table 6.1, p. 38).

Note: [a] These differences show the extent to which financial product prices, in each country, are above (represented by a positive figure) a low reference level price; the latter is the average of the four lowest prices (surveyed in 1987) for each respective financial product. Each of these price differences implies a theoretical potential price fall from existing price levels to the low reference points.

Key: B Belgium; D Germany; E Spain; F France; I Italy; L Luxembourg; NL Netherlands; UK United Kingdom.

to a whole range of new pricing strategies (Vittas, 1985)[7]. There will no doubt be a greater move towards transactions-based and relationship pricing in the future.

Finally, the EC commitment to completing an internal market in financial services has helped polarize many of the above issues. The creation of the so-called 'level playing field' is expected to increase competitive conditions in banking markets as a whole. Table 6.7 shows the price differences, computed by the Cecchini study (Cecchini, 1988), for four representative retail banking services in all member countries; the greatest differences are in the area of consumer credit. 1992 could help to reduce these differences and move European retail banking products more in line with the law of one price i.e., where a common price obtains for each financial product throughout the EC. Nevertheless, the Cecchini results must be interpreted carefully, especially in the case of retail banking which is highly segmented and organized in the main on national lines.

Technology

Technological developments over the 1980s have already had a significant impact on the core business of commercial banks. New technology has been reducing costs in what has traditionally been a high-cost business. The networking of computer systems has transformed the speed, accuracy and economics of both retail and wholesale payments and delivery systems. It is thought that over two-thirds of basic transactions can in some way be electronically automated. Retail customers can now apply for loans, enquire about deposit balances and order a plethora of other services through ATM networks or through home and office banking (HOBS) facilities. New technology also provides customers and management with better information. With new technology banks can now establish customer information files (CIFs) and household information files (HIFs), which they use for segmentation and marketing purposes. Banks can provide customers with information and guidance relating to their products and services, and they can now meet customer needs for accurate, timely on-line information.

Technological developments have transformed payments systems and services throughout Europe. In general, the facilities range from 'bricks-and-mortar' branches, through predominantly paper-based to electronically operated systems. In countries like Germany, Switzerland and the Benelux countries, where they do not rely on cheques as heavily as, say, in the United Kindom, France or Italy, consumers prefer paper or automated credit transfer instead. In these countries over half of the non-cash transfers are paperless and are electronically processed through a giro system. As we mentioned earlier in this chapter, the Eurocard/Eurocheque, which can be used in ATMs and various cash dispensers, has increasingly replaced conventional cheques in these countries.

Cheques are the dominant forms of payment in France, Italy and the United Kingdom. Even though between 1980 and 1986 UK automated clearings had grown by more than 17 per cent a year (compared with 4 per cent for paper-based transactions), cheques still accounted for nearly 60 per cent of the total volume. In France the same proportion of payments are made by bank cheques as in the United Kingdom, but the French write more cheques per head than almost any other nationality. Over 5 billion cheques a year in France account for more than 80 per cent of non-cash payments (Stevenson, 1986[8]). This, together with substantial government

Table 6.8 Overview of payment systems and services in EC member states, 1986

Country	Branches	Cheques	Cheque Guarantee Cards	Giro Transfers	Pre Auth-orised Payments	Credit Cards	ACTs	Truncation	ATMs	EFT-POS	HOBs
United Kingdom	W	H	H	W	W	H	W	L	H	V	V
France	H	H	L	W	W	W	W	L	H	L	L
Ireland	W	W	W	W	W	W	W	V	W	N	N
Belgium	H	W	H	H	H	W	H	W	W	L	V
Luxembourg	H	W	H	H	H	L	H	W	L	E	V
Netherlands	H	W	H	H	H	L	H	W	V	E	E
Germany	H	W	H	H	H	L	H	W	L	E	V
Denmark	W	W	W	H	H	L	H	W	L	L	V
Spain	W	L	L	L	L	W	W	V	W	L	V
Italy	L	L	L	L	L	L	W	V	L	E	V
Greece	L	L	L	L	L	L	W	V	V	N	N
Portugal	L	L	L	L	L	L	W	V	V	N	N

Source: Vittas (1986).
Note: H = High, V = Very Limited, W = Widespread, E = Experimental, L = Limited, N = Non-existent.

support, probably helps to account for the rapid development of card-based EFTPOS systems and smart card technology in France. Table 6.8 illustrates the development of payment systems and services in EC member states.

Even though automated clearing is growing in all European countries, paper-based transactions still account for the majority of payments. The trend has been towards the development of electronic networks which support and eventually replace burdensome paper-based systems. Cheque truncation (where cheques go no further than into the branch in which they are paid and the related information is electronically transmitted) is now widely used in the Benelux and Northern European countries. Branch counter terminals and desk-top terminals with screen monitors are widely used in Spain and Italy for information retrieval and management information services. Payments systems are generally more developed in the Northern European countries compared with their Southern counterparts (*Banking Technology*, 1988). This gap will probably be narrowed over the next ten years or so.

New technology has helped free the customer from having to go into the bank. Widespread usage of ATMs now enables customers to withdraw cash from a range of accounts, make deposits, enquire about balances, make transfers and pay bills, order cheque books and issue statement printouts – and these kinds of services are being continually extended. As banks find they can offer a broad range of products and access new localities through this automated facility, the need for a comprehensive branch network of the traditional kind becomes less necessary. ATM markets are rapidly becoming mature. Table 6.9 shows the number of ATMs in the European Community, the United States and Japan. In the United Kingdom there are some 11,000 machines installed by banks and there will be nearly as many machines as bank branches in a few years' time. As a result, banks are rapidly increasing the siting of new installations at remote locations such as 'university campuses, factories, industrial estates, hospitals, military bases and shops/shopping centres' (*Banking World*, 1988, p. 52). With harmonization moves in the run-up to 1992 there could

Table 6.9 ATMs in the EC, US, and Japan, January 1987.

Country	No. of ATMs	ATMs per mn pop.
Belgium	723	74
Denmark	462	90
France	9 480	172
Germany (Fed. Rep.)	3 300	54
Greece	70	7
Ireland	270	75
Italy	2 539	45
Luxembourg	30	82
Netherlands	240	17
Portugal	320	31
Spain	5 423	140
UK	10 845	192
USA	67 000	303
Japan	60 000	496

Source: Battelle International ATM Research, *World ATM Survey*, (London: Battelle Institute, 1987).

well be a fully integrated European system if reciprocal agreements are signed between proprietory ATM networks. Eurocheque is a leading player linking these networks: it expanded its 1987 network of around 4000 ATMs (in Spain, Portugal, United Kingdom, Denmark and West Germany) to 10 000 in 12 countries by the end of 1988. At present, Spain's Sistema 4B system is one of the most versatile, accepting Visa, Eurocheque and a host of other cards (Tutt, 1988).

EFTPOS and HOBS are less operationalized than ATM networks. The majority of experiments and systems being tried for EFTPOS involve connecting a retailer's cash register so that electronic messages can be transmitted to the bank. The customer's account is automatically debited and the retailers credited; there is no need for any paper transaction. France, with over 65 000 terminals, leads the market. In fact, French banks are committed, with the government, to one national system for electronic funds transfer based on the chip or 'smart' card by the end of the 1990s. At present around two-thirds of French EFTPOS terminals are bank-owned while the remainder are owned by retailers themselves. In the United Kingdom and Germany there are similar plans for national schemes (Vittas et al., 1988)[9].

France also leads the world in HOBS which enable customers to access cash management services, balance enquiries, funds transfer, bill payment and so on with the use of a TV screen, personal computer or variable-tone, push-button telephone, depending on the system available. The French post and telephone services has given out free over 2 million Minitel videotex terminals. As the equipment is free and home banking charges are negligible (if non-existent), home banking continues to grow in France. The French system, however, does not allow transers of funds to be made. In the United Kingdom, home banking is offered by Bank of Scotland's Home and Banking Services, and a number of banks and building societies started offering low-cost home banking via the telephone during 1987. The trend to offer HOBS by this method has been widely followed in Spain, Italy and Sweden.

Experiments with HOBS are more advanced in some European countries than in others. However, a sophisticated HOBS offering a broad range of retail products and services on a national scale has not yet been developed. The present service throughout Europe is essentially first-generation offering a limited range of services. If those services can be made more comprehensive and, more importantly, cheaper, it seems likely that this type of banking will grow rapidly. In the Arthur Andersen (1986) study respondents believed that the home banking market would not be fully developed even by 1995. Attention in Europe will clearly focus on the French market.

In 1987 the European Commission published the EC Accord for Payments Systems which established a code of conduct relating to the harmonization of electronic payments systems and services throughout member countries. The Commission intends to leave co-ordination to the banks themselves, and future legislation will legally enforce the code. The main objective is to improve the 'inter-operability' of payments systems as well as providing uniform consumer protection regulations. At present the Accord excludes non-bank financial intermediaries, such as building societies, from the harmonization process, thus maintaining the exclusivity of banks' running payments systems. This restriction is felt by many not to be in the spirit of the EC Commission. The ultimate imposition of uniform standards in the provision of payments and delivery systems will enable small banks to access large networks. This suggests that economies-of-scale arguments that have previously been used to justify large banks providing national payments systems may be rendered redundant.

All the above developments, together with the advent of the smart card and its associated electronic funds transfer (EFT) services, have major implications for the traditional bank branch. In a climate of rising operating expenses (mainly staff costs) and money transmission costs plus declining margins in retail business, banks will have to reassess the size and functions of their branches. As automated accounting and processing systems have revolutionized the back-end of branch banking business, so EFT facilities, ATMs and HOBS are beginning to alter the front-end. Throughout Europe, banks will be expected to reduce their branch networks and re-emphasize through technology their role as sales outlets in the future.

Balance-sheet implications

Retail banking business has been the mainstay of European commercial banks' profits over the last twenty years and will continue to be so until the end of the twentieth century. Retail banking profits have funded the forays of commercial banks into investment banking and securities trading and have cushioned them against major problems in corporate and international banking. For example, the strong retail business of three Nordic banks, Bikuben (Denmark), Götabanken (Sweden) and Dennorske Creditbank (Norway), helped balance their substantial investment banking losses (mainly in options) at the end of 1987 (Shegog, 1988). The strong retail profits growth of the UK clearers throughout the 1980s helped fund (before Big Bang) and sometimes cushioned (after the Crash in October 1987) the activities of their investment banking and securities trading arms. This scenario typified many commercial banks that entered these new activities during the 1980s.

As we noted in Chapter 3, banks earned higher average interest margins in countries where the main focus was on retail banking, such as Spain, Italy and the United Kingdom. High interest margins tended to be translated into high net income ratios, although operating expenses tended to be higher in these countries.

On the liabilities side of the balance sheet we would expect to see an increasing proportion of retail deposits paying interest more in line with money market rates. This trend was also noted in Chapter 3, and it is part of the so-called marketization of finance that characterizes most European financial systems. In addition, consumer lending and especially mortgage finance will become more closely linked to wholesale rates as secondary mortgage markets and securitized assets business develop throughout Europe. With the increasing trend towards the securitization of traditional retail products such as mortgages and other receivables, this will have the effect of shifting assets from pressured balance sheets and will provide banks with greater funding flexibility. The unitization of various retail banking services may well lead to a declining in banks' traditional deposit bases, as consumers increasingly demand investment-type returns from their deposits. Nevertheless, despite these probable future developments, the growth in the balance sheets and profitability of European banks is expected to be almost entirely generated by retail banking business in the immediate future.

Conclusion

Three overriding trends in the European retail banking market are clear: competition will increase between banks, competition will increase between financial institutions, and competition will increase in the market for retail financial services. Although various banks have made small acquisitions or agreed reciprocal stakeholdings with other European banks, a general view seems to be that the major benefit of 1992 will be the ability to market retail products across national borders with little or no presence in other countries. Probably the easiest and most efficient way to perform such cross-border activities is by the use of plastic cards. Harmonization of European plastic card (whether credit, debit or smart card) technology will enable consumers to use their cards in virtually any retail location. UK banks view mass-market life and other insurances/mortgage-related products as underdeveloped in various Continental European countries and these are the businesses they aim to develop, so long as they can obtain low-cost bases from which to sell them. At the other end of the market, private banking and the selling of stockbroking and investment banking services to wealthy customers are also perceived as potential profitable markets. Banks throughout Europe are probably making similar decisions vis-à-vis their retail banking strategies for 1992. There is no doubt that the retail market will continue to be the mainstay of commercial banking business throughout Europe during the 1990s despite increased competition, lower margins and the increased technological, servicing and packaging content of retail banking products.

Notes

1. The Arthur Andersen study argues that by 1992 the worldwide financial marketplace is expected to consolidate so that wholesale services will be predominantly provided on a global basis and retail services will be primarily for national markets. It is likely that less than 200 multinational financial institutions will handle 65–75 per cent of the world's depository assets and an even smaller number will handle 75–80 per cent of all global financial market transactions.
2. Such as Treasury instruments which account for over 20 per cent of consumer credit in Italy.
3. Niche operators appear to be more common in corporate and capital market activities. For example, in the United Kingdom prior to 'Big Bang', Cazenove, one of London's major brokers, resisted all takeover advances, and has preserved its traditional role in the market. Nevertheless, it has developed well-publicized links with large institutional investors which it will use if it requires more capital.
4. For example, the Mortgage Corporation (linked to Salomon Brothers) and the UK National Home Loans (which concentrate more on dealing with institutions) have built up a considerable share in the UK mortgage market. Several foreign operators have recently entered the market: Nykredit (Danish) and UCB (the mortgage finance subsidiary of France's Compagnie Bancaire) sell their products through insurance agents and brokers. Wholesale funded mortgage finance accounted for 10 per cent of the UK market at the end of 1987.
5. Visa operates in Europe through regional associations, which negotiate directly with member banks. MasterCard has to operate at arms-length in Europe through reciprocal agreements with the Joint Credit Card Company in the UK and Eurocard in the rest of Europe.
6. In the United Kingdom the clearing banks (and to a lesser extent, insurance companies through a boom in endowment business) entered the home mortgage market in a big way

in the early 1980s and have more recently purchased estate agencies (e.g. Lloyds Black Horse chain), which dovetail with their traditional business. The house purchase market offers substantial cross-selling opportunities, such as mortgage finance, insurance/ assurance etc.

7. The author argued that there are nine deposit-taking pricing strategies available to commercial banks. These are:
    a) pay no interest; levy no charges – e.g. Belgium, France and the Netherlands.
    b) pay no or little interest; levy explicit charges on most services but at levels much below operating costs – e.g. Germany. Bank charges vary considerably between banks.
    c) pay no interest; levy charges at relatively high prices but allow a notional interest rebate against imputed charges – e.g. United Kingdom.
    d) pay no interest; levy no charges if the account is kept in credit or if a stipulated minimum daily balance is maintained but otherwise levy relatively high charges – e.g. known as 'free banking' in the United Kingdom.
    e) pay high interest, levy no charges – e.g. once available on special salary accounts in Nordic countries.
    f) pay low interest on low balance; levy no charges on first five or ten transactions a month. Pay good interest on high balance. Introduced in Scandinavian countries to replace above.
    g) pay high interest; levy offsetting charges based on withdrawal fees – e.g. Sweden. The Svenska Handelsbanken offers the famous General Account (Allkonto) where this is used.
    h) pay high interest; levy high charges – e.g. Italy and the United Kingdom.
    i) apply relationship pricing; no charges if specified balances kept in specified accounts – United Kingdom.
8. At the end of 1985 it was estimated that French bankers spent $2.2 billion a year in providing this payments facility. They are still not legally allowed to charge for cheque processing, although the law can be circumvented (see Stevenson, 1986).
9. This study provides a detailed account of EFTPOS systems in France, Germany, Italy, the Netherlands, Sweden and the United Kingdom.

References

Arthur Andersen (1986), *The Decade of Change: Banking in Europe – The Next Ten Years* (London: Lafferty Publications).

Arthur Andersen (1988), *The Globalisation of the International Financial Markets: Implications and Opportunities* (New York: Arthur Andersen).

Banking Technology (1988), 'Scandinavia switches on', vol. 5, no. 9, (September), pp. 28–33.

Banking World (1988) 'Annual ATM Survey', vol. 6, no. 11, (November), pp. 49–61.

Bouveret, Andreas M. (1988), 'New strategies and current changes in the German banking system', *IEF Research Papers in Banking and Finance* RP 88/15, (Bangor: Institute of European Finance).

Cecchini, P. (1988), *The European Challenge 1992: The Benefits of a Single Market* (Aldershot: Gower).

Davis International Banking Consultants (1988), Seminar on 'Bank Strategy and 1992' (24–25 November), London.

Frazer, Patrick and Vittas, Dimitri (1982), *The Retail Banking Revolution: An International Perspective* (London: Lafferty Publications).

Frazer, Patrick (1985), *Plastic and Electronic Money* (London: Woodhead-Faulkner).

Houghton, Diana (1988), 'Global banking report predicts big surge of interest in retail banking'. *Retail Banker International*, no. 162, (30 May), pp. 6–7.

Hunter, Teresa (1989), 'Soapsud-sell with interest', *The Guardian* (7 January), p. 10.

Kleinwort Grieveson Research (1988), *1992: Financial Sector*, (July). Kleinwort Grieveson Securities Ltd.

Metaxas-Vittas, Thymi (1988), 'Mutual institutions face challenge but are set to survive', *Retail Banker International*, (27 June), no. 164, pp. 9–13.

Nicholson, Geoffrey (1988), 'Local sensitivity key to Pan-European growth', *Financial Services International*, Issue 8, (September), pp. 4–7.

Newman, K. (1984), *Financial marketing* (Holt Rinehart and Winston with the Advertising Association: London).

Nevans, Ron (1988), 'Battle lines drawn in Europe as card companies vie for market shares', *Retail Banker International*, (4 April), pp. 11–13.

Retail Banker International (1986), 'French retailers move en masse', no. 126, (November), pp. 7–8.

Revell, Jack (1985), 'New forms of competition and new competitors', *Revue de la Banque*, vol. 49, no. 2, (February), pp. 45–53.

Shegog, Andrew (1988), 'Strong retail business balances investment banking losses', *Retail Banker International*, no. 156, (7 March), pp. 12–13.

Smart, Eynon (1988), 'Second revolution', *Banking World*, (July), p. 41.

Smith, C. P. (1984), *Retail Banking in the 1990s: The Technology Suppliers View* (London: Lafferty Publications).

Stevenson, M. (1986), 'A survey of international banking: the consumer is sovereign', *The Economist*, vol. 1298, no. 7439, pp. 1–45.

Tutt, Nigel (1988), 'Europe schedules plastic card pact', *Banking Technology*, vol. 5, no. 1, pp. 22–5.

Vittas, Dimitri (1986), 'Electronic finds transfer and the stakes in Europe', *Paper given at the Symposium on Europe and the Future of Financial Services*, 5–7 November, Brussels.

Vittas, Dimitri (1985), 'Pricing Strategy for retail banking products', *Banking Technology*, vol. 1, no. 10, (February) pp. 28–30.

Vittas, Dimitri; Frazer, Patrick and Metaxas-Vittas, Thymi (1988), *The Retail Banking Revolution. An International Perspective*, 2nd edition (London: Lafferty Publications).

Chapter seven
Corporate banking

Introduction

The history of banking is inextricably linked with the corresponding history of trade and industry: changes in corporate banking are concerned with these related histories. Corporate banking in Europe has experienced significant changes during the past three decades. A greater role for market-based intermediation has raised the spectre of a growing disintermediation of some kinds of traditional bank credit intermediation. The rapid growth of international banks has increased financial integration, but it has threatened the traditional dominance of domestic banks within certain segments of national corporate banking markets. It is difficult to analyse comparatively changes in corporate banking because of the marked heterogeneity of the market. With these problems in mind, the focus of this chapter is on changes in domestic corporate banking, with a particular emphasis on bank lending and the provision of ancillary banking services to companies by domestic institutions. Chapters 8 and 9 will explore international banking in greater detail, and Chapters 10 and 11 will focus more directly on investment banking and capital market aspects of corporate banking.

A perspective of corporate banking

Historical context

Corporate banking may be defined broadly as the provision by banks of a collection of services to companies, industrial and commercial companies (ICCs) or 'corporates', of all kinds. These services encompass a wide range of financial products and services, including facilities like cash and portfolio management. Corporate finance has been traditionally classified by maturity into short, medium and long; permanent finance (like equity-type finance) may also be distinguished from long-term lending. These 'maturity classification models' are increasingly fluid in many countries, a reflection of important changes in methods of corporate financing and the respective roles of banks.

Banks in Europe have always been important providers of finance to industry at all levels. In the nineteenth century, for example, British banks are often pictured as freely discounting commercial acceptances, but not making loans to industry. Kindleberger (1984, p. 93) points out that in practice this did not always obtain, because at various times and in different parts of the country the banks did make

110

loans to industry. The popular view that British banks only engaged in short-term financing is an oversimplification. French banks also developed close links with industry during the nineteenth century. In Germany banks and industry were closely interconnected; German industrialists were represented on the boards of banks and *vice versa*.

Cameron *et al.* (1967) in their study of the banking histories of England, Belgium, France, Germany, Scotland and Russia concluded that appropriate financial institutions and related organizations were important to the process of development. Development in this context is intimately concerned with the provision of finance to industrialists and the associated role of entrepreneurship. Banks were viewed as fostering or even acting as substitutes for entrepreneurship. A later study (1972), that included the cases of Austria, Italy and Spain, modified this conclusion. Banks were seen generally in this study as a necessary but not sufficient condition for economic development to occur.

Considerable historical differences have existed – and in some cases persisted – between different European countries in corporate banking and the financing of industry. In some cases the regulatory environment has encouraged specific developments or restrained others. In countries like Italy, for example, a legal separation is still maintained between different kinds of bank and other financial institution.

Unlike Canada, Japan and the United States, however, many of the leading European countries do not require banks to separate their commercial lending and securities activities, although Norway has recently (1988) legislated to separate them. West German 'universal banks' have long combined banking and securities business. The regulatory and fiscal regime in West Germany has been conducive to the evolution of universal banks: for example, the accounting system has allowed banks to smooth their profit fluctuations. Universal banking of this kind evolved in other European countries like Austria and Switzerland. The UK clearing banks also had their own merchant banking capabilities from the 1960s, although these have typically been kept managerially separate within subsidiary, affiliated or associated companies.

Universal banking in countries like West Germany, Austria and Switzerland evolved in response to a collection of environmental factors besides regulation. The direct involvement of West German banks in industry through equity holdings, for example, was the result partly of banks converting their loans into equity stakes in companies experiencing financial pressures during the inter-war years. A combination of environmental factors and unique historical events enabled banks in different European countries to establish themselves in particular segments of the corporate financing market. The banks developed the expertise and established the kind of business relationships that helped to preserve their comparative advantage in providing corporate finance and other services over many decades.

The pattern of company financing varies significantly between different European countries, and there have been many studies on the provision of corporate finance in Europe and other countries: examples include Samuels, Groves and Goddard (1975), Vittas and Brown (1982) and Arthur Andersen (1986). General company financing patterns in Europe have also been in a state of considerable flux since the 1960s. Table 7.1 provides an historical profile of corporate gearing ratios within the major industrial countries and illustrates the differences in corporate gearing

111

Table 7.1 Debt/equity ratios of the non-financial corporate sector.

Countries	1966–73	1974–79	1980[a]	1985
United States	0.54	0.96	0.77	0.83
Japan	3.08	3.31	3.14	1.82
Germany[b]	2.38	3.36	3.85	2.39
France	1.17[c]	1.33	1.23	-
United Kingdom	0.67	1.38	1.13	0.70[d]
Canada	0.99	1.22	1.14	1.08[d]

Source: Adapted from BIS (1987, p. 70).
Notes: a Gross liabilities excluding equity and trade credit as a proportion of equity prices, except for France and Canada where equity is at book values.
b All enterprises excluding housing.
c 1970–73.
d Estimated.

between European and other countries. These data also depict some of the broader trends in European corporate financing; the rise in corporate gearing ratios during the 1970s and early 1980s is clear. The comparative higher corporate gearing ratios in Japan and West Germany are generally indicative of a greater corporate willingness (and ability) to use debt financing, whether bank-supplied or through bond markets.

Differences in the patterns of corporate funding make it difficult to standardize the sources and uses of company finance in Europe. Internationalization and other trends are imposing a greater commonality on the financing facilities available to various segments of the corporate market, but important country differences still persist. The traditional distinction between short-, medium- and long-term finance is also increasingly difficult to maintain for comparative purposes in deregulating financial markets. This is particularly evident in those countries that are moving towards a stronger market orientation within their financial systems. In countries like the United Kingdom the banks have extended their corporate facilities beyond short-term (or working capital) finance, especially since the early 1970s. Short-term facilities may also be 'rolled over' into *de facto* longer-term finance.

Other changes have also weakened traditional distinctions in bank corporate finance. A greater use has been made of new techniques like factoring and leasing. The rise of the Eurobond and Eurocredit markets during the 1970s opened up new channels for banks to be involved in corporate financing. Trends like securitization have weakened the traditional, strict segmentation of money and capital markets. Some longer-term, capital-market facilities for companies are structured nowadays as a series of short-dated, essentially money-market papers.

Historically, European countries have experienced markedly different trends in the financial position of their corporate sector. Nevertheless, large swings in corporate financing patterns occurred in both the early 1970s and early 1980s. In the United Kingdom companies relied increasingly on the banking system for funds throughout the 1970s and 1980s. Companies in Europe generally found that conditions were not favourable for borrowing on traditional, fixed-rate capital markets during much of the 1970s. Companies also faced problems during this period in raising new equity capital.

These environmental conditions helped to stimulate a resurgence of traditional

112

bank lending to companies. Banks in many European countries lent a growing volume of short- and medium-term loans at variable rates of interest. From the early 1980s there has been a noticeable, though not universal, trend back towards traditional forms of corporate finance like equity and longer-term debt maturities. From 1982 until the October 1987 downturn in the world's major stock markets – the so-called 'crash of 1987' – a growing volume of corporate financing flows was being directed through financial markets.

European trends

Table 7.2 indicates generally the changes and comparative trends in funds raised by the business sectors in major European countries from 1980; a small sample of important non-European countries are included for comparative purposes. These data confirm some of the major changes in corporate financing from around 1982: particularly the movement back towards traditional capital-market finance in many (but not all) countries.

A European perspective of the main structural changes in corporate banking is summarized below:

Table 7.2   Funds raised by domestic non-financial borrowers.

(as percentage of GNP/GDP)

| Countries | Years | Business sector | | | |
		Equities[a]	Bonds	Loans[b]	Total
United States	1980–84	−0.2	1.2	3.9	4.9
	1985	−2.0	2.4	3.7	4.0
	1986	−1.9	2.4	3.8	4.3
Japan	1980–84	0.7	0.5	7.0	8.2
	1985	0.5	1.0	7.7	9.2
	1986	0.4	1.3	8.0	9.7
Germany	1980–84	0.3	0.1	5.1	5.5
	1985	0.4	0.3	3.9	4.6
	1986	0.6	0.4	2.0	3.0
France	1980–84	1.6	0.7	5.8	8.1
	1985	2.2	0.8	3.8	6.8
	1986	3.0	0.8	3.5	7.3
United Kingdom	1980–84	0.5	0.2	2.2	2.9
	1985	1.0	0.5	2.2	3.7
	1986	1.4	0.6	1.6	3.6
Italy	1980–84	1.5	0.3	6.4	8.2
	1985	1.2	0.2	5.6	7.0
	1986	1.3	0.6	4.7	6.6
Canada	1980–84	1.6	0.8	2.8	5.3
	1985	2.3	0.4	2.0	4.7
	1986	2.6	0.9	1.4	4.9

Source: BIS (1987, p. 72).
Notes: a For Italy, net issues less purchases of equity to the business sector plus changes in publicly funded endowments.
      b Includes money-market paper and foreign borrowing.

- the entry of new institutions (especially foreign banks) into the top end of the corporate banking sector (e.g. top-1000 companies in the United Kingdom);
- a strong movement towards investment banking and securities business, especially at the top end of the corporate market;
- an intensifying drive towards the formation of financial conglomerates in many European centres in order to service fully corporate needs;
- a continued blurring of traditional lines of demarcation between traditionally separate financial institutions;
- continued concentration of banking institutions in many countries;
- increasing pressure on middle-sized institutions involved in corporate banking, squeezed between the large conglomerates and the smaller, specialist niche institutions;
- the formation of new (sometimes *at hoc*) arrangements by banks and other institutions to service particular corporate customers or segments of the market;
- a renewed emphasis on the middle corporate market;
- increased application of treasury and associated risk-management techniques in products and services to middle segments of the corporate banking market;
- increased emphasis on venture capital provision in many European countries;
- the continued rise of corporate 'in-house' banks and more sophisticated corporate treasury divisions that increasingly by-pass the traditional banking system for many kinds of finance;
- a reduction in the size of total branch networks, but more regional-based corporate branches manned by specialist staff and with a higher and more sophisticated marketing profile.

All these developments are taking place in an environment in which customers' demands for financial services have generally become more sophisticated. Technology continues to exert a strong influence on the structure and evolution of corporate banking in Europe.

Although various views exist on the likely trends influencing the size of different banking institutions in Europe (see Chapter 3), there has been a substantial growth in the size of the main banking institutions. One important stimulating factor has been the importance of banks' large customers. The growth of the MNC (multinational corporation) and the internationalization of business have produced new pressures on banks to finance the growing needs and sophistication of their large business customers.

Relations with industry
The relationship between banks and industry is a fundamental characteristic of corporate banking in any country. These relations are invariably complex, particularly for large corporate customers. A bank's relations with a single company may typically encompass a wide variety of financial and other services, ranging from corporate advice to cash management facilities.

Despite the complex nature of these relationships it is possible to identify different European 'models' of banks' relationships with industry. These models are based on criteria like bank lending volume to industry, the extent of allowable gearing by bank borrowers and the propensity of banks to take direct equity participations in

Table 7.3 Lending to industry by the banking sector.

Country	% growth[a] 1970–80	% of GDP 1970	1975	1980
France	332	31.8	34.5	30.0
West Germany[b]	259	28.5	31.2	33.6
United Kingdom	545	17.5	23.7	21.7

Source: Vittas and Brown (1982, p. 14).

Notes: a Computed using each respective domestic currency estimate; 1980 value expressed as a % of respective 1970 value.

b Universal banks, which comprise commercial banks, savings banks sector and the credit co-operatives sector.

companies. In the late 1970s and early 1980s these differences stimulated a heated debate in the United Kingdom that the country's leading domestic banks were not lending enough and on the most appropriate terms to industry: this was the famous Lever and Edwards argument – see Vittas and Brown (1982) and Edwards (1987) – and Table 7.3 summarizes the kind of data used in this analysis. In order to provide an insight into the type of differences that persist in European corporate banking, it is useful to focus initially on the financial systems of the United Kingdom and West Germany.

The German banking system is dominated by the universal banks, which cover the whole range of financial services. As a result the bulk of funds in Germany has been intermediated through the banks who also dominate the organized capital markets (see also Chapter 10). In the United Kingdom, on the other hand, there exists a wide range of non-bank financial institutions. The UK capital market has also functioned largely independently from the banks and has been another important source of external finance to companies.

German banks are the biggest issuers and (on average) the biggest investor group in the bond market. In the United Kingdom it is the public sector that comprises the bulk of fixed-interest securities, and the insurance and pensions fund are the dominant investor group. The UK equity market is generally more active (*Bank of England Quarterly Bulletin*, 1984) than the German market. Although banks' direct investment in equity shares are fairly limited in both countries, the banks' influence in Germany goes beyond their own direct holdings. German banks often exercise (with the customer's consent) the voting rights on shares deposited with them.

These kinds of institutional differences in the external provision of corporate finance have led to a distinction, as already mentioned earlier in this book, between so-called bank-based and market-based financial systems. It will be recalled that a bank-orientated (or bank-based) system is one in which banks play a major role in the financing of industry, and the securities markets are comparatively less active. A market-orientated (or market-based) system is one where the securities markets play a more important role and the banking sector is less dominant. Countries like Italy, France, Germany and Japan are commonly classified as broadly bank-orientated, whereas the United States and United Kingdom are more market-orientated (Vittas, 1986).

The degree of closeness of a banking relationship is defined by Vittas (1986, p. 4) as the 'frequency and level of contact between financial institutions and industrial companies, the interest taken in the affairs of industrial companies and the extent of influence exerted over company affairs'. Banking relations are naturally closer in bank-based systems compared to market-based systems, but this does not always hold. Other important determining factors include the relationship of institutional investors with industry and banks. The structure of the industrial sector is also important: different kinds of institution[1] have different needs. Another important factor is the role of public authorities, which are generally less important in the United Kingdom and the United States compared to Continental European countries like Germany.

A particularly high degree of bank closeness with corporate customers is practised in Japan (Vittas, 1986): frequent and comprehensive contact is maintained between the banks and many levels of the corporate hierarchy. Relations are also very close in Germany, where the universal banks have traditionally taken an active interest in the business of their company clients. German banks regularly discuss management plans, although the banks emphasize the independence of corporate management boards. In France and the United States, relations are not so close. Relations have been much less close in the United Kingdom compared to all these other countries, but this historical pattern has begun to change. The UK clearing banks developed much closer working relations with companies during the past decade, with the growth in corporate reliance on bank funding.

The traditional, one-bank relationship[2] with big companies has given way to multiple banking in all five of these countries: Japan, Germany, France, the United Kingdom and the United States. There are marked differences in the way these multiple relationships work in different countries, but a strong emphasis is placed on the role of the lead bank in Germany, Japan and, to a lesser extent, France. Multiple banking relationships are dominated by the so-called house bank in Germany[3]. Japanese industrial companies maintain relationships with a large number of banks and there tends to be a well-ordered bank hierarchy within this group: the main bank acts as the company's financial adviser. The average number of relationship banks in Japan is five, which is less than half the Western average: see Ireland (1987, p. 47). Lead banks in the French financial system[4] do not appear to have the same general influence as the house bank in Germany or the main bank in Japan.

Intensifying competition in both the United States and the United Kingdom has encouraged the spread of multiple banking relationships. Companies in the United States increasingly allocate their business to the bank most competitive for a particular service. This 'transactions approach' has been accompanied by greater pressures for banks to unbundle and price separate facilities. One result has been to consolidate relationships with a smaller number of banks. Similar trends are also under way in the United Kingdom. Companies have tended to adopt a structured approach towards multiple banking in order to eliminate excessive relationships.

The UK corporate finance market has been radically transformed in recent years by the pressures of Big Bang and a buoyant takeover wave. Traditional relationships between banks and their corporate clients are breaking down under the pressures of competition. Nevertheless, the '1987 crash' has revived – at least temporarily – the attractions of traditional commercial banking. It has also served to emphasize the operational importance of a good banking relationship with companies. Banks tend

116

not to be the 'fair-weather friends' of an impersonal, open market; a good banking relationship may help a company through bad times as well as good. More fundamental economic forces have also led to a growing internationalization and globalization in important segments of the corporate finance market. They have also stimulated a growing market orientation in more traditional bank-orientated financial systems, like those of West Germany and Japan.

Market environment

Products and services

An important aspect of the relation between banks and companies is the kinds of lending relationship assumed by banks. These range from providing overdrafts, short- and longer-term loans, project finance, bond and equity finance, leasing and venture capital. But corporate banking encompasses many other financial products and services. Examples include deposits, trade finance credit, investment management, foreign-exchange and money-market services, information services and cash management. The growth in the complexity and range of these facilities has reflected the development of industry from relatively simple manufacturing to the highly complex industrial organiations of today.

In the large corporate market there have been two revolutionary products during the past decade or so. The first is the growing range of interest-rate and currency swaps; the second is the generic Euronote facility. An expanding array of 'bells and whistles' and new financial instruments have developed from these two sets of products. At the same time new risk-management facilities – like futures and options – with a high 'technology content' have developed rapidly. Corporate bankers and treasurers have engineered caps, collars, floors and other arrangements through the use of the new hedging technology.

Transactions-based products, unbundling, explicit pricing and the growth of market-based intermediation have put pressures on bank margins. One associated change at the top end of the corporate banking market has been a much greater emphasis on investment and merchant banking compared to traditional banking (see Chapter 11). Another related change in countries like the United Kingdom with a strong market-orientation has been a greater banking emphasis on the middle corporate market. A traditional presence and track record in this sector, coupled with an extensive branch network, has given the clearing banks within the United Kingdom a dominant position in this market segment. A renewal of pre-1987 securitization trends is likely to enhance the middle and lower segments of corporate banking, including venture capital, in European banking strategies.

Financial links between banks and companies are indicative of comparative differences between countries and in banking products and services. Bank finance is generally much more important in European countries than in the United States where it tends to assume a residual financing role. Like the United Kingdom, direct equity holdings in companies by US banks are comparatively limited. Equity holdings in companies by banks are much more important in Germany, but less important in Japan (where banks' holdings are more widely spread over group-affiliated companies), and they are even less significant in France.

Selected country comparisons

In the United Kingdom, France, Germany and Japan the external provision by banks of short- and longer-term finance is important. The provision of external equity and bond finance is still limited in France, Germany and Japan, but it is expanding in all countries, expecially Japan. Companies in the United Kingdom tend to have a greater comparative reliance on equity than in many other European countries. UK corporate bond issues have been low, but there has been some renewed issuing activity in this market.

Most large European banks offer the same broad array of corporate products and services: these include factoring, asset finance, treasury services, leasing and lease-back, stock-market services, investment banking and mergers and acquisition ser-vices. In bank lending the overdraft is still one of the most important credits – especially in terms of volume – for shorter-term purposes. In West Germany, Denmark, the Netherlands and the United Kingdom, for example, overdrafts on current accounts figure highly as shorter- to medium-term lending instruments. Although there has been a strong growth in medium-term lending within the United Kingdom, overdrafts remain the traditional method of credit extension.

The overdraft is a flexible and comparatively cheap form of funding. In many countries overdrafts are made without security to good borrowers. Interest rates are differentiated to reflect factors like the size of the credit granted and the customer relationship. Interest rates are typically fixed to one of the central bank rates, the banks' base rate or (for larger customers) market rates like LIBOR may be used.

Alongside overdraft facilities for shorter-term finance there are a wide range of discount facilities in different European countries. These facilities are important to companies in West Germany and France. In order to attract good rates, bills in Germany must be rediscountable at the Bundesbank. Short-term credit (maximum maturity of two years) in France is often extended through the discount of com-mercial bills or similar paper, which may be discountable (subject to specific criteria) at the Bank of France; promissory notes called *crédits de campagne* cover seasonal financing needs. Other kinds of short-term credit available in many European countries include factoring, guarantee and acceptance credits and Lombard credit (short-term money market credit available through the central bank which is more costly than normal discounting of government paper, com-monly used in Germany).

UK banks have followed a policy of persuading their ICCs to move from hard-core overdraft borrowing to longer-term facilities, with maturities of up to 20 years and at floating or fixed rates of interest. Medium-term credits in West Germany were used in the years immediately following the 1948 currency reform as a kind of substitute for unobtainable longer-term finance; these medium-term credits are now used primarily as bridging finance. UK banks, like their German counterparts, offer a wide range of short-, medium- and longer-term financing facilities. French banks are also moving in the same general direction of 'universalization' in corporate lending.

In France, medium-term credits are extended jointly by the commercial banks and the Crédit National, Crédit Foncier de France and the Banque Française du Commerce Extérieur. These credits are in the form of promissory notes acceptable to the Bank of France. Nevertheless, the banks have developed facilities alongside this kind of official system. Medium- and long-term credits that are not eligible for official refinancing have been developed for business and industry. These credits are in the form of overdrafts or the discounting of bills.

The traditional role of French banks in the financing of industry is now subject to especially rapid changes. The French government has been an important engine of development as the authorities have moved expeditiously to ensure that Paris retains a place in global, deregulated capital markets. The major part of corporate financing in France up to the early 1980s was from bank loans and financial intermediation. The Bank of France largely refinanced the banking system and closely regulated the overall financial structure. The result was that the economy was typically debt-based. Between 1974 and 1985 bank credits comprised around 70 per cent of the growth in the external resources of non-financial enterprises: see Fenton (1987, p. 35). By 1987 this had reduced to around 40 per cent. French banks are moving from straight deposit and lending business into a wide range of corporate and investment banking services. Like the German universal banks and the UK clearing banks, the French commercial banks offer the typical wide array of corporate banking products and services.

A number of institutions have traditionally supplied medium-term credit in the Netherlands: these include the commercial banks, rabobanks and some specialized financial institutions, like the Nationale Investeringsbank. Privately placed promissory notes (*Schuldscheindarlehen*) are important in Germany for large credits: these notes have increasingly displaced industrial bonds. In Greece, the banks occasionally provide long-term loans, and (under specific conditions) they may participate in the capital of firms which they sometimes control. But it is the three investment banks in Greece that dominate in the provision of medium- and longer-term finance to industry.

Italian banking has also been characterized by particularly rigid lines of demarcation between financial institutions in providing corporate finance. The commercial banks have specialized (under legislation) in short-term credits (up to 18 months); special credit institutions provide the medium- and longer-term financing. Nevertheless, the commercial banks have been able to operate around this legislation. They can grant medium-term loans not exceeding 8 per cent of their deposits or when individually authorized by the Bank of Italy. Nevertheless, a recent survey (see Lane, 1988) suggested that Italian local banks are still bureaucratic and that they lack the stimulus of competition. Italian corporate banking has not changed under the influence of deregulation at anything like the pace of the French system, which has also been traditionally compartmentalized. Many Italian companies appear unhappy with the services available from the local banks.

As in the United Kingdom many European banks provide corporate financial services through a range of associated and affiliated companies. Leasing, for example, has grown strongly in Italy during the 1980s. Of all the EC countries, however, leasing grew most rapidly in the United Kingdom, although the 1984 Finance Act lessened its attractiveness to banks. Leasing is provided through hire purchase and leasing institutions, and insurance companies have also made their mark in this sector.

Competition

A marked feature of change in European corporate banking is the continued erosion of traditional lines of demarcation between different kinds of bank, the so-called de-compartmentalization phenomenon. Traditionally specialist commercial banks, savings banks and co-operative banks, for example, are increasingly competing with each other in corporate banking. This liberalization process involves not only traditionally segmented institutions doing each other's business, but also the development of new products and services. Intensifying competition is the motive force of these changes.

Table 7.4 indicates the extent to which different European financial institutions are significant[5] in providing business loans. Business loans are used here as a proxy for corresponding activity in corporate banking[6]; providing loans to ICCs is a traditional activity of the core commercial banks in most countries. An interesting feature of Table 7.4 is the wide range of different financial institutions active in corporate lending within different European countries.

Savings banks and credit unions in particular have increased their general involvement in corporate banking. Savings and mortgage institutions, insurance companies, stockbrokers and financial intermediaries, leasing and hire purchase companies, and government and related institutions are also active in commercial lending in different European countries. An even wider range of institutions competes for corporate funds.

During the 1970s and early 1980s foreign banks made a significant impact in some domestic corporate banking sectors in Europe, and this penetration was particularly marked in the United Kingdom. Future new entrants into domestic corporate banking markets in Europe, however, are expected to come mainly from the domestic banking arena: see Arthur Andersen (1986, p. 16). Only in the case of stockbrokers and other financial intermediaries are foreign institutions believed likely to pose a serious

Table 7.4 The extent to which different European financial institutions are significant in providing business loans.

	1	2	3	4	5	6	7	8	9
West Germany	a	c			c	c	c	c	c
France	a		c		b				
Italy	a		c		b				
United Kingdom	a	b	c	c					
Belgium	a		c		b				
Luxembourg	a		a		c				
Netherlands	a	a	c		b	c	c	c	c
Spain	a		c		b				

Source: Update of Statistical Report submitted by the Institute of European Finance to Price Waterhouse Management Consultants (Dublin) in Spring 1987.

Key:

Institutions
1 clearing/commercial traditional banks
2 merchant banks
3 savings banks
4 postal and giro banks
5 credit unions
6 mortgage, credit institutions/ building societies
7 HP finance companies
8 leasing companies
9 factors

Cell key
a very significant
b significant
c of minor significance

120

Table 7.5 Corporate banking products offered by new entrants in selected European countries.

Type of Institution	Product/service							
	Deposits	Commercial Lending	Trade Finance Credit	Leasing	Foreign Exchange Money Markets	Electronic Funds Transfer	Information Services/ Markets	Investment Managment Cash Mgmt.
Savings &/or Mortgage	D,E,L NL,UK	B,D,E L,NL,UK	B,L		E,L	L		F
Insurance	D,F,L,UK	D,L,NL,UK		F,NL				D,F,L, NL,UK
Retailing	L				L	L		
Stockbroking & Financial Intermediaries	F,L				E,L,UK		E,L,UK	D,E,L, NL,UK
Hire Purchase/ Leasing	L	L		B,D,S,L UK				
Information Technology						F	D,F	
PTT	D,E,F, L,NL	NL				E,F,NL	NL	
Government & its institutions		E						

Source: Adapted from Arthur Andersen (1986, Diagram 3 series on country studies).
Note: In these countries the respondents to the Arthur Andersen survey estimates a likelihood exceeding 40 per cent that the products would be attained by the respective new entrants.

Key: B, Belgium; D, Germany; E, Spain; F, France; NL, Netherlands; L, Luxembourg; UK, United Kingdom.

challenge to the established domestic operators. Nevertheless, foreign banks will continue to be a serious threat to the business of the large companies and, to an increasing extent, in the market for medium-sized corporate customers.

1992 is expected to stimulate renewed competitive pressures from foreign banks in European corporate banking. The Japanese in particular appear to be well placed to invade European banking markets, both retail and corporate. The Japanese buzz word for this European strategy is *dochakuka*: in a literal sense it means farmers adapting to local conditions. This kind of European banking strategy by the Japanese is one of 'global localization', where local offices are established with products that are tailored to local market conditions.

Most of the top Japanese city banks, long-term credit banks, life insurance and Big Four securities houses are already represented in some way within the major European financial centres. Japanese banks have been active recently in the United Kingdom, Germany and Italy. Nomura ranks Spain as second only to the United Kingdom as a prospective major growth area (Brady, 1988). During 1988 many Japanese institutions upgraded their corporate banking operations in various European centres from branch or affiliated status to full subsidiary status in anticipation of 1992.

Table 7.5 provides a summary of corporate banking products that are expected to be offered by new entrants in selected European countries. It not only confirms the competitive picture depicted in Table 7.4, but also illustrates the growing collection of new competitors that are likely to develop within European corporate product and service sectors. These estimates were derived from a detailed survey (in 1985 and 1986) of banks and others throughout Europe. The expectation from this survey is that the banks in Europe will continue to dominate in the corporate sector. They are predicted to retain clearly (50 per cent or more) their dominant market share in commercial lending and corporate funds. Table 7.6 summarizes the key competitive strengths and weaknesses in the European corporate sector. Contemporary changes suggest that banks will need more than ever before to harness their competitive strengths and seek to reduce corresponding competitive disadvantages.

The securitization challenge
During the past decade corporate banking, especially towards the top end of the market, has generally been much more market-orientated than retail banking. European banks have had to develop a more integrated approach to service provision: this has been important for cross-selling products. Market segmentation, relationship marketing and pricing, and the unbundling of products and services are becoming critically important in order for banks to compete effectively.

The large corporate customer has more options and a wider choice of services than ever before. The increasing movement towards securitization by large corporates has raised new challenges. Large corporate customers have increasingly by-passed the traditional banking system in favour of financial markets. The stock market crash of 1987 has slowed down this trend for a time, but it is unlikely to deflect it for long if countries remain committed to structural deregulation. This securitization movement has stimulated important new competitive pressures. We have already seen that transactional banking, especially by large corporates, has assumed a higher significance.

Investment banking activities and capital market products have become much more important in the corporate banking strategies of banks. The post-1982 growth

Table 7.6 Competitive strengths and weaknesses in European corporate banking.

Corporate funds	Corporate lending
Bank advantages	
Security	Availability of other banking and
Prestige/image	financial services
Availability of other	Accessibility/location
banking and financial	Prior relationships
services	Security
Prior relationships	Prestige/image
Accessibility/location	Use of advanced technology
Use of advanced technology	Interest rate offered
	Service charges
	Ease of making application
Bank disadvantages	
Service charges	Personal service
Personal service	Product attractiveness
Product attractiveness	Speed of approval
Interest rate offered	

Source: Arthur Andersen (1986, Diagram 20, p. 20).

of securitization in international financial markets and London's Big Bang, for example, stimulated the formation of new 'financial conglomerates' in which securities business is a key activity (see Gardener, 1987). Traditional bank lending became increasingly displaced by arranging, placing and underwriting activities. Many of the large banks moved into these new activities in a big way. Indeed the big commercial banks and leading investment banks were innovators in developing new financial products, such as Euronote facilities. Banks had lost their comparative advantage to financial markets in the intermediation of some credits; they sought to protect their profits through building up fee and commission income associated with the new financial products. They also responded to these competitive threats by emphasizing relationship banking and transactions pricing.

The movement by European banks into securities business and the growth of securitization generally have brought important new competitors into the corporate banking arena; stockbrokers and securities houses are examples. The traditional bank lending business at the top end of the corporate market has been subject to profit squeezes as margins have tightened with intensifying competition. With the movement of the most creditworthy top corporate borrowers to capital markets, banks also faced an adverse selection problem: they tended to be left with the poorer credit risks.

These competitive pressures have stimulated concerns about the profitability of traditional corporate banking in some segments of the market. Squeezed margins at the top end of the corporate market, together with associated adverse selection problems and the resource commitments needed to be a global institution, are already stimulating a renewed emphasis on the middle corporate market. More bank resources are being devoted towards the smaller business sectors, and bank venture capital activities are also growing. Pressures on corporate and international banking profits also prompted UK as well as other European banks to re-emphasize their retail banking profits in 1987 (Molyneux, 1987).

123

Technology

Rapid technological developments have been especially important stimulants of change in corporate banking. Technology has already altered some of the basic economics that have underpinned the operations of European corporate banking for many decades. Costs have reduced for many traditional operations, and the new technology has spread from the back to front-office banking.

The ubiquitous nature of technological developments has brought new competitors into banking markets. Information technology (IT) companies and the post office (PTT) have entered into competition with banks in corporate banking product areas like foreign exchange and money markets, electronic funds transfer, information services, cash management and investment management. Entry into these important product areas allows the new competitors to penetrate into other corporate product activities. The PTT, for example, is also active in corporate deposits and commercial lending in many European countries (see Table 7.5).

Electronic banking has allowed banks to exploit new opportunities for fee and commission business at a time when traditional interest margin profits are under pressure. Information provision and dissemination are important common elements in these new services. European banks have developed new electronic cash management systems that enable treasurers to monitor domestic and overseas accounts in order to invest any idle balances.

In this respect European corporate treasurers have tended to lag behind their US counterparts (Krzyzak, 1986). History has again been important in shaping these developments. The US restrictions on interstate banking under the McFadden Act, coupled with an inefficient postal system, stimulated banks to develop efficient communication channels with their corporate customers. Extensive branch banking systems in Europe made these needs less pressing. Early treasury experiences in Europe also used US systems, which did not address European needs like multicurrency reporting. US banks learnt that they could not simply offer US treasury products and systems in Europe and by 1987 they had pulled out of some markets: *Euromoney Corporate Finance Supplement* (1987, p. 3). Nevertheless, the growth and application of electronic cash management systems have accelerated recently in Europe.

The core elements of electronic cash management systems are balance and transaction reporting. All the major banks in Europe now have an EBATRS (electronic balance and transaction reporting systems) system of some kind, but full co-operation or balance reporting has not yet been achieved, although SWIFT and BAI are beginning to dominate as the two main reporting standards: see *Cash Management News* (1986, p. 1). A recent survey (*Cash Management News* (1986) and also Whitmarsh (1988)) identified the following European trends:

- intra-day reporting (provided by around 50 per cent of all systems) is increasing;
- 44 per cent of all banks now use SWIFT balance reporting standards;
- resistance to balance reporting is diminishing (only a few banks surveyed said they would never report to other banks' own systems);
- there is a 30 per cent per annum growth in data exchange of balances and transactions in Europe.

124

Integrated financial packages in which technology is a key component have become an important area of competition in European corporate banking. EBATRS is one example where a range of services may be provided: these can include money transfers, payments and the purchase of foreign exchange. Some European banks are concerned about the future profitability of their cash management services, but demand is increasing and the banks are unlikely to ignore it.

Although the European market in electronic cash management is not so mature as its US counterpart, it started to develop rapidly from the middle of the 1980s. The big banks in Europe are now pushing aggressively in this market, but most of the systems on offer in Europe are domestic ones. Some US banks regard Europe as a particularly innovative market in cash management. Many US banks found to their cost that Europe cannot be regarded in this respect as a homogenous unit: different companies have differing product needs. This has emphasized the need for banks to think more in terms of individual companies. In recent years (especially from 1987 onwards) the European market in electronic banking has become more mature. Additional opportunities for US and other foreign banks are likely as foreign investment grows in emerging European stock exchanges – especially in countries like Spain and Italy – as effective settlements procedures are developed (see Chapter 10).

European banks have responded strongly to the US challenge: France has been particularly dynamic. As we saw earlier, the French corporate style is to share out business among a number of banks. As a result, French companies have sought multibank reporting. The principle of *interbancarité* (interbank co-operation) stimulated a group of the top 20 banks in France (led by Société Générale) to develop a common payments system, the Messagerie sécurisée entreprise-banque (MSB), which began operation on 1 April 1987. MSB is used only for urgent or low-volume transfers. Thirty of France's top companies agreed to participate in this project.

The German electronic banking and treasury market is dominated by the banks' proprietary networks. This market is particularly difficult to enter by outsiders because of the close domestic bank relationships with corporate customers. Non-domestic banks also lack significant branch networks. Some German banks are more sceptical (than French bankers) about the future of work stations. Nevertheless, leading German banks (and some corporations) have developed sophisticated in-house systems. One practical problem in the development of comprehensive electronic banking in Germany has been telecommunications: the Post Office has a monopoly on modems and this results in supply delays.

In Belgium[7] Banque Bruxelles Lambert has been a pioneer in cash management, followed by Kredietbank and Societé Générale de Banque: see *Euromoney Corporate Finance Supplement* (1987, p. 3). Several Dutch banks have also developed multilateral netting centres, and Amro Bank is regularly cited as a leader in the provision of cash management services. It is interesting to note that some of the most sophisticated electronic banking services have been developed in Scandinavian countries. Union Bank of Finland, for example, has been offering corporate electronic banking services since 1979. An interesting feature of several European systems is that they have been developed by third-party vendors. For example, Barclays and Bank of Scotland in the United Kingdom are licensees of Banklink, a system developed by Chemical Bank.

Mid-to-large companies are now moving towards fully integrated trading, dealing and information systems[8]. This futuristic scenario may not be so far distant; the required technology already exists. Although banks have developed an impressive capability of EDI (electronic data interchange) through systems like SWIFT, they have not yet linked these systems effectively to the corporate customer. One important lesson that has been learnt has been the comparative failure of complex, expensive US-type treasury systems in favour of the simpler, information-orientated approach of UK banks. Moves are now under way to open up international bank data networks for direct access by customers and new support products are being developed for treasurers.

Technology is a fundamental element in the financial innovation process that has characterized European and international financial markets from the early 1970s. Present trends suggest that banks in Europe will increase their expenditure on technology. One strategic development has been increasingly to automate some branches and 'regionalize' corporate banking in selected branches. The UK banks, for example, have all tended to centralize corporate banking in certain large regional branches. Some banks have developed specialist, corporate branches. European banks recognize the need for a much greater harnessing of technology in order to remain competitive in the corporate market; this is particularly emphasized in securities business. The costs and associated risks, however, are high. At the same time, electronic banking in countries like the United Kingdom is now reaching increasingly into the middle corporate market.

Conclusion

Corporate banking is one of the most competitive sectors in European banking. Growing competition, the rise of wholesale banking and an increasing marketization of financial business are indicative of fundamental changes for banks in some sectors of this market. One scenario is that the top end of corporate banking will be increasingly dominated by a small number of large institutions, global in their orientation, servicing the top ICCs. Competition in the middle and lower ends of the market will intensify, new competitors will appear and consolidate, and the sophistication of banking products and services will grow[9].

Notes

1. The most important distinction here is between large MNCs, national public utilities, medium-sized national or regional companies and small firms.
2. Although it is still the pattern in the case of smaller firms.
3. This role tends to be assumed by banks in Germany with substantial equity holdings in the company. These banks lead syndicated credits and lead manage securities issues.
4. French industrial companies (unlike their German or Japanese counterparts) tend to appoint different banks to act as lead banks for particular syndications.
5. These 'relative significance scales' (a, b and c) were derived by the Institute of European Finance through examining bank-country data and from a field survey (in 1987 and 1988) of banking practitioners and academics in leading European countries.
6. There is no presumption that involvement in business lending necessarily means involvement in other areas of corporate banking. Nevertheless, business lending is a fundamental characteristic of corporate banking in all European countries.

7. A country that has had a sophisticated automated retail network – like the Mister Cash ATM network – for some time.
8. This trend in turn has encouraged the amalgamation of traditionally separate bank accounts in one account: the Swedish Allkonto account is a well-known example.
9. Some big UK banks are already beginning to train branch and regional corporate managers to market and sell treasury-related facilities to middle-sized (and lower level) corporates.

References

Arthur Andersen & Co. (1986), *The Decade of Change: Banking in Europe – the Next Ten Years* (London: Lafferty Publications).
Bank of England Quarterly Bulletin (1984), 'Business finance in the United Kingdom and Germany', (September), pp. 368–75.
Bank for International Settlements (1987), *Fifty-Seventh Annual Report* (Basle: BIS).
Brady, Simon (1988), 'The sun rises again in the West' *Euromoney* (December) pp. 41–51.
Cameron, Rondo, with the collaboration of Crips, Olga, Patrick, Hugh T., and Tilly, Richard (1967), *Banking in the Early Stages of Industrialisation: A Study in Comparative Economic History* (London: Oxford University Press).
Cameron, Rondo (ed.) (1972), *Banking and Economic Development: Some Lessons of History* (London: Oxford University Press).
Cash Management News (1986), 'Electronic balance reporting in Europe', no. 18, (April), pp. 1–9.
Commission of the European Communities (1988), *European Economy: The Economics of (1992)* (Brussels: Commission of the European Communities).
Committee of London Clearing Bankers (1978), *The London Clearing Banks* (London: Committee of London Clearing Bankers).
Edwards, George T. (1987), *The Role of Banks in Economic Development* (London: Macmillan).
Euromoney Corporate Finance Supplement (1986) 'Electronic banking and the corporate treasurer', (October), pp. 1–48.
Euromoney Corporate Finance Supplement (1987) 'Electronic banking: deciphering the future', (October), pp. 1–20.
Fenton, Martin (1987), 'A sea change in the Paris markets' *The Banker*, (May), pp. 35–41.
Gardener, E. P. M. (1987), 'Structural and strategic consequences of financial conglomeration', *Revue de la Banque*, no. 9, (November), pp. 5–16.
Ireland, L. (1987), 'Banking relationships: a soft touch or an iron hand?' *Euromoney Corporate Finance*, (July), pp. 43–50.
Jones, David (1989), 'Electronic banking reaches the middle market', *Banking World*, (June), pp. 34–5.
Kindleberger, Charles P. (1984), *A Financial History of Western Europe* (London: George Allen & Unwin).
Krzyzak, Krystyna (1986), 'European treasurers take to electronic services slowly', *Banking Technology*, (May), pp. 16–19.
Lane, David (1988), 'Calling for major change' *The Banker*, (September), pp. 38–43.
Molyneux, P. (1987), 'Credit where it's due' *International Correspondent Banker*, (December), pp. 11–12.
Organization for Economic Co-operation and Development (1985), *Trends in Banking in OECD Countries* (Paris: OECD).
Samuels, J. M., Groves, R. E. V. and Goddard, G. S. (1975), *Company Finance in Europe* (London: Institute of Chartered Accountants).
Vittas, D. and Brown, R. (1982), *Banking Lending and Industrial Investment: A Response to Some Recent Criticisms* (London: Banking Information Service).
Vittas, D. (1986), 'Banks' relations with industry: an international survey', *National Westminster Bank Quarterly Review*, (February), pp. 2–14.
Whitmarsh, Jerry (1988), 'Electronic delivery of corporate banking services – future trends', *The Treasurer*, (September), pp. 55 and 59.

Chapter eight

International banking and foreign banks

Introduction

After a period of practically three decades of virtual hibernation international banking began to re-awaken during the early 1960s. Although it is often difficult and unrealistic to be 'country-specific' in analyzing recent developments in international banking, the post-1960 internationalization of banking has undoubtedly been one of the major changes in West European banking. In this respect it is a kind of pan-European phenomenon. New banks have expanded into international banking, and many have used their international networks to penetrate into overseas banking and financial markets. One effect has been to diffuse financial innovations more widely across country borders; another has been to complicate fiscal, monetary and banking regulation. We shall begin with a brief historical perspective.

The internationalization phenomenon

Historical perspective
The beginnings of international banking as we know it today are commonly traced to the Middle Ages. Merchant bankers began to appear in Italian towns and cities during the thirteenth century. A number of the large international merchant banking houses were active by the fourteenth century in trading precious metals and foreign currencies, and the financing of imports and exports by discounting bills. They also established many new industrial and trade ventures. Short- or medium-term loans were advanced to reputable manufacturers or merchants. The Medici Bank, together with other Florentine banking houses like Bardi and Peruzzi, developed rapidly with the burgeoning of the international silks and wool cloth trade. These houses established branches, subsidiaries and representative offices across Europe. The Medici Bank, for example, had branches in Rome, Venice, Milan, Pisa, Avignon, Bruges, Geneva and London.

These typically family-owned merchant banks used the deposits of wealthy noblemen and clergy to expand abroad and develop their business activities. By the late fifteenth century, however, Mediterranean banking houses like Medici entered a period of decline: this resulted from a combination of bad loans, inadequate management and problems in co-ordinating foreign branches. The sixteenth century

128

saw the emergence of merchant banks further north in Europe, like the Welsers and Fuggers in Germany and Jacques Coeur in France. Antwerp and Lyons developed as international money centres.

Europe experienced a strong growth of nationalism and mercantilism during the seventeenth and eighteenth centuries. International banking declined during this period of political, economic and financial turbulence. Amsterdam emerged as the major European money centre, but by the first half of the eighteenth century London and Paris had become the dominant centres.

Throughout the nineteenth and early twentieth century, London vied with Paris (see Chapter 9) for the position as the leading financial centre in Europe. The practice became established of raising loans for foreign governments and foreign investments in London. In London Baring Brothers, later overshadowed by the Rothschilds, was one of the most energetic banks of the day in these international activities. France, Prussia, Russia, Austria, Portugal, Spain and Greece were among the first countries who came to London for finance during this period. British and European bankers were also involved increasingly in providing finance for the 'new world' throughout the nineteenth century.

During this time, leading British merchant banks – like Barings, Hambro and Rothschild – arranged, underwrote, placed and held issues of foreign bonds. Some of these bond issues were similar to modern Eurobond issues. Many others were issued in the traditional way and taken up by private investors on the London Stock Exchange. The nineteenth century was also a period of numerous bond defaults, political turmoils, speculation and financial panics. An international monetary system that was operated on the gold standard and generally free currency convertibility often exacerbated the recurrent financial crises of the day; large numbers of new international banks collapsed. During the second part of the nineteenth century, however, many consortium banks were established.

Merchant banks were also active in lending directly from their own resources during the nineteenth century. The British overseas banks – including Hong Kong and Shanghai and Standard of South Africa – were established primarily to lend funds to the Empire. Deutsche Bank was set up in Germany to challenge British supremacy in foreign finance: see Kindleberger (1984, p. 124). Britain, France and Germany[1] dominated international lending up to the First World War; much of this lending was imperial and colonial in nature.

The rise of the United States and the corresponding economic decline of Europe after the First World War had important repercussions on international banking. The United States became the main capital supplier to the world, US banks expanded abroad, and US dollar acceptance credit displaced the sterling draft drawn on London in international trade. Foreign government bond issues in the United States far exceeded those in London, and New York replaced London as the most important financial centre.

The banking collapses during the Great Depression, together with huge foreign loan defaults, heralded an era of extreme conservatism in international banking, which entered a long period of quiescence. The period immediately following the Second World War laid the foundations for the development of modern international banking. The establishment of new international organizations (like the IMF and the World Bank), the GATT in 1948, and a more favourable international economic and political environment were conducive to the re-emergence of international banking. World trade and foreign direct investment increased, and in 1958 the major European currencies again became convertible.

Modern international banking

The rise of modern international banking was the product of a number of important environmental developments. During the 1960s and 1970s, the Eurocurrency market[2] grew at a phenomenal pace. This development stimulated the growth of international banking activities such as foreign-exchange trading, trade financing and short-term international loans. Eurobanks and Eurobanking burgeoned. The development of Eurobanks was stimulated in large part by their exemption from comparatively strict domestic banking regulations. Eurobanks bid for Eurocurrency deposits in order to on-lend them.

Large US balance-of-payments deficits and Regulation Q interest-rate ceilings on bank time deposits (including CDs) in the United States stimulated large US dollar outflows to Europe. The US authorities introduced the Interest Equalization Tax (IET) in 1963, and the Voluntary Credit Foreign Restraint (VCFR) programme was launched in 1965 to restrict dollar outflows from the United States. These measures increased the demand for Eurodollars by US corporations operating overseas. Indeed, the rapid growth of MNCs during the post-war years was another important stimulant of the expansion of international banking (see also Chapter 7).

The 1963 IET was also important in the development of the Eurobond[3] market. International banks acted as syndicate managers and underwriters, and many became active in secondary market trading. The Eurobond market established itself as one of the least regulated capital markets in the world. Another significant development for international banks during this time was the emergence of the floating-rate Eurocredit, the syndicated loan, in the 1970s. The Eurocredit was distinguished from a short-term Eurocurrency bank loan by its floating-rate formula, the syndication technique and its medium-term maturity. During the 1970s the Eurocredit assumed the centre stage of international banking activities with the recycling of Arab oil money, or petrodollars – although the recycling of petrodollars was only a comparatively small part of Eurocurrency market growth during the 1960s and 1970s: see Metais in Gardener (1990).

During this period, international banking activities grew rapidly and expanded in scope. The growth of world trade and income, trade liberalization and currency convertibility were important factors in these developments. Regulation asymmetries stimulated the growth of the Euromarkets and associated international banking activities, but technological advances and the innovative drive of banks themselves were also important factors.

The internationalization of banking was originally confined to the larger banks and a number of smaller, specialist institutions. They set up branches and offices abroad in order to operate in the Euromarkets and service their MNC customers. Many banks, like Citicorp and Bank of America, began to develop global strategies. The barriers between domestic and international banking began to weaken. This globalization process has accelerated during the 1980s with improvements in technology, continued structural deregulation by governments and the development of important financial innovations, especially the growth of the swaps market.

Nevertheless, the 1970s, the so-called 'golden age' of international banking, had its casualties. The floating of exchange rates produced new risk-control problems for banks. The difficulties of Herstatt, Franklin National and other banks sent shock waves throughout the system; interbank rates became markedly tiered. General fears were expressed about banks' international exposures and the solvency of financial markets, and new initiatives were launched in international banking supervision. By the late 1970s the international debt crisis had begun to dominate concerns in international banking.

The debt crisis that emerged in August 1982 with Mexico's massive payments deficit and moratorium on repayments was another watershed in the modern development of international banking. It was one of the 'trigger mechanisms' for the burgeoning of securitization in international financial markets. A flight to quality in international finance after 1982, together with increased supervisory demands for improved bank capital adequacy, were particularly important stimulants of the so-called 'liquefaction of the Euromarkets'. The result was a shift of credit intermediation away from the international banking system into international capital markets: market-based intermediation began to replace increasingly institution-based intermediation.

Investment banking became emphasized in the strategies of international banks. A remarkable wave of financial innovation emerged as the market pressures and new technology stimulated new financial instruments. Banks were highly innovative in the development of new facilities like Euronotes or note issuance facilities (NIFs). Fee and commission income associated with bank activities in these new instruments began increasingly to displace interest-margin profits. The comparative high liquidity of the new markets, coupled with the drive towards securitization, operated effectively to improve the liquidity of the Euromarkets.

The crash of 1987 halted the strong bull run that had developed in the world's financing markets from the early 1980s. It also exposed the illusion of a Euromarket perceived to have virtually unlimited liquidity. 1987 was a bad year for international banks with a heavy writing down of Third World debt losses and the stock market crash. Securitization and associated market trends, however, are now well-established; they are unlikely to disappear, much less go into reverse. Syndicated lending revived strongly during 1987. Flexibility has been improved for borrowers and lenders through the development of multiple option facilities (MOFs) and a growing secondary market in loans and commitments. Many believe that the revival in syndicated loans is more fundamental than just the short-term reaction of the market to the crash. They have proved a flexible and competitive financing vehicle, for example, in the 1980s corporate M&A wave in the United Kingdom.

Internationalization and globalization

Internationalization refers generally to the rapid growth in the international business of banks, especially since the middle of the 1960s. A distinguishing feature of this trend has been the marked growth of Eurocurrency business and the concurrent development of multinational banking. The latter refers to activities that are carried out through branches and other offices located abroad. The faster growth of offshore financial markets and increased foreign participation in domestic financial markets have been characteristic of the internationalization of financial markets.

Table 8.1 Euromarket financial activities (US$ bn).

	1973	1980	1986
Eurobonds	4.2	20.4	187.0
International bank loans[a]	20.8	81.0	82.8
Issuance facilities[b]	-	-	92.2
Equity-related bonds	-	-	22.3

Source: OECD, *Financial Statistics Monthly* and *Financial Market Trends* (various).
Notes: a Defined here as credits advanced by commercial banks wholly or in part out of Eurocurrency funds.
  b Excludes merger-related stand-by agreements.

Table 8.1 depicts the rapid growth of international banking from 1973. The growth of multinational banking is also reflected in the growth of international banks operating in London, which developed as the apex of Euromarket financial activities (see Chapter 9). At the end of 1975 there were 310 reporting banks in London: these grew to 448 by the end of 1987. Table 8.2 shows the average size of international banks in London during the decade 1975–85, together with respective growth data. Concentration of international banking activity in London has generally declined over the period 1975–85 and thereafter.

The internationalization of banking and the concurrent growth of multinational banking have had an important impact on the structure, conduct and performance of the banking industry. A good example of this is in the United Kingdom where the top end of the domestic corporate banking market was penetrated markedly by US banks during the 1970s: intensifying competition and new kinds of competition resulted. During the 1970s it became fashionable for banks to have a significant international presence, and they made important organizational moves in this direction. Some banks even purchased banks in other countries, and many set up new, separate international businesses. Growth of international banking has been exceptionally high in France, Switzerland and the Netherlands. Although the United Kingdom

Table 8.2 Average size of 'international' banks in London, $ m. (at year end).

Size ranking of bank at each date	Average size of international liabilities			Growth of international liabilities (%)
	1975	1980	1985	1976–85
1–10	5,991	14,727	20,020	+234
11–25	2,637	7,115	11,546	+338
26–50	1,432	3,695	6,101	+326
51–100	637	1,909	2,653	+316
101–200	187	580	929	+397
201 +[a]	24	93	158	+558

Source: Bank of England Quarterly Bulletin (1986, Table F, p. 372).
Note: a 110 banks at end-1975; 144 at end-1980; 272 at end-1985.

dominates, France is now second in importance in terms of the external positions of banks.

Internationalization has been accompanied recently by another important trend, globalization: the world's financial markets have become increasingly integrated and inter-connected on a worldwide scale. Internationalization is concerned generally with cross-border flows of capital. The globalization phenomenon refers to the emergence of a broadly integrated, international but practically single market in finance. This 1980s phenomenon is the product of a number of contemporary forces. Financial volatility, economic imbalances, economic growth, technology, and the information revolution are some of the important stimulants.

Deregulation and the opening up of domestic capital markets have also been important stimulating factors to both internationalization and globalization trends. Big Bang on the Stock Exchange in London and the opening up of Japanese financial markets are examples of contemporary stimulants. A global financial market is one in which savers and investors everywhere are linked with the most attractive funds' outlets. In this respect the swaps mechanism has been a particularly important factor in the globalization of the Euromarket. Important features of the emerging global market include the integration of capital and credit markets, disintermediation of the lending process and increasing securitization of credit assets.

Most European countries have already responded to the challenge of globalization; no country can ignore these fundamental developments. The approach of 1992 has re-emphasized the challenge of globalization, the single market concept. But 1992 is unlikely to have a major direct impact on international banking and finance. These areas of wholesale banking are becoming globalized under the influence of strong international developments and other fundamental forces that appear outside the control of any single country or group of countries.

International and multinational banking

Foreign banks and Europe

Foreign banking presence in most European countries has grown rapidly from the early 1960s and Table 8.3 confirms this trend. The comparatively high growth of foreign banks in the United Kingdom reflects London's special position as one of the three leading international financial centres in the world. During the 1970s London maintained a liberal attitude towards the establishment of new banks from abroad. Entry restrictions were minimal and the regulatory treatment of foreign banks in London was very flexible.

It is clear from Table 8.3 that the extent and development of foreign banking presence in different European countries is heterogeneous. One factor in these different country patterns of foreign banking presence has been the policies adopted towards the entry of foreign banks. Another stimulating factor has been the comparative sophistication and degree of openness of a country's economic and financial system.

Countries like Switzerland, the Netherlands, France and Belgium also attracted foreign banks from the early 1960s. The penetration of MNCs into these countries attracted foreign banks to service their financial needs. These countries also had

Table 8.3 Foreign banks in selected European countries.

Host Country	Number of banking institutions			Assets of foreign banks relative to bank assets in country		
	1960	1981	1985	1960	1981	1985
Belgium	14[a]	56	57	8.2[a]	46.8	57.0
France	33	131	147[b]	7.2	17.4	18.2[b]
West Germany	24	148	95	0.5	3.6	2.4
Italy	2	38	36	–	2.3	2.4
Netherlands	–	40	40	–	18.0	23.6
Switzerland	8[c]	107	119	–	11.6	12.2
United Kingdom	51[d]	229	472	–	60.2	63.1

Source: Pecchioli (1983, Table 2, p. 69) and Lewis and Davis (1987, Table 8.7, p. 243).
Notes: a 1958.
   b End 1984.
   c Foreign branches only.
   d 1962.

comparatively sophisticated financial systems and pursued relatively liberal entry policies. In France and Belgium increasing foreign bank presence reflected the rise of Brussels and Paris as Eurocurrency centres. In some other European countries, however, offshore banking has only been a marginal factor. Banks have been attracted to West Germany, for example, by the strength of its economy and the importance of its foreign trade. European countries like France have traditionally welcomed foreign banks. The French consider that foreign banks play a beneficial role in the financing of the economy. With the present strong policy commitment towards modernizing the French capital market, foreign banks are also seen as important channellers of new financial techniques and instruments.

Entry restrictions affect the extent and nature of foreign bank presence in different European countries. All OECD member countries have allowed the establishment of representative offices by foreign banking organizations. In many countries no prior authorization has been needed to set up a representative office, although the authorities must be notified in some countries. The opening of agencies, branches and subsidiaries is generally permitted in most European countries, although the Nordic countries have traditionally been more restrictive in this area. Agencies and branches of foreign banks may be licensed, subject to a number of specific requirements. The same applies to the subsidiaries of foreign banks. Reciprocity tests have been applied by several countries with regard to foreign bank entry.

But even those European countries that have traditionally not allowed foreign banks to enter have deregulated. In Sweden, for example, the authorities changed their minds on foreign bank entry in 1985. On 9 January 1986 twelve foreign banks were granted licences to operate in Sweden. Although Sweden was the last of the Nordic countries to open up its market in this way, it was probably the least uninhibited. All banks that applied for licences got them, and the authorities set out to give foreign banks the same opportunities as the Swedish banks.

The growth of foreign banks in Europe has not been a one-way phenomenon.

European banks have expanded abroad. Foreign banks have had a major presence in the United States for many decades: like foreign banks operating in European countries, their activities are mainly wholesale. At the end of 1986 there were over 250 foreign banks operating in the United States. In many respects this reflects a reversal of the 1960s and 1970s trend of aggressive US bank expansion abroad. Many in the United States argue that it should adopt a stricter policy towards reciprocity in banking and finance.

Nationality structure of international banking and the expansion of networks
The tremendous growth in international banking presence within selected European countries from 1960 was summarized in Table 8.3. There has been a strong, sustained growth in international banking presence throughout the 1970s and the first half of the 1980s. Growth in international banking has generally exceeded that of domestic banking liabilities by a significant margin. Besides its comparative freedom from national controls, the expansion of international banking has also allowed banks to tap new sources of funding.

This growth has continued into the second half of the 1980s. During 1987 the external positions of banks reporting to the BIS grew more rapidly (expressed in current US dollars) than ever before. Assets and liabilities expanded by $885 and $959 billion, respectively. A large part of this growth was the result of currency

Table 8.4 International bank assets, by nationality of banks[a].
End-December figures

Parent country of bank	US $ billion			Percentage share of total bank assets		
	1985	1986	1987	1985	1986	1987
France	244.0	289.6	375.5	9.0	8.4	8.6
Germany	191.2	270.1	347.9	7.0	7.8	7.9
Italy	113.3	145.1	185.0	4.2	4.2	4.2
Japan	707.2	1,120.1	1,552.1	26.1	32.4	35.4
Switzerland	109.2	152.0	196.1	4.0	4.4	4.5
United Kingdom	192.9	211.5	253.9	7.1	6.1	5.8
United States	590.2	599.2	647.6	21.7	17.3	14.8
Other	566.8	666.4	823.2	20.9	19.4	18.8
Total	2,714.8	3,454.0	4,381.3	100.0	100.0	100.0
of which:						
vis-à-vis non-banks	*785.0*	*954.4*	*1,200.1*	*28.9*	*27.6*	*27.4*

Source: BIS (1988, p. 121).
Note: a This table shows the international assets, i.e. the cross-border assets in all currencies plus the foreign currency assets vis-à-vis local residents, of banking offices located in the following seventeen countries: Austria, Belgium, Luxembourg, Canada, Denmark, Finland, France, Germany, Ireland, Italy, Japan, the Netherlands, Spain, Sweden, Switzerland, the United Kingdom and the United States (cross-border assets in domestic currency only). The international assets of US banks also include the cross-border assets reported by US banks' branches in the Bahamas, the Cayman Islands, Panama, Hong Kong and Singapore. The international assets in this table are classified according to the nationality of ownership of the reporting banks.

appreciations (like the yen and Deutschmark against the US dollar). As usual, the largest single component of bank foreign currency assets and liabilities reflects interbank positions within the BIS reporting area.

Growth in international bank assets from 1985 to 1987 is summarized in Table 8.4, together with the nationality structure of international banking. Several important trends are evident. The exceptionally strong growth of the Japanese in international banking is dramatic. International assets of Japanese banks expanded by 39 per cent in 1989, compared to a range of 27.5 to 30 per cent for the French, German, Italian and Swiss banks. The international assets of US and Canadian banks expanded by only 8 and 2.5 per cent, respectively, over the same period. The rapid comparative decline of US banks is the result of exchange-rate developments and bank balance-sheet cutbacks resulting from credit exposures and other problems.

We have already seen that a large number of environmental influences have contributed to the growth of international banking. Regulations, the growth of world trade, the rise of the MNC and the growing interpenetration of the OECD economies and of their financial markets have been important general stimulants. Nevertheless, Tables 8.3 and 8.4 show that foreign bank presence and the importance of international banking vary widely. Various theoretical attempts have been made to explain the expansion of international banking networks, using the tools of applied economics, like those of industrial organization theory and trade theory.

Industrial organization theory, for example, has been suggested (Aliber, 1976) for appraising bank market structures in different countries by comparing bank profits. If one accepts the assumption that there is an inverse relationship between bank profits and concentration (see Chapter 3), banks should generally be more profitable in countries where banking concentration is highest. *Ceteris paribus*, banking efficiency will be highest in those countries where profits are lower.

It is notoriously difficult to obtain reasonably comparative data in order to test this kind of hypothesis. Nevertheless, an OECD study – Revell (1980) – has produced some data that may be used to explore initially some of these explanations. This study computed the ratios of gross earnings margin (GEM) to volume of business (VB), total assets, for 1968 through to 1977. Using the ratio GEM/VB as a kind of proxy for banking profitability, Table 8.5 summarizes some illustrative data. It is interesting to note that the GEM of banks in the United States was comparatively high even though the United States had a low concentration ratio. The opposite seems to hold for countries like Austria and Switzerland that have a high concentration ratio. These data on margins, therefore, do not seem to match our *a priori* hypothesis.

Although there have been many theoretical attempts to explain the expansion of international banking networks, they have been generally unsuccessful. We can identify important causal factors, but no economic theory has emerged that is empirically supported. Individual banks view international banking as a part of their overall corporate strategy. Banks may also move abroad to seek direct access to customers in local markets. Foreign banks in Europe have successfully tapped the top end of various domestic corporate sectors and (with much more limited success) the HNWI segment of retail banking markets. Horizontal integration can also be an important factor in a bank's strategic decision to move abroad. The objective is often to channel the bank's resources to those centres where the net marginal returns are the highest. Vertical integration may also be sought to 'add value' through the

Table 8.5   Gross earnings margins[a] of banks.

Country	1977[b]
Austria (4 large banks)	2.28
Belgium (3 large banks)	3.86
France (All commercial banks)	3.06
Germany (Big banks)	3.26
Italy (All commercial banks)	3.65
Netherlands (All commercial banks)	3.46
Switzerland (All large banks)	2.81
US (FDIC insured)	3.84

Source: Revell (1980, Table 10.1, pp. 129–30).
Notes: a Ratio of gross earnings margin (GEM) to volume of business (VB).
   b Although these data were subsequently updated by Revell to 1981, only the data for
   Italy (3.55) were available to update the above 1977 data to 1981.

exploitation of economies of scale and scope. In this respect banks seek to combine efficient deposit-gathering and similar (upstream) activities with (downstream) customer (user)-orientation services, like advisory services and cash management.

Products and services
Modern international banking covers a wide range of activities: see Lewis and Davis (1987, Table 8.1). These products and services encompass financial intermediation (taking deposits and making loans) in domestic and foreign currencies to domestic and foreign economic units, managing and acting as agents for syndicated loans, foreign-exchange transactions, international money transfers, dealing in precious metals, and the design of special financial packages for international trade and project finance. International banking also covers advisory services, the provision of documentary letters of credit, arranging stand-by facilities, involvement in various other forms of guarantee and commitments, the underwriting and placement of a diverse variety of new issues and trading in a wide range of financial instruments. These products and services cover both on- and off-balance sheet activities. Many of them are essentially investment banking activities.

We have seen that the growth of international banking has reduced the traditional compartmentalization between national banking and financial markets, and between different kinds of financial markets. National boundaries have become increasingly irrelevant in international wholesale finance and the traditional dividing lines between specialist money and capital markets have eroded. The result is that banks have been able to offer a growing variety of more sophisticated financial products and services. A taxonomy of these products and services is beyond the scope of this chapter – see, for example, Dufey and Giddy (1978, 1981); Baughn and Mandich (1983) and Williamson (1988) – but we may focus usefully on some broad characteristics.

One such characteristic has been the growth of new funding opportunities for banks and the rise of the interbank market. Liability management strategies vary between banks, but a distinguishing feature of modern international banking is the comparative importance of interbank deposits as a funding source compared with

Table 8.6 The currency composition of reporting banks' cross-border positions[a]. Changes[b]; US $ bn

Currencies		Assets				Liabilities				Stocks at end-1987	
		1984	1985	1986	1987	1984	1985	1986	1987	Assets	Liabilities
US dollars	A	22.0	52.9	188.8	186.4	40.1	41.3	210.1	196.1	1,238.2	1,377.9
	B	8.8	1.4	43.2	13.5	27.9	33.5	63.1	63.4	458.2	477.4
Other	A	47.5	77.9	72.8	107.2	43.1	90.7	110.1	136.5	893.1	996.2
	B	32.4	46.4	90.0	113.5	30.2	34.8	52.9	123.3	689.2	517.2
of which:[c]											
Deutschmark	A	10.6	13.5	1.1	33.8	16.4	16.0	28.7	43.1	297.7	338.8
	B	4.2	15.5	26.4	4.0	2.9	3.0	2.3	4.4	147.9	80.7
Swiss francs	A	2.9	15.3	7.8	−1.8	2.7	18.9	17.5	10.0	139.2	181.5
	B	1.6	2.8	3.3	3.5	1.0	2.4	1.4	4.7	66.4	25.3
Japanese yen	A	6.4	21.0	20.9	30.9	1.8	19.4	21.2	23.9	147.8	137.2
	B	11.9	22.1	43.9	92.6	11.3	17.9	29.4	89.9	288.6	223.8
Pound sterling	A	5.0	4.8	8.7	5.8	4.7	7.1	10.3	14.5	48.3	67.0
	B	6.7	2.3	8.8	8.3	8.3	5.6	9.4	14.9	72.2	94.0
ECUs		12.8	13.7	7.4	9.9	10.5	12.4	4.2	8.7	78.5	69.4

Source: BIS (1988, p. 119).

Notes: a   Positions of banks in industrial reporting countries only.

b   Excluding exchange rate effects.

c   Excluding positions of banks in the United States.

A   Eurocurrency positions.

B   External positions in domestic currency.

domestic banks. Negotiable CDs and FRNs are also important sources of funds for international banks. Another characteristic is the relative importance of transactions in foreign currencies. Table 8.6 shows the currency composition of BIS reporting banks' cross-border positions. Foreign currency business is especially important for those banks in leading Eurocurrency centres like London, Brussels, Paris and Luxembourg. It has been much less important for countries like Germany. In this latter case reserve requirements have not been conducive to the growth of the Eurocurrency market.

International banks have also been characterized by their lack of success in penetrating domestic retail markets. This has not been an altogether unresisted trend. Citicorp, for example, has announced on a number of occasions its strategic intention to secure a significant retail presence in the United Kingdom. So far these strategic initiatives have not been successful: there are many reasons why this is so. The reliance of international banks on wholesale funding, stiff domestic retail banking competition and the required expense of extensive branch networks are particularly important constraints. In many respects retail banking is a kind of 'last bastion' in modern globalization trends. The EC 1992 internal market objectives might help to erode this traditional resistance of domestic retail markets to foreign banks. Just as the so-called retail banking revolution really started in Northern Europe during the late 1950s (see Chapter 6), the modern globalization of retail banking may be stimulated by another 'European factor'. Chase Manhattan, for example, announced in November 1988 that it was adjusting its European strategy in anticipation of the post-1992 unified EC market (Lascelles, 1988). Chase has decided to focus on wholesale banking services for major corporations (especially corporate finance) and upmarket private banking in the personal sector. 1992 is likely to figure increasingly in the strategies and associated products and services offered by major international banks (see Chapter 12).

A major characteristic of the strategies and business mix of international banks in Europe has, of course, been associated with the growth of the Euromarkets. Eurocurrency market growth has far outstripped that of banks' domestic currency banking business. Euromarket business[4] now encompasses a wide range of currencies (including the ECU) and different kinds of financial activity, and is conducted on a large scale in various locations outside Europe. During the 1970s the syndicated Eurocredit occupied 'centre stage' during the so-called 'golden age' of international banking.

Post-1982 securitization trends shifted the strategic focus of international banks away from the syndicated loan market to capital market products. Many banks in London disbanded their syndicated loan teams built up during the 1970s and replaced them with capital market groups. London's Big Bang consolidated this strategic emphasis. Nevertheless, we saw earlier that the syndicated loan has fought back in recent years, and the 1987 crash has helped to revive its post-securitization popularity. A record $100 billion of new credit lines was raised in the first quarter of 1988 (Pavey, 1988).

The syndicated loan market has changed markedly from the days when banks (including the smallest ones) were lending term money for good returns. It is now a market practically dominated by the largest institutions. Margins are very small and over 50 per cent of the finance is for the provision of cheap, stand-by credits. The post-crash period has been a good time for borrowers to take advantage of the attractive terms on offer by banks anxious to secure mandates. New lending structures have been developed; banks have often been stimulated into tight margin business with the promise of attractive relationship business. Acquisition and leveraged buy-out financing has also increased in popularity.

Securitization and globalization trends in financial markets have been accompanied by so-called 'global banking strategies'. International banks like Citicorp and Bank of America have long practised global banking strategies, but the post-1982 European approach has been distinctive. Many European banks have formed financial conglomerates, all-purpose financial groupings (see Chapters 11 and 12). In many respects these bank 'financial conglomerates' or 'universal banks' are a kind of European model. The Japanese and US 'model' is inclined more towards specialist banking institutions: to a great extent this is reflective of the US and Japanese legal separation of investment and commercial banking.

In London a bank financial conglomerate trend developed rapidly with the approach of Big Bang: investment banking aspirations were the 'strategic driver' for the institutions involved. The objective of these new groupings that formed rapidly in London was to provide the bulk of a client's needs – 'one-stop' financial shopping – through the organizational construction of an integrated securities business. London is the largest deregulated capital market where these new-style (European) financial conglomerates face the full competitive challenge of the more 'specialist' US and Japanese investment banks and securities houses. Although the 1987 stock market crash has dented somewhat the concept of conglomeration in London, it is still a convenient label for distinguishing organizationally the 'European model' in international and investment banking from that of the US and Japanese. New kinds of bank financial conglomerate are being constructed in Europe with the approach of 1992 (see Chapters 3, 6, 11 and 12).

Innovation and fragility

Modern international banking has been characterized by comparatively high rates of innovation. New financial instruments and new financial markets have helped to stimulate corresponding strategic reactions by banks. One such organizational response has been that of conglomeration. Another has been the increased emphasis given to their own innovation capability by banks in the field of capital-market products. Events during the 1980s have repeatedly stimulated concerns about the risk implications of all these developments in international banking.

New technology, internationalization, deregulation and securitization have opened up new opportunities in banking and finance, but there are associated risks. The 1987 stock market crash exposed the dangers of over-capacity and over-commitment by many institutions. In 1986 the Bank for International Settlements published its famous 'Cross Report', which expressed concern at the risk implications for banking of many new financial innovations. This is a complex topic and we can do no more than outline here (see also Chapter 5) the broad balance-sheet implications of recent trends.

High on-balance-sheet growth during the 1970s was displaced increasingly from 1982 by a high rate of OBS growth (see Chapter 5). Various international US banks, for example, typically hold OBS positions over 100 per cent and beyond of their corresponding on-balance-sheet positions. Although the growth of active ALM (asset and liability management) and treasury functions in banks has been a response in part to the complexities and opportunities of these innovations, the risks remain; Harrington (1987, p. 134), for example, emphasizes the risks associated with the growth of OBS commitments. The recent (July 1988) Basle initiatives for the convergence of capital adequacy (see Chapter 4) have sought to capture the OBS dimension of banks' total (or economic) balance sheets.

British banks and a number of leading European banks have been exposed to these intensive competitive pressures in international banking since the early 1970s. French banks (like the Japanese) have been pushed since 1984 by official deregulatory reforms into the competitive international financial arena. December 1985 saw the launch of several new instruments in France, including negotiable CDs, CP and treasury bills; a new financial futures market, the MATIF (Marché à Terme d'Instruments Financiers) was established in 1986. Two important challenges from French banks in this new environment are privatization, and the need for the banks to reduce their own lending spreads.

West German banks have experienced their share of problems in the new international arena. Two of the handful of recent world banking disasters have involved German banks. Two of Germany's big three banks – Dresdner and Commerzbank – were badly affected by interest-rate mismatching in 1980 and 1981. Nevertheless, the big universal banks[5] are currently in the top league of world competition and they have had time to build up considerable experience in areas like securities business. Even so, the big German banks are likely to be exposed to more intense competition as foreigners obtain greater access to German financial markets.

Swiss banks are archetypal strong risk-takers in international banking. The Swiss universal banks have a reputation for conservative lending and a very conservative provisioning approach to Third World loans. Nevertheless, the big three Swiss banks are involved in the leading and most innovative financial markets worldwide: see *The Economist* (1987, p. 14). Although their traditional strength has been in placing paper, the Swiss are moving into trading. The enormous equity strength of the Swiss banks has been demonstrated on a number of occasions when losses have been experienced.

Conclusion

International banking and foreign banks have been an important focus of change in European banking. Internationalization and the more recent globalization phenomena have been important stimulants of deregulatory changes in European banking (see Chapter 4). Supervisory re-regulation has also been shaped by wider global pressures. Innovations have diffused more rapidly to domestic markets through the international banking network. Later chapters will cover other aspects of European international banking, especially the post-1982 focus on investment banking and capital market products. The following chapter continues in the same vein by exploring the rise of European financial centres.

Notes

1. In Germany and France the banks dominated the provision of foreign investment.
2. Its forerunner was the Eurodollar market that developed in the late 1950s.
3. Eurobonds are bonds issued in the international Euromarket and underwritten by an international banking syndicate. They are not subject to any single country's securities laws and may be denominated in any major national currency or artificial currency unit.
4. Euromarkets in this context encompass Eurocurrency, Eurocredit and Eurobond business – the full gamut of banking Eurobusiness.
5. Deutsche, Dresdner and Commerzbank.

References

Aliber, Robert (1976), 'Towards a theory of international banking', *Economic Review*, Federal Reserve Bank of San Francisco, Spring, pp. 5–8.

Bank for International Settlements (1986), *Recent Innovations in International Banking*, April (Basle; BIS).

Bank for International Settlements (1988), *59th Annual Report* (1 April 1987–31 March) (Basle: BIS).

Bank of England Quarterly Bulletin (1986), 'International banking in London, 1975–85', September, pp. 367–78.

Baughn, William H. and Mandich, Donald R. (1983), *The International Banking Handbook* (London: Dow Jones-Irwin).

Dufey, G. and Giddy, I. H. (1978), *The International Money Market* (London: Prentice Hall).

Dufey, G. and Giddy I. H. (1981), *The Evolution of Instruments and Techniques in International Financial Markets*, SUERF Series 35A.

Economist, The, (1987), 'Survey: International Banking' (March 21) pp. 1–70.

Gardener, E. P. M. (ed.) (1990), *The Future of Financial Systems and Services* (London: Macmillan).

Harrington, R. (1987), *Asset And Liability Management By Banks* (Paris: OECD).

Kindleberger, Charles P. (1984), *A Financial History of Western Europe* (London: George Allen & Unwin).

Lascelles, David (1988), 'Chase adjusts European strategy', *Financial Times* (15 November), p. 35.

Lebègue, Daniel. (1985), 'Modernising the French capital market', *The Banker* (December), pp. 23–9.

Lewis, M. K. and Davis, K. T. (1987), *Domestic and International Banking* (Oxford: Philip Allan Publishers).

Pavey, Nigel, (1988), 'Razor-thin returns on cheap standbys' in *Syndicated Loans: A Competitive Business, Euromoney Supplement*, (May), pp. 1–24.

Pecchioli, R. M. (1983), *The Internationalisation of Banking: The Policy Issues* (Paris: OECD).

Revell, J. R. S. (1980), *Costs and Margins in Banking – An International Survey* (Paris: OCED).

Williamson, J. Peter (ed.) (1988), *Investment Banking Handbook* (London: John Wiley and Sons Ltd.).

Chapter nine

Financial centres

Introduction

There has been a marked growth of interest in the development of European financial centres during recent years mainly because of the benefits that are believed to accrue to the domestic economy from hosting such centres. The aim of this chapter is to analyze the role and development of such centres and to examine the various trends that have affected them in recent years. The first part of the chapter deals with the major financial centres and the second part looks at small centres, the reasons for countries hosting such centres and the expected effects of 1992.

Major European centres

The history, role and development of major European centres
The traditional explanation for the development of financial centres in the nineteenth and early twentieth centuries revolves around the way in which various centres tended to dominate international trade financing and capital export, and the important role they have played in the world economy. London is usually used as the role model to highlight the main features of this type of development. From the mid-nineteenth century onwards, the United Kingdom was the world's largest exporter of capital; sterling acted as a reserve currency and the majority of the world's business was done in sterling. So much so that there was little need for major foreign-exchange transactions to take place and those that did invariably took place in London, which became the main market for them. The pre-eminence of London in the financing of world trade encouraged the development of other activities such as the Lloyd's insurance market. The scale and subsequent growth of these activities generated a whole panoply of complementary businesses – import and export agents; accounting and legal services; agents and brokers; specialist printers; and a wide range of other services allied to London's international financial business.

Some commentators (Economists Advisory Group, 1984) refer to the development of London during the nineteenth century as the 'classical' model, primarily because of its predominance in international finance and its implied role as a 'super central bank' to the world. There has been, however, considerable debate as to whether London or Paris was the leading financial centre during the nineteenth and early twentieth centuries. One statistical study (Morgenstern, 1959) found that Paris was the 'strongest' financial centre in the world before 1914 if one accepted the view that a relatively low short-term interest rate was an indication of financial strength. Bagehot (1873) stated that between 1850 and 1870 London (through the Bank of England) and Paris (through the Bank of France) held the two greatest stores of cash in Europe. He believed that the pre-eminence of London arose from the change to suspend the convertibility of the French franc into gold and silver in 1870. In fact, the general position was that Paris had substantial stocks of capital and gold, whilst London (through its well-established money markets) had the ability to transfer funds efficiently. The consensus view is summed up as follows:

London was a world financial centre, Paris was a European financial centre. London was an efficient financial market, handling an enormous body of transactions on a small monetary base. Paris was a rich money and capital market, efficient in the sense that it could mobilise savings and pour them in a given direction, ..., but inefficient in its much higher ratio of gold reserves to total financial transactions as compared with London (Kindleberger, 1984, pp. 63–4).

Historically, financial centres tended to develop as significant capital-exporting centres and this was more or less directly related to the relative importance of the host country economy and the international payments and reserve characteristics of its currency. During the 1800s and up to the early part of the present century gold was the legally recognized international means of payments and reserves, although sterling was widely used as a close substitute. This helped reinforce London's position as an international financial centre.

Today, however, no one currency takes the place formerly held by gold as both a universally accepted means of payment and ubiquitous reserve asset. The US dollar is the most widely used for both purposes but New York is by no means the sole or most important source of dollar finance, as the developoment of the Euromarkets has exemplified. In other words, the development and continuance of New York as an international financial centre cannot be attributed solely to the concentration of international dollar exchange transactions in this centre.

There are various reasons why financial centres have become less dependent on their domestic economies. Firstly, no country can now be relied upon to be a substantial exporter of capital year after year, decade after decade, as was the case for London during the nineteenth century. As a result, this has led to the growth of an entrepôt trade whereby international financial institutions mobilize the savings of surplus countries and distribute them to deficit countries. The growth in entrepôt trade results in a corresponding increase in the number and type of foreign institutions operating in important financial centres, the development of consortia arrangements, and the growth and deepening of markets such as the interbank, certificate of deposits, and Eurocurrency markets in which institutions can transact between themselves (Economists Advisory Group, 1984, p. 12). Secondly, the internationalization of finance has meant that the close links that once existed between the currency in which financial claims were denominated and the country in which they were issued, owned and traded, no longer apply.

Although every international financial centre has its own special characteristics – with different business mixes, regulatory frameworks, time zones and so on which give each centre an individual flavour – one may conclude that there are a variety of general

Table 9.1 Economies of scale and financial centres.

Economies of scale for individual firms	Economies of scale for particular markets	Economies of scale for the centre as a whole
Spreading of risk	Substantial business volume means that transactions can be made quickly at low cost with little disturbance to prices.	Average of having markets in close proximity
Access to capital		
Advertising & marketing		Development of specialist ancillary services
Personnel specialization	Increased volume = increased information	
Employment of costly technology		Pool of specialized skills that can be drawn upon both by existing undertakings and by new firms entering the market
	Narrow bid and offer prices	
Firm-specific economies of scale are considered to be important in banking, insurance, investment business and capital markets activities	Any centre that establishes a market in any financial asset that is bigger than those existing elsewhere will probably enjoy some of the above advantages, thus attracting business away from its rivals. This would further increase scale economies.	
		Reputation, firms will be attracted mainly because of the number of firms already established there
Firm-specific economies are not considered to be important in various niche financial operations such as specialist brokerage, and computer software		Economies through concentration.

Source: Adapted from Economists Advisory Group (1984, pp. 15–17).

factors behind the development of such centres. Many financial centres maintain their *status quo* because of a *laissez-faire* attitude towards banking and financial markets. Deregulated financial markets are perceived as being more favourable than heavily regulated ones. Political stability is another important factor, as is the ability of centres to adapt to new financing techniques and technological innovations, and to change in general.

Overall, international financial centres have developed according to a whole range of such factors, and momentum has been sustained largely from advantages gleaned from various types of economies of scale. Table 9.1 illustrates the three types of economies that can be earned from operating in a financial centre. The first type relates to firm-specific economies, the second to market size and growth, and the third to the financial centre as a whole. Although all of these are difficult to quantify, the general consensus appears to be that the second and third (and most likely the third) are where most of the economies are obtained. The self-sustaining nature of financial centres strongly implies that once such factors as reputation, customer loyalty, specialized ancillary services and a whole range of high volume financial markets are concentrated in close proximity, the centres generate substantial economies of scale. This is reinforced through their pulling power *vis-à-vis* the location decisions of new firms; it also makes it more difficult for new centres to become established.

145

London

London is by far the most important financial centre in Europe and even more of an international centre than either Tokyo or New York. A survey conducted in 1989 by twenty central banks reported that daily turnover in the foreign-exchange market amounted to $450 billion, of which $187 billion took place in London. The figures for New York and Tokyo were $129 billion and $115 billion, respectively. Foreign-exchange business in Zurich, Europe's largest rival market to London, was estimatged to be worth about $57 billion[1]. The position of London as the world's major foreign-exchange centre is reinforced by its position as capital of the Eurocurrency markets. London had a share of just over 30 per cent of overall Eurocurrency business in 1986, although its relative position as the main centre for Eurocurrency operations has declined somewhat in recent years *vis-à-vis* the growth of New York and Tokyo.

It is the position of London as the world's major foreign-exchange market and its dominance in the Eurocurrency markets that continue to reinforce its position as a major financial centre: this is why so many foreign banks and securities set up shop in London. At the end of 1988 there was a total of some 448 foreign banks represented in London by branches, representative offices, subsidiaries and joint ventures. In addition, there were some 120 securities houses. The substantial increase in the number of employees in banks and security houses that preceded Big Bang in October 1986 was almost wiped out during 1988. At the end of 1987 foreign banks and securities houses employed over 72 000 people, a 35 per cent annual increase since 1985, but during 1988 employment in the sector fell to 58 000. Despite this substantial fall, resulting mainly from the October 1987 stock market crash, there has been no 'mass exodus': only 15 banks and security houses decided to leave London. Lyon (1988, p. 82) suggests in this context:

> Many believed the cumulative effect of the Financial Services Act, the Securities and Investments Board's plans to monitor the resources of foreign branches, and the October crash would precipitate large scale departures; other European centres, said the Jeremiahs, would become more attractive. *The Banker's* listing does not bear this scenario out.

Table 9.2   UK banking sector deposits, 1988.

Banks	Sterling		Other currencies	
	£ million	%	£ million	%
Foreign banks				
American	15,269	5	79,692	14
Japanese	19,285	6	213,462	38
Others	58,088	19	184,823	33
	92,642	30	477,979	85
British banks	215,753	70	82,476	15
	308,395	100	560,455	100

Source: *Bank of England Quarterly Bulletin*, February 1988 (various tables).

Foreign banks in London account for the major part of bank activity in the foreign-exchange market. In 1989 they accounted for 80 per cent of the dollar-related transactions and over 50 per cent of those against sterling. In general, non-UK banks tend to do business in the currency of their country of origin. In terms of domestic banking business, by 1988 foreign banks held around 30 per cent of total sterling deposits. Table 9.2 shows the deposit breakdown for the UK banking sector and illustrates the relative strength of the Japanese banks.

During the 1970s banks were the most important foreign financial institutions in the UK markets; they were attracted to London because of punitive US restrictions and the burgeoning Eurocurrency market. Since 1982, however, Euro-syndicated lending has slowed down and some US banks have come under increasing pressure because of large exposures to international lending and problems with their domestic loan books. US banks have increasingly focused their attention on their own domestic business whilst the Japanese banks and securities houses have continued to expand into the United Kingdom, as well as continental Europe. In December 1979 American banks held over 22 per cent of London's total banking sector assets compared with 11 per cent for Japanese banks. By the end of 1988 the position had reversed with Japanese banks holding over 25 per cent compared with 10 per cent for US banks.

'Other overseas banks', according to the Bank of England's classification, have had a relatively stable market share ranging between 20 and 25 per cent of total banking sector assets throughout the 1980s. Continental European banks constitute the lion's share of this category. By the end of 1988 there were 116 EC banks operating in London employing nearly 10 000 staff. Banks from other West European countries account for another 4000 staff – 21 Swiss banks employ 2700 and five Swiss securities houses employ a further 400. 'Other overseas banks' accounted for around 30 per cent of foreign currency advances and 15 per cent of bank sterling advances in the United Kingdom by the end of 1988. Changes in the regulations affecting capital market operators have also had a significant impact on the character of London's financial markets.

The deregulation of the UK securities market in October 1986, known as 'Big Bang', witnessed the abolition of dual capacity between jobbers and brokers on the Stock Exchange floor. In March 1986, the authorities announced that foreign banks could take controlling interests in Stock Exchange firms and this, together with the abandonment of dual capacity, encouraged a wave of merger and takeover activity in which well-capitalized UK and foreign banks swallowed relatively under-capitalized (compared with their US and Japanese counterparts) broking houses, jobbers and merchant banks. This large-scale rush into the capital markets, coupled with the deregulation of the gilt-edged market, led to a more competitive environment and substantial over-capacity in certain market-making areas.

Despite the well-publicized wave of exits from the equities, gilts and Eurobond market-making sectors, the Stock Exchange stated in September 1988 that net job losses among the 40 000 employed in the securities industry amounted to only 3000. Nevertheless, it is still the view that the UK markets are operating at well over capacity. One study[2] has reported that the securities industry is losing £500 million a year on its mainstream institutional business, and this implies that there will continue to be more firms leaving the industry. The restructuring of the City has suggested that only two or three world-class investment banks (such as S. G. Warburg and Kleinwort Benson) will be able to face up to the Tokyo and New York giants in global markets, although previous niche players (Schroders, Rothschilds, Lazards) are thriving (*Financial Times*, 1988a).

Various other markets have played an important role in maintaining London's position as a major international financial centre. The London International Financial Futures Exchange (LIFFE) has established itself as one of the leading European futures exchanges and turnover has continued to grow despite the October 1987 crash. On the other hand, trading volumes are down at the London Traded Options Market (LTOM), which operates as a division of the International Stock Exchange (ISE). The initial expectation that London would easily become the most important futures and options exchange in Europe has not materialized. Paris has had much greater comparative success with its financial futures market, and regional options exchanges, such as Amsterdam, are also of significant importance. Wilson (1988, p. 66) points out that plans are currently under way to establish London as the 'main centre for derivatives trading in the European time zone'.

Probably one of the most important recent developments was the introduction in September 1988 of a futures contract on West German government *Bunde* (bonds) at LIFFE. The Bunde market is the fourth biggest government debt market in the world, after US Treasury bonds, Japanese government bonds and UK gilts. Futures contracts that are already offered on these latter government instruments have all been successful. It is hoped that LIFFE Bunde futures contracts will emulate this success. The main difference between the Bunde futures and similar other contracts is that it is being traded only in London, not in Frankfurt. A second major development has been a co-operation agreement between LIFFE and LTOM, which could reduce transaction costs and improve liquidity in both markets, and might well lead to a merger between the two. It is also hoped that if they come together, London should be able to provide a unique combination of futures and options services that other European centres may find difficult to rival.

Other markets also help to consolidate London's position as a major financial centre. Lloyd's of London is still the most important international market for direct insurance and reinsurance business; there is little doubt that this market will strongly benefit from the increased flow of financial services that is expected throughout the 1990s. In addition, there is a broad range of metal and commodities markets, such as the London Metal Exchange, London Commodity Exchange, International Petroleum Exchange and the gold bullion market which all contribute to the international flavour of the centre.

Despite the regulatory constraints imposed on the City by the Financial Services Act 1986 and the new 'investor protection' regulatory structure – comprising the Securities and Investment Board (SIB) and the various self-regulatory organizations – London still remains a thriving international financial centre. According to Peat Marwick McLintock (1988) it will continue to remain so for the following specific reasons:

● London is geographically well-positioned in terms of the world's time zones. It is conveniently situated between Tokyo and New York and overlaps part of its working day with the financial markets in both these centres;

148

Table 9.3 External position of banks in individual banking centres, end–1988.

Country	US$ bn	%
Belgium	164.8	4.02
Denmark	17.1	0.42
France	266.4	6.49
Germany	206.0	5.02
Italy	63.4	1.55
Luxembourg	182.3	4.44
Netherlands	115.3	2.81
Spain	25.5	0.62
Sweden	17.1	0.42
Switzerland	130.2	3.17
United Kingdom	875.6	21.34
Other European[a]	21.4	0.52
Europe	2,085.9	50.83
Japan	576.9	14.06
United States	508.9	12.41
Canada	52.9	1.29
Other reporting countries[b]	878.5	21.41
Total	4,102.3	100.00

Source: Bank for International Settlements, *58th Annual Report* (p. 118).

Notes: a Finland, Ireland and Norway.

b Banks engaged in international business in the Bahamas, Cayman Islands, Hong Kong, Singapore, all offshore banking units in Bahrain, all offshore banks operating in the Netherlands Antilles and the branches of US banks in Panama.

● concentration of foreign institutions in London, comprising 448 banks and 120 securities houses;

● availability of well-qualified staff with financial sector experience;

● a large number of specialist professional advisers such as accountants, lawyers, information technology experts;

● availability of adequate office space and premises equipped to current standards. The City of London's boundaries are currently being extended by developments in other parts of London (Canary Wharf in the Docklands) and the relocation of bank back-office operations to provincial centres (Chemical Bank to Cardiff, Barclays to Coventry, etc.);

● London is in a convenient location and has well developed transport links with other parts of Europe and the world.

Just so as to reinforce the relative importance of London compared with its European counterparts, one can see from Table 9.3 that international banking business booked out of the United Kingdom (virtually all through London) is at least three times as large as that of its nearest European rival. Stock market capitalization is also much larger than that of its European competitors. Given these features, it is difficult to find any compelling reasons (Gunn, 1988; McMahon, 1988) why London will decline as a major financial centre over the next decade.

Frankfurt and Paris

Frankfurt As the financial capital of Europe's largest and most stable economy, Frankfurt has established itself as the second most important centre after London. In recent years the Bundesbank's slowly evolving reform of the country's capital markets has attracted a plethora of the world's major investment banks as well as a whole range of other foreign banks and securities houses. The role of Frankfurt as a major centre for foreign banks is not new and Frankfurt has consolidated its position in recent years. Leading US and Swiss banks have been established there for some time, although one of the main reasons why foreign institutions moved into Frankfurt is that withholding tax on securities was abolished in April 1984 and, since 1985, foreigners have been allowed to lead-manage Deutschmark bond issues from within Germany.

By 1988 all but 70 of the 250 or so foreign banks and securities houses in Germany did their business in Frankfurt (Jones, 1988a) and most of these firms concentrated on investment banking and top corporate business. Foreign banks' presence in Frankfurt was given a boost in April 1986 when the Federal government bond (*Bunde*) underwriting consortium was expanded to include a large foreign presence. In 1987 the consortium was widened to include twenty foreign banks (Jones, 1988b). As over 60 per cent of these federal bonds are held by foreigners, there was an even greater incentive for foreign banks to enter Frankfurt. Despite the slow opening-up of German capital markets, the three largest banks, Deutsche, Dresdner and Commerzbank, account for 40 per cent of total turnover, whilst half the trade in shares is transacted off the floor of the exchange. The dominance of these banks is attributable to the fact that they have very large fund management arms (with close links to insurance companies) and in order to trade shares on behalf of clients you need a banking licence in Germany.

In September 1989 these three banks shocked the nation's financial community by announcing plans to set up a new computerized stock exchange for international investors. They have developed a three-pronged strategy which will transform the stock-exchange structure. Firstly, a new screen-based pre- and post-bourse trading system called Inter-Banken-Informations-System (Ibis) started operation in December 1989. Ibis trades blue-chip and federal government bonds, and is switched off during the official two-hour floor session and will be mainly restricted to interbank activities. Secondly, Ibis complements the long-planned Deutsche Termin-börse (DTB), a computerized futures and options exchange, by improving transparency in the underlying cash market for its bonds and share contracts. Finally, Ibis will eventually be upgraded into a computer trading network for international investors.

It is likely that Ibis will gradually deprive the old exchanges of more and more business. The banks concerned argue that the aforementioned developments are necessary because West Germany's stock exchanges have failed to respond in an appropriate way to increased competition from other European centres. It is hoped that Ibis will redress the competitive disadvantage. From January 1989 a 10 per cent withholding tax on investment income was introduced, and this was deducted at source. It affected all domestic bonds (including Federal bonds), mortgage bonds, Eurobonds of all currencies issued by German borrowers, but not Euro-Deutsche-mark bonds issued by foreigners (Shale, 1989). The 1989 tax lasted only six months but it has already shifted investment banking business activity away from the domestic towards the international arena. The government intends to maintain a 0.25 per cent turnover tax until January 1993.

Frankfurt is one of the largest foreign-exchange markets (in terms of volume) in the world and probably comes fifth after London, New York, Tokyo and Zurich. Foreign exchange is traded in Hamburg and Düsseldorf (the country's second financial centre), but Frankfurt is by far the most important centre. There are some 400 banks operating in Frankfurt and over 50 per cent are active in the foreign-exchange markets. In standard Deutschmark/dollar trading Frankfurt has no domestic competitors: Deutschmark/sterling, Deutschmark/French franc and Deutschmark/Swiss franc trading rank next in volume terms (*Euromoney Corporate Finance Supplement*, 1988, p. 9). Although the market is very competitive for corporate spot business, there is only negligible trade in hybrid foreign-exchange products such as futures.

Frankfurt has slowly been monitoring the success of London's LIFFE and MATIF in Paris, but there is no doubt that it was the development of the SOFFEX (the Swiss Options and Financial Futures Exchange) which spurred Frankfurt and its authorities to establish a West German futures and options market (Simonian, 1988). The new exchange, known as the Deutsche Terminbörse (DTB), began operating in January 1990. The potential competitive threat posed by SOFFEX, which might extend its interest to German equities, obviously quickened the German authorities' plans to develop the new exchange[3]. At present only banks can operate in options markets, and options and futures are still considered to be covered by a law which stipulates that forms of gambling debts cannot be recovered.

At the beginning of 1988 there were 574 domestic companies and 409 foreign companies listed on Germany's eight stock exchanges. Around 40 per cent of stock-exchange turnover can be attributed to non-resident transactions, which illustrates the international flavour of the capital markets. Table 9.4 shows the combined capitalization of these exchanges as the second largest in Europe and the fourth largest in the world. There is a poor degree of integration between the exchanges in Berlin, Bremen, Düsseldorf, Hamburg, Hanover, Frankfurt, Munich and Stuttgart, and over 50 per cent of total turnover is believed to take place in Frankfurt. The Frankfurt exchange is open to both domestic and foreign banks and currently has 116 member banks, of which 45 are foreign (Von Rosen, 1988, pp. 18). Despite the size of the market and its international complexion, however, it is considered to be thin – 'one large order can push the market up by five per cent' (Jones, 1988b, p. 10) – there are few institutional investors, and private household trades account for only 5 per cent of the market. Almost half the trading in equities and four-fifths of that in bonds takes place off the market. It is predominantly commercial banks and savings banks that operate in the market, although various mutual fund related products are being developed to help woo private investors.

Frankfurt has three major advantages as an international financial centre. Firstly, the Deutschmark is a stable internationally respected currency that is widely used as a means of international payment and reserve currency. Secondly, Germany has long had a relatively liberal capital market, a tradition of universal banking and no exchange controls. Finally, Frankfurt is the financial capital of the wealthiest country in Europe with a strong export-orientated economy. Nevertheless, the cautious

Table 9.4 How Frankfurt compares with other stock exchanges.

| | Listed securities end–1987 | | | Companies introduced in 1987 | | Market value of local companies' shares end-87 (DM bn) |
	Shares Domestic no.	Foreign no.	Bonds Total no.	Local no.	Foreign no.	
New York	...	...	3,348	138	16	3,505c
Amex	1,020	58	325	145	7	...
NASDAQ	44,330a	301a	...	715	47	476
Tokyo	1,533	88	1,192	37	36	4,382
Osaka	1,072	0	892	21	0	3,775
London	1,964	613	4,170	155	34	1,085
Toronto	1,628b	67b	219	167	13	346
Montreal	1,166	30	...	121	2	294
Frankfurt	410b	310b	6,643	19	27	...
W.Germanyd	679b	432b	15,018	19	27	345
Paris	650	207	2,363	69	10	285
Amsterdam	283	290	1,325	19	12	138
Zurich	296	271	2,355	55	18	205
Brussels	591	229	14,935	5	8	66
Milan	316	0	1,280	23	0	190
Vienna	113	50	1,952	4	4	12
Stockholm	263	7	1,626	8	0	112
Copenhagen	...	...	2,167	4	1	32c
Helsinki	100	3	544	3	0	32c
Luxembourg	56b	180b	4,893	4	14	...

Source: Jones (1988b, p. 51).
Notes: a Ordinary shares only.
b Excluding warrants, etc.
c Including foreign companies.
d All stock exchanges.

attitudes of both investors and policymakers are inhibiting Frankfurt's ability to keep up with the more sophisticated developments that are taking place in London and in other European financial centres.

Paris Throughout the nineteenth century Paris vied with London for the position as the leading European financial centre, and some commentators (Bonelli, 1981, p. 42) suggest that Paris was the 'real' centre for regulating world liquidity at the turn of the century. The relative position of London has strengthened, and that of Paris weakened, since these times, but the French authorities are now introducing various reforms to counteract this trend. Widespread nationalization of the banking system under the Socialist government from 1981 onwards did little to dispel the view that Parisian financial markets and banking systems were over-regulated and uncompetitive. In the light of two important 1986 European phenomena, London's Big Bang and the French government's 'about-face' on state ownership, considerable changes in the financial system have sought to regenerate the importance of Paris as a European financial centre.

The rate of change in the French capital markets has been remarkable. In 1985 equity prices were fixed daily by two-hour daily sessions on the floor of the exchange.

By 1988 the trading system had completely changed and now almost all stocks are traded on a continuous screen-based system known as CAC (Continuous Assisted Trading). As in other European countries, exchange controls have been lifted; the MATIF, the stock options and futures market, is well ahead of other continental rivals; and the brokers' monopoly has been abolished, leading in principle to a substantial number of takeovers by domestic and foreign banks and various securities houses. The monopoly held by 45 Paris firms over all transactions put through the exchange will not end until 1992, and banks will not take 100 per cent of their broking partners until the end of 1990. Of these 45 firms, at least 25 brokers are either negotiating or are already 30 per cent owned by the new banking partners (McDougall, 1988, pp. 38–9). Fixed commissions were abolished in July 1989 and from October brokers have also been permitted to make markets in some stocks.

Compared with London, however, the market capitalization of the Paris bourse is quite small. This was practically demonstrated in 1987 when a variety of large privatization issues came to the market and these were too large for the Bourse's system to handle, thereby contributing to the 15 per cent or so of French shares traded outside the country, mainly in London. By mid-1988, most main market stocks are quoted on the Bourse's own and the CAC system. As with London, a large proportion of business has moved off the floor of the exchange. Apart from a minor scandal that broke in 1987[4] reforms of the exchange has established a more professional and competitive environment.

A brief look at the make-up of the capital market shows us that at least 80 per cent of turnover of the main market is related to bond transactions, and corporate issues account for a very small proportion. The pre-eminence of bond trading is reinforced by various fiscal requirements which state that various mutual funds – like SICAVs (Sociétés d'Investissement à Capital Variable) and FCPs (Fonds Communs de Placement) – have to hold at least 30 per cent of their portfolios in bonds. This industry, the largest mutual fund market in Europe, has developed partly because of specific domestic tax incentives and also because of the Monory Law which encouraged individual investment in equities. Other types of investment funds based on money market funds have also developed (see Graham, 1988; Jeancourt-Galignani, 1988; Rambossen, 1988), but there are stringent government contraints on the portfolio characteristics of such funds.

The role of foreign banks in Paris is not significant and is geared primarily to niche market business such as private banking, specific areas of top-rank corporate business, and activities in derivative options and futures products (Large, 1988, p. 35). Over the last year or so foreign banks operating in France have seen their margins fall on corporate banking business, and they find it difficult to compete with large domestic banks that all have substantial 'free' deposit bases which they can use to fund corporate business.

Switzerland, Luxembourg and Amsterdam

Switzerland Switzerland is a financial centre where third countries raise capital and use it as a base for international portfolio management activities. This business takes place in a number of centres: international transactions in Basle focus on Germany

153

and Alsace; Geneva on France and the Arab countries; Lugano on Italy; and Zurich on Germany, the United States and the rest of the world (Schuster, 1987, p. 2). Although it may be more accurate to focus on Zurich, Basle and Geneva as international financial centres in their own right, for the purpose of this section we shall view the whole country as a financial centre.

The historical development of Switzerland as an international financial centre is not a post-World War II development but is founded on an old tradition of capital export. Iklé (1972, p. 14) reports that even before the introduction of the Swiss franc in 1850 Basle had become an important 'storehouse' of domestic as well as foreign capital; Geneva was 'already in the thick of European transactions' (p. 16) and Zurich was establishing itself as a major economic and financial centre.

Switzerland has always been able to attract substantial amounts of foreign capital. The reasons for this include the stability of the country's political, social and economic infrastructure, together with its well-established institutions, the 'legendary banking secrecy' provision and the numbered account system. Another attraction is the traditionally low interest rates, which, far from being an isolated phenomenon, are the result in part of the abundant liquidity in the banking system. As the Swiss economy is relatively small, a large proportion of capital that enters the country has to be re-exported, and this is why Switzerland is renowned as a centre where countries raise interest and capital.

The domestic Swiss capital market is less important than the foreign sector. Since 1985, transactions in foreign bonds and shares have exceeded those of Swiss stocks. Despite the international flavour of Swiss capital markets, Zurich (the largest stock exchange) has a narrow market with a mere 23 stocks accounting for around 78 per cent of total market capitalization (Dullforce, 1987, p. 4). Various levies and withholding taxes are imposed on many types of securities transactions. The international capital markets, consisting mainly of bonds and notes issued by foreign borrowers and various fiduciary transactions[5], accounted for 14 per cent of all international issues between 1981 and 1985. Over 50 per cent of these were Eurodollar issues. By the end of 1987 Euromarket and foreign issues accounted for 93 per cent of the total stock and bond issues values at SFr 248 billion (Pearson, 1987, p. 6).

One of the more recent and innovative developments has been SOFFEX, the fully-automated Swiss Options and Financial Futures Exchange. The five largest Swiss banks and the three largest stock exchanges invested $48 million to equip the new exchange. It opened for operation in 1988 and has over 50 members with nearly 20 market-makers. The SOFFEX exchange is different from the US and UK futures exchanges in that it integrates trading and clearing operations in one automated system. The Swiss authorities do not levy stamp duty and investors are exempt from withholding tax. It can be seen that the establishment of SOFFEX is an indication that the Swiss banks and bourses are determined to keep a significant European securities trading centre in Switzerland.

Over 600 domestic and foreign banks, including private banks and various finance companies, now operate in Switzerland. Their total assets amounted to US $592 billion at the end of 1988. Foreign banks' sector assets accounted for 11 per cent of the total. As much of the foreign capital flowing into Switzerland is primarily for long-term investment, Swiss banks have built up a reputation second to none in the area of investment advisory services and portfolio management. It is estimated that there is some $1100 billion under management in Switzerland, of which 45 per cent is managed by the three largest banks, Union Bank of Switzerland, Swiss Bank Corporation and Crédit Suisse. Put into perspective, at the end of 1987 Pearson (1987) noted that Union Bank of Switzerland managed $167 billion of funds compared with $62 billion by J. P. Morgan, $19 billion by Société Générale and $14 billion by Barclays. This explains the enormous placing power of Swiss banks in the international securities markets.

Beusch-Liggenstorfer (1987, p. 230) reports that about one-third of Eurobond new issues 'go straight into portfolios administered by Swiss banks'. Over the last few years Swiss bankers have had to compete more aggressively to hold on to their share of the portfolio management business. Luxembourg has witnessed a marked decline in Eurocredit business and is attempting to make up by competing with Switzerland for more portfolio business. Another interesting development for Swiss international bankers is the increasing importance of the relationship between Switzerland and Liechtenstein. As bank secrecy laws become marginally more transparent, business is being increasingly routed through the principality which ensures total secrecy.

Despite Switzerland's secrecy laws preventing an accurate comparison of its relative importance as an international financial centre, estimates suggest that it still invests more than any other financial centre, including London and Tokyo. Competition from other financial centres has led the Swiss authorities to increase scrutiny of domestic banks' performance, and this could well lead to greater disclosures of the operations of the banking system (Braillard, 1987).

Luxembourg   Up to the mid-1960s, the Luxembourg economy had been dependent upon two industries, agriculture and steel, and the majority of banks existed mainly to serve the needs of the local community. Over the last two decades, however, developments in European financial and capital markets have helped Luxembourg to become one of the major centres for Eurobanking. The Grand Duchy's share of Euromarket business was approximately 10 per cent of the assets and 8 per cent of the liabilities in 1987, according to the BIS. This helps to explain why nearly 90 per cent of banks and savings institutions operating in Luxembourg are foreign. By June 1987 there were 125 banks operating there, of which 110 were foreign. As Luxembourg was one of the pioneers in developing the Eurobond market and holding company status was found to be an ideal corporate vehicle for raising capital in the international markets, this encouraged foreign banks to enter the market, primarily to undertake Euromarket business. Most local business is undertaken by domestic banks, whereas international business is dominated by foreign financial institutions. Typically, a universal banking system prevails.

The strength of Luxembourg as a financial centre lies with the growth of the Euromarkets and the start in 1969 of international bond quotations in the currency of issue. Blanden (1987) notes that by the end of 1986, 421 companies (152 of them foreign) were listed in Luxembourg and around 4500 different securities, issued by 1800 companies from 55 countries, were quoted. Luxembourg is particularly strong in Euro-Deutschmark and Euro-French franc issues and is the home of Cedel, the clearing organization set up for international capital market transactions.

It has all the characteristics that are necessary for a successful financial centre: geographically well placed; good communications; multi-lingual community; guaranteed bank secrecy; holding company law which exempts companies from tax on dividend and interest income as well as capital gains; and a favourable tax regime in general. Nevertheless, Luxembourg's position as an onshore tax haven is its greatest asset. Barrett (1988, p. 92) points out:

> For example the EC Undertaking on Collective Investment in Transferable Securities (UCITS) regulations, which will come into force in October 1989, led to the number of funds in Luxembourg rising from 261 to 495 in calendar-year 1987 – representing some \$36 billion in total funds. The UCITS directive requires that only funds registered within the EC may be marketed inside the Community.

Although Luxembourg has established itself as an important financial centre over the last twenty years it is still cynically viewed by many as merely a booking and clearing centre, whereas the 'real' business is being undertaken in London and other major centres. It is expected to maintain its significance as a financial centre by concentrating more on private client business and investment banking as well as consolidating its position in the Euromarkets.

Amsterdam International finance emerged in Amsterdam in the sixteenth century concomitant with the growth of the substantial merchant fleet. Trade financing was well established there when King William I set up the Netherlands Trading Society in order to promote trade with the Dutch East Indies. The Netherlands, and Amsterdam in particular, has been an international centre of finance and trade for at least two centuries. 85 banks were operating in 1988 and of these, over 40 were foreign. Many entered this market in the late 1970s and early 1980s for some of the following reasons (Peat Marwick, 1984, pp. 53–5):

- the Netherlands has a comparatively large number of multinational companies (Shell, Unilever, Philips) and these can utilize the sophisticated technology-based services offered by international banks;
- because the country is geographically rather small, one bank office can deal with all that bank's Dutch business;
- holding companies operate under a favourable fiscal regime and many treaties exist to prevent double taxation;
- the Dutch guilder is a stable currency to invest in;
- general reasons relating to: foreign direct investment in the Netherlands; financing Dutch trade, entry to the capital markets, English as the main business language, etc.

The foreign banks primarily undertake high-level corporate banking and investment banking business. Of the 40 or so foreign banks operating in Amsterdam, 8 are Japanese. It was the two largest Swiss banks, Credit Suisse First Boston and Swiss Bank Corporation which were believed (Brown, 1988, p. 3) to be the main instigators of change in the Dutch capital market by lead managing issues along Euromarket rather than traditional domestic country lines.

156

Amsterdam's capital market ranks tenth in the world, but it has moved much more quickly than some of its larger competitors towards global trading in the shares of major companies. The Amsterdam Security Account System (ASAS) set up in 1980 makes markets in American and Japanese stocks. Foreign membership of the Amsterdam Stock Exchange (ASE) has been allowed since 1986 and various structural and regulatory reforms have taken place, aimed at improving the global position of the exchange and trying to entice back the 20 per cent or so dealings in Dutch stock that take place in London. In regard to the supply and demand for funds on the Dutch capital market, foreigners play a greater role in the demand for funds rather than supplying them, although as a proportion of the total neither amounts to more than 10 per cent. Both Amsterdam and London established listed options markets in 1978. The European Options Exchange (EOE) is LIFFE's main European competitor, being the sixth largest options exchange in the world with a daily turnover at least twice that of London.

Despite the international flavour of capital markets business in Amsterdam the stock exchange announced a major liberalization programme in May 1988. The new scheme will abolish the antiquated 'Van Camper' underwriting system under which the Dutch primary bond market operates. The new market will operate on the same lines as Euromarket practices. The general view, however, is that Amsterdam's capital market will have to liberalize further if it wants to maintain its competitive position against rival markets. Brown (1988) notes that, amongst other things, listing costs should be reduced and stamp duty, paid on all securities trades, should be abolished.

Other financial centres and 1992

In addition to the above major financial centres, various other European countries have sought to promote their capitals as developing centres aimed at providing a more limited range of services compared with their larger competitors. This section deals with developments in these centres.

Other European financial centres

Copenhagen Danish financial markets have been undergoing a gradual process of deregulation over the last two decades, with the final restrictions on inward and outward investment being lifted in 1985. The National (Central) Bank has also adopted more market-based controls which have helped to stimulate an increasingly competitive marketplace. The banking sector, however, is still dominated by domestic banks. There were only eight foreign banks in Copenhagen by mid-1987, and Bank of America pulled out in late 1986 because the securitization phenomenon had undermined its loan business (*Financial Times*, 1988b, p. 3). Talks about whether Copenhagen is an international financial centre have focused on stock exchange reforms and the country's large bond market.

In 1986 the Danish Parliament introduced stock exchange reforms which led to three important developments: an electronic commercial system; an electronic registration system; and liberalization of firms entering the market. The reforms aimed to make the Copenhagen exchange one of the most sophisticated in the world. Rostung (1987, p. 37) notes:

> Danish bankers disagree among themselves about the role the Copenhagen Stock Exchange will play after the introduction of the reforms. Some bankers think that after a few years Copenhagen will be able to compete with cities like Frankfurt as a financial centre ... The sceptics claim that Europe has absolutely no need for another financial centre; and that Copenhagen has too few products to offer anyway.

A distinct feature that Denmark and Copenhagen can offer is a very large bond market, about two-thirds the size of the Eurobond market. It is a very liquid market and about 60 per cent of outstanding bonds are mortgage bonds which are fixed-interest annuity loans. At the end of 1986 business volume in this market amounted to DKK 4449 billion, although only just over 3 per cent of this was traded on the Copenhagen exchange. Further exchange reforms could move more of this business towards the stock exchange.

In general, Copenhagen could well become the financial centre of the Nordic countries as long as it can exploit the opportunities provided by its current plan gradually to deregulate its financial markets. For example, from 1 October 1988 more liberal currency regulations were introduced which meant that there are no longer any restrictions on how to achieve financing via the Euromoney market. Other deregulation has freed activity relating to private bank accounts held abroad. During 1989 the stock exchange experienced fundamental changes in its dealing arrangements. In addition, it could be argued that, because the non-EC Nordic countries have no direct access to the ECU market, Denmark is the most sensible place for this market.

Although some commentators believe that Copenhagen's European look will be the most important ingredient of its future success as the major North European financial centre, it has also been suggested that the Danish centre is too small and restricted by too many regulations (Kanji, 1987, p. 36). Some believe that Stockholm is a 'more suitable' financial centre because it is less regulated and hosts more big international companies. Despite these views, Stockholm's presence as an important financial centre will continue to be limited because of the small number of foreign banks operating there.

Stockholm Foreign banks were not allowed to operate in Sweden until January 1986 when the government conferred charters on a dozen banks, two of which (French banks) have subsequently given notice that they intend to close down. The banking law precludes Swedish ownership of foreign banks operating in Sweden and also prohibits foreign banks from establishing branch offices. Foreign bank establishment is solely through wholly-owned subsidiaries or the setting up of consortium banks. The initial 12 foreign banks comprised 5 from France, 2 from the United States, 2 from Finland, 2 from Norway and 1 from the Netherlands. Only the two Finnish-owned banks provide traditional retail banking services, whereas the rest have concentrated on corporate banking activities. By 1988 the foreign banks had over 350 staff, and their assets constituted about 3 per cent of the total banking sector. As would be expected, a substantial proportion of the assets and liabilities of the foreign banks are denominated in foreign currencies, around 54 per cent in 1987, compared with 29 per cent of the total for all Swedish-owned commercial banks.

Foreign banks account for only 2 per cent of total bank lending. Their presence is most marked in the foreign-exchange market. In 1987 they accounted for around 12 per cent of its total business, although much of this was interbank dealing, and subsequently their share of dealing with commercial and industrial companies was considerably smaller. Given the short history and limited success of foreign bank activity in Sweden, it seems unlikely that the international flavour of banking activity will be enhanced by a flood of new entrants into Stockholm in the near future (Jochnick and Norman, 1988, p. 8).

Stockholm's position as the leading Nordic financial centre is more likely to be promoted by developments on the stock exchange (and to a lesser extent on the options exchange[6]), rather than by any rapid increase in foreign bank presence. Rydén (1988) notes that the proportion of trade conducted on the Stockholm Stock Exchange by foreign investors during the 1980s increased from around 4 per cent in 1980 to a maximum of nearly 12 per cent by the end of 1986. The corresponding figure for 1987 was 9 per cent but this proportion has drastically fallen since October 1987: it amounted to only 5 per cent of turnover in the second quarter of 1988. Despite this downturn, the stock exchange authorities have recently announced a series of developments which intend to make it 'one of the best national stock exchanges and a leading market place for trade in Swedish shares' (Ryden, 1988, p. 92).

In 1986 the exchange established guidelines for electronic trading and a new trading system – the Stockholm Automated Exchange (SAX) – was introduced during 1989. This will be supplemented by another automated system to deal with small trades taking place outside the stock exchange. By the end of 1990 it is expected that all shares will be traded on SAX and there will be a new automated registration system known as the Securities Register Centre. The present stock exchange·information system is also being updated. In addition to screen-based trading, plans are also under way to link Nordic stock exchanges so as to allow market information to be transferred between the four exchanges. Stockholm should be well equipped to meet the demands of international investors over the coming decade.

Sweden lifted its ban on the foreign ownership of Swedish banks, finance companies and stock brokerage firms, while also allowing foreign banks to open branches from 1 July 1990. The opening up of Sweden's long-protected financial sector to foreign competition is unlikely to witness a flood of foreign bank entrants if historical evidence is anything to go by. Nevertheless, foreign ownership of stockbroking firms could give Swedish firms a much needed capital boost and provide greater access to foreign investors. The change in legislation is clearly aimed at giving Swedish banks unfettered access to EC markets.

There are, however, two main factors that have limited the growth potential of the Stockholm market. Fristly, the turnover tax on bond, money market and share transactions. The turnover tax on shares made it cheaper for large investors to trade in Swedish stocks in London and New York than in Stockholm. Secondly, onerous foreign-exchange restrictions remain that deter foreign investors. The controversial turnover tax on the bond and money markets was abolished on 15 April 1990, and it is to be halved on share dealing and options from 1 January 1991. This, along with the abolition of the foreign-exchange restraint, should help to generate a more vibrant marketplace and would also promote Stockholm as the premier Nordic financial centre.

Brussels   Brussels is particularly European in its outlook as it is the home of the EC Commission, the European headquarters of NATO, and the base for many large international corporations. Although it is nowhere as big as London or Frankfurt, it has managed to attract many subsidiaries and branches of foreign banks and is fifth among European financial centres measured in terms of Eurocurrency deposits. In March 1988 there were 84 banks operating in Belgium of which 28 were subsidiaries and 31 branches of foreign banks. The Japanese (15) are most heavily represented in Belgium, followed by the French (11) and the Americans (8). All the foreign banks concentrate on doing wholesale and corporate business and they have contributed to the substantial increase in the size of the interbank market in recent years.

Belgium has a developed financial system and is ideally located in Europe, but nevertheless its financial system is relatively sluggish compared with other European financial centres. Shegog (1987) notes that the lack of innovation, high taxation and large government debt are regarded as the main explanations for the poor performance of Brussels as an international financial centre. The argument continues that unless a radical change of attitude takes place, Brussels will continue to lag behind.

Milan   Milan is one of the most heavily regulated international financial centres in Europe. Short-term international capital flows and investments such as bank deposits are subject to restrictions which are expected to be lifted by the end of 1990, although banking activities in general are heavily regulated. US and Japanese banks are based in Milan, because they can underwrite debt securities and (under various restrictions) equity securities as well. On the other hand, there are no plans to introduce any futures or options markets and hedging instruments are very limited.

There appear to be many official impediments to the development of new markets. A recent report (*Euromoney Supplement*, 1988, p. 8) states that foreign banks are selling their Italian branches because corporate lending is no longer profitable, mainly because the largest Italian corporations are so cash-rich that they rarely need to borrow. Those that have not pulled out are concentrating on merchant banking, such as commercial paper issues and investment management business, but there is very little M&A business. The foreigners are concentrating on niche markets.

The Milan stock exchange, the Borsa, is very small in relation to the domestic economy. There are only 200 listed companies and despite moves by the CONSOB (Commissione Nazionale per le Società e la Borsa), the exchange ruling body, to introduce new rules, share trading on the exchange is inefficient and antiquated. The market is also volatile, owing to a distinct lack of 'depth and transparency'. Around 70 per cent of all share trades are undertaken off the market by banks. The narrowness of the market can be illustrated by the fact that, of the 30 per cent of shares traded, the ten most traded stocks account for 50 per cent of all trades (the five largest companies account for 70 per cent of market capitalization) (Drury, 1989). The change in law proposed by the CONSOB would permit brokers to form joint-stock companies and to have banks as partners. Brokers argue that the reforms will result in a variety of conflicts of interest as banks participate in the underwriting of securities and finance most of the listed companies. Istituto per le Ricerca Sociale (IRS) (1988, p. 8) also found that over recent years the foreign sector, relative to other investors, has continued to 'withdraw' from the Italian capital markets; this could be attributable, however, to a decline in direct investments which would have little effect on the depth of the capital market. Many of the above features indicate that there is currently a de-internationalization trend in Milan.

Madrid The financial markets in Spain, and Madrid in particular, have been dramatically transformed since 1979 when foreign wholesale banks were allowed limited access to the Spanish marketplace. At first the law insisted on a minimum of three branches and only those who purchased troubled Spanish banks could go into the retail branch banking business. Of the 40 or so foreign banks doing business in Spain, and predominantly in Madrid, most originally sought to do business with Spain's large state-owned multinationals, concentrating on traditional wholesale corporate banking activities. By 1988, however, virtually all of these foreign operators had substantial retail operations and the Bank of Spain became so worried that it has stopped issuing licences to foreigners for the time being (Lascelles, 1988, p. 5).

The Madrid stock exchange (which accounts for approximately 75 per cent of total business), together with the small provincial exchanges, also faces a series of major legislative reforms which will no doubt improve its attractiveness to outside investors. A new Capital Markets Bill, Ley de Mercado de Capitales, was introduced in February 1988 and this was followed by a second barrage of legislation in April which was concerned with corporate law. The former introduced various innovations which aim to link by computer the markets of Madrid, Barcelona, Bilbao and Valencia by setting up a continuous and simultaneous trading system. There will also be provision for an electronic book-keeping system for automatic settlements: the *modus operandi* of the Madrid and other exchanges will be considerably transformed as will the role of '*agentes*' that currently operate on the exchange floor. By late 1989 outsiders were permitted to set up as agency brokers or integrated securities houses and were able to underwrite issues and trade on their own account. Members still have monopoly access to the floor of the exchange but they can now be part-owned (30 per cent) by outsiders.

Burns (1988, p. 5) suggests that the eventual outcome is '... unlikely to be more than a dozen market firms, the majority of these will have to look to partnerships and most of the new tie-ups willl be international ones'. The April 1988 company law legislation introduced provisions that allowed companies for the first time to issue non-voting shares; abolished a procedure whereby existing shareholders had preferential rights to new issues; and also increased the number of companies' accounts subject to professional audit. This legislation is in place to bring Spain's corporate law into line with that of other EC countries by 1992.

No doubt the above reforms are partly aimed to maintain the considerable growth of foreign investors on the exchange as well as trying to tempt Spanish companies to obtain listings. At the beginning of 1987 only 60 of Spain's top 500 firms were listed on the market, and the volume of trading amounted to only 5.4 per cent of gross domestic product (Smith, 1987, p. 6). To date it is estimated that no more than 15 per cent of Spanish companies have any listing at all. Foreign investors accounted for

161

approximately 50 per cent of total stock market transactions by the end of 1989, compared with 15 per cent in 1984. It is hoped that further development of the screen-based dealing system known as the Continuous Automated Trading System (CATS), which began in the summer of 1989 and currently quotes 33 stocks, will help to boost business further.

The above features indicate that Spanish capital and banking markets are changing rapidly and that the presence of international operations is also markedly increasing. Despite the Bank of Spain placing a moratorium on new bank licences to foreigners, it seems likely that Madrid will continue to develop its international character and will no doubt become a much more important financial centre.

Smaller financial centres

In addition to the above, there are also a range of much smaller financial centres that generally do not offer a broad range of servies but provide certain facilities, such as tax-free zones, to encourage commercial and financial activity. These would include Cyprus, Malta, Ireland, Liechtenstein, Monaco and Andorra. Cyprus offers various tax incentives and exemptions are available to branches of foreign institutions and to Cyprus-based branches of foreign banks. Since 1987 the Maltese government has been constructing a system of incentives for foreign companies to locate in Malta and during 1988 it enacted legislation to turn the island into an offshore centre. The main benefits offered to offshore businesses include: a special rate of income tax (5 per cent on chargeable income); exemption from all exchange controls, stamp duties and customs duty; special treatment with regard to bank regulation.

In 1987 the Irish government announced plans to establish Dublin as an international financial centre. By offering attractive tax rates, low rental values and inexpensive telecommunications links Dublin could provide a secondary or ancillary service to firms operating in London, New York and Tokyo. A 27-acre site in the city's dockland was earmarked as a commercial and residential development site, the focus of which will be the International Financial Services Centre (IFSC). The government originally hoped that 7500 jobs would be created in the five years following 1987, although current projections suggest that half that number is a more realistic target. The IFSC seeks to develop international banking business post-1992 as well as international fund management and insurance business.

Liechtenstein has already an international reputation for its favourable tax system as well as its stringent banking secrecy laws. Monaco and Andorra offer similar advantages, such as no personal income tax, low death duties and so on. The latter offers more favourable operating conditions but it is limited from becoming a 'utopian' tax haven because of the constraints imposed by its governors, the President of France and the Spanish Bishop of Urgel.

Why host an international financial centre?

From recent trends and developments in the financial capitals in Europe there does appear to be a unanimous presumption that developing an international financial centre is inherently a 'good thing' and must benefit the economy in some way. There is, however, little statistical support for this presumption; most of the evidence is either theoretical or anecdotal. A general view would be that a successful financial centre should help improve the balance of payments and also add to government tax

162

revenues. It should provide substantial direct and indirect employment effects as well as substantial welfare gains from the efficient trade in international financial services. In addition, because trade in financial products is relatively unhindered in many of these centres, various economies of scale should be earned at the level of the individual firm, market and 'centre as a whole'.

An international financial centre should provide the benefits of wide and deep financial markets with narrow bid and offer prices. Allocative efficiency gains should also be high. The disadvantages of hosting an international financial centre relate to concentration; the concentration of population and high income earners in one area may lead to pressure on house prices, transport systems and so on. Macroeconomic policy and monetary policy in particular may be made less effective if the influence of international capital flows makes the demand for money endogenous. These flows may also have a perverse effect on interest and exchange rate levels and relativities, and may also cause periodic overshooting in the markets. Many of the above costs, however, would accrue in centres of dense population or in small open economies whether they hosted an international financial centre or not. As such international financial centres are generally viewed as being beneficial to economies as a whole.

General implications of 1992

As barriers to trade and establishment in banking and financial services continue to be dismantled throughout the 1990s, London seems in the best position to confirm its role as the major financial centre in Europe. Certain doubts, however, have arisen about London's future because of the proposed EC treatment of non-EC banks as encapsulated in the Commission's Second Banking Co-ordination Directive. The legislation does not make it clear whether non-EC banks would benefit from the planned single market in financial services, even if they were already licensed to operate in an EC member country (see also Chapter 4). The unofficial line (*Financial Times*, 1988c) is that the Community would wish to negotiate some form of bilateral agreement with the non-EC banks' governments to require reciprocal treatment for EC banks. 'Reciprocal', however, will not mean 'identical', the general view being that non-EC financial services law should not discriminate unfairly against EC institutions.

This attitude towards the reciprocity issue has already raised 'hackles' in the City of London as some view it as a major drawback in maintaining London's comparative advantage amongst EC capitals as an international financial centre (*Financial Times*, 1988d). The second banking directive has made it clear that licences will not be granted to non-EC banks unless their home country allows the licensing of EC banks. This would effectively prevent new, third-country (non-EC member) banks from coming to the EC (and London in particular). It may also involve the revoking of already established licences. A concern in the City is that operators do not want to see London penalized if, for example, a Greek bank is refused a licence to operate in Japan. London does not want Brussels telling it who can do business in the City. Recent comments made by senior EC trade officials (*Financial Times*, 1988e) have sought to allay fears by stating that narrow and rigid reciprocity agreements will not be required and 'national treatment' will prevail.

Despite this possible drawback there does not appear to be any viable European alternative to London: Blanden (1988, p. 66) suggests that '... deregulating Paris may be the only possible starter – but there may be a danger that markets now centred in London will tend to move back to their countries of origin'. This was illustrated by the October 1988 decision by Morgan Stanley International to transfer the Swiss franc warrant and convertible bond trading team from London to Zurich. Excessive supervisory re-regulation has been cited as the main impetus which could generate such a trend (Gardener and Molyneux, 1989).

On the other hand, EC centres that have developed through operating 'lax' regimes will also be affected by the 1992 proposals. The harmonization of tax treatment throughout the EC would have a deleterious effect on Luxembourg's position as a major financial centre, but the majority of other EC centres, especially Frankfurt, would benefit from such developments. Non-EC financial centres may seek to offer tax and other operating conditions that are more favourable than those of their EC competitors in order to maintain some form of comparative advantage. The increased uniformity of operating conditions within the EC may well help to consolidate the importance of already well-established centres such as Zurich, and to a lesser extent Stockholm, and may also promote the financial-centre aspirations of places as diverse as Cyprus, Malta and Liechtenstein.

Conclusion

The economic and political significance of financial centres is inextricably linked to the growth of the financial services industry and to the benefits which this provides for the economy as a whole. We have seen that there are many factors that determine the development of such centres, of which the main ingredients appear to be a liberal attitude towards regulation, a stable political environment, and the ability to adapt to change. The growth of financial centres has been sustained largely from advantages gleaned from various types of economies of scale. It appears that in the run-up to 1992 London will continue to maintain its position as the dominant international financial centre in the European time zone. Other European centres such as Paris and Frankfurt are its nearest rivals, although operating conditions in the latter, especially tax treatment on securities business, will have to be liberalized if it is to keep up with the leaders. Switzerland will continue to consolidate its position as by far the most important investment management centre, and Luxembourg could be severely disadvantaged by the EC 1992 tax harmonization proposals. Overall, the uniform regulatory frameworks that may eventually be established after 1992 could well encourage markets operating in London (and other centres) to move back to their European countries of origin – an example is the LIFFE Bund futures market – as well as the development of new financial centres in such places as Cyprus and Malta.

Notes

1. Next comes Paris ($26 billion), Amsterdam ($16 billion) and Brussels ($13 billion). No figures are available for Frankfurt because the Bundesbank was unable to participate in the survey for constitutional reasons.
2. The study was undertaken by Scrimgeour Vickers (owned by Citicorp) in December 1988.
3. It could also be argued that the decision of LIFFE on 29 September 1988 to start trading in

German government bond futures also put pressure on German authorities to establish quickly a futures and options exchange.

4. In the summer of 1987 the Parisian stock exchange lost FFr 614 million of its own reserve funds on the MATIF.

5. A fiduciary transaction is a special Swiss phenomenon: it relates to investments in credits made by a bank in its own name but on account and risk of the customer. The customer bears all the risk, earns the full profit and pays the bank a commission for its troubles. They are OBS items, and some estimates suggest they account for almost 33 per cent of the consolidated balance sheets of all Swiss banks.

6. The Swedish Options and Futures Exchange closed in February 1989. Taxation and an inefficient trading system based on electronic transfers between traders are seen as the main reasons for closure. On the other hand, the rival Option Market Fondkommission remains very active.

References

Bagehot, Walter 1873 (1978), *Lombard Street, The Collected Works of Walter Bagehot* (ed. N. St. John Stevas) vol. 9 (London: *Economist*), pp. 63–4.

Bank for International Settlements (1988), *58th Annual Report* (Basle: BIS).

Bank of England Quarterly Bulletin (1988), vol. 28, no. 1, (February).

Barrett, Matthew (1988), 'Feather-footed shuffle in the Grand Duchy', *Euromoney*, (July), pp. 91–4.

Beusch-Liggenstorfer, Christine (1987), 'International banking centres', *Butterworth Journal of International Banking and Financial Law*, vol. 2, no. 5, (December), pp. 230–4.

Blanden, Michael (1987), 'Fortress Luxembourg', *The Banker*, vol. 137, no. 741, (November) pp. 33–5.

Blanden, Michael (1988), 'Can London really compete?', *The Banker*, vol. 138, no. 753, (November), pp. 65–6.

Bonelli, Franco (1971), *La crisi del 1907: una tappa dello sviluppo industriale in Italia* (Turin: Einaudi).

Braillard, Phillipe (1987), *La Place Financière Suisse* (Geneva: Georg).

Brown, David A. (1988), 'Capital markets in the throes of great chance', *Financial Times Survey on Netherlands Banking*, (30 June), p. 3.

Burns, Tom (1988), 'Stock markets face a series of major legislative reforms – a watershed year', *Financial Times Special Survey on Spanish Banking*, (23 June), p. 5.

Commission of the European Communities (1988), 'Proposal for a Second Council Directive on the co-ordination of laws, regulations and administrative provisions related to the taking-up and pursuit of the business of credit institutions and Amending Directive 77/780/EEC' COM (87) 715 Final, 16 February (Brussels: Commission of the European Communities).

Drury, Barbara (1989), 'Italians hasten slowly', *Investors Chronicle*, vol. 90, no. 1141, pp. 24–5.

Dullforce, W. (1987), 'Foreign influence is confirmed', *Swiss Banking: Financial Times Survey*, (14 December), p. 4.

Economists Advisory Group (1984), *City 2000: The Future of London as an International Financial Centre* (London: Lafferty Publications).

Euromoney Corporate Finance Supplement (1988), 'West Germany: guarding her own', (January), pp. 8–10.

Euromoney Supplement (1987), 'European stock exchanges', (August).

Euromoney Supplement (1988), 'Italy – joining the world's markets' (April).

Financial Times (1988a), UK Banking Survey Part 2, 'Investment banking was shaken by the crash', (26 September) p. 40.

Financial Times (1988b), Denmark: Special Survey, 'Setback on bond yields', (9 November) p. iii.

Financial Times (1988c), 'Call to limit banks' access to EC market', (13 July) pp. 1 and 44.

Financial Times (1988d) 'Reciprocity in Financial Services', Editorial, (12 July) p. 22.

Financial Times (1988e) 'EC to apply reciprocity in financial services', (12 October) p. 7.

Gardener, E. P. M. and Molyneux, P. (1989), 'Banking regulation in the UK – converging towards complexity', *Banking World*, vol. 7, no. 2, (February), pp. 35–7.

165

Graham, George (1988), 'Sicavs prepare for a wider market', *Financial Times Survey of French Banking*, (10 November), p. iv.

Gunn, John (1988), 'London's future as a financial centre', *Treasurers Yearbook 1988*, (London: Association of Corporate Treasurers), pp. 33–6.

Iklé, Max (1972), *Switzerland: an International Banking and Finance Centre*, (Strondsburg: Dowden, Hutchinson, and Ross Inc.).

Istituto per la Ricerca Sociale (1988), *The First Report on the Italian Stock Market* (Milan: IRS).

Jeancourt-Galignani, Antoine (1988), 'French aspirations for Paris as a financial centre', *The Treasurer*, vol. 10, no. 11, (December). pp. 7–9.

Jocknick af Kerstin and Norman, Peter (1988), 'Foreign banks in Sweden', *Sveriges Riksbank Quarterly Review*, no. 2, pp. 26–33.

Jones, Colin (1988a), 'Time to take a stormy role – Frankfurt as a financial centre', *The Bank* vol. 138, no. 751, (September), pp. 49–57.

Jones, R. (1988b), 'Deutsche bank calls the tune', *Euromoney Supplement on German Finance and Industry*, (July), pp. 23–7.

Kanji, Shireen (1987), 'A new start?', *The Banker*, vol. 137, no. 742, (December), pp. 36–42.

Kindleberger, Charles P. (1984), *A Financial History of Western Europe* (London: George Allen and Unwin).

Large, Andrew (1988), 'Foreign banks discreet bourgeoisie', *The Banker*, vol. 138, no. 746, (April), p. 35.

Lascelles, David (1988), 'Foreign banks – moratorium halts the 'inrush'', *Financial Times Special Survey on Spanish Banking*, 23 (June), p. 5.

Lyon, Simon (1988), 'Still worth staying', *The Banker*, vol. 138, no. 753, (November), p. 82.

McDougall, R. (1988), 'Après le déluge', *The Banker*, vol. 138, no. 746, (April), pp. 34–47.

McMahon, Kit (1988), 'London as a financial centre – problems and opportunities', *The Treasurers Yearbook 1988*, (London: Association of Corporate Treasurers), pp. 29–32.

Morgenstern, Oscar (1959), *International Transactions and Business Cycles* (Princeton NJ: Princeton University Press), pp. 128–37.

Pearson, C. (1987), 'The 'big three' stage a comeback as issuing volume falls', *Swiss Banking, Financial Times Survey*, (14 December), p. 6.

Peat Marwick (1984), *Banking in the Netherlands* (Amsterdam: Peat Marwick Nederland).

Peat Marwick McLintock (1988), *Banking in the United Kingdom* (London: Peat Marwick McLintock).

Rambosson, Jacques (1988), 'The French financial revolution', *The Treasurer*, vol. 10, no. 11, (December), pp. 10–13 and 23.

Rostung, Henning (1987), 'Copenhagen aims to be an international centre', *Banking World*, (April), p. 37.

Rydén, Bengt (1988), 'The Stockholm Stock Exchange. Well equipped for the future', *Skandinaviska Enskilda Banken Quarterly Review*, vol. 4, pp. 92–5.

Schuster, Leo (1987), 'The role of Swiss banks in international finance', *IEF Research Papers in Banking and Finance* RP 87/7 (Bangor: Institute of European Finance).

Shale, T. (1989), 'Frankfurt trembles for its future', *Euromoney*, (March), pp. 77 and 80–84.

Shegog, Andrew (1987), 'Boom leaves Brussels behind', *Euromoney*, (February), pp. 137–43.

Simonian, Haig (1988), 'West German Banking 3', *Financial Times Special Survey*, Swiss influence plan for new exchange, (13 July) pp. iii–iv.

Smith, Diana (1987), 'Banking records as economy expands', *Financial Times Special Survey on Spanish Banking and Finance*, (17 July), p. 6.

Von Rosen, Rudigir (1988), 'The German Stock Exchanges Building for the Future: German finance and industry', *Euromoney Supplement*, (July).

Wilson, Neil (1988), 'Local heroes', *The Banker*, vol. 138, no. 753, (November), pp. 66–74.

Chapter ten
Securities markets and business

Introduction

Earlier chapters have already confirmed the growing orientation by European banks towards securities markets and related business. Securitization is one generic label for this trend, but it only depicts a part of the story. Continental universal banks, for example, have always been active in securities markets. And nowadays many major European countries are becoming more strongly market-orientated as market-based intermediation continues to grow, often at the apparent expense of traditional, institution-based intermediation. Even in European retail banking, there is also a growing strategic emphasis on capital market products. We saw in Chapter 6, for example, that 'unitization' – the linking of deposit and other facilities to unit trusts – is expanding rapidly. This chapter will focus on securities markets and securities business in Europe. It builds on the preceding chapter by focusing more specifically on particular markets and related business. Chapter 11 will go on to examine investment banking in Europe.

Capital markets

Historical perspective and the economic role of stock exchanges
The development of stock exchanges and the wider capital market is an important process in the evolution of all financial system. In a 'logical historical-order model' of financial development (Revell, 1973, pp. 24–6) financial markets appear at a comparatively early stage. Markets facilitate the process of direct finance, the movement of funds from investors (surplus units) to borrowers and entrepreneurs (deficit units). Early models of financial development implied that the emergence and subsequent evolution of financial intermediaries (indirect finance) alongside financial markets was the highest, *extant* state of financial development. The Rybczinski (1985) model, on the other hand, implies that increasing breadth and efficiency within modern financial markets may lead to a growing disintermediation of banks and other financial intermediaries. 'Strongly market-orientated' financial systems, like those of the United States and the United Kingdom, are characterized *inter alia* by correspondingly large capital markets. Growing market-based intermediation (securitization) is a characteristic of strongly market-orientated systems.

Securities markets have played an important part in the development of the British financial system. The evolution of the Stock Exchange in London – The International

Stock Exchange of the United Kingdom and the Republic of Ireland (ISE), formerly the London Stock Exchange – is intimately linked to government finances and the rise of private corporate finance (Briston, 1975). In many European countries the coming of the railroad and its associated financing needs were important stimulants (Kindleberger, 1984) to joint-stock company formations; this was certainly the case in countries like Sweden and France. In Germany, joint-stock companies were rare before 1850, but once again the railroad was an important factor. Nevertheless, the German historical experience in this respect is quite different from that of the United Kingdom and France. In Germany the large banks maintained particularly close relationships with large-scale industry. A combination of banking finance and ploughed-back profits provided German industry with its capital. One result was that the volume of industrial financial paper in a city like Frankfurt was comparatively small.

It is possible to group the historical evolution of the world's equity markets into three kinds: private-type, banking-type and state-controlled (see Jacquillet in George and Giddy, 1983, p. 3). The UK and US markets typify the private type of organization, and this general 'model' is sometimes referred to as a 'market-orientated, capital market' or Anglo-Saxon system. In the banking-type system, the market is dominated by the banks. Germany is an archetypal example, and this model is sometimes called a 'bank-orientated capital market' system (see Chapter 7). State-controlled markets are invariably the pattern for Latin and some major European stock markets. The French equity market has been largely state-controlled until the recent reforms.

These models are reflective in part of different policy views about the economic usefulness and role of stock exchanges. The 'Anglo-Saxon model' has been characterized by a growing acceptance of the benefits of the free enterprise system, but this was not always the case. Industrial-banking links in Britain were very strong during the eighteenth and nineteenth centuries (see Edwards, 1987, p. 31). Since this period, these close links between the banks and industry have been weakened compared with more authoritarian regimes, like those in Germany and, to a lesser extent, France and Spain.

Alongside the many strong supporters of the economic usefulness of stock exchanges there have been severe critics; Keynes (1936, pp. 159–60) was one of them. In recent years others (Edwards, 1987) have questioned the Anglo-Saxon view that a free enterprise ethos, translated into a strongly committed policy of deregulation on stock exchanges, will improve the allocative functions of capital markets. These more critical views invariably embody a critique of the role of banks in industrial development; the post-war economic records of Germany and Japan are often cited as evidence of the economic advantages of their closer bank-industry linkages (see also Chapter 7).

A comparative overview
In the previous chapter, Table 9.4 compared European exchanges at the end of 1987. A major structural and historical difference between Continental systems and that of the United Kingdom has been that, unlike the United Kingdom, Continental countries have markets of considerable importance in several major cities. In West Germany, for example, there are eight stock exchanges, located in Frankfurt, Düsseldorf, Münich, Stuttgart, Hamburg, West Berlin, Hanover and Bremen. Smaller European countries

Table 10.1   European stock market performance (%)

Market	Sept 1982 low to Dec 1982	Calendar 1984	Calendar 1985	Calendar 1986	Sept 1982 low to end 1986
Belgium	+12.1	+16.3	+36.4	+39.1	+147.4
Denmark	+17.9	−21.9	+41.5	−18.9	+5.7
France	+6.8	+16.4	+45.7	+49.7	+171.1
Germany	+18.2	+8.3	+76.1	+4.9	+136.5
Italy	+12.0	+19.2	+100.3	+58.1	+322.8
Netherlands	+17.1	+18.0	+ 40.6	+8.8	+111.4
Norway	+5.4	+29.1	+37.1	−9.1	+69.6
Spain	+1.2	+40.7	+35.3	+108.3	+301.3
Sweden (From 16.9.80)	+157.2	−6.3	+28.3	+41.5	+337.5
Switzerland	+21.6	+0.5	+52.5	+0.2	+86.7
UK	+24.5	+25.3	+19.7	+22.3	+128.4
World comparisons					
Japan	+17.0	+16.0	+13.6	+39.7	+115.4
US	+34.7	−4.3	+28.4	+22.3	+102.4

Source: Davies (1987, p. 4)

tend to have a single dominant stock exchange; even in larger countries where there are several exchanges, however, there is invariably a dominant, leading one.

We saw in the previous chapter that the rapid growth of international securities markets has stimulated fundamental changes in most European stock exchanges. Exchanges like the Milan Borsa have installed the latest technology in order to modernize traditional trading systems. Exchanges across Europe are modernizing their outdated systems in order to cope with the growth in equity trading. Since the ending of foreign-exchange controls in the late 1970s and the concomitant, rapid development of communications technology, fund managers across the globe have increasingly 'internationalized' their portfolios. Nevertheless, foreign direct investment still only comprises a small proportion of total stock market capitalization in Europe (see *Euromoney*, 1987, p. 2).

International equity flows in major European countries increased markedly during 1986 (see Davies, 1987, p. 3). In Continental Europe better-known markets – like those of Germany, the Netherlands and Switzerland – were among the first to feel this surge of new internationally-orientated activity by fund managers. Other major European centres soon felt the pressures of international demand. France has experienced massive inflows of foreign money since 1985; Italy and Spain have also received similar huge inflows. These various developments helped contribute to the differential performance of capital markets throughout Europe. Markets worldwide also experienced a strong bull-run from the early 1980s up to October 1987.

The comparative performances of European stock markets are summarized in Table 10.1, which shows that France, Germany, Italy, Spain and Sweden have experienced particularly high growth. The securities markets in other European countries, like Portugal, are also burgeoning. Many European exchanges have found it difficult to cope with the huge increase in securities trading. Particular areas of difficulty include regulation and settlement procedures. Investors have also been deterred from some markets by local taxes and ceilings on foreign ownership. Only London, New York and Tokyo have so far developed the capabilities to capitalize on the equity boom in Europe.

Exchange reforms

The International Stock Exchange of the United Kingdom and the Republic of Ireland (ISE) has the distinction of being the most rapidly changing exchange in Europe. More major changes occurred in the London market during the 1980s than at any other time in the preceding two centuries. Walmsley (1988, p. 33) has put these changes into perspective:

> In US terms, it is as if Glass-Steagall had been abolished, Mayday took place, the SEC were set up, primary dealerships set up in the government bond market, NASDAQ was introduced, most securities houses were sold to foreign banks, the NYSE merged into an international exchange and the trading floor abolished – all in the space of three years.

Probably no other major financial centre has initiated the scale and kind of changes experienced in London since the start of the 1980s. The reforms were designed to help make London a truly International Stock Exchange. Table 10.2 shows the market value of securities listed on the ISE. On 31 March 1989 there were 388 ISE member firms.

The four major markets in the ISE are international equities, UK domestic equities, traded options, and gilts (Davies, 1987). All these markets have grown in size and liquidity since Big Bang. The Exchange's Foreign Equity Market Committee plans to make London the leading market in the world for trading in international equity and equity-related instruments. Technology figures highly in plans to develop London, one indication of its key role is that the ISE is the first major exchange to move from a trading floor to a screen-based market.

Big Bang brought new players into all the major market segments of the ISE and the London market now has the longest opening hours in Europe. London's Traded Options Market is currently the third largest such market outside the United States. The comparatively high yield on UK gilts has attracted Japanese investors, who are

Table 10.2 Market value of securities listed on the ISE (US$ bn).

Official list	As at 31 March 1989		As at 31 March 1988	
	Number of securities	Market value	Number of securities	Market value
British funds	119	137.2	126	151.2
Other fixed interest	4,321	203.1	3,982	153.0
Equities: UK and Irish	1,987	458.3	2,013	380.7
Equities: overseas	673	1,062.5	635	742.4
Total	7,100	1,861.1	6,756	1,427.3
USM	450	9.2	422	6.7
Third Market	69	0.6	43	0.3
Total capitalisation	7,619	1,870.9	7,221	1,434.3

Source: ISE Fact Card.

diversifying into gilts from UK T-bonds. There is little doubt that the increased turnover in the London market has been stimulated partly by the deregulation-induced, competitive cuts in transactions costs. Combined dealing costs have been slashed by around 50 per cent (see *Euromoney*, 1987, p. 8).

Chapter 9 emphasized that London is not the only major European stock exchange to have experienced important reforms and changes during recent years. Smaller (but still significant) 'Bangs' have been exploding throughout Europe. Paris has set out to challenge world markets and the new reforms (especially since 1985) have been styled 'France's financial revolution'. These reforms are designed to establish Paris as Continental Europe's leading financial centre, and to restrict the growing European dominance of London. Privatization initiatives led to a policy of denationalization up to 1988. This is a marked contrast to the policy of 'Gaullist France'. The privatization programme has brought millions of new investors on to the French market. Major groups like Saint-Gobain, Paribas and Sogenal have been sold off to the public. President Mitterrand was re-elected in May 1988 and has made it clear that there will be no more privatizations (or nationalizations) during the next five years. In addition, rapid monetary deregulation since 1984 has led to the almost complete abolition of exchange controls and the abandonment of direct credit control (*encadrement du crédit*) for monitoring money growth. A sign of the increasing competition in the Paris markets has been the failure, by the beginning of 1990, of three Paris brokers. Allowing the entry of new foreigners into the market, the abolition of fixed commissions and the introduction of market-making have all boosted competition.

The West German exchanges are dominated by the country's biggest banks and only around 50 per cent of the trade in shares is effected on the floor of the exchanges. The West German approach to deregulation and innovation has been more conservative than that in London or Paris. Despite the occasional criticism about being excessively parochial, various changes are taking place to strengthen the efficiency of West Germany's stock exchanges (Von Rosen, 1987). These reforms are designed to ensure that Germany becomes one of the three or four leading financial centres of the world and this ambition is further helped by the stability and strength of the Deutschmark which has made it a major investment, reserve and transactions currency.

Despite the comparatively healthy volume of foreign equity and bond stocks listed and traded on the German stock exchanges, there has been increasing German concern at the drift of equity business abroad, especially to London. It is often easier to trade a large amount of well-known stock, like Siemens, in London than in Frankfurt. Competition from London and the comparatively low level of domestic share buying, which has led to an increasing reliance on foreigners, have prompted increasing recognition of the need for reforms. The role played by equities in German corporate finance is not improved through the seeming complexities of the country's stock exchange system.

The present reforms focus on modernizing spot trading in shares and securities and the creation of a German futures exchange. A heavy investment in technology is planned in order to extend the depth of the market for each individual security. Although the universal banking system dominates the German stock exchanges, there is a clear trend towards a loosening of the link between industry and the banks. Nevertheless, their traditional dominance of the exchanges has given German banks enormous placing power and related expertise, and the decision by the 'Big Three' banks to set up their own screen-based trading system, Ibis, as described in Chapter 9, will help to consolidate their position in the market.

The Swiss are adopting a cautious view towards the financial revolution in the world's securities markets. Although Swiss capital markets have maintained their international status, the equity market in Switzerland is a comparative backwater. Switzerland has apparently lost out on the growth of retail equity ownership seen in the United Kingdom, France and the United States. Black Monday also shook the Swiss market badly: a market that rose by only 11 per cent in the first eight months of 1987 had dropped by 35 per cent by the end of December.

The Swiss have been spurred to innovate under the pressure of international competition. In January 1986 the authorities announced preferential commission rates on transactions in excess of SwFr 2 million. There is a growing recognition of the need for greater market transparency. Increasing concern has also been shown about stamp duty. Switzerland's three leading bourses – Zurich, Geneva and Basle – have been stimulated into working together for greater technological integration. We have already referred several times to the launch in early 1988 of SOFFEX, which is a market for options and financial futures. It is the first, fully automated, computer-based options and futures exchange in the world (see Chapter 9).

The Dutch have made it clear that they are prepared to innovate in order to boost Amsterdam's status internationally. In early 1986 the guilder bond market was freed, allowing FRNs, CDs, bullet bonds and CP. In early 1988 the Ministry of Finance announced that zero coupons and MTNs (medium-term notes) were also to be allowed. With over three centuries of trading to its credit, the ASE lays claim to be one of the most international and innovative of the Continental markets. Nevertheless, Amsterdam has also had to respond to increasing competition from London. Commissions on trades have been reduced, the AIM (Amsterdam inter-professional market) was introduced to allow direct trading between institutions, and corporate tax has been reduced. The ASE has grown rapidly in sophistication. It is automating increasingly, but has retained its central trading floor. One of the strengths of the ASE is that it is the principal market for government bonds in the Netherlands. In 1987 bond trading on the ASE overtook share trading for the first time since 1983.

Italy is opening up its financial markets in preparation for 1992. Nevertheless, its stock markets are in clear need of innovation and new regulations if they are to be competitive internationally. Lack of competition and skilled investors on the Milan Borsa has led to stagnation and an equities glut (see MacLeod, 1987, p. 2). Insider trading is still legal in Italy. The settlements system is inefficient: six-month delays are not uncommon. In 1985 CONSOB prepared a global project for reform which was presented in April 1987. The main objectives of the reforms (IRS, 1988) are to concentrate trading on the exchange floor and to regulate intermediaries. This new environment will lead to a revision of negotiation techniques in the market and stock-price fixing.

All exchanges throughout Western Europe are responding to the pressures of international competition. Other countries – including Spain, Austria, Scandinavia and Portugal – are modernizing their exchanges and trading methods. Within the next three to four years the Spanish market is expected to match the sophistication of the leading developed markets in Europe. The Portuguese market has even further to go, but the Lisbon and Oporto exchanges are learning fast. The Austrian government embarked on a privatization programme in late 1987. The Nordic exchanges are small, and Stockholm (the largest) still uses an auction system. The Swedish government has recently abandoned the turnover tax payable on the trading of bonds and equities. Within the EC, there is growing talk of linking the major exchanges throughout the Community. Technology will play an increasing role within Europe in both the management and delivery of capital market products.

Securities business

New issues and trading

During 1988 most European exchanges outperformed the ISE. A recent survey (Wilkinson, 1988) showed that buoyant growth and activity in M&A allowed some Continental exchanges to exceed their pre-crash peaks, whilst London only reached 25 per cent below its October 1987 level. Despite the setbacks of 1987, European stock markets generally have experienced high new issue and trading activity since the early 1980s. Table 10.1 confirmed the good performances achieved from 1982. Privatization and large inflows of foreign money have boosted expectations of continuing high new issues and trading activity.

Recent statistics on new issues activity confirm the general upward trend. In Spain, for example, new companies have recently been coming to the market at the rate of two a month. The French privatization programme boosted share ownership up to 9.5 million shareholders by the end of 1987. Even in West Germany the 'cult of the equity' is beginning to strengthen (Jones, 1988). Another important stimulant has been the ageing population in most European countries, with their increasing demands for pension and contractual savings products already encouraging a more performance-orientated investment culture. A recent forecast (Arthur Andersen, 1989, p. xiii) is that European equity markets are expected to show growth in capitalization and turnover of 10–15 per cent per year over the years to 1992. This is in contrast with the 30 per cent a year average growth over 1984–7.

New issues and trading structures reflect the structural and related characteristics of different stock markets. In London company securities are usually issued with the help of a 'team' that includes a merchant bank and a stockbroker. This team manages the new issue and arranges the underwriting. A specified portion of shares issued must be made available to dealers in order to ensure market liquidity. In France a single *agent de change* (*société de bourses* from 1988) is responsible for a new equity issue. The *agent de change* sets the issue price, and placement is carried out by the *agent* and the banks. The banks in Germany manage new equity and bond issues and are responsible for setting up underwriting groups. The company and the bank determine by negotiation the price for equities, which cannot be issued below their nominal value.

Equity and bond issues are again underwritten and managed by banks in the Netherlands. Banks can take over or guarantee the entire issue. In Italy the CONSOB has laid down new procedures for the placement and public offer of bonds, equities and stakes in public banks; the main requirement of the new regulations is the issuing of a prospectus and the advertising of public offers.

173

As we have seen, trading structures have recently been reformed in major markets like London. The London gilt-edged market now operates along similar lines to the US government bond market. GEMMs (gilt-edged market-makers) act as primary dealers and make markets in government stocks. Whereas Big Bang in London witnessed the US invasion, 1988 saw the Japanese invasion of the UK gilts market with the arrival in the market of Nomura and Daiwa Securities. Equities in London are now dealt through competing market-makers, who are required to make continuous markets in the stocks in which they deal throughout the daily quote period. Margin trading in London is much more limited than in the United States.

Stock borrowing is allowed in London for market-makers only, and must be conducted through the recognized money brokers. Borrowing and lending of government shares and equities is monitored closely by the Bank of England. Although stock borrowing is prohibited in France (except through the Contango System), margin trading is permitted by domestic and foreign investors. In order to trade in margins, a coverage is required of 20 per cent cash in Treasury bonds, 25 per cent in French bonds or in gold and 40 per cent in shares. Margin trading is not allowed in West Germany, except in exceptional circumstances. Under Dutch law, securities may not be purchased with borrowed money, but limited margin trading is possible as securities may be used to secure a loan. Margin trading is allowed in countries like Sweden, Denmark and Switzerland. There is no margin trading in Luxembourg and Portugal.

The process of innovation in equity markets has not been so extensive as in the bond markets, especially the Eurobond market. Nevertheless, there have been several innovations in recent years and these include floating-rate preferred stock, equity commitment and contract notes, puttable equity, equity whose dividend is linked to the performance of key subsidiaries, and convertible exchangeable preferred stock (convertible into equity, exchangeable into debt). US investment banks and securities houses have been important innovators in these kinds of instruments throughout the 1980s. The rise of the Euroequity market has been one of the important developments for many stock exchanges during the 1980s. This is more a change in the trading structure of the market, rather than the development of a new form of equity.

Rise of the Euroequity

The development of international equities, or Euroequities, may be viewed in many respects as the next logical step after the development of the Eurobond market. The growth of the international equity market has been explosive during the 1980s. In 1986 almost $12 billion was raised through international, publicly underwritten equity issues. This was a 300 per cent increase over the corresponding 1985 issue volume (see *Euromoney*, 1987, p. 1). The breakthrough in the market probably took place in 1985 with various issues by Nestlé, Eselte and British Telecom (Walmsley, 1988).

Table 10.3 confirms the importance of overseas companies for major exchanges. International equities have been the main growth area for many exchanges. Some investment bankers compare the international equity market to the Eurobond market of twenty years ago. We saw earlier that the explosion in international equity trading was a major impetus to the reform of many of the traditional stock exchanges in Europe. The economic effects of this phenomenon include a further erosion of

Table 10.3   International equities.

	1984	1985	1986	1987
London International Stock Exchange – Full Listing				
Foreign companies listed	477	473	482	505
Total companies listed	2,738	2,671	2,670	2,658
Percentage of foreign companies	17	18	18	19
New York Stock Exchange				
Foreign companies listed	42	44	52	67
Total companies listed	1,511	1,541	1,575	1,647
Percentage of foreign companies	2.8	2.8	3.3	4.1
Paris Bourse – Cote Officielle				
Foreign companies listed	164	177	183	192
Total companies listed	683	678	677	680
Percentage of foreign companies	24	26	27	28
Tokyo Stock Exchange				
Foreign companies listed	11	21	52	75
Total companies listed	1,790	1,806	1,834	1,882
Percentage of foreign companies	0.6	1.2	2.8	4.0

Source: Austen and Russell (1988, p. 27).

national frontiers in finance so that suppliers and users of share capital are linked increasingly across national frontiers.

Companies and other major institutions seek new finance from the market. The large institutional investors and fund managers look for price, liquidity and efficient settlements procedures. Where domestic exchanges are unable to meet these needs, trading is likely to move to other exchanges. Although Paris, Frankfurt and other leading European markets are becoming more competitive, only London, New York and Tokyo currently have the resources to make continuous two-way prices in the burgeoning numbers of Continental stocks (see Davies, 1987, p. 4). One result is that shares like Unilever, Royal Dutch and Siemens are now almost as freely traded in London as they are in their respective domestic exchanges.

Euroequities have been the fastest growing market in London. The ISE plans to have around 1400 international equities quoted on SEAQ by the end of 1989; over half of these will be European. A lower estimate of $1 billion has been suggested for the volume of international equities traded daily in London. Trading in London probably comprises around 15 per cent of the total volume in major European stocks. One forecast (Arthur Andersen, 1989, p. xiii) is that the wholesale trading of international equities will be increasingly concentrated in OTC (over-the-counter) markets.

The dramatic trend towards foreign listings appears to be the result of four related factors. Issuers are increasingly aware of the attractiveness of being able to tap overseas markets. Some foreign markets may also give a higher rating to a particular sector than that obtainable in the domestic market. Institutional investors have been steadily increasing the geographical diversification of their portfolios. International equity listings appear to have been boosted through the use of Eurobond-type distribution arrangements. Many stock exchanges have also encouraged the trend towards international equities by adopting a more commercial approach (Austen and Russell, 1988). In some instances the listing requirements have been relaxed for international equities.

The October 1987 crash was a major blow to the market, but it had recovered substantially by the end of 1988. Table 10.4 lists the Top Twenty lead and co-lead managers in 1987 and their corresponding (where relevant) 1986 positions. Many of the top rankings in 1987 were affected by the award of the British Petroleum mandate. This relationship-orientated market has been difficult for the Japanese to penetrate. Up to 1987 Nomura Securities and Daiwa managed to do so only through business generated by Western privatization programmes. CSFB (Credit Suisse First Boston) and Morgan Stanley syndicated the majority of issues in 1987. CSFB won most mandates outside its domestic market by lead-managing issues from Australia, Austria, Canada, Finland, Italy, Spain and the Netherlands.

New international equity issues have been distributed through two major routes, the Euroequity syndicate (similar to a Eurobond syndicate) and the 'geographically targeted' syndicate. In the latter syndicate members can sell only in a restricted geographical area, thereby preventing multiple solicitations to investors. With a general syndicate distribution the members are able to sell stock without restriction to any client.

Many regard syndication as essential for a good distribution to foreign investors and an important characteristic of international equities or Euroequities. Although international equity distribution practices have been moulded to some extent by Eurobond experiences, they have had to take account of the peculiarities of the security. Some investment bankers are happy with the label Euroequity, but others are more cautious. This reflects the fact that domestic market practice still tends to dictate how issues are distributed internationally.

Market practice has adapted to the fact that issuing and distributing risk capital invariably requires adjustments to the techniques commonly used for investment grade paper. As a result, distribution practices have adapted accordingly. Syndicates now tend to be smaller, and end-placing is becoming more important than fast syndication. Many investment banks emphasize the importance of placing power and the ability to create a new market in a stock outside the issuer's domestic base. There have been several well-publicized cases of flowback (or reflow)[1], where shares held abroad have come back to the issuer's home country.

Securitization developments

The trend towards securitization has been particularly prevalent in the international capital markets, and it was emphasized in Chapter 8. The stock market crash in 1987 halted for a time the increasing proportion of funds raised directly by borrowers issuing their own paper to investors. Bond issues dropped by around 20 per cent in 1987 and international bank lending reached levels not seen since the late 1970s.

By the middle of 1988, however, securitization was beginning to re-establish itself. This trend has been generally encouraged by the flexibility of the instruments developed, lower costs and the increasing globalization of financial markets. These characteristics have lowered the comparative advantage of banks in more traditional forms of credit intermediation. Securitization in Europe has taken three main forms:

176

Table 10.4 Top lead and co-lead managers: international equities, 1987.

Ranking		Bank	Amount US$ million			Number of issues			Percentages of total amount		
1987	1986		Lead	Co-lead	Total	Lead	Co-lead	Total	Lead	Co-lead	Total
Lead-managed and co-lead managed											
1	10	Goldman Sachs Int.	1,653.33	316.98	1,970.31	14	18	32	9.15	1.76	10.91
2	4	Shearson Lehman Bros Int.	375.51	869.14	1,242.65	14	18	32	2.07	4.81	6.88
3	7	Salomon Brothers	455.47	771.16	1,226.62	12	11	23	2.52	4.27	6.79
4	3	Swiss Bank Corp. Int.	872.73	304.82	1,177.55	11	16	27	4.83	1.69	6.52
5	5	Morgan Stanley Int.	269.22	796.42	1,065.64	17	14	31	1.49	4.41	5.90
6	16	SG Warburg	639.79	411.12	1,050.91	12	19	31	3.54	2.28	5.82
7	1	Credit Suisse First Boston	705.86	245.23	951.08	23	18	41	3.91	1.36	5.27
8	8	Merrill Lynch Capital Markets	723.94	173.45	897.39	17	11	28	4.01	0.96	4.97
9	19	Daiwa Securities	667.15	137.22	804.37	4	6	10	3.69	0.76	4.45
10	2	Deutsche Bank	352.79	387.97	740.76	5	17	22	1.95	2.15	4.10
11	9	Banque Paribas	638.61	73.97	712.57	11	3	14	3.54	0.41	3.95
12	6	Union Bank of Switzerland	401.60	193.66	595.26	3	12	15	2.22	1.07	3.30
13	14	Wood Gundy	500.59	42.22	542.81	6	4	10	2.77	0.23	3.01
14	13	Nomura Securities	32.37	454.32	486.68	1	9	10	0.18	2.52	2.69
15	11	Dresdner Bank	173.90	168.84	342.74	3	9	12	0.96	0.93	1.90
16	–	MacLeod Young Weir	104.98	182.92	287.90	7	5	12	0.58	1.01	1.59
17	–	Dominion Securities	94.35	187.90	282.25	6	5	11	0.52	1.04	1.56
18	–	Banque Indosuez	231.83	21.05	252.88	2	2	4	1.28	0.12	1.40
19	–	J Henry Schroder Wagg	162.91	25.51	188.42	3	3	6	0.90	0.14	1.04
20	–	Crédit Commercial de France	88.33	97.58	185.91	2	3	5	0.49	0.54	1.03
Lead-managed											
1	9	Goldman Sachs International		3,763.70			14			20.84	
2	2	Credit Suisse First Boston		1,268.03			23			7.02	
3	4	Merrill Lynch Capital Markets		1,055.40			17			5.84	
4	–	SG Warburg		1,010.64			12			5.60	
5	3	Swiss Bank Corporation Int.		998.71			11			5.53	
6	–	Banque Paribas		983.18			11			5.44	
7	–	Daiwa Securities		977.50			4			5.41	
8	–	Wood Gundy		746.74			6			4.13	
9	–	Salomon Brothers		665.95			12			3.69	
10	1	Deutsche Bank		618.74			5			3.43	

Source: Euromoney Annual Financing Report March 1988 (p. 32).
Note: Each issue is equally apportioned between lead and co-lead managers.

issuance of securities that act as a substitute for loans, the rise of domestic commercial paper (CP) markets, and the issue of asset-backed securities.

The rise of the Euroequity and the burgeoning of equities issues in European exchanges are aspects of the securitization phenomenon. In countries like Germany there are signs of a movement by companies towards a greater proportional use of equity funding in their financial structures. The previous section explored the growth of Euroequities in some detail.

The first form of securitized loan, however, was probably commercial paper (CP). In the international capital markets the Euronote, or generic note issuance facility (NIF), paved the way for the development of a Euro-commercial (ECP) paper market. The ECP, or Euro-CP, and generic Euronote facility have been important factors in the increasing securitization of lending in the Euromarkets since 1982.

The CP market in the United States is a powerful and long-established competitor to US banks. Until the 1980s CP was largely a US phenomenon. Throughout Europe, however, CP markets have been established in many countries. In 1982 a CP market opened in Spain. New CP markets were also established in Sweden (in 1983), France (1985) and Finland (1986). These markets have grown strongly. A CP market started in Holland in January 1986, but its impact has been comparatively small. Dutch companies actively place intercompany loans direct, and this restricts the demand for guilder CP.

Table 10.5 summarizes the size of the global CP market. The sterling CP market was launched on 20 May 1986, and the Bank of England prescribed rules in order to ensure an orderly market. Sterling CP is issued in the form of a promissory note. Paper has a minimum face value of £100,000, and maturities range from seven days to a maximum of five years. An issue may be made direct to investors or to a dealer or group of dealers. Dealer(s) can be appointed to manage an issue or act as underwriters.

Despite initial high expectations, however, the sterling CP market has not matched the optimistic growth expectations held by some when it was first launched; Table 10.5 confirms this picture. The other major European CP market is in US dollars. The sterling CP market is unlikely to experience the kind of growth rates seen in the USCP and ECP markets for a number of reasons. In the United States, for

Table 10.5 Global commercial paper market.

Country	Volume outstanding ($ bn equivalent)
United States	323
Euro-CP	36
Canada	11
Sweden	7
Spain	5
France	4
Australia	4
Hong Kong	1
United Kingdom	1
Netherlands	0.3

Source: Bank of England Quarterly Bulletin, February 1987.

example, $395 billion of paper from over 1500 programmes was outstanding by April 1988. The US domestic market has been boosted by the costs of comparatively high reserve requirements on the banks. Concern over bank risk has also allowed yield levels on CP to be driven markedly below bank deposit rates in the United States and the Euromarkets, and still attract investors.

Another important example of securitization has been the explosive growth of mortgage securitization in the United States. Although it might be argued that CP was the first securitization, the development of mortgage-based securities was undoubtedly a major development of securitization techniques. In the United States growth of the secondary mortgage market was fuelled by the interest-rate volatility of the period and the increasing support of agencies like GNMA (Government National Mortgage Association) and FHLMC (Federal Home Loan Mortgage Corporation). An important initial development in this connexion came in 1970 when the GNMA developed the 'Ginnie Mae' pass-through, a mortgage-backed security collateralized by single-family FHA (Federal Housing Administration) and VA (Veterans Association) mortgage loans.

Three kinds of loan-backed securities have developed from the US secondary mortgage market (Gardener and Revell, 1988). These are the pass-through (of which the Ginnie Mae is the most common type), the MBB (mortgage-backed bond) and the pay-through bond. The pass-through represents direct ownership in a portfolio of mortgages that are similar in quality, maturity and interest rate so that holders receive some proportion of capital and interest as it is paid on the mortgages. Mortgage pass-through techniques in the United States grew from 12.8 per cent of 1–4 year family mortgages in 1980 to 24.9 per cent in 1985.

MBBs are once again collateralized by a portfolio of mortgages or, occasionally, a portfolio of mortgage pass-through securities. Mortgage banks in Europe have used a similar kind of technique for many years. For example, West Germany and all the Scandinavian countries have established mortgage banks that provide housing finance through the issuance of mortgage-backed bonds (similar smaller-scale mortgage banks exist in Spain and Italy). Unlike pass-throughs, MBBs remain a debt obligation of the issuer. A pay-through bond, the third category, combines some of the features of the pass-through with some of those of the MBB.

One basic problem with US mortgage-backed securities is that pre-payments affect the maturity date of the paper. The CMO (collateralized mortgage obligation) – first issued in 1983 – was an attempt to circumvent this problem. The US market has grown rapidly. During 1986 the investment banks moved aggressively into the market in order to take advantage of arbitrage possibilities between it and the corporate bond market. Mortgage-backed bonds of this kind heralded the era of Euromortgages during 1985 and 1986.

Various European countries can boast certain forms of secondary mortgage markets. France has long had a type of secondary mortgage market. The Caisse de Refinancement Hyopothécaire (CRH) has pooled mortgages for many years and placed these with institutional investors. However, this is not a true securitization in the modern sense. Mortgage loans are not negotiable in France under the Napoleonic Code. In December 1988, however, a legal framework was established that created common claims funds (CCF). Securitization here is based on transferring ownership of claims by the transferring institution to the CCF. Securitization (*titrisation*) of this kind is being pushed by the French government *inter alia* in order to help the larger French banks meet the new Basle capital-adequacy rules (see Chapter 4).

Strong interest in a UK secondary mortgage market began around 1985 (*BSA Bulletin*, 1985, p. 7). Since then five mortgage companies[2], each with an interest in secondary market operations, have been formed. The institutional and structural factors behind the strong growth of the US secondary mortgage market do not exist in the United Kingdom and much of Europe. In the United States, the secondary mortgage market was a vehicle to help manage the resultant interest-rate risk exposure of savings institutions borrowing in a volatile interest-rate environment and lending longer-term at fixed rates of interest. Another 'US factor' has been the restrictions on banking institutions to operate within state borders: demand and supply of funds may not be matched within a state. As a result of these constraints, nowadays between 25 and 50 per cent of all new US housing loans are subsequently traded in the secondary mortgage market.

Although these institutional and structural characteristics do not exist in the United Kingdom, it is already clear that a limited secondary mortgage market is developing (Gardener, 1989). This market will be a vehicle for building societies and other lenders to meet increasing loan demand in the face of funding and capital-adequacy constraints. Other financial institutions (like insurance companies) may also use the technique to originate mortgages and cross-sell other products. Already so-called 'new lenders' with restricted equity bases have used securitization to penetrate the UK residential mortgage market. The first issue of UK mortgage-backed securities (MBS) in the Euromarkets took place in 1987 with a £50 million issue by NHL First Funding Corporation[3]. Since then the market has grown rapidly. By the end of 1988, £4.2 billion had been raised through 27 bond issues: issuers have deployed the MBS structure to transfer the ownership of mortgages originated by them.

Most of these issues have been effected by new lenders like the TMC, NHLC and HMC. By the end of 1987 these lenders accounted for 8 per cent of total net advances (Bank of England, 1988). It is believed that banks are major investors in MBS and the volume of secondary market trading of these bonds is quite low. MBS issues[4] are usually FRNs that offer investors a spread over three-month sterling LIBOR. All these issues have been rated AAA or AA by Standard & Poors. Future prospects for the MBS market are clearly linked to the corresponding level of activity in the housing market in general.

In the United States securitization has been extended to a wide range of loans. These include credit card receivables, motor car loans and C&I (commercial and industrial) loans. Although the US financial system has been characterized by distinguishing features not generally found in Europe, the prospects for increased securitization in Europe seem good. These increases are likely to be modest initially, however, compared with US experience. The new UK secondary mortgage market may be the forerunner of a wave of securitization innovations in domestic European financial systems.

The selling or trading of loans is not a new need in banking, but it is only recently that any kind of structured approach has begun to evolve in the London market (Barratt, 1988). Securitization and other developments have helped to stimulate a huge increase in the volume of loans traded in London. The strong securitization trend has encouraged banks to structure lending arrangements to include techniques[5] that allow the ready transferability of loan assets. This creates trading opportunities and improves the flexibility of portfolio management. In 1987 the Bank of England proposed capital-adequacy rules for certain loan assets where, previously, a bank would have regarded the risk as transferred to another bank in the London market.

European companies and banks are now gearing themselves to exploit US and UK financial technology in order to establish asset-backed finance that suits their own local conditions. Many of the banks that are active in the field have imported staff from the United States. The early 1990s are the years that securitization is likely to establish itself in Europe beyond the United Kingdom. Although some are cautious in predicting a high rate of growth along US lines in Europe (Gardener, 1989), many believe the technique could grow even faster there once it is established.

Securitization may be a vehicle for banks (as in France) to help them meet the new Basel capital-adequacy rules. Other kinds of European banks, such as savings banks, may also deploy the technique to help them relieve increasing capital-adequacy pressures. Securitization is a technique that may also be very attractive to the financial services divisions of non-financial companies. These divisions may use it to move from margin-based to fee-generating units. The market for securitization has now become truly global.

Risk-management products

Securitization is a financial innovation that has helped to make financial markets more liquid. We have seen on several occasions that globalization trends have operated to integrate increasingly financial markets that were once fragmented. The growth of the Euromarkets and the development of the swaps market have been particularly important in this respect. In this new world of increasing market sophistication and opportunities, the penalties and potential risk exposures have also increased.

Risk management emerged as an important financial market trend of the 1970s and 1980s. Increased volatility of interest rates, exchange rates and market prices, coupled with important developments in the financial markets themselves, have encouraged a more active approach to risk management. A widening range of derivative financial products has emerged. The most important kinds of instruments under this heading are financial futures and options. Important advances in technology have been necessary in order to support the enormous volumes traded in these markets. Financial futures and options, together with currency and interest-rate swaps, are the most successful of recent financial innovations.

Since financial futures and options started to trade in the early 1970s, exchanges have attempted to secure the biggest share of volume in the new instruments. By the end of 1987 there were 22 exchanges across the world trading in financial futures and options contracts of all sizes, denominations and maturities. Volumes have soared and new records are set practically every month. Eight new exchanges have been established since 1984. The majority of European countries will have a financial futures and/or traded options exchange by 1992.

The most important European futures and options markets are the EOE (European Options Exchange), LIFFE (London International Financial Futures Exchange), LTOM (London Traded Options Market) and MATIF (Marché à Terme des Instruments Financiers). As we have also seen, the leading Swiss securities firms have formed in Switzerland an automated futures exchange called SOFFEX. The Swedish Options and Futures Exchange (SOFE) started in 1986, but closed in late February 1989 (Shale, 1989) as its rival exchange – Stockholm's Options Marknad Fondkommission (OM) – prospered.

There are no futures or options markets in Spain, Portugal or Luxembourg, but in the latter country certain brokers deal on the EOE in Holland or LIFFE in London. Up to 1990 there was no financial futures market in Germany, the Deutsche Terminbörse (DTB) started operations in January 1990 – but there was a forward market in currencies outside the Frankfurt Stock Exchange. Options trading is conducted under the rules of the Stock Exchanges Act (*Börsengesetz*) and the *Special Regulations for Options Dealings on the German Bill Market*. Comparatively active options markets exist on the Italian stock exchanges, but there are no links with overseas markets.

The EOE in Holland is a member of the International Options Clearing Corporation. The EOE was established in 1978 and began to trade options immediately. It has over 200 registered members, and around 9.8 million contracts were traded in 1986 (compared with around 6 million on LTOM). Trading in AMEX Major Market Index (XMI) options began in August 1987. AMEX and EOE became the first major options exchanges in the world to trade options on a leading stock-exchange index in two different time zones. XMI also became the first UK index option available for trading before the opening of the New York market. On November 1986 a financial futures market – the Financiël Termijnmarkt Amsterdam (FTA) – was established. The FTA is wholly owned by EOE.

In London, financial futures and options are both traded on LIFFE, and options are also traded in the ISE. Alongside the traditional options market, the LTOM was set up in 1978. As a result, there are now two kinds of options market in London: 'traditional' options and traded options. The former are traded 'over the counter' and positions may be closed only with the original counterparty. The traded options market encompasses a limited range of securities, although the options are fully transferable. LIFFE was set up in 1982 and now trades 20 futures and options contracts; there are over 200 member firms.

MATIF opened for business in February 1986. In its first two years of operations its performance has exceeded the most optimistic forecasts. MATIF has achieved a world ranking of number three in terms of number of daily contracts. In 1987 a negotiable options market (MONEF) was established. The two main kinds of futures contract available on the MATIF are the National Government bond futures contracts and the Treasury bills futures contracts.

Exchanges compete among themselves for business and with the OTC market. Sales of OTC risk-management products have been growing rapidly in bank trading rooms in New York, London and (to a smaller extent) Tokyo. The OTC market is taking business away from the exchanges, although some bankers feel that the OTC and exchange markets are complementary (see Commins, 1987, p. 6). Portfolio insurance has been an area in which the OTC market has done particularly well.

Conclusion

We have seen that internationalization, globalization and technology developments have brought new challenges for Europe's securities markets and related business. Internationalization and globalization pressures are moving business away from domestic exchanges. Technology has facilitated trading away from the floor. Another major challenge is the approach of 1992, the completion of the European internal market. The EC Directive on the mutual recognition of listings (due in late 1990), for example, will increase the pressures on Europe's stock exchanges. A recent report suggests (Fidler, 1989) that European capital markets are not prepared for the growth in demand for securities in the years up to 1992 and the projected dismantling of the barriers to capital flows. Many believe that international equity trading will be increasingly concentrated in London, Tokyo and New York. The following chapter will examine the implications of these developments for investment banking in Europe and, at the same time, explore further the related market environment.

Notes

1. Like the British Telecom issue in 1984.
2. The National Home Loans Corporation (NHLC), the Household Mortgage Corporation (HMC), The Mortgage Corporation (TMC), the Mortgage Funding Corporation (MFC) and First Mortgage Securities (FMS).
3. NHL is effectively controlled by the NHLC: see note 2.
4. MBS structures in the UK have been issued by special purpose NIVs (note-issuing vehicles) set up by the specialist lenders. The NIVs' assets are a pool of residential mortgages that are (funded) matched to the issued MBSs.
5. The common basic methods of selling participations are by assignment, novation or sub-participation. Sophisticated variants include the TLI (transferable loan instrument), TLC (transferable loan certificate), TPC (transferable participation certificate) and the Master Participation Agreement.

References

Arthur Andersen & Co. (1989), *European Capital Markets: A Strategic Forecast*; Special Report no. 1161, January (London: The Economist Publications Ltd).

Austen, Mark and Russell, Robin (1988), 'Issues in international listings', *The Treasurer* (December) pp. 27–9.

Bank of England (1988), *International Capital Markets Report, Q4* (London: Bank of England).

Barratt, Jeffery (1988), 'Selling loan assets – some guidelines and some problems' *Butterworths Journal of International Banking and Financial Law*, vol. 3, no. 3, (June) pp. 367–74.

Briston, R. J. (1975), *The Stock Exchange and Investment Analysis* (London: George Allen & Unwin).

BSA Bulletin (1985), 'Secondary Mortgage Markets', no. 41, (January) pp. 7–13.

Commins, Kevin (1987), 'OTC market: help or hindrance', *Supplement to Euromoney and Corporate Finance: Futures and Options* (November) pp. 6–7.

Davies, Ben (1987), 'Reveille for Europe's exchanges', *Euromoney*, Supplement, (August) pp. 2–5.

Edwards, George T. (1987), *The Role of Banks in Economic Development* (London: Macmillan).

Euromoney (1987), *European Stock Exchanges*, A Supplement to Euromoney (August) pp. 1–86.

Euromoney Corporate Finance (1987), 'International equities take wing', *Supplement* (June) pp. 1–24.

Fidler, Stephen (1989), 'Europe falls behind in the securities race', *Financial Times* (25 January), p. 27.

Gardener, E. P. M. (1987), 'Structural and strategic consequences of financial conglomeration', *Revue de la Banque*, no. 9, (November) pp. 5–16.

Gardener, E. P. M. (1989), '1992 and the future of securitisation in Western Europe', *IEF Research Papers in Banking and Finance* (Bangor: Institute of European Finance).

Gardener, E. P. M. and Revell, J. R. S. (1988), *Securitisation: History Forms and Risk, IEF Research Monographs in Banking and Finance* no. 5 (Bangor: Institute of European Finance).

Gardener, E. P. M. and Molyneux, P. (1988), *Structure and Regulation of UK Financial Markets, IEF Research Monographs in Banking and Finance* no. 6 (Bangor: Institute of European Finance).

George, Abraham M. and Giddy, Ian H. (eds) (1983), *International Finance Handbook*, Volumes 1 and 2, (London: Wiley Interscience).

Istituto la Ricerca Sociale (IRS) (1988), *First Report on the Italian Stock Market* (Italy: IRS).

Jones, Nicholas (1988), 'The cult of the equity, a believer at last', *The Treasurer* (June) p. 31.

Keynes, J. M. (1936), *The General Theory of Employment Interest and Money* (London: Macmillan).

Kindleberger, Charles P. (1984), *A Financial History of Western Europe* (London: George Allen & Unwin).

MacLeod, Allison (1987), 'The Borsa and a wary world' *Euromoney Supplement*, (August) pp. 38–9.

Phillips, Patrick (1987), *Inside The New Gilt-Edged Market* (Cambridge: Woodhead-Faulkner).

Rambosson, Jacques (1988), 'The French financial revolution', *The Treasurer* (December) pp. 10–13 and 23.

Revell, J. R. S. (1973), *The British Financial System* (London: Macmillan).

Rybczynski, T. (1985), 'Financial systems, risk and public policy' *The Royal Bank of Scotland Review*, (December) pp. 35–45.

Shale, Tony (1989), 'Why did SOFE have to die?', *Euromoney*, (March), pp. 49–52.

Spicer & Oppenheim International (1988), *The Spicer & Oppenheim Guide to Securities Markets Around the World* (Chichester: John Wiley & Sons).

Von Rosen, Rüdiger (1987), 'Finanzplatz Deutschland' *Euromoney*, Supplement, (August) pp. 23–76.

Von Rosen, Rüdiger (1988), 'The German Stock Exchanges – building for the future', *Euromoney*, Supplement, (July), pp. 18–22.

Walmsley, Julian (1988), *The New Financial Instruments* (Chichester: John Wiley & Sons).

Wilkinson, Terry (1988), 'European bourses beat London', *The Independent* (31 December) p. 21.

184

Chapter eleven

Investment banking

Introduction

Earlier chapters have emphasized repeatedly the modern evolution of investment banking. Securitization trends and the associated strategic orientation towards capital market products have heightened its strategic profile in most European banking systems. Privatization, unitization and other developments have reinforced the strategic importance of capital markets and treasury products in retail banking sectors. Investment banking in Europe, however, is not a new phenomenon. We have seen, for example, that the Continental universal banks have traditionally undertaken many important investment banking functions. This chapter explores the evolution, structure and market environment of European investment banking. More detailed attention is then focused on changes and developments in investment banking products and services in Europe.

Industrial structure and competition

Definitions

The role of London as a leading international financial centre and the events leading up to Big Bang emphasized the strategic importance of investment banking. A growing adoption of the 'Anglo-Saxon model' in the financial systems of many continental European countries has reinforced the position of London as the European centre of many modern investment banking activities. The British have been one of the strong driving forces in the modern evolution of merchant/ investment banking in Europe. The US investment banking industry has also enjoyed historical close ties with the United Kingdom. Of the several hundred banks that operate in London, around 100 would probably classify themselves as merchant banks. Sixteen of these make up the exclusive Accepting Houses Committee, and all of these are members of the (58-strong) Issuing Houses Association.

It is practically impossible to find an accurate definition of a merchant bank. The title has often been used wrongly as a kind of generic label for firms operating in the wholesale corporate financial sector, irrespective of the character of their banking or merchanting services. A definitional problem is that the activities of merchant banks are constantly being re-shaped and extended as financial markets evolve and customers' needs alter. Indeed, this changing business mix reflects an important characteristic of London's merchant banks, their flexibility and nimbleness in adapting to changing conditions.

Some observers (Clay and Wheble, 1985, pp. 9–10) emphasize the distinction between the old established houses and the newer arrivals in London who variously described themselves as merchant banks. Many of the former may be grouped conveniently as the members of the Accepting Houses Committee. An important part of their traditional business consisted of accepting bills of exchange in order to provide short-term finance for the trade of third parties. More generally, the merchant banker was a merchant who extended his credit to others in a variety of ways[1]. The majority of these banks started as merchants trading on their own account and their business evolved gradually into a mercantile bank. The UK Radcliffe Report (1959) emphasized the high measure of responsibility and reputation that London's accepting houses have traditionally enjoyed:

> These firms are nearly all companies, including some public companies, but all of them retain a strong element of their traditional ownership and management by families, some of whose names have stood high in world finance for a century or more.

London's accepting houses now provide a wide variety of financial services. Nevertheless, many of the accepting houses started as merchant ventures, although, merchant financing today makes up a very small portion of overall merchant banking profits.

In the United States the terms investment and merchant banking have more specialist meanings. Investment banking generally involves comparatively less use of a firm's own capital, and business is generally orientated towards trading and merger advice. Traditionally, investment banks have been involved in areas like capital markets and hedging products, specialized services and advice on areas like mergers and acquisitions, restructuring and leveraged buyouts (LBOs). Merchant banking is a term used in the US to describe banking activities where large amounts of individual firms' own capital, as well as investors' capital, is 'put on the line' to support LBO and M&A business. In this sense merchant banking is merely a special type of investment banking business and is generally only undertaken by the top rank investment banks. A further operational distinction would be between securities houses and merchant and investment banks. The former (Nomura Securities is a good example) are represented by comparatively simple and specialized organizational structures that are centred on stockbroking.

In both the United States and the United Kingdom the traditional institutional segmentation between merchant, investment and commercial banking has eroded rapidly. No formal definition, legal or regulatory, exists in Britain. In Europe generally it is practically impossible to define merchant and investment banking neatly. We shall use the two terms interchangeably to refer to modern investment banks. Under this pragmatic approach an investment bank is a financial institution that is active in securities and advisory services. It covers institutions like the UK merchant banks, the US investment banks, French *banques d'affaires* and Japanese securities houses.

Perhaps one of the most significant characteristics of a modern investment bank concerns its size, the kind of staff it employs and its corresponding organizational structure. Investment banks are typically smaller than the leading commercial banks, although investment banking may also be conducted by banks or units ultimately owned by commercial banks. Staff are often given high responsibility at an early age and a premium is invariably put on flexibility, innovation, experimentation and adaptability. As a result, organizational structures are typically characterized by swift decision-making, substantial delegation of authority, flexibility and short chains of command. Financial decisions and related advisory services within an investment bank typically embody comparatively high levels of sophistication. These characteristics are not altogether unique to investment banks, but they are important. No definition unaided can adequately capture the essence of modern investment banking, but a consideration of its historical evolution provides further important insights.

Historical background

Although the UK merchant banks have been strong driving forces in the evolution of modern investment banking, merchant banking did not begin in the United Kingdom. It had its roots in Italy and the Northern European non-financial trading houses. During the late Middle Ages, European merchants found it profitable to add other activities to normal trading business: these included money lending and foreign-exchange dealing. Italian traders were geographically well located to exploit these new activities fully. Traders in Florence were the most active because of that city's role in the international wool trade.

The history of merchant banking is inextricably linked to that of international banking and Chapter 8 has already traced the historical evolution of the emergent, international merchant banking houses in some detail. Italian merchants dominated European international trade for several centuries. The result was that many kinds of merchant bank and even the first modern commercial banks have their origins in Italy; famous names included Medici, Bardi and Peruzzi.

Over time Italy started to lose out to the English and Northern European banks. The German houses emerged strongly by the seventeenth century. This growth was stimulated through profitable commercial ventures and diversification objectives by the houses. The German Rothschild's initial business was in textiles and coins: it was first established in the mid-1700s in Frankfurt. Baring was first established in Bremen in 1717, Warburg (in 1798) and Schroder (in 1804) in Hamburg. Rothschild was the most diversified with offices in Frankfurt, London, Paris, Naples and Vienna.

During the seventeenth and most of the eighteenth century Amsterdam was the centre of international finance. The growing importance of the Dutch as carriers of international trade allowed Dutch commission agents[2] to increase their expertise in financing trade. Intensifying competition between Dutch and British merchants encouraged many of them to shift their capital into financial business. It was really the Amsterdam merchants who developed many of the financial techniques that were later to become associated with the emergent merchant banker.

The expansion of trade in the eighteenth and nineteenth centuries markedly stimulated the development of the 'international house', essentially a family business that operated simultaneously in two or more centres of trade (Chapman, 1984, pp. 3–4). This was not a new kind of business structure; it was familiar from at least the later Middle Ages. Nevertheless, it grew rapidly in popularity as international trade evolved. Another impetus was the preference for this form of organization by ethnic trading groups that had been geographically dispersed through religious persecution. Examples of these groups include Dutch, French and Sephardic Jewish *émigrés*; Ashkenazi Jews from Hamburg, Frankfurt, Berlin and Leipzig; and the French Huguenots who were attracted to London by the strong growth of the British textile trade.

The influence of Dutch finance and merchant banking techniques was considerable in London throughout the early period of strong growth in the British economy and trade in the eighteenth century. In many respects Amsterdam was used to support the growth of British overseas trade during this period. Many merchant bankers in London and Amsterdam moved gradually from generalized commerce into specialized commerce, and from there into finance. The merchant venturer evolved into the accepting house. British and US trade flourished throughout the nineteenth century and it was the London-based merchant banks, for example, who financed much of the American railway system.

During the eighteenth century, Rothschilds and Barings emerged as the two dominant houses in London. Chapman (1984, p. 39) dates the emergence of merchant banking as we know it today to the period 1825–36, a decade of crisis. During that time a few rich firms altered their status from commission merchants to commission bankers. During the boom period in Anglo-American trade throughout the early 1830s a number of young houses grew very quickly. Many of the younger firms attempted to emulate the Barings and Rothschilds. Barings tended to be copied by those British merchants who were evolving towards pure finance. Rothschilds was the model for a number of German-Jewish and American-Jewish family-run merchant banks.

The development of European investment banking had an important influence on the character of US investment banking (see Hayes III, Spence and Marks in Williamson, 1988, p. 12). Joint ventures between European and US houses, for example, influenced the development of financial services within the United States. Some bankers also pursued transnational careers. In Europe the emergence of the early investment bankers may also be dated by changes in financing practices. British and Continental practice in handling new securities issues differed up to the early nineteenth century.

Although many of the families that were later to dominate British finance were Continental by descent and some international co-operation did exist in banking and finance, these inter-relationships were neither extensive nor dominant. During the decade from 1780, loan contractors developed in Britain to buy up share subscriptions outright in order to re-sell them for gain. The Continental European practice, on the other hand, was not to take shares outright like the English loan contractors. The Continental middleman negotiated entire issues on a commission basis and then disposed of the securities.

The apparent divide between British loan contracting and these Continental practices was effectively breached after the Congress of Vienna, 1814–15. Investment banking came into existence when professional middlemen (rather than ultimate investors) took over the original market for new subscriptions. From the perspective of modern investment banking the real significance of this movement of ultimate investors from the original securities market is that a small number of leading investment houses began to dominate the flow of long-term capital into public securities. This 'apex industrial structure' in investment banking did not obviate competition; intense competition existed at the apex of the industry and at its base. The leading firms competed within the oligopolistic apex stratum of the industry; chains of middlemen from the apex to the base of the industry competed strongly for business and alliances.

During the latter part of the nineteenth century the French developed their own kind of investment bank called *banques d'affaires*. These banks were formed primarily for investment in industry. The Banque de Paris et des Pays-Pas (Paribas), for example, was formed in 1872 through the merger of the Banque de Paris with the Banque des Pays-Bas. Although the bank had its main branch in Paris, its nominal head office was in Amsterdam. Kindleberger (1984, p. 112) suggests that this organizational structure was an interesting early prototype of the twentieth-century Eurocurrency market.

Early private bankers in Germany (the Rhineland) were subject to strong French influence. From 1833 many German banks developed along French Crédit Mobilier lines. These were often distinguished from note-issuing banks and those banks that combined both functions. The Dresdner Bank, for example, was formed for the same purposes as the industrial banks of the Crédit Mobilier type. We saw earlier (Chapter 7) that close links between the large banks and big industry have characterized German banking. The private banks gradually lessened in importance in Germany during the nineteenth century. The universal bank model increasingly distinguished the approach of the German and several other continental European countries (like Switzerland and Austria) to investment banking. Nevertheless, profits from industrial stakes now contribute less than 10 per cent of the profits to German banks. Although the German banks retain their representation on the boards of industrial companies they are slowly running down these interests.

Modern evolution and structure

London dominated the world financial system until the First World War. Just as its merchant bankers had been such an important part of its success up to that time, so, some commentators have suggested, they were partly to blame at least for London's reduced dominance in international finance up to the 1950s. From the 1950s they again played an important role in developing the City as the centre of the fast-growing Eurodollar market. By the late 1950s London had re-asserted its premier position as a world financial centre.

The growth of the Euromarket has been a particularly strong influence on the evolution of modern investment banking. The Euromarket, with its headquarters in London, has helped to coalesce various national and regional financial markets around the world. It links all the major financial centres and has created the world's first, truly global capital market. London has emerged as the major European centre for investment banking.

Big Bang in London was prompted in large part by the major challenge of the new international capital market. After 1982 securitization trends in international finance emphasized the strategic importance of investment banking to European and other banks. The revolution associated with Big Bang led to the rapid build-up of new 'bank financial conglomerates' in the City. A bank financial conglomerate is an organization that conducts a number of separate financial activities under common ownership. The continental European universal banks are good examples of this organizational model. These banks, however, are the product of a long evolutionary process; the conglomerates that emerged in London with the approach of Big Bang evolved in a much shorter time span.

The distinguishing feature of London's financial conglomerates is that they were driven primarily by investment banking considerations. Many of them set out to provide most of the clients' needs – one-stop financial shopping – through the organizational construction of an integrated securities business. These new 'super banks' were the result, then, of a strong strategic drive by banks into securities business and capital market products. All these developments reflected banks' strategic reactions to the challenges of deregulated capital markets. They comprise one of the major developments in the industrial structure and strategies of world banking.

One of the striking characteristics of the conglomerates that formed in London up to Big Bang day was their different organizational groupings. Hardly any two were alike. Apart from Shearson Lehman Brothers and Citicorp Investment Bank (CIBL), most of the US investment banks did not buy brokers in London in the build-up to Big Bang. The Japanese also held back. The UK merchant banks were active purchasers, and they may legitimately come under the generic label of financial conglomerate. In this respect the European 'model' in modern investment banking is the conglomerate, although we may distinguish many different species within the genus. The corresponding US and Japanese 'models' are more specialist institutions.

Many of the new financial conglomerates in London spanned new-style capital market product business, merchant banking, stockbroking operations, and traditional banking (primarily commercial and retail banking). The massive investments in these new banks confirmed their view of London as the apex of global money and securities markets. It was felt that banks generally had to choose one of two strategies: become a full-service bank or pursue a niche strategy. Global status was the strategic target of many leading banks. A large number of them believed that strong synergies existed between the different parts of their widely-diversified and integrated operations. The consensus view was that a critical mass of talent and resources was needed, and that these should be typically bought in to be effective.

This view led to a kind of generally perceived 'barbell model' of industrial structure in world investment banking (Gardener, 1988). It comprised two groups of participants, the global institutions and the smaller niche firms. Medium-sized institutions were seen as 'falling between two stools'. They did not have the resources to compete with the global league players and they lacked the dedicated expertise to compete effectively with the niche institutions. This kind of 'strategic folklore' certainly influenced the strategy followed.

Banks also displayed 'herd instinct' as they followed perceived market leaders into a widening spectrum of capital market business. The immediate pressures of competition and a desire for 'strategic position' stimulated many of them into new kinds of investment banking. Post-crash attitudes on investment banking strategies, however, have led to a new kind of revisionist thinking in which banks are increasingly focusing on their own strengths. Synergy has been downgraded and

190

so-called 'cluster strategies' are in vogue. Medium-sized institutions are now seen as being competitive so long as they play to their strengths (see Chapter 12).

London is an especially interesting market for students of investment banking strategies. We saw earlier that it is the largest capital market where specialist investment banking and securities houses face the new-style, financial conglomerates in open competition. The specialist and conglomerate models each have comparative advantages and disadvantages. Institutions that perform specialist functions have operations characterized by a long record in securities business and capital market products, developed expertise, established information-gathering capabilities and a strong cultural affinity with capital markets. On the other hand, financial conglomerates have a wider portfolio diversification, good capital strength, wide expertise, extensive international networks and good placement capabilities. Nevertheless, many of the financial conglomerates were comparative newcomers to the kind of commitments made to investment banking in the build-up to London's Big Bang.

Industrial structure may be analyzed in a number of ways. Concentration measures are a usual starting point for appraising the competitive market environment. Table 11.1 summarizes some data on concentration trends in the primary Eurobond market, an important market for modern investment banking. Although the Herfindahl index and related measures imply some increase in concentration from 1980 to 1987, the number of firms with over 1 per cent of the market rose from 1980 to 1985, and fell back in 1987.

Two interesting features of the market environment revealed by Table 11.1 are the seeming inexorable rise of the Japanese and the post-crash emphasis on placement power compared to innovation. The marked demise of the United States in these kinds of league tables has been more than exceeded by the dramatic growth of the Japanese presence. The European conglomerates have steadily increased their market share. The Japanese have also made dramatic inroads since 1988 into international equities, especially in issues with equity warrants attached and equity-linked Eurobonds (see Barnett, 1988, p. 94). The decline in the comparative attractiveness of the US dollar from the middle of the 1980s allowed banks that focused on the non-dollar segments of the market to do well. Swiss and German banks, together with Japanese securities houses, flourished. The latter managed a large number of issues for Japanese companies; these debt-with-equity warrants allowed the warrants to be sold off to investors within Japan whilst the corresponding debt was re-packaged with interest-rate swaps and sold to Japanese banks within Europe. The Japanese houses became market leaders as these activities grew rapidly.

It is interesting to note that, with the exception of CSFB (Credit Suisse First Boston), 1988 was the first time in three polls of corporate treasurers' (excluding Japanese corporates) assessment of top banks that non-US banks have featured (as runners-up) in the overall top ten banks; corporate treasurers still seem to prefer the expertise of the US banks. The European banks appearing as runners-up in various segments of the market included UBS, S.G. Warburg, Deutsche Bank, BZW, Midland Bank, NatWest and Swiss Bank Corporation. The latter two banks were ranked within the overall top-ten banks. Nomura was the only Japanese bank to appear as a runner-up in these polls (*Euromoney Corporate Finance*, 1988b).

Table 11.1   Selected indicators of primary Eurobond concentration.

	5-firm proportion	Herfindahl index[a]	Numbers equivalent	Number over 5%	Number over 1%	Nationality of top 5 lead managers
1975	40	0.052	19	8	21	D, US, B, D, CH
1980	34	0.039	26	4	29	CH, D, UK, US, F
1985	37	0.048	21	6	29	CH, US, US, US, D
1987	36	0.043	22	5	22	J, CH, D, J, J

Source: Gardener (1988, p. 8, Table 2).
Note: a Based on shares of the top 20 firms.
Key: D   Germany
     CH   Switzerland
     J   Japan
     US   United States
     B   Belgium
     F   France

Products and services

Market environment

The market environment for investment banking in Europe is now subject to important changes. New risks and opportunities are emerging with the approach of 1992 and the projected completion of the European internal market. Despite its undoubted significance, 1992 should not be viewed in isolation. It is the latest step in a series of deregulation moves that started at least a decade ago in Europe.

We have already emphasized on several occasions the growing adoption of the 'Anglo-Saxon model' in many continental European (and other) countries. This movement towards a stronger market-orientation is reflected in a corresponding diminution of state interference and the centralized direction of industry. Popular socialism has been increasingly displaced by shareholder democracy models and associated government and banking policy targets. Privatization is one aspect of the trend. Another is the loosening of traditional strong ties between banks and industry in countries like West Germany.

Europe 1992 may rival London's Big Bang in its impact on the investment banking industry. These effects should flow not only from the financial sectors themselves, but also from the resultant effects on those sectors using financial services. The volume and pattern of demand for investment banking services will undoubtedly be affected. Demand for capital-raising is likely to increase as major companies restructure. The corresponding demands for corporate financial advice and investment management services, together with brokerage and trading activities, are all likely to increase through the stimulus of 1992. New kinds of investment banking competition will appear as banks and other financial services firms restructure in the new evolving market. Europe 1992 has already stimulated a new industrial restructuring movement within the European banking industry (see Chapters 3 and 12).

Many studies and commentators have suggested that 1992 will produce a more integrated, homogenous market. A recent study (Centre for Business Strategy, 1989) has argued, however, that there is nothing in the 1992 proposals themselves that can achieve such an aim. Trade liberalization of the kind promulgated within the 1992 proposals has its main effects on supply. Demand is the product of other character-istics[3] that are likely to be largely unaffected by 1992. This suggests that the popular myth that European production will be concentrated in a smaller number of larger organizations that offer consumers a smaller choice of products with lower prices induced by scale economies is unlikely to be realized.

The 1992 measures are directed economically more towards the increase of trade flows, rather than market unification *per se*. The Centre for Business Strategy (1989, p. 7) argues that there are three main ways that the 1992 plan will affect the structure of European markets. First, companies that export to other Community states are likely to find their costs reduced relative to their domestic competitors. Secondly, existing market segmentation strategies may be undermined through completing the internal market. Finally, the 1992 plan may bring new competitors into previously closed, or unattractive, markets.

These developments in their turn impact on the investment banking environment in Europe. We saw in Chapter 10 that globalization and other trends are already encouraging greater capital market integration. It is likely that 1992 will reinforce these trends, although greater co-operation among European central banks and other regulatory agencies may be required for an integrated EC market in key investment banking markets like new issues and secondary market trading.

Significant industrial restructuring may be expected as companies adapt to the new competitive environment. A new wave of industrial M&A activity within Europe is already under way. This will increase activity in the debt and equity segments of EC investment banking markets. Privatization will probably reinforce these trends. As European markets enhance their breadth and liquidity, they are likely to stimulate increasingly a displacement of bank (institution-based) finance by market-based finance. The growth of securitization will help to accelerate this process.

The demand for greater and more specialist investment banking advisory services will grow alongside these trends. Trading volumes will expand as financial institu-tions increase their participation in capital markets in order to boost portfolio performance. Mutual funds, international in their orientation, are likely to displace increasingly the private account management services of the universal banks. Increased capital-market liquidity and the pressures of an increasingly competitive marketplace will be important stimulants in this respect. Broker-dealers will need to have increasing linkages across EC markets in order to exploit trading opportunities. Futures and options trading, together with derivative and associated products, are other likely strong growth areas in European investment banking. These same kinds of developments – particularly intensifying competition and a stronger market orientation – will also boost the demand for investment management services.

Any scenario is bound to be speculative, but earlier analysis (see, for example, Chapters 9 and 10) seems to confirm this view of a buoyant and rapidly expanding investment banking market in Europe. Traditional distinctions between bank and bond market finance are likely to be eroded significantly in several market segments. Commercial banks will face growing competitive threats from new entrants to investment banking markets like savings and/or mortgage institutions, stockbrokers and financial intermediaries, and insurance companies. If US experiences are any guide, leading accountancy firms may also encroach increasingly into traditional and the newer investment banking fields.

Europe's large corporations are already penetrating increasingly into banking territory. Our earlier study of the history of merchant and investment banking confirmed the logic and precedent of such moves. Early merchants used their contacts and financial resources to diversify into financial services. Several large, cash-rich European corporations are now effectively developing in-house banking operations. These trends are much more advanced in the United States. Corporate treasury divisions are becoming profit rather than cost centres. European companies like British Petroleum and Volvo now have their own in-house banks. BPFI (BP Finance International), Fortos (in Volvo) and GEC Finance confirm a developing trend that banking is not an unnatural outgrowth of corporate activity.

Another important development is the increased interest of the large US and Japanese investment banks in Europe. The majority of European companies are loyal to their retained merchant banks, but there are signs of change. US investment banks based in London can be expected to exploit this emerging trend (Purnell, 1989, p. 3). Although the Japanese did not buy into stockbroking firms in London's Big Bang or rush into the Paris market when the rules were relaxed on the acquisition of *agents de change*, they now seem to be making their long-awaited 'European move' (see Brady, 1988, pp. 41–51 and Dignan, 1989, pp. 4–5). In December 1988, for example, Nomura announced two moves that suggested an expansion into European securities: a stockbroker acquisition in Paris and a planned expansion of staff in London.

Capital raising

The previous chapter confirmed the growing maturity of European capital markets, although the Continental markets have a considerable way to go before they compete strongly in areas like equities with London, New York or Tokyo. We also charted in Chapter 10 the recent spectacular growth of the international equities market in Europe. From September 1982 to April 1987 the market capitalization of Europe's stock markets (excluding London) increased by 515 per cent: from US $194 billion to US $1000 billion (Davies, 1987, p. 2).

European banks have been highly competitive for some time in new issues and related business. These banks were quick to exploit the new techniques that developed in the Euromarkets from the early 1980s. A banking culture that put an increasing emphasis on performance and innovation was soon absorbed into the major European banks as the 1970s and 1980s developed. One need only recall their positions in global league tables that were discussed in an earlier section.

The provision of finance at all levels has always been a key investment banking function. Finance provision covers short-term finance, medium-term finance, long-term and permanent finance (including mergers and acquisitions), international issues and venture capital. European companies have had a traditional orientation towards domestic issues in their own home markets. Domestic debt issues have been especially important in countries like France, Germany and Italy. Equity issues have been particularly important in the United Kingdom and, in recent years, within France; privatization programmes have given these issues a powerful boost.

There is little doubt that the comparatively underdeveloped capital markets in Continental Europe and the traditional dominance of bank-linked finance shaped corporate attitudes to capital market finance. All this has been changing throughout the 1970s and (especially) the 1980s. The Continental banks (particularly the Germans and Swiss) were important participants in the Euromarkets virtually from the beginning. Intensifying bank competition in Euromarket business and the development of the market itself soon attracted European companies to the increasing array of Euromarket financing vehicles.

European companies increased their use of Euromarket financing instruments throughout the 1980s. They became more aware of new financing techniques and the increasing worldwide interest in international equities. Equity and equity-linked issues burgeoned from the middle of the 1980s. A much wider variety of debt instruments – ranging from an expanding array of Euronote facilities through MTNs (medium-term notes) up to longer-term Eurobonds – became available. Companies became increasingly familiar with the technique of raising CP in one currency in that international centre where rates happened to be most attractive, and then swapping it into the desired currency.

Corporate restructuring within Europe throughout the 1980s increased the demand by companies for all kinds of external finance. This increased use of the Euromarkets for external finance and a growing awareness of the attraction of the Euroequity market enhanced the experience and expertise of European companies in new issue activity. Nevertheless, national debt markets have traditionally been dominated by home country firms.

From 1982 the increasing use of swaps and other arbitrage techniques led to an accelerated globalization of the Euromarkets. This has had an inevitable impact on new issues in domestic markets. Up to ten years ago competition in the Eurobond market between banks of different nationalities was only evident in the Eurodollar bond market, which has been truly offshore since its birth. New bond issues in currencies like Deutschmarks, for example, were generally lead-managed by one of the big West German houses. From 1982, however, local banks in most countries have faced growing competition in debt securities in their own currencies.

Deregulation in countries like the United Kingdom, France, Germany and Switzerland has increased the penetration of foreign houses in national markets. In the United Kingdom, for example, foreign houses handle a very significant slice of the external finance business of the top 1000 companies. Most of this business has been international, but some houses are strategically orientated towards national issues. The US Goldman Sachs and Swiss UBS, for example, have clear aspirations (and an impressive track record) in this direction within the United Kingdom.

Deregulation of European stock exchanges, the increasing globalization of financial markets, intensifying bank competition and an increasing role for external issues in European corporate finance suggest a buoyant new issue market in Europe in the run-up to 1992 and beyond. There are proposals for an EC common prospectus for new issues, but conduct-of-business rules at an EC level have still to be formulated. The rules for foreign securities issues in national capital markets within the EC still differ markedly (Terry, 1987).

195

Concern has already been expressed by the AIBD that any EC rules should be consistent with the principle of self-regulation. This is the *modus operandi*, of course, of the Eurobond market and it is in keeping with the new, international capital market thinking that has been a significant stimulating factor in the movement towards deregulation on European stock exchanges. From April 1989 UK-based AIBD members are required to report to the Association all transactions in international securities[4]. Once again, the challenge of reconciling structural deregulation (of exchanges) with corresponding re-regulation initiatives (in this case, conduct-of-business rules) emerges as a key policy issue in Europe for 1992 and beyond.

An interesting question is the shape of the new, more integrated new issues market after 1992. We seem a long way off harmonized conduct-of-business and investor-protection rules in Europe, but a fully liberalized capital market is now within the EC's grasp. This is likely to be achieved shortly and wider globalization pressures are accelerating this movement.

Europe 1992 and other developments seem unlikely to herald the demise of the Euromarket as we know it today. It seems more likely that national capital markets in Europe will themselves form part of a wider, global capital market that encompasses the Euromarket. The ability of funds managers, companies, governments and other participants to access an increasing variety of alternatives will undoubtedly enhance investment banking opportunities within Europe. Capital-raising is likely to provide increasingly attractive opportunities in Europe. This prospect is linked to transactional activities (like M&A) and increasing demands by companies for advisory services from investment banks.

Advisory services, mergers and acquisitions

London's Big Bang, deregulation in other major European centres and the approach of 1992 have focused corporate thinking in Europe on new expansion possibilities and new organizational forms and links. Continental European companies may also see this as a way of competing with the giant US and Japanese companies. Mergers and other forms of link-ups are already buoyant as the market for corporate control continues to become more active and liquid in Europe. Fee-based advice to companies and related banking services appear especially attractive market segments with the approach of 1992. These fee services cover areas like M&A, defence against takeovers, LBOs and other corporate financial restructurings.

There is still a long way to go in Europe before the kinds of US waves of M&A activity are experienced, but the signs are clear that M&A business in Europe is growing rapidly (see Rybczynski, 1989). Historically, intra-European M&A activity has been a comparatively small part of total, worldwide M&A business: certainly less than 5 per cent. EC companies, however, spent $44.8 billion in the year to June 1988 on foreign acquisitions (McDougall, 1989, p. 33). The most active European M&A markets have been in the United Kingdom, followed by France, Italy and Germany. Most European deals have been small (below $50 million) by US and world standards. Many ascribe the UK's industrial revival during the 1980s in large part to the marked wave of corporate M&A activity during that period. In addition, contested takeovers have historically been much more important in the United Kingdom (and of course the United States) than in other European countries.

The approach of 1992 has focused corporate attention on the need to re-position for aggressive and defensive purposes. A merger or at least a joint venture appears to have good economic logic in an intensifying competitive environment. Larger institutions are better positioned to achieve economies of scale and scope. It may be cheaper to acquire production and marketing facilities and brand names than to make investments *de novo*. Competitive pressures in the market for corporate control will be intensified as investment managers and deregulated capital markets continue to put a premium on performance.

London's corporate merger wave in the period leading up to Big Bang and beyond confirms the potential of M&A activity in the European 1992 environment. It also confirms that a great deal of the needed investment banking 'technology' is already in place within Europe. The surge of UK takeover activity penetrated several traditional business and industrial sectors. M&A activity in the United Kingdom had already reached $7 billion by the end of 1985 (*Euromoney Corporate Finance Supplement*, 1986, p. 22). In the latter part of 1987 increasing amounts of debt (gearing) began to figure in UK takeovers. The role of debt in the financing of the bid by UK retailer Barker and Dobson for the UK Dee Corporation is indicative in this respect, but the Bank of England appears to retain a cautious attitude towards the effects of large increases in corporate leverage[5].

One of the most dramatic visionary signals of the potential for a more united Europe was, perhaps, the recent activities of the Italian entrepreneur, Benedetti. Benedetti virtually saved the Olivetti company by himself, and Benedetti companies now have substantial interests in Italy, France and Spain. It was Benedetti's attempts to take control of Société Générale de Belgique that was, perhaps, prophetic of post-1992 Europe. Benedetti saw this takeover as the first stage in the creation of the first truly pan-European holding company.

The Benedetti bid failed, but it exposed some of the major challenges in opening up the market for corporate capital in Europe. One issue was the concern that a foreigner should take over an important domestic institution. This kind of concern, together with historic entrenched management attitudes in many companies, is still a characteristic of the European market for corporate control. A related issue is the different legislation that exists on monopolies (anti-trust) and development policies aimed at stimulating various sectors. In many EC countries there is still a lack of clear rules and regulations on contested, open market takeovers. Rybczynski (1989) emphasizes the need to resolve the new and important question raised by this form of corporate restructuring in the 'new' Europe.

These kinds of constraints are certainly not unique to Belgium. Even in the United Kingdom where the authorities have actively encouraged a system of self-regulation and level playing fields in takeovers, there have been some well-publicized blockages of deals on public interest and competitive grounds. A good example was the blocking of the HongKong and Shanghai Corporation's attempt to acquire the Royal Bank of Scotland in 1981. Nevertheless, since 1987 the UK has sought increasingly to level the playing fields for M&A activity. Many hostile bids have been allowed to continue in the United Kingdom.

Although some takeover rules are incorporated into national laws, this is not the general pattern in the majority of EC countries. Nevertheless, anti-competitive, national interest and other devices have been used historically throughout Europe to constrain M&A activity, especially hostile bids and those by 'outside' companies. In Switzerland, for example, the first sign of aggressive M&A activity was uninvited overtures in late 1986 by Jacobs Suchard towards the Swiss confectionery company Hero. This particular deal did not go through in its original form, but it served notice of a new wave of aggressive M&A activity in Europe. Out of 600 takeovers in continental Europe in 1988, however, only two were hostile and both of these failed. Much remains to be done in developing the European market for corporate control.

The signs are that EC monopoly control will become more flexible under pressures from the large corporate lobby[6]. There is a movement now towards individual EC countries easing restrictions, often in advance of Commission proposals. In December 1988 the EC Commission proposed a draft directive to harmonize takeover rules within the Community. It contained a number of significant and contentious proposals. Big bids[7], for example, will have to be notified to Brussels. Some kinds of anti-takeover devices will be prohibited or heavily constrained. These include the issue of new shares that carry voting rights or engaging in 'operations of an exceptional nature' (loss-making deals) after a bidder has appeared. Companies that initiate takeover attempts will have to specify their intentions about the financial structure, debt levels and future activities of the target firm. Only a small number of EC countries currently have even the basic regulatory framework in place to implement the new EC proposals when they become law. The most heavily protected M&A markets in Europe are in Germany and the Netherlands. Change is likely to be resisted most strongly in these countries.

The increasing use of debt in UK M&A activity is indicative of a general European trend towards more leverage. This debt-driven M&A activity does not appear to be approved by Brussels, but market forces are setting the pace. Increased leverage opens the way for public flotations starting as buy-outs. In the United Kingdom, around 25 per cent of new flotations are initiated through former LBOs (McDougall, 1989, p. 37). Table 11.2 confirms the growth (especially in the UK) of management buy-outs (MBOs) and buy-ins (MBIs). A growing proportion of European M&A activity in the future can be expected at the seller's initiative as the market becomes more liquid.

Table 11.2 Management buy-outs and buy-ins in Europe, 1980–87.

Country	Estimated number of deals
United Kingdom	2,000[a]
France	200
Netherlands	175
Sweden	75
Belgium	30
West Germany	20
Switzerland	20
Italy	18
Spain	15
Norway	11
Denmark	7

Source: McDougall (1989, p. 37).
Note: a To end-1988: 2,350.

The competitive structure of the European M&A industry can be broken down into two broad groups: the European conglomerates and third-country institutions. The former group comprises British and continental European merchant banks and the specialist investment banking units of the large commercial banks. The third-country institutions are dominated by the US houses who offer a 'fully integrated' financial services package to companies.

In the M&A market the US investment banks have already penetrated significantly. The biggest single UK M&A deal in 1986, for example, went to Goldman Sachs, which was ranked top or second in the list of advisers on M&A within the United Kingdom during the first six months of 1988 (see Wolman, 1988, p. 5). UK merchant banks argue that the US houses have no significant appeal in a domestic UK merger or acquisition; the US institutions, however, are able to add value through the addition of services from their established, London-based capital market groups.

From 1987 there has been a strong drive by US banks into UK and European takeovers. US banks have been winning a growing number of mandates. Several of them have made the United Kingdom their base for M&A work in Europe. A growing UK presence and targeting for medium-sized UK companies are likely to be the next stages in US investment banking strategy. The Japanese have also been reported as wishing to acquire M&A teams in London. Another new and important competitor for corporate advisory fees is accountancy firms. Although corporate finance in accounting firms is comparatively new, cross-border M&A business in Europe is one of their expected growth areas. Two recent surveys by Peat Marwick confirm the large potential size of the European M&A market (European Investment Banking Report, 1988, p. 7). If Wall Street experiences are any guide, accountancy firms are likely to increase their role in corporate financial advice and transactional activities that have up to now been the preserve of the investment banks.

Brokerage, trading and investment management

The growth of European capital markets and investment banking activities like M&A will create a corresponding requirement for more highly developed secondary markets for intra-European securities transactions. Broker support services for portfolio managers, pension funds, brokers and other banks will increase correspondingly. We saw earlier that the large institutional investors and portfolio managers – especially the US, UK and Japanese institutions – have substantially increased their interest and activity in continental European securities. Given the current, comparatively low level of foreign investment in Europe, many believe that the modern boom in European stock markets is just beginning (see also Chapters 9 and 10).

The continued globalization of financial markets and London's Big Bang have been important stimulants to secondary market trading in Europe. These developments took place against the backcloth of the world stock market boom up to the 1987 crash. Increased opportunities developed in the non-dollar segment of the world's financial markets as the US dollar began its precipitous decline from the mid-1980s.

From 1986 onwards there was a strong growth of market-making in continental European stocks within the London market. Like the earlier Wall Street 'May Day' reforms, Big Bang effectively re-capitalized the London brokerage industry and

Table 11.3 Growth of cross-border portfolio investment: pension and tax-exempt funds.

Year end	Total	Of which US
1975	6	0
1980	21	3
1985	85	27
1987		
(Nov. est.)	150	50
1990		
(projected)	300	100

Source: Bunker (1987b, p. 10).

brought in negotiated commissions. We have already noted the substantial M&A activity that took place in the build-up to London's Big Bang. The French reforms have also been characterized by this same kind of activity among financial firms and the freeing up of commissions.

The crash came before London had fully adjusted to the new regime. It was already clear that over-capacity in gilts and equity market-makers in London would produce a shake-out. The freeing up of commissions and aggressive price fixing put enormous pressures on profits. Institutions like Midland and Lloyds Bank withdrew from market-making. Wall Street experiences confirm the resultant squeeze on broking profits and the corresponding pressures on investment banks' securities research capabilities in an environment of negotiated commissions. A common criticism of investment research was that it moved towards a shorter-term perspective after Big Bang, and the crash has at least consolidated this trend.

Investment management services in Europe cover a wide spectrum of activities including securities distribution, asset management, finance for investors and general support services. The three main groups of investment portfolios within the European investment banking market are the management of European and non-European securities portfolios for European institutions, the management of European private investor portfolios and the management of portfolios of European securities for non-European institutions.

The stock market crash slowed for a time, but did not stop the movement towards overseas investment funds. This, together with intensifying competition and growing awareness of performance, is likely to be the pattern for European investment-management services through 1992 and beyond. The sustained growth of cross-border portfolio investment is confirmed in Table 11.3. Table 11.4 depicts the strong movement overseas by the top US pension fund managers. Competition for this business by European institutions has been particularly intense. Around one-third of the top US fund managers were European in 1987. Recent survey evidence also confirms the vigorous growth overseas by UK and Japanese pension funds. Tables 11.3 and 11.4 substantiate the strong growth expectations for cross-border portfolio investment in general.

With the movement towards more investment overseas by European institutional investors, competition to manage these funds will increase. This competition will intensify from foreign institutions, especially in those major centres (like Tokyo and

Table 11.4 Top 15 international ERISA fund managers.

Rank			Manager	Assets under international management (US$ million)			Number of accounts		
1987	1986	1985		1987	1986	1985	1987	1986	1985
1	5	9	State Street	3,885	2,380	1,000	19	16	14
2	1	1	JP Morgan	2,866	3,159	3,100	36	35	31
3	3	2	Capital Guardian	2,754	2,599	1,900	29	25	22
4	2	3	Morgan Grenfell	2,378	2,693	1,800	45	42	41
5	7	6	First Chicago Investment	2,286	2,148	1,400	13	15	12
6	4	4	Templeton International	2,118	2,395	1,800	97	53	45
7	9	7	Rowe Price Fleming	2,006	1,790	1,400	23	21	21
8	12	12	Baring International	2,006	1,370	819	24	16	13
9	8	8	Grantham Mayo	1,857	1,944	1,100	11	28	27
10	6	5	Fidelity International	1,800	2,200	1,700	17	21	19
11	11	14	Schroder Capital	1,635	1,420	800	34	25	18
12	16	NA	WorldInvest	1,535	766	NA	18	7	NA
13	14	15	NM Rothschild	1,421	1,021	604	11	10	9
14	13	10	Batterymarch Financial	1,164	1,070	880	7	7	8
15	15	20	Warburg Investment Mgt.	1,132	886	375	27	20	15

Source: Financial Times (1988, p. 6).
Note: (all mandates) ranked by international assets under management.

New York) where investments are directed. Within Europe, UK, Swiss, German and Dutch institutions are likely to be especially competitive. Several continental European institutions – particularly the Germans and Swiss – could see the management of international pension fund portfolios being increasingly attractive as pressures mount on the management of European private investors' portfolios.

One of the important traditional components of 'value added' by European institutions to the management of European private investors' portfolios has been secrecy. Private investors have cherished secrecy for tax-evasion and capital-mobility purposes. National bank secrecy laws in countries like Luxembourg and Switzerland have put a premium on the corresponding portfolio management services of the banks in those countries. The value of banking secrecy is likely to be reduced with the EC 1992 initiative. The growth of an intra-EC capital market, the concomitant deepening and extension of investment banking in Europe and the entry of new competitors with continued deregulation and globalization will all increase the competitive pressures on continental European banks for the management of private clients' portfolios.

Conclusion

The investment banking market in Europe is now evolving through an intensifying competitive phase (see Walter and Smith, 1989). Continued deregulation and globalization pressures will increase business opportunities in all major market segments. As in other important banking markets in Europe, no institution is unaware of these pressures and the need to adapt to them and position accordingly. More so than many traditional banking activities, modern investment banking is a fast-moving business. It typifies the need for forward thinking and the organizational need to foster internal dynamics to adapt easily to change. Strategy and planning are becoming increasingly important in the evolving European environment. In the following chapter we shall focus more specifically on this managerial and related organizational aspect of change in European banking.

Notes

1. These included issuing letters of credit that merchants could use to draw bills of exchange, buying and selling outright bills of exchange created by trade, and making advances to producers before the goods were sold.
2. These agents did not own the commodities in which they traded; instead, they sought out customers.
3. Like language, preferences, habit, national culture and incomes.
4. The AIBD is the designated exchange for Eurosecurities.
5. One reason is the possible effect on companies with high gearing of a possible downturn in the economy.
6. Only three EC countries – the United Kingdom, Germany and France – have trust-breaking regulators.
7. Comprising more than one-third of the shares in a target company.

References

Barnett, Matthew (1988), 'Alive – but barely twitching', *Euromoney* (May) pp. 92–8.

Brady, Simon (1988), 'The sun rises again in the West', *Euromoney* (December) pp. 41–51.

Bunker, Nick (1987a), 'Four causes for satisfaction in the M&A zone', *Financial Times, (Corporate Finance Supplement)*, (27 July), p. vii.

Bunker, Nick (1987b), 'The Crash will mean closer scrutiny of fees', *Financial Times, International Fund Management*, (16 November), p. 8.

Campbell Committee (1980), *Australian Financial System: Interim Report of the Committee of Inquiry* (Canberra: Australian Government Publishing Service).

Centre for Business Strategy (1989), *1922: Myths and Realities* (London: London Business School).

Chapman, Stanley (1984), *The Rise of Merchant Banking* (London: Unwin Hyman Ltd).

Clarke, Tim and Thorne, Peter (1987), *The Magnificent Seven* (London: Citicorp Scrimgeour Vickers).

Clay, C. J. J. and Wheble, B. S. (1983), *Modern Merchant Banking* (Cambridge: Woodhead-Faulkner).

Committee on the Working of the Monetary System (1959), *Report* (Radcliffe Report), Cmnd 827, (London: HMSO) (August).

Davies, Ben (1987), 'European stock exchanges', *Supplement to Euromoney* (August) pp. 1–56.

Dignan, Janet (ed.) (1989), 'Nomura strengthens its European operations', *European Investment Banking Report*, Issue no. 36, (January) pp. 4–5.

Euromoney Corporate Finance Supplement (1986), M&A, (July), pp. 1–36.

Euromoney Corporate Finance Supplement (1987), 'The changing face of Swiss finance', (February), pp. 1–48.

Euromoney Corporate Finance Supplement (1988a), 'Treasurers top team' (March), pp. 20–33.

Euromoney Corporate Finance Supplement (1988b), 'Mergers and acquisitions: corporate big cats stalk the global jungle', (May) pp. 1–24.

European Investment Banking Report (1988), 'Corporate finance advice from accountants?', Issue no. 35, (December), pp. 5–7.

Financial Times (1988), *International Fund Management Survey*, 28 November.

Gardener E. P. M. (1987), 'Structural and strategic consequences of financial conglomeration', *Revue de la Banque*, 9, pp. 5–16.

Gardener E. P. M. (1988), 'A strategic perspective of bank financial conglomerates in London after the crash', *IEF Research Papers in Banking and Finance* RP 88/22, pp. 1–19 (Bangor: Institute of European Finance).

Kindleberger, Charles P. (1984), *A Financial History of Western Europe* (London: George Allen & Unwin).

McDougall, Rosamund (1989), 'Whatever you do, keep it friendly', *The Banker* (March) pp. 33–7.

Purnell, Sonia (1989), 'The Americans in Europe', *European Investment Banking Report*, Issue no. 35, (December) pp. 1–3.

Rybczynski, Tad (1989), 'Corporate restructuring', *National Westminster Bank Quarterly Review* (August), pp. 19–28.

Skully, Michael T. (1987) *Merchant Banking in Australia* (Oxford: Oxford University Press).

Terry, Brian (ed.) (1987), *International Finance and Investment* (London: The Chartered Institute of Bankers).

Walter, Ingo and Smith, Roy C. (1989), *Investment Banking in Europe: Restructuring for the 1990s* (Oxford: Basil Blackwell).

Williamson, J. Peter (ed.) (1988), *Investment Banking Handbook* (Chichester: John Wiley & Sons).

Wolman, Clive (1988), 'US innovation has been slow to diffuse into the UK', *Financial Times* (25 July) *Corporate Finance*, p. 5.

Chapter twelve

Banking strategy and 1992

Introduction

Strategy and strategic management have become increasingly important for European banks during recent years. The new financial environment that started to develop in the 1960s has emphasized the need for planning and strategy in modern banking. The preceding chapters confirmed that all the main banking sectors – retail and wholesale, domestic and international – are now subject to intensifying competition and rapid change. The approach of 'Europe 1992' will help to accelerate many of these processes and, simultaneously, confirm the importance of sound banking strategies. This chapter focuses on European banking strategies with the approach of 1992. In this respect it draws together and summarizes the strategic implications of much of the foregoing analysis. Following on from the preceding chapter, we shall begin by examining investment banking strategies after the 1987 crash.

Strategic management challenges

Investment banking strategy after the crash
The stock market crash exposed the weaknesses of some of the 'Big Bang' era investment banking strategies adopted by many of the investment banks in London. The previous chapter discussed the formation of bank financial conglomerates in London up to Big Bang and the emergent 'barbell view' of industrial structure in world investment banking. These organizational design changes have been an important feature of investment banking strategies in London (Gardener, 1988, pp. 5–6). The rapid evolution of more market-driven organizational designs in banking is largely a phenomenon of the past two decades. We shall see in the following section that this has also been a feature of retail banking in Europe.

The stock market crash has led to new, revisionist thinking about investment banking strategies. In Chapter 11 we alluded to the emergence of so-called 'cluster strategies', and we shall explore these shortly. The crash emphasized the apparent lack of strategy in many investment banks and the weaknesses of some kinds of internal control systems. Risk-based pricing, for example, was apparently not the general rule; 'strategic positioning' appears to have been the main objective in pricing. The Japanese houses, however, were distinguished by their longer-term planning commitment (*The Economist*, 1988). The stock market crash highlighted three important barriers to competing that are now helping to influence post-crash banking strategies: capital adequacy, the role of information in OTC markets, and placement power.

The rise of the 'bought deal' in the business mix of modern investment banks has emphasized the role of capital adequacy. The recapitalization of the Stock Exchange in London (with Big Bang) and in Paris (with the new reforms) endorsed the particular significance of capital backing in the capital market and related activities that characterize contemporary investment banking. Banks need to ensure that they have the capital resources to hold portfolios on their own books and carry them through temporary market downturns. This need has been emphasized with the new supervisory developments in London and the associated increasing formality of position risk rules. We have already suggested (Chapter 4) that the convergence of capital-adequacy rules for investment banks will be one of the big supervisory challenges in the new post-1992 Europe. A related pressure has been the increasing importance of trading-related profits for houses in London and New York.

Unlike London and New York, commissions are still fixed in Tokyo. Position-taking in the majority of Japanese securities houses comprises only around 5–15 per cent of total revenue. Japanese houses were still able to record a 56 per cent increase in profits after tax for the year to September 1987 (Jones, 1988). Negotiated commissions in London and (particularly) New York have squeezed profits. This has been a factor in encouraging high trading volumes and has probably helped to restrict the amount of research undertaken by houses. US houses were already suffering from the burden of speculative excesses before the crash.

The crucial role of information in OTC markets has also become emphasized since Big Bang. Feldman and Stephenson (1988) argue that failure to recognize this fundamental barrier to competing in OTC markets:

> ... makes becoming a successful large volume player difficult; they render many niche strategies indefensible long-term; and they make becoming a medium-sized player virtually impossible.

The reason is that success in these markets requires controlling access to supply and demand information. Market share and trading volumes do not ensure access to the appropriate markets. In certain kinds of markets – called 'opaque' by Feldman and Stephenson – pockets of 'proprietary information' may develop[1]. Supply and demand change quickly and erratically in these markets, and there is no centralized mechanism for the dissemination of reliable information to market participants.

The 1987 crash has markedly reduced the emphasis on more exotic financial instruments. In the new environment placement power – the third of our suggested barriers to competing – has been highlighted. Table 12.1 provides some illustrative data that confirm the rise of those banks with known, extensive placement capabilities. US investment banks have been noted for their innovation abilities, but they have been increasingly displaced by firms with strong placing capabilities. Access to a good retail investor base has been especially emphasized. So-called 'farmers' (less innovative banks, but with good placement abilities) are displacing as market leaders the 'hunter-gatherers' (the highly innovative investment banks) of the pre-crash era.

Table 12.1 Top lead managers of Eurobond new issues.

1987	Value $bn	1982	Value $bn
Nomura Securities	17.9	Crédit Suisse First Boston	7.2
Crédit Suisse First Boston	10.4	Deutsche Bank	5.2
Deutsche Bank	7.8	Morgan Stanley	3.8
Nikko Securities	7.1	JP Morgan	2.0
Daiwa Securities	6.7	Swiss Bank Corp.	1.7
Morgan Stanley	5.0	Merrill Lynch	1.7
JP Morgan	4.4	S. G. Warburg	1.6
Salomon Brothers	4.4	Goldman Sachs	1.2
Industrial Bank of Japan	4.1	Société Générale	1.0

Source: Euromoney Bondware.

Within this new environment and thinking, many investment banks have undertaken a significant reappraisal of their strategies. Pre-crash thinking stressed the importance of alleged 'synergies' within financial conglomerate strategies, but these have been downgraded in the new thinking. Synergies are at least temporarily out of fashion in post-crash London. This has led to the emergence of so-called cluster strategies. A cluster strategy approach is a simple concept. Essentially, banks are exhorted to play to their strengths. It is characterized by a bank specializing in a number (cluster) of different services, locations or customer segments. The important requirement for inclusion in the cluster is that each 'cluster activity' should be profitable in its own right. Synergies between component cluster activities are given a comparatively low weighting.

Alongside this view has emerged a growing acceptance that an institution no longer needs to build integrated investment banks in each of the world's major financial centres. Physical presence for trading in banking products like Treasury

Table 12.2 Planning issues – country/comparisons.

Issues		Countries			
		UK	Spain	Italy	Switzerland
	Marketing^a	1	1	1	1
Competition					
	–from European banks	5	2	4	
	–from non-European banks				3
	interest-rate fluctuations	3	3	5	
Credit risk:	–domestic	4	4		
	–international			1	5
	cost of technology	3		2	4
	sources of capital				2
	world recession/growth				
	personnel policy		5	3	

Source: Arthur Andersen (1986, Diagram 54, p. 59).
Notes: a including product development and market segmentation.
The scale 1–5 denotes a comparative ranking, where 1 is the most important and 5 depicts the least comparative importance.

bonds and swaps is no longer viewed as so important. Location is more important for products like equities. The emergence of the cluster strategy approach has under-mined the pre-crash 'barbell model'[2] of the industrial structure of world investment banking (see Chapter 11). The crash has led to an increasing acceptance of the view that a large number of 'global niche' institutions may be successful in world investment banking markets and many of these will be medium-sized institutions. Over 100 successful firms have been predicted (see *The Economist*, 1988 and Gardener, 1988 and 1990).

Strategic marketing orientation

New competitors and new forms of competition have consolidated the attractions of strategic planning in European banks. In this environment, marketing is likely to become one of the single most important planning issues. This is the finding of an important recent survey, and some comparative results are summarized in Table 12.2. On a scale from 1–5, marketing (including product development and market segmentation) was consistently ranked a number one planning issue for the four countries surveyed. It consistently came second (to management quality) in a survey of the key success factors in banking across Europe (Arthur Andersen, 1986, p. 65).

Although bank marketing is not a new concept in Europe, sophisticated marketing is an innovation for the majority of banks. Deregulation, intensifying competition and an increasingly sophisticated and mobile customer base have been important factors in the enhancement of the importance of marketing in banking. In a bank strategic perspective, marketing is defined by Reidenbach (1986, p. 1) as 'an integra-ted business activity directed at identifying, creating, and servicing demand'. The work 'integrated' within this definition emphasizes that marketing should not be divorced from other bank activities. The remainder of the definition focuses on the customer. As we have seen on many occasions, banking in Europe is moving rapidly from its traditional, supply-led orientation to a much stronger demand orientation (see, for example, Chapter 6).

A strategic marketing orientation is concerned operationally with matching a bank's resources to the customer market. Marketing is a kind of link in the equation between market opportunities and bank capability. A bank must ensure that it has the resources – financial, human and technological – to create, satisfy and service customers' needs at a profit. This is not a random process, and it is not free from constraints. This modern concept of marketing is the latest stage in an evolutionary process within banking (see Clarke *et al.* 1987, 1988).

The first stage (probably up to the early 1960s) in this 'logical historical order' model of the evolutionary process may be labelled the production era, when the emphasis was on producing and selling financial services. Banks were generally supply-led and had an inward-looking focus during this phase. From the early 1960s to the early 1970s banks entered the so-called promotion era. The emphasis began to focus more on product quality and the impact of competition. Marketing's potentials were increasingly recognized by banks and other FSFs. Banks started to recognize the need to identify customers and to advertise.

Some time during the early 1970s banks entered the third stage, the market-orientated era. More resources were diverted towards promotion and the selling concept became much more strongly emphasized. This era consolidated strongly in

207

those European countries that were in (like the United Kingdom) or rapidly approaching (like France, the Netherlands, West Germany and Sweden) a 'strong market orientation' within their financial systems. We saw in Chapter 6 that many continental European countries were leaders in the development of retail banking, and they were often more 'market-orientated' in this particular sector than other countries like the United Kingdom. The selling concept became much more emphasized during this stage, and marketing increased in importance within the organizational structure of banks. Marketing experience began to figure in many senior bank appointments.

'Marketing control' is a kind of intensification of the marketing-orientation concept. The entire organization becomes increasingly shaped by marketing and associated profitability considerations. Longer-term strategies are influenced to a growing extent by marketing. At this stage marketing becomes more strongly identified with senior management. The ultimate in marketing control is where marketing considerations drive the whole organization.

European banks are now entering this latest stage of their organizational development (see Priestley, 1987). 'Europe 1992' will accelerate this process as the range of alternative financial services is increased in all European market segments. Technological advances and deregulation will allow new delivery techniques, such as 'trade without establishment', to encourage this movement. In one sense this historical transition from the production to the marketing control stage is also one from a seller's to a buyer's market. As we have seen, at another level it is also positively correlated with the evolution of a stronger market-orientation in financial systems.

Bank marketing in Europe and in other countries has traditionally been biased in favour of retail banking. One result is that the full implementation of marketing control within specialist retail organizations may be swifter and perhaps less painful than in larger and more diverse financial conglomerates. The reason is simple. It may often be easier to focus senior management policies and adapt organizational design in those organizations that are more dedicated to retail banking. Intra-organizational conflicts between different power groups are likely to be less acute than in larger conglomerates, where international, corporate and other specialist units may be competing strongly for resources. Marketing in all product/market segments is undoubtedly one of the major strategic challenges for banks in Europe, and this is likely to be intensified with the approach of 1992.

The build-up to 1992

The single European market in financial services is already forming as FSFs assume defensive or offensive links. A sample of recent country trends confirms the importance of organizational design in the competitive strategies of FSFs with the approach of 1992. Invariably, the result is to consolidate or enhance the organizational model of a FSM (financial services supermarket). We have seen that the FSM model of organizational design – typified in the German universal bank – is very much a European banking feature. Within these strategies – like the build-up to London's Big Bang – a wide variety of different organizational models are emerging (see *The Banker*, September 1989). Table 12.3 shows the five main types of strategies that have emerged and provides a comprehensive list of the banks and other financial institutions involved in these activities.

Table 12.3 Recent merger and acquisition activity in key European markets.

Category/Investor	Target country	Date	Transaction
1. Alliances (non-predator minority interests)			
San Paolo Bank (Italy)	UK	1986	Acquired 6% interest in Hambros Bank
Deutsche Bank (Germany)	UK	1987	Acquired 5% interest in Morgan Grenfell
San Paolo Bank (Italy)	France	1987	Acquired 1% interest in Compagnie Financière de Suez
Generale Bank (Belgium)	France	1987	Purchased 1.55% of Compagnie Financière de Suez
Cariplo (Italy)	Spain	1988	Acquired 1% interest in Banco Santander
Commerzbank (Germany)	Spain	1984	Purchased 10% of Banco Hispano-Americano, BHA, acquired at 5% of Commerzbank
Banco de Bilbao (Spain)	UK	1987	Acquired 5% of Hambros Bank
Proventus (Sweden)	Finland	1988	Intends to acquire 2% of KOP as part of asset swap
Banco Santander (Spain)	UK	1988	Acquired 10% interest in Royal Bank of Scotland The latter owns 2.5% of Santander's equity
Banque Nationale de Paris (France)	France	1989	Share-link and cross marketing deal with the state-owned Union des Assurance de Paris insurance company
Paribas (France)	Denmark	1989	Link with Hafnia (insurance company)
Verenigde Spaarbank (VSB) (Netherlands)	Netherlands	1989	Alliance with Amex, the third biggest Dutch insurer
Dresdner Bank (Germany)	Germany	1989	Agreement with Allianz (Europe's largest insurance group) to distribute its products in various regions
DG Bank (Germany)	Spain	1989	Linked with Spain's rural savings banks in a joint venture, Banco Co-operativo Español
2. Blocking/strategic minority interests			
Hongkongbank (HK)	UK	1987	Acquired 15% interest in Midland Bank
Cartera Central (Kuwait, Spain)	Spain	1988	Purchased 12% of Banco Central
Cariplo (Italy)	Spain	1988	Acquired 30% interest in Banco Jover from Banco Santander
Banco Santander (Spain)	Italy	1988	Purchased 30% of IBI from Cariplo
Skandinaviska Enskilda Bank (Sweden)	Denmark, Norway, Finland	1986	As part of Scandinavian Bank partnership, S-E-Banken acquired 5% of Privatbanken, 6% of Bergen Bank, and 3% of Union Bank of Finland
Kansallis Osake Pankki (Finland)	Sweden	1988	Intends to acquire equivalent of 16% of Gotagruppen from Proventus Holding Company

Table 12.3 (*cont*).

Category/Investor	Target country	Date	Transaction
Banque Indosuez (France)	UK	1989	Acquired 15% of Morgan Grenfell
Hypo Bank (Germany)	Spain	1989	Owns 1.7% of Banco Popular
3. Cross-border acquisitions			
Banco Populare di Novara (Italy)	France	1988	Acquired 80% of Banque de l'Union Maritime from CCF
National Australia Bank	UK/Ireland	1987	Purchased Clydesdale Bank and other interests from Midland Bank
Bank of Ireland (Ireland)	UK	1987	Acquired Bank of America's UK mortgage loan subsidiary
Banque National de Paris (France)	UK	1988	Purchased Chemical Bank's UK mortgage loan subsidiary
Dresdner Bank (Germany)	UK	1988	Acquired 70% of Thornton Fund Management Group
Deutsche Bank (Germany)	Italy	1986	Purchased Banca d'America e d'Italia from Bank of America
Banco Santander (Spain)	Germany	1987	Purchased CC Bank from Bank of America
Citicorp (US)	Spain	1983	Acquired Banco de Levante
Citicorp (US)	Italy	1984	Acquired Banco Centrosud from Banco di Roma
Chase Manhattan (US)	Spain		Purchased Banco de Finanzas from Regulatory Authorities
Barclays (UK)	Spain	1981	Acquired Banco de Valladolid from Regulatory Authorities
Crédit Lyonnais (France)	Netherlands	1987	Purchased Nederlandse Credietbank from Chase Manhattan
Banco Santander (Spain)	Belgium	1988	Acquired Belgian subsidiary of Crédit du Nord
San Paolo Bank (Italy)	France	1987	Acquired control of Banque Vernes from Suez Group
Lloyds Bank (UK)	Germany	1984	Acquired failed Schroeder, Muenchmeyer Hengst Merchant Bank
Midland Bank (UK)	Italy	1989	Controlling stake in Euromobiliare merchant bank
Westdeutsche Landesbank (Germany)	Various	1989	West LB is buying Standard Chartered's European branches, except those in Frankfurt and Switzerland. The two firms intend to co-operate in international and merchant banking
Société Générale (France)	UK	1989	Purchase of Thornton, Touche Remnant (UK) (fund management firm) from Dresdner Bank
Hypo Bank (Germany)	UK	1989	Acquired 50% of fund managers Foreign and Colonial
Deutsche Bank (Germany)	UK	1989	Purchased Morgan Grenfell

Banque Nationale de Paris (BNP) (France)	Spain	1989	Acquired 85 branches of Banco Bilbao Vizcaya (see below for related deal)
Banco Bilbao Vizcaya (Spain)	France	1989	Acquired 85 branches of BNP's Crédit Universel consumer finance chain
Crédit Lyonnais (France)	Italy	1989	Purchased 30% of Credito Bergamasco
Société Générale (France)	Germany	1989	Acquired SG Alsässische Bank
Société Générale (France)	Netherlands	1989	Acquired Ingurersen (a broking firm)
Deutsche Bank (Germany)	Netherlands	1989	Acquired Albert de Bary merchant bank
NMB (Netherlands)	Belgium	1989	Acquired Royal Bank of Canada's Belgian banking operations
Banco Bilbao Vizcaya (Spain)	Belgium	1989	Acquired Banque Crédit Commercial
Banco Hispano (Spain) and BACOB (Belgium)	Belgium	1989	Joint acquisition of Continental Bank
Banque Bruxelles Lambert (Belgium)	France	1989	Fully acquired the French investment bank Dreyfus
Deutsche Bank (Germany)	Spain	1989	Fully acquired Banco Commercial Transatlântico
Deutsche Bank (Germany)	Portugal	1989	Acquired 100% of merchant bank MDM in Portugal
Dresdner Bank (Germany)	France	1989	Arranged to acquire specialist arbitrage and treasury management firm, Banque Internationale de Placement
Crédit Agricole (France)	Italy	1989	Acquired 13.3% stake in Nuovo Banco Ambrosiano
Banesto (Spain)	Portugal	1989	Holds 3.3% in Banco Tottae Acores
S. G. Warburg (UK)	Portugal	1989	Acquired stake in merchant banking firm Efisa
Baltica (Denmark)	UK	1989	Acquired 9% of Hambros
4. National mergers/acquisitions			
Westdeutsche Landesbank	Germany	1988–	(Proposed) Projected merger with Hessische Landesbank (failed mid-1989). Other mergers of Landesbanken expected to follow
Banco de Bilbao/Banco de Vizcaya	Spain	1988	Merged November 1988
Banco Español de Credito/Banco Central	Spain	1988–	(Proposed) Projected merger (failed in March 1989)
ABC Bank	Norway	1985	Leading Oslo savings bank merged with central savings bank in Norway; known internationally as Union Bank of Norway
NMB	Netherlands	1989	Merger with Postbank. Gives the government 49% of the combined group (half of the holding is to be sold off to the public)
Risparmio di Roma	Italy	1989	Acquired 51% of Banco Spirito Santo from IRI heading up to a full merger

Table 12.3 *(cont).*

Category/Investor	Target country	Date	Transaction
Credito Italiano	Italy	1989	Built up a sizeable stake in Banca Nazionale dell' Agricoltura
Nuovo Banco Ambrosiano	Italy	1989	Purchased Banca Cattolica de Veneto
San Paolo	Italy	1989	Large stake purchased in Crediop (a specialist corporate finance institution)
La Caixa	Spain	1989	Proposed merger with Caixa de Ahorros de Barcelona. (If merger takes place it will become Spain's largest bank)
Den Norske Creditbank	Norway	1989	Planned merger with Bergen Bank to create a new Den Norske Bank
Sparekassen SDS	Denmark	1989	Planned merger with Privatbanken to form a new bank called UNIBank Danmark
Amro	Netherlands	1990	Planned merger with ABN
5. Cross-border mergers to create supranational group			
Generale Bank (Belgium)/ Amro (Netherlands)	Netherlands/ Belgium	1988	Exchange of 10% equity holdings with intent to increase to 25% and possibly merge in future. (Planned merger failed, October 1989. Holding to be reduced to 5% each)

Source: Davis International Banking Consultants (1988) and authors' updates.

The five main strategies are as follows:

- alliances (non-predator minority interests),
- blocking/strategic minority interests,
- cross-border acquisitions,
- national mergers/acquisition,
- cross-border mergers to create supranational groups.

It is clear from Table 12.3 that the majority of activity to date has related to cross-border acquisition, mainly large banks purchasing much smaller firms. Non-predatory alliances appear to be undertaken by similar large-sized institutions, whereas projected national mergers between large-sized banks tend on the whole to be less common. But alliances are by no means as widespread as many authors often imply. It should also be noted that the term 'alliances' has a specialist meaning in the context of Table 12.3; on other occasions in this book this term is used in a more general way to cover any general form of institutional co-operation.

These new acquisitions and other institutional forms of co-operation have received much publicity. A great deal of speculation exists on which banks are likely to be acquired (see also Chapter 3), but the opportunities for bank takeovers (especially of large banks) in Europe seem limited even with the approach of 1992. Molyneux (1989, p. 364) predicts that if acquisition activity is focused anywhere in the EC, it is likely to be in the United Kingdom, Germany, Italy, Spain and (possibly) Luxembourg. Limited large bank takeover opportunities may encourage more joint ventures of the kind already described, the establishment of limited, niche branch networks overseas and the greater cross-border delivery of financial services.

Nevertheless, there appears to be a growing view in some quarters that a continued wave of bank takeovers and mergers in Europe should not be discounted too heavily (see Crabbe, 1989). So far, certain banks have shown an apparent preference for limited share swaps and technology-sharing agreements. One reason is the perceived difficulties of running a branch network in another country. But there is growing evidence that an increasing number of regulators hold the view that their banks should not be excessively protected from foreign purchasers. In this general connexion, share swaps may be flawed as a defensive strategy. These links increase bank size, and that might make them more attractive to a predator.

Although there are no specific laws forbidding bank acquisitions by foreign institutions in countries like Italy, France and West Germany, there are other barriers. For example, a powerful anti-trust philosophy exists in West Germany through the state cartel office. Probably the most severe restriction on major banking acquisitions across Europe is the new Basle capital-adequacy convergence rules. The deductibility from Tier 1 capital of any premium (or goodwill) above the asset value acquired in an acquisition is likely to precipitate a need for fresh capital. This enhances the attractiveness of share exchanges or mergers of the capital and assets of the FSFs involved. It may also increase the likelihood that those acquisitions which do occur will usually be the larger banks purchasing smaller ones.

Towards 1992 and beyond

Organizational design and strategy

Many FSFs have already realized that operating successfully in post-1992 Europe will require much more than finding a foreign partner or opening a few new outlets. The vulnerability of the big universal banks in countries like West Germany has already been demonstrated, albeit on a small scale (see Andrews, 1989). The danger of a business mix where, for example, profitable business helps to subsidize unprofitable business is that highly focused competitors may poach away the profitable business. A McKinsey expert suggests (see Andrews, 1989, p. 45) that in many large banks up to 80 per cent of revenue comes from only 20 per cent of the customers. FSFs like the American Express Company's bank in West Germany and France's Compagnie Bancaire have already demonstrated the potential for tightly organized and highly focused companies to take business away from their much bigger domestic competitors. These kinds of FSF typify one end of the organizational spectrum in the new kinds of FSM that are emerging with the build-up to 1992.

The West German Deutsche Bank's strategy is seen by many as the archetypal structure at the other end of the spectrum, and it has been characterised by the following *inter alia*:

- purchase of Banca d'America e d'Italia,
- increased holdings in both a Portuguese and Spanish bank,
- purchase of the remaining shares of H. Albert de Bary in the Netherlands,
- opening a mortgage bank in Luxembourg,
- setting up an insurance company and buying a management consultant in West Germany,
- purchase of the UK merchant bank Morgan Grenfell.

Deutsche Bank has also stated that it wants to buy a French bank. Deutsche emphasizes that its strategy is highly selective and conditioned largely by potential returns; it is also supported by a strong capital base.

Organizational design changes have been an important feature of change in all financial systems during the past two or three decades. The organizational design of a FSF is concerned with the structuring of two basic tasks: specialization and co-ordination. In this respect it is concerned fundamentally with sub-dividing activities into different departments or divisions (specialization) and then managing these (co-ordination) in such a way that the organization fulfils its strategic objectives.

The recent strategic activities by FSFs throughout Europe have incorporated various important kinds of organizational innovations. Some institutions have aimed at an increased scale and a wider spread of financial services: we may label these the global financial supermarkets (GFSMs)[3]. At the other end of the size spectrum are the much smaller niche and narrowly focused organizations: we shall simply refer to these as niche financial supermarkets (NFSMs)[4]. One may be forgiven for thinking that European strategic thinking in the run-up to 1992 appears to be dominated by this kind of 'barbell model' of organizational design. Medium-sized players do not seem to figure highly as attractive alternatives in this particular view of the world. An important characteristic feature of all these changes in organizational design, however, is that they represent a form of 'interchange system' with a more market-orientated financial environment. This rapid evolution of more market-driven organizational designs in banks and other FSFs is largely a phenomenon of the 1970s and 1980s.

Viewing FSF organizational design as a kind of interchange system between FSF strategy and the external environment is informative and analytically useful. A significant innovation, external or internal to the FSF, may render obsolete part of the existing organization. In this setting, innovation is likely to generate organizational crises, a need to change organizational design. Controlled organizational crises can help stimulate desirable innovations, but uncontrolled or inappropriate organizational changes, on the other hand, can be disastrous.

FSFs throughout Europe are now faced with continuing and increasing pressures to overhaul their old managerial approaches and strategies. Organizational design changes are an essential part of this process, and the success of particular kinds of FSM organizational models will hinge in large part on them. But all these changes by themselves are part of a more fundamental programme of managerial adaptation. A greater demand (or market) orientation, harnessing technology, cost cutting, the disposal of unprofitable business and better internal risk and return allocation systems for increasingly expensive capital are likely to be essential features of these changes.

The size issue

Adoption of the GFSM strategy suggests that a strategic view prevails that size is a desirable organizational characteristic. It implies that the large FSMs must strive to become even bigger, and the medium-sized institutions, the 'regionals', must also grow rapidly or suffer the consequences. In the European context, size appears to be a contemporary objective not only to defend the strategic position of the institutions involved, but also to enlarge their geographic, customer and product market penetration. It is also, of course, a defence against predators as the European market for corporate control becomes more liquid and active.

Investment banking experiences in New York and London have demonstrated the severe management problems that can arise as different corporate cultures are brought together in a single organization. The kind of European GFSM that is emerging carries with it the potential for two important kinds of culture clashes: these may be labelled business/product and geographic/national. The former (business/product) kind of culture clash concerns the different managerial styles of specialists from different financial services fields. Despite globalization trends and the increased profile of marketing, these differences exist and they matter. They may be compounded by geographic/national differences between managers: different strategic viewpoints, conditioned by individual country experiences and national traits, in tackling different problems.

Europe 1992 will lead to a more international financial services sector and the prospect of outsiders entering some previously uncompetitive markets. A great deal of the discussion about the 'economics of 1992' from a microeconomic perspective, however, focuses on alleged economies of scale and scope. As we have seen, the FSF industry is similar to many others in often exhibiting a belief (implied at least) that

215

size is an essential factor for success. It is often suggested, for example, that the fixed costs of running a large branch network may be spread over a larger customer base, although the EC aim of inter-operability in technological standards may weaken or eliminate this kind of argument (see Centre for Business Strategy, 1989, p. 99). Unit transactions costs may also be reduced in the case of larger business volumes.

Financial economists have long questioned the view that larger banks are more efficient. The basic hypothesis investigated in this research has been whether there is an advantage, in terms of cost, in being big: this is the operational meaning of economies of scale. Economies of scale exist if existing output (Qe) is increased (by expanding existing operations or merging with another producer) so that, ceteris paribus, the average cost of Qe falls.

The many empirical studies have found limited evidence for economies of scale of this kind in banking. Generally, the evidence suggests that scale economies in banking are limited to smaller institutions, and the average cost curve for producing the main products of banking (loans and deposits) seems to be U-shaped. Berger, Hanweck and Humphrey (1986) found evidence that large unit state banks in the United States suffered from scale diseconomies, and they suggested that these institutions would probably '. . . have to alter their output configurations to survive interstate banking' (p. 58).

A recent study by Humphrey (1987) produced some new evidence and insights into the measurement of cost dispersion economies in banking. He pointed out that there are two components of the observed variation in costs among banks: scale economies across different sized banks and cost differences between banks that are similar in size. Using 1984 data, Humphrey found cost economies in US banking, but only for smaller and/or higher-cost banks. He concluded that these cost economies do not confer competitive advantages for large banks over small banks.

The evidence from the majority of research studies does not seem to support the view that larger banks are necessarily more efficient in cost terms. Although many empirical studies imply that there are some economies of scale with larger banks, these are generally small. Also, when banks are large because they have branches, the extra costs of branching may offset the savings in operating costs.

Beyond economies of scale?

Investment banking experiences in London after Big Bang confirmed that size by itself does not guarantee profit and survival, but is is clear that size has other potent attractions. A large FSF, for example, may boost public confidence and attract superior management, a necessary factor of production in reducing operating costs. A large FSF is better able to service the needs of its large customers. In the face of growing competition, size may also be important in matching the 'fire power' of big domestic and foreign competitors.

A large FSM, for example, may be in a better position to engage in a price war against its competitors, existing and potential. As financial markets become more contestable, this may be an increasingly important factor. Complaints during the mid-1980s about the aggressiveness and related pricing tactics of the Japanese institutions in international financial markets are a reminder of the viability of the strategy. A so-called 'level playing fields' regulatory strategy at EC and international levels may increase the likelihood of such price wars.

A recent study – Centre for Business Strategy (1989) – on the impact of 1992 on EC financial sectors suggested that large size can make a positive contribution to performance in three ways: lower administration costs; increase intermediation skills through economies of scale in research; and reduce marketing costs (because consumer recognition is a by-product of size, and recognition is an important determinant of sales). However, these possible contributions may be limited. The administrative benefits of size can be exaggerated; local knowledge is especially valuable in risk management; and the benefit of size for increased recognition may be limited in a world where names are already established in national markets.

Diversity is a more pervasive characteristic of European FSMs than size. An FSM may be small, but it has a diversified business mix by definition. There are (at least) two basic economic rationales for such a strategy: portfolio effects and economies of scope. 'Portfolio effects' are used as a label here to refer to the possibility of improved risk management, a better risk and return profile. Although the potential for such managerial economies may exist, realizing them is not an automatic consequence of greater product diversity.

The Chief Executive of Lloyds Bank in the United Kingdom has recently – see Hewitt (1988, p. 27) – emphasized that diversity does not necessarily imply greater strength. Once again, the experiences of the new financial conglomerates in London after Big Bang confirm the relevance of this message. Increased size and diversity have brought more than proportionate increases in problems, reduced productivity and losses for many institutions. There are some clear lessons here for European FSM strategies as we approach 1992.

We have already seen that one apparent problem for many of London's financial conglomerates was their apparent failure to understand the difficulties of overcoming information flow asymmetries in order to secure a profitable market share in sectors where over-capacity was being expanded at a rapid rate. This latter 'overshooting behaviour' appears to be a characteristic of deregulated markets – at least for a period (until the bubble finally bursts) following deregulation. These information asymmetries in OTC markets are such that size alone is no guarantor of success. Indeed, Feldman and Stephenson (1988) demonstrate that a strategy of market penetration and profit growth based primarily on increased size may produce the opposite effect for a time, a period in which it may be hard to survive without the hypothesized profits that originally led to the strategy. Similar kinds of overshooting behaviour by FSFs, a build-up of over-capacity in financial markets and potential information asymmetries (in relation to attempts to penetrate foreign national markets) appear to be emerging features also in the build-up to 1992. Surely history will not repeat itself so soon?

This leads us finally to economies of scope and synergy. Economies of scope may exist when an FSF adds a new product Qn to its existing output (Qe), either through new product development or acquisition of a producer of Qn. If the following condition obtains:

$$C(Qn, Qe) < Cn\,(Qn) + Ce\,(Qe)$$

(where C (Qn, Qe) is the respective cost function), then economies of scope are said to exist[5]. The empirical evidence on the existence of economies of scope in FSFs, however, is even more tenuous than that for economies of scale (see Berger, Hanweck and Humphrey, 1986 and Revell, 1987). This appears to be reflective partly of methodological problems in definition and measurement. Nevertheless, Kolari and Zardkoohi (1987) report scope economies for the joint production of loans and deposits (but not for demand and time deposits or securities and loans). Interestingly enough, they also found (as in some of the economies of scale studies) that small banks are not disadvantaged relative to large banks in the joint expansion of outputs.

The competitive strategy analogue of the search for economies of scope is synergy, the celebrated '2 + 2 = 5' effect. A seasoned financial journalist refers to the present strategic drives of Europe's FSMs as 'the quest for synergy' (see Fairlamb, 1989). He examines four case studies of institutions that are trying to solve the daunting challenges of harnessing potential synergies in different ways[6]. Once again, it may be noted that the quest for synergy was the alleged strategic driver of many of London's Big Bang financial conglomerates.

Synergy is an elusive concept, but it is probably the biggest single challenge facing Europe's FSMs in the run-up to 1992 and beyond: competing successfully with a strategy of differentation requires that FSMs must recognize what Ballarín (1986, p. 30) calls 'value chain analysis'. In this kind of strategic analysis each activity undertaken by the FSM can be viewed as a link in a chain that determines the final profitability of the whole enterprise. Each of these activities, or links, must be analysed separately in terms of its cost determinants and natural geographic areas. The competitive analysis of any product or business will be unavoidably superficial if total cost behaviour is seen as the result of a single cost driver (like economies of scale or capacity utilization). It is important to recognize – through value chain analysis – the individual components of costs and the differential impact that a single driver may make on different parts of the value chain.

The search for synergy is not an easy one. However, the experiences with London's Big Bang financial conglomerates have demonstrated clearly the strategic challenges of synergy and the consequences of getting it wrong. Post-crash thinking in London on organizational design has developed into a new revisionist thinking in which 'cluster strategies' are in vogue. Size, a global presence and geographical position are not viewed as strategic objectives *per se*. FSFs should focus on their own profitable 'cluster' of products. It is the characteristics of these products/markets that determine, for example, whether a geographical presence is necessary in particular centres. Recognition of the viability of these kinds of 'cluster strategies' has interred the previous belief that only the global and niche players can survive and prosper in deregulated capital markets.

Conclusion

Deregulation, shortened financial product life cycles and the entry of new, highly focused competitors have increased the need for European FSMs to ensure that they have the best cluster of products and markets in relation to their own internal resources. Technological developments are continuing to erode one of banking's traditional advantages, personal contact with the consumer, besides allowing new competitors and forms of competition to emerge. Recent experiences confirm the attractions of committed and focused FSF policies compared with the dangers of competition-led, follow-the-leader strategies into everything and everywhere.

This scenario implies that intensifying competition will inevitably weed out those banks whose strategies are ill-conceived and inappropriate within the new Europe. Particular pressures are likely to arise in retail and the middle (and lower) corporate markets as these segments become more globalized[7]. In these segments, margins will be squeezed as prices fall, and there will be unprecedented opportunities to offer financial services across Europe. One important constraint will be the increasing problems of successfully managing the large and diverse FSMs that are likely to emerge. A small group of 'Euro-universals' will, of course, emerge and consolidate, but many super-regionals, regionals and focused niche players will be successful. New institutional groupings and co-operation arrangements are already forming; new inter-country and inter-institutional linkages are being developed. European banking structure is likely to be characterized by a steady growth of these organizational models in the quest for synergy and competitive advantage. Change looks set to be a permanent feature of European banking for the foreseeable future.

Notes

1. This is not insider information but the privileged access some trading firms have to information about investors' willingness to sell (namely, supply) and their willingness to buy (demand) a given range of securities.
2. A world dominated by a small number (20–30) of global players and a few, very small, niche players.
3. This broad category would include the so-called 'Euro-universals' (like NatWest, Deutsche, Barclays and Lloyds): see Andrews (1989).
4. We may also decompose this category into two finer sub-categories: the 'regionals' (like Commerzbank and Banco Popular) and the 'niche players (like Paribas and Indo-suez).
5. If the FSM expands proportionally its outputs, Qe, and Qn, and its Ray Average Cost (RAC) declines, economies of scale are also said to exist for the multiproduct firm.
6. They are Royal Bank and Santander; San Paolo and Guardian; Société Générale and Touche Remmant; and Deutsche Bank.
7. Although these market segments will not yield easily to European globalization pressures. National differences and preferences, for example, are likely to remain important influences on preferred products and institutions.

References

Andrews, Suzanna (1989), 'Banks' winning gambits for 1992', *Institutional Investor*, (June), pp. 41–52.

Arthur Andersen & Co. (1986), *The Decade of Change: Banking in Europe – The Next Ten Years* (London: Lafferty Publications).

Ballarín, E. (1986) *Commercial Banks Amid the Financial Revolution*, (Cambridge, Mass: Ballinger Publishing Company).

The Banker, (1989) '1992 update' (September), p. 6.

Berger, Allen N., Hanweck, Gerald and Humphrey, David B. (1986) 'Competitive viability in banking: scale, scope and product economies', *Research Papers in Banking and Financial Economics* (January), Board of Governors of the Federal Reserve System.

Centre for Business Strategy Report Series (1989), *1992: Myths and Realities*, (London: London Business School).

Clarke, P. D., Gardener, E. P. M., Feeney, P. and Molyneux, P. (1987), 'The genesis of strategic marketing control in British retail banking', *IEF Research Papers in Banking and Finance* RP 87/6 (Bangor: Institute of European Finance).

Clarke, Paul D., Gardener, E. P. M., Feeney, Paul and Molyneux, Phil (1988), 'The genesis of strategic marketing control in British retail banking', *International Journal of Bank Marketing*, vol. 6, no. 2, pp. 5–19.

Crabbe, Matthew (1989) 'Which banks in Europe can be bought?', *Euromoney* (August), pp. 59–64.

Economist, The (1988), 'The City of London survey', (25 June), pp. 1–34.

Fairlamb, David B., (1989) 'The quest for Eurosynergy', *Institutional Investor*, (June) pp. 54–69.

Feldman, Lynn and Stephenson, Jack (1988), 'Stay small or get huge – lessons from securities trading', *Harvard Business Review*, (May–June), pp. 116–23.

Gardener, E. P. M. (1988), 'A strategic perspective of bank financial conglomerates in London after the crash', *IEF Research Papers in Banking and Finance* RP 88/22 (Bangor: Institute of European Finance).

Gardener, E. P. M. (ed.) (1990) *The Future of Financial Systems and Services* (London: Macmillan).

Hewitt, Garth (1988), 'Brian, Pitman – guiding the dark horse', *Banking World*, (April), p. 24.

Humphrey, David B. (1987), 'Cost dispersion and the measurement of economies in banking', *Federal Reserve Bank of Richmond Economic Review*, vol. 73, no. 3, (May/June), pp. 24–38.

Jones, Colin (1988), 'Profits under pressure, but still hunky', *The Banker* (January) pp. 63–4.

Kolari, James and Zardkoohi, Asghar (1987), *Bank Costs, Structure, and Performance*, (Lexington, MA: Lexington Books).

Molyneux, Philip (1989), 'An analysis of the structure and performance characteristics of top EC banks and their strategic implications for 1992', *Revue de la Banque*, 6 (June), pp. 359–65.

Priestley, L. W. (1987), 'Profitable growth in a changing market', *IEF Research Papers in Banking and Finance* RP 87/8 (Bangor: Institute of European Finance).

Reidenbach, Eric R. and Pitts, Robert E. (1986), *Bank Marketing: A Guide to Strategic Planning* (Englewood Cliffs, NJ: Prentice Hall).

Revell, Jack (1987), *Mergers and the Role of Large Banks*, Institute of European Finance Monographs in Banking and Finance, No. 2.

Statistical and country appendix

This part of the book summarizes some of the key features of the banking systems of 17 European countries. This is useful background for the main text of the book and is available for the readers to draw on if they wish. It is more the 'standard model' for comparative studies of banking. We have sought to make it comparative by standardizing the treatment of each country and in the data that we present. Once again, we have drawn heavily on the extensive resources of the Institute of European Finance at Bangor. A postal survey (1989) was also conducted of banking associations in Europe.

Each country chapter lists (summarizes) the central bank and regulatory bodies, and examines the main banking institutions. We have attempted to supplement each country section by a series of three tables that show the following:

i)   institutional breakdown (1983 and 1988),
ii) sectors of ownership (1983 and 1988),
iii) key performance/condition data for the top five banks in that country (1988).

However, data availability has meant that there are some country exceptions to this target series.

We felt that this structure provided the essential skeletal information on the banking systems of each country. It is, admittedly, a partial approach, because it is inappropriate generally to analyse a banking system in isolation from the wider financial, monetary and credit system within which it operates (see, for example, Chapter 2). Nevertheless, there are many other textbooks and directories that do this job.

We have drawn heavily in this respect on the style (and some of the data) used by Revell in his 1987 study on *Mergers and the Role of Large Banks*. The full source of each table is listed at its foot. The criterion for Table 3 is that these banks are included in *The Banker* (1989) Top 500 banks in Europe. We believe these data in the Tables 1–3 series provide at least a useful 'feel' for the structure and major changes in the banking system concerned.

Appendix one

Austria

The Austrian National Bank is the central note issuer and state bank of the Republic of Austria. Authority for bank supervision rests with the Federal Ministry of Finance. Banking institutions in Austria can be split into four main groups:

a)   Groups linked by a central institution which comprises:
     The savings bank sector
     The Raffeisen sector (agricultural banking co-operatives)
     The Volksbank sector (banking co-operatives for the small business sector)
     Provincial mortgage banks.
b)   Joint-stock banks and private banks not organized into groups;
c)   The Building Societies;
d)   Specialized banking institutions.

These are shown in Table A1.1

The savings banks accounted for 25 per cent of total banking sector assets in 1988. There are around 120 such institutions and they have more than 1000 branches. The three largest – the Girozentrale, Zentralsparkasse and Kommerzialbank Vienna – and the Erste Österreichische Sparkasse are situated in Vienna. Girozentrale is the second largest bank in Austria with assets amounting to $22.7 billion: it concentrates not only on retail business but on financing for the central government, provincial and local authorities, and for large and medium-sized business as well as for the savings bank sector as a whole. In contrast to other large Austrian banks, it does not have any substantial industrial holdings. Zentralsparkasse and Kom Bank are Austria's main retail banking institutions and act mainly as financiers to the trade and crafts sector as well as to the housing construction industry.

The Raffeisen banks are agricultural banking co-operatives and comprise over 17 per cent of total banking sector assets. There are over 2000 of these banks and they are located mainly in rural areas dealing with agricultural enterprises. The central institution of the sector, Genossenschaftliche Zentralbank AG, is the seventh largest bank in the country and acts as the clearing house for the whole sector. Its main commercial interests involve financing agriculture and forestry, industry and trade. The Volksbanken are co-operative banks doing business with the small firm sector, and are mainly involved with financing small business development, trade and tourism.

The joint-stock banks and private banks not organized into groups include: the joint-stock banks, the private banks, the provincial mortgage banks and the building

Table A1.1 Austrian banking system: institutional and sector breakdown by assets.

Institutions	Balance sheet total				Sector ownership					
	Percentages		Schillings billion		Schillings billion				Number of Institutions	
	1983	1988	1983	1988	Private	Public	Mutual	Foreign	1983	1988
Commercial banks										
Joint stock banks	36.4	36.0	994.5	1284.1		1284.1			42	50
Private banks	1.6	0.4	41.6	12.5	12.5				9	5
Other banking institutions										
Savings banks	24.3	25.0	629.5	889.9			889.9		128	126
Provincial mortgage banks	4.8	5.4	123.8	194.0			194.0		9	9
Rural credit co-operatives (Raffeisen)	16.7	17.6	432.4	627.0			627.0		940	860
Industrial credit co-operatives (Volksbanken)	4.6	4.3	119.2	153.1			153.1		115	103
Building societies	4.0	3.6	102.4	126.9			126.9		4	4
Specialized banks and Postal Savings Bank	7.6	7.7	196.0	277.6					68	74
Total	100.0	100.0	2589.4	3565.1	12.5	1561.7	1990.9		1315	1231

Source: Austrian Nationalbank: *Annual Report 1988*, Table *Monatsausweise der Osterreichischen Banken*, pp. 18–29.

societies. Joint-stock banks comprise the largest portion of total banking sector assets, amounting to 36 per cent in 1988. Creditanstalt Bankverein and Länderbank are the two main joint-stock banks, the former being Austria's largest bank. The government has a majority shareholding in these two institutions as a result of the 1946 First Nationalization Act. Their main activities consist of financing industry and trade in both the public and private sector. They also have a wide variety of shareholdings mainly in banks based outside Vienna. Private banks or 'banking houses' form a very small proportion of total banking sector assets. They are owned by personally liable partners and their main business consists of international transactions. Provincial mortgage banks have the function of promoting loans which are secured by title deeds as well as lending to local authorities. There is one mortgage bank for each federal region. In Austria there are four building societies which concentrate on housing finance. In the early 1980s they had more than 40 per cent of the housing loans advanced by Austrian banks, but this share has subsequently fallen.

Finally, the specialized banking institutions include: Österreichische Kontrolbank which is responsible for export financing, and the Postsparkasse (Postal Savings Bank) whose main objective is to clear postal cheques and effect money transfers as well as taking deposits and helping to administer the national debt. Other specialist firms include those involved in long-term financing to industry as well as those doing factoring, leasing and equity financing business.

Table A1.2 Sector ownership 1983–8: Austrian banking system.

Category	Total banking sector assets Percentages		
	1983	1988	Change
Private	1.6	0.4	−1.2
Public	44.0	43.8	−0.2
Mutual	54.4	55.8	1.4
Foreign	–	–	–
Totals	100.0	100.0	–

Table A1.3 Top five Austrian banks, 1988.

	Units	Creditanstalt Bankverein	Zentralsparkasse and Kommerzialbank	Österreische Länderbank	Girozentrale Vienna	Genossenschaftliche Zentralbank
Rankings (by capital)						
Country		1	2	3	4	5
Europe		46	97	98	105	119
World		105	221	225	241	279
Measures						
Assets	$m	39,041	17,585	20,670	22,721	13,767
Capital	$m	1,695	778	759	699	596
Pre-tax profits	$m	131	109	77	82	48
Pre-tax profits on assets	%	0.36	0.62	0.37	0.36	0.35
Capital/assets ratio	%	4.34	4.42	3.67	3.08	4.33
Pre-tax profits per employee	$	12,625	21,848	14,259	47,481	50,955
Number of employees		10,376	4,989	5,400	1,727	942

Sources: The Banker (1989) Europe's Top 500 Banks, October, p. 101.
The Banker (1989) World's Top 1000 Banks, July, p. 109.

Appendix two

Belgium

The two main bank regulatory bodies in Belgium are the central bank – the National Bank of Belgium (NBB) – and the Banking Commission. Banking supervision is the responsibility of the Banking Commission, which was set up by Royal Decree 185 of 9 July 1935. On 30 June 1975 the scope of the Commission was widened to include powers previously exercised by the Central Office of Small Savings. The Belgo-Luxembourg Exchange Institute (BLEI) supervises exchange-control regulations and regulates international capital movements. In practice the day-to-day management of the BLEI is carried out by the NBB.

The three main groups of banking institutions in Belgium are the commercial banks, the public credit institutions and the savings banks. The commercial banks are the biggest group in terms of balance-sheet size, as shown in Table A2.1. Under the Royal Decree 185 of 9 July 1935, banks are defined as 'Belgian and foreign enterprises which regularly receive deposits repayable at sight or at a time limit not exceeding two years, with a view to using them for their own account in banking, credit or investment operations'. At the end of 1988 there were 56 banks under Belgian law and 30 under foreign law. They operate around 3600 branches in Belgium, and their activities have diversified considerably during recent years. A significant feature of Belgium is its automated and highly efficient clearing system, which was built up during the 1970s and 1980s.

The public credit institutions were created initially to provide long-term credit to special groups or industries. They were constructed essentially to fill financing gaps left by the private sector. The main public credit institutions are the Caisse Générale d'Epargne et de Retraite, Crédit Communal and Société National de Crédit à l'Industrie. The Caisse Générale d'Epargne et de Retraite provides pensions, life insurance and mortgages, and is the largest building society in the country. Since 1970 it has been allowed to conduct all types of banking activities. The Crédit Communal is a bank for local authorities and has also developed into a full bank. The Société Nationale de Crédit à l'Industrie extends long- or medium-term loans to industry. In terms of volume of funds collected, these three major public institutions are comparable in size to the biggest private banks. There are also a number of other public institutions that play important roles in Belgium: these include the National Fund of Professional Credit, the National Institute of Agricultural Credit, the Central Mortgage Credit Board and the Post Office Giro.

The private savings banks sector also contains some very large institutions. With despecialization trends, they increasingly resemble the clearing banks, but they do have some special characteristics. Their main assets are mortgage loans and govern-

226

Table A2.1 Belgian banking system: institutional and sector breakdown by assets.

Institutions	Balance sheet total				Sector ownership				Number of Institutions	
	Percentages		Francs billion		Francs billion					
	1982	1988	1982	1988	Private	Public	Mutual	Foreign	1982	1988
Commercial banks										
Belgian law banks	45.2	37.0	3108	5616	5616				24	25
Branches & subsidiaries of foreign banks	24.1	35.2	2971	5338				5338	57	61
Other banking institutions										
Private savings banks	8.6	11.0	755	1674			1674		30	31
Crédit Communal	10.4	10.9	980	1650		1650			1	1
Caisse Générale d'Epargne et de Retraite (CGER)	8.9	3.9	783	592		592			1	1
L'Office des Cheques Postaux (OCP)	2.7	2.0	239	302		302			1	1
Total	100.0	100.0	8764	15172	5616	2544	1674	5338	114	120

Sources: (i) *Association Belge des Banques*, Les Banques am Seim du Sectur Financier en 1988, *Aspects et documents* 93.
(ii) Bulletin de la Banque Nationale de Belgique, March 1989, Table XIII–10.
(iii) Revell (1987), *Mergers and the Role of Large Banks*, Institute of European Finance Monographs in Banking and Finance, No. 2, Table 6.1, p. 157.

Note: The split for branches and subsidiaries of foreign banks is approximately 3 to 2 respectively.

ment securities, which are financed primarily by deposits on savings books. The savings banks tend to be less international in their activities compared to the commercial banks. Like the banks and the public credit institutions, they come under NBB monetary policy measures. Their operations are supervised by auditors approved by the Banking Commission. The savings banks are also subject to several constraints regarding the investment of the funds that they collect.

Besides the three principal categories of banks depicted in Table A2.1, there are several other categories of financial institution in Belgium. These are generally comparatively small and highly specialized. They include mortgage companies and finance companies specializing in consumer credit and personal loans.

Table A2.2   Sector ownership 1982–8: Belgian banking system.

Category	Total banking sector assets Percentages		
	1982	1988	Change
Private	35.5	37.0	1.5
Public	22.0	16.8	− 5.2
Mutual	8.6	11.0	2.4
Foreign	33.9	35.2	1.3
Totals	100.0	100.0	–

Table A2.3 Top five Belgian banks, 1988.

	Units	Generale Bank	ASKL-CGER Bank	Kredietbank	Bank Brussels Lambert	Crédit Commercial de Belgium
Rankings (by capital)						
Country		1	2	3	4	5
Europe		48	65	69	76	79
World		109	150	162	178	183
Measures						
Assets	$m	61,954	40,168	38,849	45,293	40,251
Capital	$m	1,601	1,233	1,108	953	929
Pre-tax profits	$m	240	223	184	182	65
Pre-tax profits on assets	%	0.39	0.55	0.47	0.40	0.16
Capital/assets ratio	%	2.58	3.07	2.85	2.10	2.31
Pre-tax profits per employee	$	14,435	24,623	16,711	21,050	18,106
Number of employees		16,626	9,057	11,011	8,646	3,590

Sources: The Banker (1989) Europe's Top 500 Banks, October, p. 101.
The Banker (1989) World's Top 1000 Banks, July, p. 109.

Appendix three

Denmark

Denmark's National Bank Act of 1936 states that it is the responsibility of the central bank to maintain a sound monetary system and to facilitate and regulate money transactions and various lending activities. Banks are supervised by a Ministry of Industry department called the Supervision of Commercial Banks and Savings Bank Division. The commercial and savings banks operate under the same legislation and undertake similar types of business.

The Danish banking system is dominated by the commercial and savings banks. Together they control the national payments system. In addition, there are a number of financial institutions performing more specialist functions and these institutions comprise the National Giro office (Postgirokontoret), mortgage credit institutions, finance houses, life insurance companies and pension funds, and authorized stockbrokers.

Commercial banks undertake a wider range of national and commercial banking business. Tables A3.1 and A3.2 show the breakdown of banking sector deposits and advances and illustrate the importance of the commercial banking sector. The commercial banks control nearly 70 per cent of banking sector deposits and over 60 per cent of total advances. Danish banking has traditionally been dominated by three commercial banks: Den Danske Bank of 1871 Aktieselskab, Privatbanken A/S and the Aktieselskabet Kjobelnhauns Handelsbank. These banks have nationwide branch networks as do the three 'second-tier' commercial banks, Andelsbanken A/S, Den Danske Provinsbank A/S and Jyske Bank A/S. (In mid-November 1989 the Danske Bank and Aktieselskabet Kjobelnhauns Handelsbank announced that they would merge. Three weeks later, Privatbanken, Sparekassen SDS and Andelsbanken announced that they would also merge.) The majority of other commercial banks are either regional or local in nature. Foreign banks are estimated to have less than 3 per cent of the total banking market. All commercial banks provide a wide range of deposit as well as credit facilities. Virtually all accounts pay some form of interest and household credit is mainly in the form of personal loans. Banks provide a very small proportion of mortgage finance; this sector is dominated by the special mortgage credit institutions. Commercial banks are also active in the money markets, security business and portfolio management.

The savings banks (Sparekassen) undertake much the same business as the commercial banks. The sector controls over one-quarter of banking system deposits and slightly less of advances. It is dominated by two major banks, Sparekassen Bikuben and Sparekassen SDS. Of the 88 savings banks operating in Denmark and the Faroe Islands only these two have nationwide branch networks. The majority of

Table A3.1 Danish banking system: institutional and sector breakdown by deposits.

Institutions	Balance sheet total				Sector ownership				Number of Institutions	
	Percentages		Kroner billion		Kroner billion					
	1983	1988	1983	1988	Private	Public	Mutual	Foreign	1983	1988
Commercial banks	69.6	69.6	186.9	335.8	335.8				78	76
Total										
Other banking institutions										
Savings banks	27.5	28.6	73.8	137.9			137.9		82	88
Co-operative banks	0.6	0.6	1.5	2.7			2.7		na	na
Postal Giro	2.3	1.2	6.2	6.4		6.4			1	1
Total	100.0	100.0	268.4	482.8	335.8	6.4	140.6		159	165

Source: Denmark Nationalbank: *Report and Accounts 1988*, Tables 24, 25, and 37.

Table A3.2 Danish banking system: institutional and sector breakdown by advances.

Institutions	Balance sheet total				Sector ownership				Number of Institutions	
	Percentages		Kroner billion		Private	Public	Kroner billion Mutual	Foreign		
	1983	1988	1983	1988					1983	1988
Commercial banks Total	56.9	61.1	125.8	294.8	294.8				78	76
Other banking institutions										
Savings banks	24.2	26.3	53.3	127.1			127.1		82	88
Mortgage credit institutions	18.9	12.6	41.8	60.9			60.9		6	5
Total	100.0	100.0	220.9	482.8	294.8		188.0		166	169

Source: Ibid.
Notes: Mortgage credit institutions do not take deposits.

savings banks have a large number of very small branches, which are regional or locally based. The savings banks are allowed to do the same business as their commercial bank counterparts although they tend to concentrate on retail banking and are generally poorly represented in the corporate banking sector. Some of the larger savings banks, however, have recently increased their activity in the Copenhagen interbank market. In addition to the savings banks, there are also various co-operative banks that provide specialist banking services to predominantly retail and small business customers. They accounted for less than 1 per cent of banking sector deposits in 1988.

The main function of the National Giro Office (Postgirokontoret) is to provide a payments mechanism for private individuals making transfers, normally to commercial firms. It also handles the payroll accounts of many state-run firms. By 1988 it held around 1.2 per cent of banking sector deposits, of which the majority were retail deposits. The National Giro has sought to improve its position in the domestic banking market by issuing a range of new products, but these have not yet been widely adopted by the retail banking public.

The mortgage credit institutions (Realkreditinstitutter) are relatively small and specialist in nature. They provide the major part of the long-term financing required by the building sector. Mortgages are bond-financed and these are quoted on the Copenhagen Stock Exchange. The mortgage credit institutions do not operate deposit facilities for their customers and they accounted for approximately 13 per cent of total outstanding advances in 1988. There are three major mortgage credit institutions: Nykredit, Kreditforeningen Danmark and Byggeriets Realkreditfond, and the remainder are quite small and specialist in nature.

Denmark also has a variety of finance houses which specialize in providing consumer and commercial finance to various sectors in the economy. The major finance houses are owned by commercial banks and savings banks. Life insurance companies and pension funds have been active periodically in providing mortgage finance although their share of this market (around 9 per cent in 1979) has fallen dramatically during the 1980s. Authorized stockbrokers are also allowed to receive deposits, make loans and deal in securities.

Table A3.3 Sector ownership 1983–8: Danish banking system

Category	1983	Total deposits Percentages 1988	Change
Private	69.6	69.5	− 0.1
Public	2.3	1.3	− 1.0
Mutual	28.1	29.2	1.1
Foreign[a]	-	-	-
Totals	100.0	100.0	-

Note: a Steinherr, A. and Gilbert, P. (1988), *The Impact of Freeing Trade in Financial Services and Capital Movements on the European Banking Industry*, mimeo (INSEAD: Fontainbleau), estimate that the foreign share was 1% at the end of 1987.

Table A3.4 Top five Danish banks, 1988.

	Units	Den Danske Bank	Copenhagen Handelsbank	BRF Bygg Realkreditfond	Sparekassen SDS	Privatbanken
Rankings (by capital)						
Country		1	2	3	4	5
Europe		43	72	77	89	90
World		99	169	180	201	202
Measures						
Assets	$m	23,339	17,995	18,202	14,846	14,920
Capital	$m	1,883	1,056	934	852	852
Pre-tax profits	$m	366	186	102	125	137
Pre-tax profits on assets	%	1.56	1.03	0.56	0.84	0.92
Capital/assets ratio	%	8.07	5.87	5.13	5.74	5.71
Pre-tax profits per employee	$	58,579	29,435	19,566	27,274	24,196
Number of employees		6,248	6,319	5,213	4,583	5,662

Sources: *The Banker* (1989) Europe's Top 500 Banks, October, p. 100.
The Banker (1989) World's Top 1000 Banks, July, p. 112.

Appendix four

Finland

The Ministry of Finance is the country's highest body supervising bank operations. The central bank, the Bank of Finland, is also consulted in connection with related banking issues like the establishment of a new bank and setting up offices abroad. Banking operations are monitored by the Bank Inspectorate, which is subordinate to the Ministry of Finance. The main role of the central bank is to formulate and administer monetary policy; this is directed particularly towards the commercial banks which have central bank drawing rights.

The Finnish banking system comprises commercial banks, savings banks, co-operative banks, the post office bank (Postipankki), foreign banks, insurance institutions and other credit institutions. Table A4.1 shows the institutional breakdown of the banking sector according to total assets in 1982 and 1988.

It can be seen that the commercial banks had 64.4 per cent of total banking sector assets in 1982 and increased their share to 65.0 per cent by 1988. These banks, of which there were seven in 1988, undertake a mix of consumer and commercial business. The two largest commercial banks, Kansallis-Osake-Pankki and Union Bank of Finland, handle national and international payments through their substantial branch networks and overseas subsidiaries. Skopbank, the savings banks' central bank, and Okobank, the central bank of the co-operative banks, increasingly act as commercial banks, providing a broad range of corporate and retail banking services as well as doing business with their 'member' banks. Postipankki, the post office bank, is classified by the official statistics as a commercial bank.

The commercial banks provide a broad range of deposit and lending facilities as well as undertaking money-market and limited securities business. (Commercial banks are not permitted to acquire shares on their own account, but they can buy and sell securities for their clients.) They also undertake a range of non-banking business. It should be noted that the majority of commercial bank lending is to the corporate sector, with the co-operative and savings banks dominating retail lending. The commercial banks and the state-owned post office bank (Postipankki) are sometimes referred to as authorized foreign-exchange banks because they are allowed to undertake foreign-exchange transactions within the limits set by the Foreign Exchange Regulations and permits granted by the central bank. The foreign-exchange transactions of the savings and co-operative banks are handled by their central institutions, Skopbank and Okobank, which have commercial bank status.

Table A4.1 shows that the savings banks' share of total banking sector assets has fallen from 18.8 per cent in 1982 to 16.2 per cent in 1988. There has also been a decline in the number of these institutions from 270 to 211 over the same period. The

Table A4.1 Finnish banking system: institutional and sector breakdown by assets.

Institutions	Balance sheet total				Sector ownership				Number of Institutions	
	Percentages		Markka billion		Markka billion					
	1982	1988	1982	1988	Private	Public	Mutual	Foreign	1982	1988
Commercial banks	64.4	65.0	116.7[a]	395.8	248.7	66.0	81.1[b]		7	7
Other banking institutions		4.2								
Mortgage Credit Institutions	-		-	25.3	25.3				-	8
Foreign banks	1.4	0.9	2.6	5.3				5.3	3	4
Savings banks	18.8	16.2	34.6	98.9			98.9		270	211
Co-operative banks	16.4	13.7	30.3	84.0			84.0		371	367
Total	100.0	100.0	184.2	609.3	274.0	66.0	264.0	5.3	651	597

Source: (i) OECD (1988) *Bank Profitability*, Statistics Supplement, Financial Statement of Banks 1982–86, pp. 30–35.
(ii) The Finnish Bankers Association.

Notes: a Commercial bank sector comprises private banks, Postipankki (publicly owned), Skopbank and Okobank (both mutual organisations)
b Central banks of savings banks and co-operative banks owned by member banks Skopbank (1988: 49.8m)

savings banks are predominantly municipal or district banks that traditionally acted as savings institutions for retail customers and provided funds for households and the agricultural sector. The 370 co-operative banks controlled 13.7 per cent of total banking sector assets in 1988, a decline of 2.7 per cent since 1982. On average they are much smaller than the average savings banks but they perform much the same function and the largest have nationwide branch networks. The post office bank (Postipankki) operates both in the consumer and corporate banking sectors and had nearly 11 per cent of banking sector assets in 1988. It holds predominantly retail deposits and lends mainly to local authorities, state corporations and households. Traditionally its primary purpose has been to deal with state payments.

Foreign banks have been allowed to operate in Finland since 1982 but as Table A4.1 illustrates, they have probably had a more psychological rather than real impact on the banking sector as a whole. Their share of total banking sector assets fell from 1.4 per cent to 0.9 per cent between 1982 and 1988. Other institutions operating in the Finnish banking market include insurance institutions that play an important role in the commercial credit market and various mortgage credit institutions that obtain their funds in the wholesale money markets and are not allowed to take deposits.

Table A4.2 Sector ownership 1982–8: Finnish banking system.

Category	Total banking sector assets Percentages		
	1982	1988	Change
Private	43.5	44.5	1.0
Public	11.8	10.5	− 1.3
Mutual	43.2	44.2	1.0
Foreign	1.4	0.8	− 0.6
Totals	100.0	100.0	-

Table A4.3 Top five Finnish banks, 1988.

	Units	Union Bank of Finland	Kansallis-Osake-Pankki	Postipankki	Skopbank	Okobank
Rankings (by capital)						
Country		1	2	3	4	5
Europe		31	54	64	87	121
World		72	122	149	198	283
Measures						
Assets	$m	31,810	34,688	17,944	15,233	10,491
Capital	$m	2,542	1,439	1,237	858	586
Pre-tax profits	$m	421	159	131	142	26
Pre-tax profits on assets	%	1.32	0.46	0.73	0.93	0.25
Capital/assets ratio	%	7.99	4.14	6.89	5.63	5.59
Pre-tax profits per employee	$	40,578	15,900	16,947	65,347	15,142
Number of employees		10,375	10,000	7,730	2,173	1,717

Sources: *The Banker* (1989) Europe's Top 500 Banks, October, p. 101.
The Banker (1989) World's Top 1000 Banks, July, p. 112.

Appendix five

France

In December 1945 the Bank of France (the central bank), together with the big banks and other credit organizations, was nationalized. The Bank of France supervises the whole of the banking system. With the Commission Bancaire, the Bank may demand from banks and *établissements financiers* any documents or other information that it feels are necessary in order to conduct its functions. The Bank also has a number of specific functions that it carries out on behalf of the Treasury. It plays an important role in the operations of *établissements de crédit* through its provision of the infrastructure and staff of the Conseil National du Crédit des Comités de la Réglementation Bancaire et des Etablissements de Crédit. The public authorities, and especially the monetary authorities, in France prescribe various limitations on banking operations. It is necessary to obtain explicit agreement for many banking changes (like significant changes in banking structures or statutes) from the Comité des Etablissements de Crédit. The Finance Ministry has national supervisory responsibility for the whole of the banking and financial system.

French banking institutions can be divided into two broad groups, the commercial banks and other banking institutions (see Table A5.1). The commercial banks (*banques inscrites*) are clearly the largest group, and they represent over 55 per cent of the system in terms of total assets. Apart from one important feature, the French banking system may be regarded in many respects as the archetypal Continental banking system. Many of its features were developed in the second part of the nineteenth century and served as role models for many other countries. The one feature that distinguishes it from other Continental systems is the programme launched in 1981 that nationalized over 60 per cent of all commercial banks (in terms of total assets) by 1983. In 1986 a re-privatization movement began and five banks – including Société Générale and the two financial companies Paribas and Compagnie Financière de Suez – have already been privatized. These so-called 'new reforms' are part of a wider movement in France towards a more market-orientated banking and financial system. Public ownership of the banking system has fallen from 62.5 per cent in 1983 to 42.2 per cent in 1988, reflecting the privatization programme.

The law of 1945 distinguished between three types of banks: *banques de dépots*, *banques d'affaires*, and *banques de crédit à long et moyen terme*. The 1984 Banking Law abolished this long-standing legal distinction. Any institution that is granted banking status – now called *établissement de crédit* under the 1984 banking law – may carry out all banking activities. Over 400 banks currently operate through a network of 9900 branches. French commercial banks offer the full range of banking services and play a dominant role in issuing all kinds of securities.

Table A5.1 French banking system: institutional and sector breakdown by assets.

Institutions	Balance sheet total				Sector ownership					
	Francs million		Percentages		Francs million				Number of Institutions	
	1983	1988	1983	1988	Private	Public	Mutual	Foreign	1983	1988
Commercial banks	4239[a]	6406	62.7	55.1	427	4411		1568	400	408
Other banking institutions										
Mutual and co-operative banks	890	1833	13.2	15.8			1833		135	178
Savings banks	550	502	8.1	4.3			502		479	300
Caisse Nationale	261	470	3.9	4.1		470			1	1
Caisse de Crédit Municipal (National Savings Bank)	8	17	0.1	0.2			17		20	21
Finance companies	301	1323	4.4	11.4	1323				425	1059
Specialist financial institutions	521	1063	7.6	9.1	1063				30	32
Total	6770	11614	100.0	100.0	2813	4881	2352	1568	1490	1999

Sources: (i) Revell (1987) *Mergers and the Role of Large Banks*, Institute of European Finance Research Monographs in Banking Finance, no. 2, Table 6.7, p. 163.

(ii) Banque de France (1988) *Statistiques Monétaires et Financières Annuelles*, Section 2.4, *Les Banques* pp. 72, 76, 82, Section 2.5, 2.8, p. 145.

Note: a Includes 282 private, 3314 public and 633 foreign-sector ownership.

Alongside the banks there are a number of groups of institutions of a mutual or co-operative (listed under mutual and co-operative banks in Table A5.1) nature that conduct banking business. These include Crédit Agricole, Crédit Mutuel, Banques Populaires and Crédit Co-opératif. The agricultural credit banks (Crédit Agricole), for example, are mutual organizations whose members operate in rural areas or are engaged in agricultural activities. There are around 3000 local associations (*caisses locales*) in this sector. A similar number of local associations operate with Crédit Mutuel, but they do not usually specialize by sector. There are 40 *banques populaires* and the activities of these banks are similar to those of registered banks. Their customers are primarily small and medium-sized firms, professional people and craftsmen. The Caisse Central de Crédit Co-opératif was created in 1938 as the central organization of the group Crédit Co-opératif.

Several official and semi-official specialized banks exist in France. Like the mutual and co-operative banks, they are governed by special laws. These specialized banks (under the control of the state) mainly provide medium- and long-term financing to the private and public sector. The 1984 law classifies the majority of them as specialized financial institutions. They include Crédit National, Sociétés de Dévéloppement Regional (SDRs), Crédit Foncier de France and Comptoir des Entrepreneurs, Institut de Dévéloppement Industriel (IDI), Crédit d'Equipment des Petites et Moyennes Enterprises (CEPME) and Banque Française du Commerce Extérieur (BFCE). The BFCE (foreign trade bank) specializes in import and export financing.

The 300 *caisses d'épargne et de prévoyance* (ordinary savings banks) operate through 6500 offices. They are in competition with the Caisse Nationale d'Epargne (national savings bank), which operates through the post office network (approximately 17 200 offices). Unlike the national savings banks, the ordinary savings banks are mutual sector deposit-takers. The PTT (postal and telecommunications service), not shown in the table, also supplies two kinds of payment: postal transfers (for collection and payment) and post office current accounts.

Sociétés financières and *établissements financiers* are classified in the official statistics as specialist financial institutions. They cover a wide range of financial institutions like hire-purchase firms, leasing and factoring companies and mortgage institutions. 1059 *sociétés financières* were registered in December 1988. Several securities and property investment companies also exist. Open-ended investment funds were introduced in 1963 in the form of Sociétés d'Investissement à Capital Variable (SICAVs); there are over 500 of these. From 1975 authorized institutions were entitled to create unit trusts and over 2500 *fonds communs de placement* existed at the end of 1988.

Table A5.2 Sector ownership 1983–8: French banking system.

Category	Total banking sector assets Percentages		
	1983	1988	Change
Private	4.5	24.2	19.7
Public[a]	62.5	42.2	− 20.3
Mutual	22.9	20.2	− 2.7
Foreign	10.1	13.5	3.4
Totals	100.0	100.0	3.4

Note: a The significant fall in the public sector is partly attributable to the privatization of Société Genérale, Paribas and Compagnie Financière de Suez in 1986.

Table A5.3 Top five French banks, 1988.

	Units	Crédit Agricole	BNP	Crédit Lyonnais	Paribas	Société Générale
Rankings (by capital)						
Country		1	2	3	4	5
Europe		3	8	10	11	12
World		5	20	22	23	27
Measures						
Assets	$m	210,601	196,955	178,878	121,617	145,661
Capital	$m	9,152	5,567	5,409	5,324	4,874
Pre-tax profits	$m	1,047	876	811	939	863
Pre-tax profits on assets	%	0.50	0.44	0.45	0.77	0.59
Capital/assets ratio	%	4.34	2.83	3.02	4.38	3.35
Pre-tax profits per employee	$	14,208	14,950	13,946	36,115	18,983
Number of employees		73,693	58,595	58,151	26,000	45,462

Sources: The Banker (1989) Europe's Top 500 Banks, October, p. 102.
The Banker (1989) World's Top 1000 Banks, July, p. 114.

Appendix six

Greece

The Bank of Greece undertakes the traditional functions of a central bank, implementing monetary policy, supervising and controlling the banking sector and dealing with the bank note issue. Bank supervision extends to commercial banks as well as to investment banks, mortgage banks and specialized credit institutions that are authorized to take deposits.

Commercial banks are the most important category of bank operating in the Greek market. Table A6.1 shows that in 1988 they controlled over 46 per cent of total credit extended by the banking system. There are 32 commercial banks operating in Greece, by far the largest being the National Bank of Greece. This bank is indirectly controlled by the state and handles more banking business than all the other commercial banks combined. The second largest commercial banking group, Commercial Bank of Greece, is also indirectly controlled by the state and handles around one-fifth of commercial banking business. All the domestic commercial banks, apart from Credit Bank, Ergo Bank, General Hellenic Bank and the Macedonia Thrace Bank, are controlled by the public sector. Credit Bank is by far the largest private sector bank.

The commercial banks offer a broad range of banking services similar to their commercial banking counterparts in other European countries. They take deposits and offer retail and wholesale banking services including foreign-exchange dealing. In addition, they grant short and medium-term loans to industry and participate in the financing of private or state enterprises. The general terms of granting loans to particular sectors as well as the interest rates on these loans, however, are determined by the Bank of Greece. Terms on loans are such as to direct commercial bank credit to sectors and activities which are viewed as having high socio-economic priorities, such as small businesses and the agricultural sector. Commercial banks are encouraged to make low-interest loans by the operation of a system of reserves and rebates on various business categories. Most of the funds lent by the commercial banks (around 70 per cent) go to the private sector. They are allowed to undertake securities business, portfolio management and trust business on behalf of their clients and also engage in commercial and industrial activities on their own account. Consumer credit business in Greece is constrained because of tight monetary policy restrictions, trust services are unsophisticated and leasing and factoring operations hardly exist.

The Agricultural Bank of Greece is the second largest category of banking institution according to its share of total banking sector advances. It was founded in 1929 in order to direct credit flows to the agricultural sector as well as to encourage the development of farmers' co-operatives. It is under the supervision of the Ministry

Table A6.1 Greek banking system: institutional and sector breakdown by bank credits.

Institutions	Total bank credits				Sector ownership				Number of Institutions	
	Percentages		Drachma million		Drachma million					
	1983	1988	1983	1988	Private	Public	Mutual	Foreign	1983	1988
Commercial banks	53.5	46.4	858.5	2003.0	235.6	1535.7		231.7	30	32
Other banking institutions										
Agricultural Bank of Greece	18.3	20.5	293.8	885.4		885.4			1	1
Mortgage banks	3.9	5.7	62.0	247.2	237.8	9.4			2	2
Hellenic Industrial Development Bank	3.8	5.4	60.3	232.8		232.8			3	3
Post Office Savings Fund	15.9	18.0	255.0	775.4		775.4			1	1
Consignments & loan funds	2.4	2.5	38.2	107.9		107.9			1	1
Investment banks	2.3	1.5	37.3	66.9		66.9			1	1
Total	100.0	100.0	1605.1	4318.6	473.4	3613.5		231.7	39	41

Source: Bank of Greece, *Monthly Statistical Bulletin*, June 1989, Table 19, p. 37.

of Agriculture and is responsible for the implementation of the agricultural policy of the government. It has an extensive network of branches, especially in the rural areas.

The two mortgage banks provide medium- and long-term mortgage finance to the general public for house and hotel construction and to the public sector to finance various building projects. The largest mortgage bank is the National Mortgage Bank of Greece, which had advances exceeding Dr 237 billion in 1988, and is a private institution. Its smaller competitor, Mortgage Bank, is a wholly-owned subsidiary of the National Bank of Greece and therefore comes under state control.

Investment banks provide longer-term finance to industry. There are three investment banks in Greece, by far the largest being the Hellenic Industrial Development Bank which is wholly owned by the state. The other two are the National Bank for Industrial Development (solely owned by the National Bank of Greece) and the Investment Bank in which the state has an indirect shareholding. As well as granting long-term loans to industry these banks take equity participations in industrial, shipping and tourist enterprises as well as providing quasi-venture capital finance. In this general connexion it may be noted that the commercial banks provide long-term finance to industry, but to a lesser degree than the investment banks.

The two remaining types of banking institutions in the Greek system are the Post Office Savings Fund and the Consignments and Loan Fund. The former has increased its share of the banking market since the early 1980s. Its main function is to attract deposits from the general public on which it pays higher rates than the commercial banks. These deposits are predominantly used to purchase government bonds or are redeposited with the Bank of Greece. The Post Office also accepts deposits on similar terms to the commercial banks and provides medium- and long-term finance to the public sector as well as housing loans to state employees. Finally, the Consignments and Loan Fund is a government institution that funds public construction projects, public activities and mortgage finance for state employees and pensioners.

Table A6.2   Sector ownership 1983–8: Greek banking system.

Category	Total banking credit Percentages		
	1983	1988	Change
Private	8.1	11.0	2.9
Public	88.8	83.7	−5.1
Mutual	–	–	–
Foreign	3.1	5.3	2.2
Totals	100.0	100.0	–

Table A6.3 Top five Greek banks, 1988.

	Units	National Bank	Agricultural Bank	Hellenic Industrial Bank	Commercial Bank	Credit Bank
Rankings (by capital)						
Country		1	2	3	4	5
Europe		107	140	152	247	375
World		246	329	493	566	803
Measures						
Assets	$m	26,125	6,857	2,535	6,227	3,141
Capital	$m	677	493	443	225	131
Pre-tax profits	$m	46	26	n.a.	17	30
Pre-tax profits on assets	%	0.17	0.38	n.a.	0.27	0.96
Capital/assets ratio	%	2.59	7.19	17.5	3.61	4.17
Pre-tax profits per employee	$	2,603	3,770	n.a.	2,462	9,591
Number of employees		17,670	6,897	n.a.	6,885	3,128

Sources: The Banker (1989) Europe's Top 500 Banks, October, p. 107.
The Banker (1989) World's Top 1000 Banks, July, p. 118.

Appendix seven

Republic of Ireland

The Bank of Ireland is the country's central bank. It is state-owned and is the financial controlling authority for all the licensed banks in Ireland. Supervision by the Central Bank covers all the licensed banks but does not cover Trustee Savings banks, building societies, credit unions, friendly societies, investment trust companies, the Post Office Savings Bank and the two state-controlled banks, the Industrial Credit Company and the Agricultural Credit Corporation.

Banking institutions in Ireland can be split into four main categories: licensed banks (which include the associated and non-associated banks), building societies, savings banks (including the Post Office Savings Banks and the Trustee Savings Bank), and state development banks. Table A7.1 shows the institutional breakdown.

The associated banks are the main sector in the Irish banking system and accounted for 47.4 per cent of total banking sector assets in 1988. There are four associated banks, two of which are Irish-owned (Allied Irish Banks Ltd and the Bank of Ireland). The remaining two are both wholly-owned subsidiaries: Ulster Bank, wholly owned by National Westminster Bank Ltd and the Northern Bank Ltd (previously owned by Midland Bank) which has been owned by National Australia Bank Ltd since 1987. Like their UK counterparts all the associated banks are referred to as clearing banks and they all have a significant number of branches in Northern Ireland. The two Irish-owned associated banks account for the majority of the associated banks' activities in Ireland. These banks control the nation's payments system and undertake a mix of retail and commercial business through their extensive branch network; they all operate merchant banking subsidiaries. The majority of associated bank lending is to the private sector in the form of overdrafts or term loans, and these four banks accounted for around 40 per cent of private sector lending in 1988. As well as providing overdrafts and term loans they also extend other credit facilities, ranging from bill discounting and acceptance credits to leasing, mortgage finance and trade finance.

The second category of banks are known as the non-associated banks. These banks undertake commercial banking, merchant banking and consumer finance activities. They include subsidiaries of the associated banks as well as branches and subsidiaries of foreign banks and a small number of other Irish banks. By the end of 1988 there were 30 non-associated banks operating in Ireland. They are classified into two main categories, comprising merchant and commercial banks and industrial banks. The merchant and commercial banks are the largest in number and accounted for 27 per cent of total banking sector assets in 1988. Banks in this category have a bias towards either merchant or commercial banking, but the larger banks tend to concentrate

247

Table A7.1 Ireland's banking system: institutional and sector breakdown by assets.

Institutions	Balance sheet total				Sector ownership				Number of Institutions	
	Percentages		Irish Punts million		Irish Punts million					
	1983	1988	1983	1988	Private	Public	Mutual	Foreign	1985	1988
Commercial Banks										
Associated banks	46.2	47.4	8436a	13992	11613			2379	4	4
Non-associated banks										
i) Merchant & Commercial	28.3	27.0	5168b	7977	4025			3952	24	20
ii) Industrial	9.1	8.8	1658	2594	2594				14	10
Other banking institutions										
Post Office & Trustee Savings Banksc	4.2	4.0	762	1178		1178			5	3
Building Societies	12.2	12.8	2226	3805			3805		11	10
Total	100.0	100.0	18250	29546	18232	1178	3805	6331	58	47

Sources: (i) Central Bank of Ireland, *Annual Report* (1988): Statistical Appendix: Tables C9–C15, C20, C21, p. 42–68.
(ii) Revell (1987), *Mergers and the Role of Large Banks*, Institute of European Finance Research Monographs in Banking and Finance, No. 2, Table 5.11, p. 150.

Notes: a Includes 6014 in respect of private and 2422 in respect of foreign-sector ownership.
b Includes 2492 in respect of private and 2676 in respect of foreign-sector ownership.
c The Post-Office Savings Bank is a public institution whilst the Trustee Savings Bank is a mutual one. The figures as aggregated are from the central bank statistics. We have no breakdown for 1988.

Figures for the state development banks are not included in this table. We estimate that they probably accounted for less than 5% of total assets in 1988.

more on merchant banking activities. They undertake syndicated and corporate lending, foreign-exchange and money-market dealing, deposit-taking, and a range of fee-income services including investment management and mergers and acquisitions business. The smaller banks tend to concentrate on retail rather than wholesale business and provide retail deposit-taking, chequing facilities and consumer lending. Industrial banks accounted for nearly 9 per cent of total banking sector assets in 1988 and they are institutions that specialize in providing instalment finance for the purchase of consumer durables, leasing finance, export/import finance and types of term lending to industry. Four of the industrial banks are wholly-owned subsidiaries of the associated banks and they all compete with their parents in the retail deposits market.

The third major category of institution is the building societies. In 1988 they accounted for 12.8 per cent of total banking sector assets, and they are the most important providers of mortgage finance for housing. They have traditionally taken deposits for the purpose of mortgage lending and they held 20 per cent of total non-bank deposits in 1988. Irish building societies are supervised by the Registrar of Building Societies and the Department of the Environment. Traditionally, they were not permitted to offer unsecured loans and current accounts, but legislation in 1986 empowered some societies (with specified reserves) to make loans not secured by a mortgage for bridging finance or home improvements. Recent legislation aims to broaden the scope of building society business enabling them to provide more types of unsecured finance.

The savings bank group includes the Trustee Savings Banks and the Post Office Savings Bank (An Post). The Trustee Savings Banks are non-profit-making, state supervised institutions, of which there are about 50 branches throughout Ireland. They are deposit-taking institutions doing predominantly retail business. They on-lend a large proportion of their deposits to the government and provide a limited range of loans, mainly short-term, to the personal sector. The state-controlled Post Office Savings Bank (An Post) has over 1400 branches throughout the country and raises finance for the government from the consumer deposit market mainly through contractual savings facilities.

Finally, there are also two state-controlled development banks which are not shown in Table A7.1. These are the Agricultural Credit Corporation (ACC) and the Industrial Credit Corporation (ICC). The main activity of the ACC is to take consumer deposits and lend to the agricultural sector, whereas the ICC raises wholesale funds and provides medium- and long-term funds to industry.

Table A7.2 Sector ownership 1983–8: Irish banking system

Category	Total banking sector assets Percentages		
	1983	1988	Change
Private	55.7	61.7	6.0
Public	4.2	4.0	− 0.2
Mutual	12.2	12.9	0.7
Foreign[a]	27.9	21.4	− 6.5
Totals	100.0	100.0	−

Note: [a] Mainly UK banks.

Table A7.3   Top two Irish banks, 1988.

	Units	Bank of Ireland	Allied Irish Banks
Rankings (by capital)			
Country		1	2
Europe		63	88
World		148	200
Measures			
Assets	$m	15,626	20,736
Capital	$m	1,254	853
Pre-tax profits	$m	181	220
Pre-tax profits on assets	%	1.16	1.06
Capital/assets ratio	%	8.03	4.11
Pre-tax profits per employee	$	19,561	16,058
Number of employees		9,253	13,700

Sources: The Banker (1989) Europe's Top 500 Banks October, p. 101.
The Banker (1989) World's Top 1000 Banks, July, p. 112.

Appendix eight

Italy

The Italian system is noteworthy for the complexity of its governing legislation and regulations. The 1936 Banking Law sets out the basic provisions that govern the credit sector. Responsibility for the guidance and control of the credit system is essentially vested in the CICR (Interministerial Committee for Credit and Savings) and the Bank of Italy. The Italian foreign-exchange office (UIC) is affiliated to the Bank of Italy, and is responsible for ensuring that foreign-exchange regulations are met.

A fundamental characteristic of the Italian banking system is the legislative distinction between short-term funding (up to eighteen months) and medium- and long-term funding. The former is provided by the commercial banks and the latter (over eighteen months maturity) by the special credit institutions. Banking institutions in Italy may be grouped under two broad headings: commercial banks and other banking institutions, as shown in Table A8.1. A number of sub-groupings can be identified under each of these two headings. The national interest banks have to be established as joint-stock companies that operate throughout Italy. They must be deemed to be of 'public interest' by decree of the President of the Republic, and their by-laws have to be approved by the Treasury Minister. Most of their capital is held by a state holding corporation IRI (Industrial Reconstruction Institute). The three banks in this group operate 947 branches.

The six public law banks operate through 1855 branches, and the largest one is also Italy's largest bank, Banca Nazionale del Lavoro. The capital of these six banks is held directly or indirectly by the government. The 108 ordinary credit banks have over 3000 branches; these banks are established in the form of joint-stock companies and/or banking firms. Some are large banks, but others are essentially local. The co-operative banks are essentially local, but some (like Banca Popolare di Milano) have extensive geographical coverage. These banks are established as co-operative, joint-stock companies; capital (equity) holdings in them are markedly fragmented.

Under 'other banking' institutions the savings banks (and first category pledge banks) are by far the biggest category. They must be recognized by decree of the Minister of the Treasury as corporate entities, and are established in the form of foundations or corporations. They are non-profit-making and engage nowadays in a full range of banking activities. The 83 savings banks and first category pledge banks operate through 3776 branches. The rural (or agricultural and craft-industry banks) are co-operative banks with at least 30 members; they operate primarily at local level, but they carry out most normal banking functions (726 of them operate 1500 branches). The other two small categories comprise a small group of central

251

Table A8.1 Italian banking system: institutional and sector breakdown by assets.

Institutions	Balance sheet total				Sector ownership				Number of Institutions	
	Percentages		Lira trillion		Lira trillion					
	1983	1988	1983	1988	Private	Public	Mutual	Foreign	1983	1988
Commercial banks										
National Interest Banks	13.0	12.8	121.6	147.3		147.3			3	3
Public law banks	18.9	19.1	177.1	218.6		218.6			6	6
Ordinary banks	27.6	19.2	258.1ª	219.9	140.7	44.8		34.4	119	108
Other banking institutions										
Co-operative banks	12.0	12.8	112.8	146.9			146.9		189	169
Savings banks	18.9	22.4	176.8	257.3		257.3			87	83
Rural banks	2.5	3.9	23.4	45.7			45.7		683	726
Central institutions	2.3	2.4	21.3	27.0		27.0			5	5
Postal administration	4.8	7.4	44.2	83.9		83.9			1	1
Total	100.0	100.0	935.3	1146.6	140.7	778.9	192.6	34.4	1092	1100

Source: (i) Italian Banking Association, 1988 year book.
(ii) Revell (1987), *Mergers and the Role of Large Banks*, Institute of European Finance Monographs in Banking and Finance, No. 2, Table 6.19, p. 182.

Notes: a Includes 199.1 trillion in respect of private, 32.3 trillion public and 24 trillion foreign sector ownership.

institutions and the postal administration. The central banking institutions promote the development of banks in the various categories and also act as a kind of central bank for those banks. They comprise the Italian Savings Bank Credit Institution (ICCRI), the Central Banks and Bankers Institution, the Italian Co-operative Banks Central Institutions and the Rural Savings Bank Credit Institution (ICCREA).

A number of special credit institutions also operate in Italy. The basic distinction between short- and medium-term funding within the banking system has resulted in a corresponding distinction between banks authorized to provide short-term, ordinary credit (up to eighteen months maturity) and those institutions allowed to provide medium- and long-term credit. A distinction is then made between '*credito mobiliare*', '*credito immobiliare*', 'public work credit' and 'credit for agriculture and fisheries'. Specialized institutions or departments of commercial banks are active in the provision of each specific form of these special credits.

Table A8.2 Sector ownership 1983 to 1988: Italian banking system.

Category	Total banking sector assets Percentages		Change
	1983	1988	
Private	21.4	12.3	−9.1
Public	60.4	67.9	7.5
Mutual	15.6	16.8	1.2
Foreign	2.6	3.0	0.4
Totals	100.0	100.0	-

Table A8.3 Top five Italian banks, 1988.

	Units	Istituto Bancario Sao Paolo	Monte dei Paschi di Siena	Cariplo	Banca Nazionale del Lavoro	Banca Commerciale Italiana
Rankings (by capital)						
Country		1	2	3	4	5
Europe		18	19	20	23	25
World		39	43	44	48	55
Measures						
Assets	$m	103,105	66,560	54,131	87,729	62,700
Capital	$m	4,075	3,625	3,504	3,352	3,178
Pre-tax profits	$m	1,048	543	823	211	484
Pre-tax profits on assets	%	1.02	0.82	1.52	0.24	0.77
Capital/assets ratio	%	3.95	5.45	6.47	3.82	5.07
Pre-tax profits per employee	$	54,737	28,605	73,944	7,883	23,009
Number of employees		19,146	18,983	11,130	26,766	21,035

Sources: *The Banker* (1989) Europe's Top 500 Banks, October, p. 107.
 The Banker (1989) World's Top 1000 Banks, July, p. 119.

Appendix nine

Luxembourg

The Luxembourg Monetary Institute (Institut Monétaire Luxembourgeois, IML) was established in May 1983, its main purpose being to regulate the financial centre and to execute monetary policy. It performs functions similar to a central bank. The Caisse d'Epargne de l'Etat (CEE), although originally a savings bank, now acts in all areas of commercial banking, but more importantly as banker to the Luxembourg Treasury. It is the only financial institution which is controlled by state law, and the government uses the CEE to influence the financial markets. The CEE also acts as a clearing house for transactions undertaken on the Luxembourg Stock Exchange. The IML supervises all credit institutions, whether banks or non-banks. It also supervises investment funds, fiduciary representatives and professional depositors of securities, as well as the public offerings and sales of securities.

Table A9.1 shows the total balance-sheet size for the Luxembourg banking system. The official statistics do not provide any formal breakdown. Banks in Luxembourg can be grouped into two categories, domestic and foreign. These banks undertake a broad mix of business activities, and no distinction is made between commercial, investment and merchant banking. By the end of 1988 out of the 143 banks operating in Luxembourg only 15 were of wholly Luxembourg/Belgian origin, the remaining 128 were foreign-owned. Of the domestic banks the state-owned savings bank, the CEE is the most important. Banque Générale du Luxembourg (BGL), Banque Internationale à Luxembourg (BIL) and Kredietbank SA Luxembourgeoise (KBL) are the three main other domestic banks that have significant branch networks and provide a wide range of services including international banking. These banks raise their funds predominantly from domestic and Belgian residents and also through the interbank markets. They undertake various types of lending ranging from overdraft

Table A9.1 Luxembourg banking system: institutions.

	Balance-Sheet Totals (Francs billion)		Number of Institutions	
Institutions	1986	1988	1986	1988
Banks	8007	9938	122	143

Source: OECD 1988, *Bank Profitability, Statistical Supplement, Financial Statement of Banks* 1982–86, p. 51.
Note: At 30 June 1988 only 19 banks were of wholly Luxembourg/Belgian origin. 124 banks had their origins in countries other than these two. Over 85% of the balance-sheet totals are denominated in foreign currencies.

255

finance to medium- to long-term loans to industry. In addition, they undertake widespread Eurobanking business. Approximately 60 per cent of the domestic commercial market is controlled by the aforementioned banks, and the remainder is held by some smaller institutions such as the agricultural co-operatives as well as branches of mainly French banks which were the first foreign banks to establish in Luxembourg.

The majority of banks in Luxembourg are foreign or Eurobanks. Foreign banks initially entered Luxembourg with the growth of the Eurobond and Eurocurrency markets. Luxembourg's favourable tax regime and holding company legislation also helped promote the Duchy as an international banking centre. Initially, foreign banks concentrated in the Eurobond and syndicated markets, but nowadays they operate in most areas of international banking; local business is undertaken only by the domestic banks. The majority of the Eurobanks' assets and liabilities are denominated in currencies other than Luxembourg and Belgian francs and these are strongly concentrated on OECD member country currencies. Over 70 per cent of Eurodeposits in Luxembourg banks come from member countries of the European Community; it is also estimated that Luxembourg's banking institutions maintain somewhere in the region of 8 per cent of all Eurocurrency deposits.

There are also a small number of specialist banks operating in the Luxembourg market. This group includes the consumer credit institutions, the Central Agricultural Co-operative Bank (Caisse Centrale Raiffeisen) and the National Credit and Investment Company. The consumer credit institutions offer hire-purchase facilities for consumers, a type of business that is not usually offered by the banks. Nevertheless, banks either own or have a controlling interest in these organizations. The Central Agricultural Co-operative, whose members are predominantly individuals involved in the agricultural industry, offers preferential lending facilities to its clients. Finally, the National Credit and Investment Company (a public group) concentrates on medium- to long-term lending to industry, export credits, guarantees and equity participation. Sectoral data were unavailable and so no sectoral breakdown, as with the other European countries, can be provided.

Table A9.2 Top five Luxembourg banks, 1988.

	Units	BCCI	Caisse d'Epargne	Générale du Luxembourg	International Luxembourg	BAII Group
Rankings (by capital)						
Country		1	2	3	4	5
Europe		83	201	226	244	252
World		192	459	527	560	578
Measures						
Assets	$m	20,638	8,965	10,311	11,476	5,394
Capital	$m	886	311	252	229	218
Pre-tax profits	$m	47	38	59	69	12
Pre-tax profits on assets	%	0.23	0.42	0.57	0.60	0.22
Capital/assets ratio	%	4.29	3.47	2.44	2.00	4.04
Pre-tax profits per employee	$	3,336	26,704	34,994	32,153	20,906
Number of employees		14,090	1,423	1,686	2,146	574

Sources: *The Banker* (1989) Europe's Top 500 Banks, October, p. 110.
   The Banker (1989) World's Top 1000 Banks, July, p. 130.

Appendix ten

Netherlands

De Nederlandsche Bank is the nationalized central bank of the Netherlands. It is charged with conducting monetary policy, and supervises the banking system.

The institutional breakdown of the Netherlands' banking system is shown in Table A10.1. This shows that by far the most important category of banks are the universal or, as they are sometimes called, commercial banks. Their share of banking sector assets increased from 66.1 per cent in 1983 to 72.1 per cent in 1988. The majority of these banks are private institutions and foreign banks are estimated to account for around 18 per cent of the universal bank sector. Only one bank in this category is not wholly private, the Nederlandsche Middenstonsbank in which the state has a minority holding. Two banks dominate this sector, Algemene Bank Nederland (ABN) and Amsterdam-Rotterdam Bank (AMRO). A proposed merger between these banks was announced in early 1990. The new bank will be the largest in the Netherlands and will comprise 40 per cent of total banking sector assets. It is estimated that it will control around two-thirds of trades on the domestic bourse, will dominate lending to the corporate sector and will be the largest provider of consumer credit.

The universal banks provide a broad variety of financial services ranging from commercial and investment banking to stockbroking and insurance business. AMRO concentrates mainly on the domestic market whereas ABN has substantial overseas interests. The larger banks offer all the usual credit facilities to the business sector: overdrafts, short-term and medium-term loans (up to 10 years), leasing and factoring services. They also provide cheap credits to small business, especially to firms operating in the retail sector. The banks' consumer lending ranges from overdraft facilities to house finance loans. Funding comes mainly from time and savings deposits as well as resources raised in the wholesale markets.

An important service provided by all the banks is the bank giro transfer system, whereby account holders can transfer funds to another institution's account by making use of pre-printed transfer forms, which are not negotiable instruments but only paying orders to the bank concerned. The banks co-operate in an administrative (clearing) centre, the Banks' Clearing Institution, where interbank transactions are processed. Banks also issue cheque guarantees and Eurocheques to their retail account holders. In addition, these banks undertake wide-ranging securities business for their clients and on their own account, foreign-exchange activities and trustee business.

The rabobanks were originally established as co-operative societies to provide savings and credit facilities for the agricultural community. They are still organized

Table A10.1 Netherlands banking system: institutional and sector breakdown by assets.

Institutions	Balance sheet total				Sector ownership				Number of Institutions	
	Percentages		Guilders billion		Guilders billion					
	1983	1988	1983	1988	Private	Public	Mutual	Foreign[b]	1983	1988
Commercial banks								97.0	80	85
Universal banks	66.1	72.1	420.4[a]	538.7	441.7		90.7		1	1
Rabobanks	18.6	12.2	118.3	90.7						
Other banking institutions										
Postbank	7.1	8.1	45.5	60.6		60.6			1	1
Mortgage banks	3.2	2.0	20.3	15.0	15.0				6	8
General savings banks	4.9	5.5	31.5	40.7			40.7		40	55
Security credit institutions	0.1	0.1	0.8	0.8	0.8				22	19
Total	100.0	100.0	636.8	746.5	457.5	60.6	131.4	97.0	150	169

Source: (i) *De Nederlandsche Bank Quarterly Bulletin* 1988, no. 4, Table 1.2, pp. 4–7.
(ii) Revell (1987), *Mergers and the Role of Large Banks*, Institute of European Finance Monographs in Banking and Finance, No. 2, Table 6.1, p. 194.

Notes: a This figure is split between 348.4 in respect of private and 68.0 in foreign sector ownership.
b Revell (1987) provides an estimate for foreign bank assets in 1983. We are unable to provide an accurate estimate for 1988. Foreign bank assets are included in the private category. The Nederlandsche Bank *Annual Report* (1987, pp. 106–7) states that foreign banks' subsidiaries (of which there are 43) accounted for 20.1% of all universal bank lending. They had 29.2% of foreign lending and 13.5% of domestic banking.

on a co-operative basis and their central bank institution is known as the Co-operative Centrale Raiffeisin Boerenleenbank or Rabobank Nederland. At the beginning of 1988 there were over 900 local banks. The rabobanks' share of Dutch banking sector assets substantially declined between 1983 and 1988, from 18.6 to 12.2 per cent. The co-operative banks offer a similar range of services to those of their universal bank competitors, although traditionally their emphasis has been on banking to the retail and small business sector. In recent years they have directed their services more towards larger corporate clients. Nevertheless, retail deposits account for around 45 per cent of their total funds and it is estimated that this sector controls somewhere in the region of 40 per cent of the Dutch savings market.

Up to 1 January 1986 the Postbank operated as two separate institutions, the Postal Giro Service and the Post Office savings institution. The latter traditionally provided savings facilities for retail customers but recently, under the aegis of the Postbank, it has become more active in the mortgage lending and consumer credit market. The Postbank is gradually offering a wider range of services more akin to those of the commercial banks.

By 1988 over 50 independent savings banks in the Netherlands accounted for just over 5 per cent of total banking sector assets. These institutions have traditionally provided a rather limited range of services to the retail sector, concentrating on deposit-taking and mortgage finance. They have recently obtained permission from the central bank to offer commercial loans.

The Dutch market has a variety of other financial institutions which include mortgage banks, whose activities concentrate on the financing and, to a lesser extent, on the developing of real estate projects. The largest of these mortgage banks are controlled by banks or insurance companies. The market also includes security credit institutions (stockbrokers operating in the Dutch market who attract deposits and lend against securities), venture-capital institutions (Particulive Participatie Maatschappij) and finance houses which are mostly owned by banks and insurance companies.

Table A10.2 Sector ownership 1983–8: Netherlands banking system.

| Category | Total banking sector assets Percentages | | Change |
	1983	1988	
Private	58.7	61.2	2.5
Public	7.1	8.1	1.0
Mutual	23.5	17.7	−5.8
Foreign	10.7	13.0	2.3
Totals	100.0	100.0	-

Table A10.3 Top five Netherlands banks, 1988.

	Units	Rabobank	Algemene Bank	Amsterdam -Rotterdam Bank	NMB Bank	Postbank
Rankings (by capital)						
Country		1	2	3	4	5
Europe		14	27	28	56	66
World		30	58	61	126	155
Measures						
Assets	$m	80,808	85,176	84,072	43,307	34,103
Capital	$m	4,666	3,130	2,961	1,390	1,176
Pre-tax profits	$m	573	417	407	203	210
Pre-tax profits on assets	%	0.71	0.49	0.48	0.47	0.62
Capital/assets ratio	%	5.77	3.67	3.52	3.21	3.45
Pre-tax profits per employee	$	17,259	13,636	17,545	17,231	19,588
Number of employees		33,200	30,580	23,198	11,781	10,721

Sources: *The Banker* (1989) Europe's Top 500 Banks, October, p. 111.
         The Banker (1989) World's Top 1000 Banks, July, p. 131.

Appendix eleven
Norway

The Norges Bank is charged in law with promoting an efficient payments system and it implements government policy with regards to the monetary system. Another body, the Banking, Insurance and Securities Commission (BISC), is entrusted with the public inspection of banks and their supervision.

The *Yearbook of Nordic Statistics* (1986) notes the similarity that exists between the credit market institutions of the Nordic countries. Table A11.1 summarizes the institutional breakdown of the Norwegian banking sector. The commercial and savings banks comprise the bulk of the banking sector, and the three largest banks – Den Norske Creditbank, Bergen Bank and Christiana Bank together with the ABC Bank, the largest savings bank – dominate (about 60 per cent of) this part of the banking sector. The 28 commercial banks and 158 savings banks provide a broad range of consumer and corporate banking products and services.

Banks like the Norwegian State Housing Bank and the State Bank for Agriculture are used by the government to achieve specific economic and social policies. Loans for these latter kinds of institution are offered at subsidized rates of interest. There are 8 state-owned banks in Norway. Although the Post Office Savings Bank is part of the Postal Services, it is managed as a separate business with separate accounts. Loan facilities are limited, but savings accounts and current accounts are available at all Post Office branches. Foreign banks have been active in the financing of activities associated with North Sea oil exploitation and shipping finance, and they were allowed to open branches in Norway in 1985. (Although we have no official estimates figures from the Norwegian Bankers Association suggest that foreign banks accounted for approximately 2.6 per cent of the total assets of all commercial banks in Norway at the end of 1988.)

The loan associations are largely funded by issuing bearer bonds. They lend primarily to companies that are not large enough to raise capital directly from the bond market. These associations are employed (through a system of government quotas) to channel funds towards specific industry sectors. The private finance companies are similar to the banks in many respects. Unlike the state banks, they largely finance their lending activities by raising loans. These funds are raised from a wide variety of depositors.

Table A11.1 Norwegian banking system: institutional and sector breakdown by assets.

Institutions	Balance sheet total				Sector ownership				Number of Institutions	
	Percentages		Kroner billion			Kroner billion				
	1983	1988	1983	1988	Private	Public	Mutual	Foreign	1983	1988
Commercial Banks	31.8	35.3	147.9	393.4	393.4				20	28
Other banking institutions										
Savings banks	21.8	24.4	101.6	271.5			271.5		253	158
State banks	25.7	14.4	119.7	160.7		160.7			8	7
Postal Giro	3.1	2.9	14.2	32.3		32.3			1	1
Post Office Savings Bank	2.8	2.5	12.9	28.2		28.2			1	1
Loans associations	11.3	14.6	52.8	162.2		162.2			15	15
Private finance company	3.5	5.9	16.2	65.4	65.4				61	76
Total	100.0	100.0	465.3	1113.7	458.8	221.2	433.7		359	286

Sources: (i) Norges Bank: *Economic Bulletin* (1985) vol. 5, Tables 5–9, 12 and 13.
(ii) Norges Bank: *Economic Bulletin* (1989) vol. 1, Tables 5–9, 12 and 13, pp. 62–6.
(iii) *Norwegian Bankers' Association Financial Review*, 1989, no. 3, p. 12.

Table A11.2 Sector ownership 1983–8: Norwegian banking system.

Category	Total banking sector assets Percentages		
	1983	1988	Change
Private	35.3	41.2	5.9
Public	31.5	19.9	−11.6
Mutual	33.2	38.9	5.7
Foreign	–	–	–
Totals	100.0	100.0	–

Table A11.3 Top five Norwegian banks, 1988.

	Units	Christiana	Bergen Bank	Den Norske Credietbank	Fokers	Union Bank of Norway
Rankings (by capital)						
Country		1	2	3	4	5
Europe		128	166	174	269	300
World		297	378	403	610	670
Measures						
Assets	$m	6,320	16,239	15,633	4,850	7,360
Capital	$m	522	401	375	203	175
Pre-tax profits	$m	18	29	(132)	(16)	(23)
Pre-tax profits on assets	%	0.28	0.18	(0.84)	(0.33)	(0.31)
Capital/assets ratio	%	8.7	2.47	2.40	4.19	2.38
Pre-tax profits per employee	$	15,734	8,696	(25,696)	(6,525)	(10,222)
Number of employees		1,144	3,335	5,345	2,452	2,250

Sources: *The Banker* (1989) Europe's Top 500 Banks, October, p. 111.
The Banker (1989) World's Top 1000 Banks, July, p. 131.
Note: Figures in parentheses represent losses.

Appendix twelve

Portugal

Banco de Portugal, as the central bank, has the responsibility of undertaking monetary and financial policy in accordance with the macroeconomic policy guidelines issued by the government. The central bank has been a state institution since 1974, and since 1975 it has been legally empowered as the supervisory body for all banking institutions.

Table A12.1 provides a broad breakdown of the institutions operating in the Portuguese banking system at the end of 1988. Banks can be classified into two categories: commercial banks and special credit institutions. By 1988 there were 22 commercial banks operating in Portugal of which 9 are state-controlled, 3 were private domestic banks and the remaining 10 were foreign. The state-controlled banks dominate the commercial banking sector, having nationwide branch networks and offering a broad range of services. By the end of 1988 they controlled over 54 per cent of total banking sector assets. They offer cheque deposits as well as time and savings deposits, raise funds in the interbank markets, are predominantly engaged in short-term lending, invest in securities and undertake foreign-exchange transactions. The private sector commercial banks accounted for 6 per cent of banking sector assets in 1988. Until quite recently time deposits with the commercial banks could not exceed maturities of longer than one year. The foreign-owned banks tend to offer limited (fee-based) wholesale services and account for just over 4 per cent of banking sector assets.

There is also a wide range of special credit institutions that operate in the Portuguese banking sector. Table A12.1 shows that this group increased their share of total banking sector assets from 30.6 per cent in 1980 to 35.5 per cent in 1988. The group includes Portugal's largest banking institution, the Caixa General de Depositos, which is a government-owned credit institution. Its main source of funds comes from retail savings deposits and it is the most important provider of credit for private and public investment. In addition, this category also includes investment banks, which specialize in medium- and long-term credit to industry; Creditor Predial Portugues, an institution specializing in mortgage credit; 13 savings banks and the Postal Savings Bank; and, finally, various agricultural credit co-operatives.

Unfortunately it is not possible to provide a breakdown of the sectoral features in 1980 and 1988 of the Portuguese banking system because no data were available for 1980. Table A12.2 shows the sectoral breakdown for 1988.

Table A12.1 Portuguese banking system: institutional and sector breakdown by assets.

Institutions	Balance sheet total				Sector ownership				Number of Institutions	
	Percentages		Escudos billion		Escudos billion					
	1980	1988	1980	1988	Private	Public	Mutual	Foreign	1980	1988
Commercial banks	69.4	64.5	1174.2	5548.0	510.2	4672.4		365.5	na.	22
Other banking institutions										
Special credit institutions	30.6	35.5	516.7	3053.7	76.1	2815.7	161.9		na.	5
Total	100.0	100.0	1690.9	8601.7	586.3	7488.1	161.9	365.5	na.	27

Source: Associação Portuguesa de Bancos.

Table A12.2 Sector ownership 1988: Portuguese banking system.

Category	Total banking sector assets Percentages 1988	Change
Private	6.8	—
Public	87.1	—
Mutual	1.9	—
Foreign	4.2	—
Totals	100.0	—

Table A12.3 Top five Portuguese banks, 1988.

	Units	Caixa General de Dépositos	Banco National Ultramarino	Banco Espirito Santo	Banco Totta & Azores	Banco Português do Atlantico
Rankings (by capital)						
Country		1	2	3	4	5
Europe		94	298	339	373	404
World		135	556	753	747	849
Measures						
Assets	$m	15,615	3,888	6,849	4,526	8,407
Capital	$m	815	176	148	132	117
Pre-tax profits	$m	180	(17)	24	7	19
Pre-tax profits on assets	%	1.15	(0.18)	0.35	0.15	0.23
Capital/assets ratio	%	5.22	4.5	2.16	2.92	1.39
Pre-tax profits per employee	$	17,647	(1,453)	3,610	1,573	2,946
Number of employees		10,200	4,816	6,649	4,449	6,450

Sources: The Banker (1989) Europe's Top 500 Banks, October, p. 111.
  The Banker (1989) World's Top 1000 Banks, July, p. 133.

Note: Figures in parentheses represent losses.

Appendix thirteen

Spain

The Spanish financial system was significantly reorganized under the basic law on the Regulation of Credit and Banking, passed on 14 April 1962. Following directives from the Treasury, the Bank of Spain is responsible for everything that relates to the private banks, savings banks, co-operative savings banks and intermediate money-market houses.

The most important group of banking institutions are the commercial banks as shown in Table A13.1. The latter may be divided into three sub-groups: the private banks, branches of foreign banks, and the Banco Exterior. The private banks are easily the biggest sub-group (around 87 per cent of total assets in 1988) under the head of commercial banks: they account for just over 53 per cent of aggregate total assets of the banking sector. The private banks extend more than 60 per cent of private-sector and public-sector financing in the Spanish banking system and practically all foreign funding. There are 139 private banks (December 1988) and 42 of these are branches of foreign banks. (The number of foreign subsidiaries classified under the private banks category is not available.)

The imposition of geographical limits allows Spanish banks to be distinguished as national, regional and local banks according to the size of their resources and the number of provinces in which they operate. The 1962 banking law also encouraged the classification of banks into industrial/merchant banks and commercial/mixed banks. The classifications are not so relevant today and size (large, medium and small) is probably a more useful classification model.

Foreign banks have won substantial market share in Spain during recent years. Domestically the only real challenges to the private banks come from the mutual sector. The savings banks (*cajas de ahorro*) and credit co-operatives have over 37 per cent of total assets in the system. The savings banks are in direct competition with the private banks and they have practically the same banking powers. They compete with the private banks across almost the full range of banking services; the largest savings banks have moved into international and corporate banking. The savings banks are closely involved with the consumer market and operate through an extensive branch network.

The Banco Exterior is one of two institutions (the other is the Postal Savings Banks) that comprise the public-sector financial institutions in Spain. The chairman of Banco Exterior is the Secretary of State for the Economy and Planning. The credit co-operatives are not so highly developed in Spain as in other countries and they are mainly composed of the rural savings banks. These institutions will be strengthened by the recent agreement between Banco de Crédito Agricola and a large number of

Table A13.1 Spanish banking system: institutional and sector breakdown by assets.

Institutions	Balance sheet total				Sector ownership				Number of Institutions	
	Percentages		Pesetas billion		Pesetas billion					
	1985	1988	1985	1988	Private	Public	Mutual	Foreign	1985	1988
Commercial banks										
Private banks[a]	56.0	53.7	22135	29803	26218			3585	97	96
Branches of foreign banks	4.6	4.5	1797	2515				2515	35	42
Banco Exterior	6.1	3.6	2425	1981	687	1294			1	1
Total	66.7	61.8	26357	34299	26905	1294		6100	133	139
Other banking institutions										
Savings banks[b]	29.7	34.6	11731	19218			19218		79	79
Credit co-operatives	3.1	3.0	1223	1676			1676		146	117
Money market intermediaries	0.5	0.6	181	260	260				41	156
Total	100.0	100.0	39492	55453	27165	20893	6100		399	491

Sources: (i) Banco de España, *Boletin Estadistico*, February, Tables II, III, IV.
(ii) Revell, (1987), *Mergers and the Role of Large Banks*, Institute of European Finance Research Monographs in Banking and Finance No. 2, Table 8.1, p. 225.

Notes: a Includes foreign subsidiaries; in 1985 this group accounted for 1092 bn pesetas.
b Less than 5% of savings bank *assets* fall in the public sector.

rural savings banks. Money market intermediaries shown in Table A13.1 are part of a varied collection of other financial institutions that compete with the banks. These institutions are not so competitive with the banks – many are linked to banks – in Spain as in other European countries.

Table A13.2 Sector ownership 1985–8: Spanish banking system.

Category	Total banking sector assets Percentages		
	1985	1988	Change
Private	53.3	49.0	− 4.3
Public	7.9	2.3	− 5.6
Mutual	31.5	37.7	6.2
Foreign	7.3	11.0	3.7
Totals	100.0	100.0	-

Table A13.3 Top five Spanish banks, 1988.

		Banco Bilbao Vizcaya	Banco Central	Banco Español de Crédito	Banco Santander	Hispano Americano
Rankings (by capital)						
Country		1	2	3	4	5
Europe		17	24	33	45	52
World		38	54	79	104	120
Measures						
Assets	$m	63,340	40,659	27,385	29,462	27,772
Capital	$m	4,138	3,200	2,332	1,703	1,451
Pre-tax profits	$m	1,077	663	352	559	454
Pre-tax profits on assets	%	1.70	1.63	1.29	1.90	1.63
Capital/asset ratio	%	6.53	7.87	8.52	5.78	5.22
Pre-tax profits per employee	$	33,510	27,883	21,333	35,962	25,352
Number of employees		32,140	23,778	16,500	15,544	17,908

Sources: *The Banker* (1989) Europe's Top 500 Banks, October, p. 112.
　　　　　The Banker (1989) World's Top 1000 Banks, July, p. 133.

Appendix fourteen

Sweden

The Swedish Central Bank is the Riksbank. Banking supervision is effected by the Swedish Bank Inspection Board, which is responsible for commercial banks, savings banks and co-operative banks, mortgage institutions and credit companies. Supervision was extended to the collective investment institutions in 1975 and to the finance companies in 1986.

The Swedish financial system is one of the most sophisticated in the world and is characterized by an unusual mix of private and public sector institutions. Table A14.1 summarizes the institutional structure. The banking sector comprises the commercial banks, savings banks, foreign banks and the co-operative banks. The commercial banks dominate the deposit-taking sector. They are universal institutions that provide an extensive range of services to all sectors of the economy. The banks have wide interests covering stockbroking, insurance broking, unit trusts and estate agency.

The Swedish banking system is highly concentrated. The four big nationwide banks account for a large slice of the business of the commercial bank group: they are Skandinaviska Enskilda Bank, PK Banken, Swedbank and Svenska Handelsbank. (It was announced in December 1989 that PK Banken would merge with Nordbanken, Sweden's most profitable bank.) Eleven of the (14) domestic commercial banks are privately owned, limited companies; PK Banken is 85 per cent government-owned. Two of the other commercial banks are the central institutions of the savings and co-operative banks, respectively, and they also play a key role as clearing institutions for payment transfers and the collection of the surplus liquid funds of their member banks. By the end of 1988 there were 10 foreign banks operating in the Swedish market. The commercial banks comprised around 70 per cent of the total balance sheet of Swedish banking institutions in 1988.

The savings banks have close links with the local communities and are self-owned, independent institutions. Although they operate as foundations, they have the same legal rights as commercial banks. A change in the banking law in 1969 allowed the savings banks to compete on an equal footing with the commercial banks and offer the same range of services. Since then the savings banks have evolved into universal institutions similar to the commercial banks. Swedbank, the central institution of the savings banks, is now the third largest bank in Sweden. The co-operative banks were known originally as agricultural credit institutions. Meeting the savings and credit requirements of the agricultural sector has remained their main focus of activity, but their lending powers have been widened since 1969. Foreign banks have been allowed into Sweden since January 1986. On 15 January 1990 the Swedish authorities

Table A14.1 Swedish banking system: institutional and sector breakdown by assets.

Institutions	Balance sheet total				Sector ownership				Number of Institutions	
	Percentages		Kronor billion		Kronor billion					
	1983	1988	1983	1988	Private	Public	Mutual	Foreign	1983	1988
Commercial banks	68.0	68.9	513.2[a]	804.6	502.0	225.7	43.2	33.7	15	24
Other banking institutions										
Savings banks	16.9	17.2	127.3	201.0			201.0		154	110
Co-operative banks	4.3	4.0	32.4	47.3			47.3		392	391
Finance companies	8.7	9.9	65.3	115.9	115.9				220	164
Postal Giro	2.1	-	16.0	-					1	1
Total	100.0	100.0	754.2	1168.8	617.9	225.7	291.5	33.7	782	690

Sources: (i) Sveriges Riksbank, Quarterly Review, vol. 1, (1989) p. 54.
(ii) Bankerna (1988) Tables 1.3, 2.4, 3.4, pp. 18, 46–47, 72–3.
(iii) Revell, (1987), *Mergers and the Role of Large Banks*, Institute of European Finance Research Monographs in Banking and Finance No. 2, Table 6.30, p. 199.

Notes: a Includes 345.9 bn Kronor in respect of private, 123.9 public, 43.4 mutual-sector ownership.

proposed lifting the ban on the foreign ownership of Swedish banks, finance companies and stock brokerage firms while also allowing foreign banks to open branches. These changes came into effect from 1 July 1990.

There are several other kinds of financial institutions in Sweden. The Postal Giro does not engage in lending business, but it is important in money transmission. The National Pension Insurance Fund (AP-fund) was set up to administer the pension contributions that are paid into the supplementary income-related pension system (ATP). There are also a wide variety of special credit institutions that lend to specific sections of the economy. These institutions operate in the housing sector, business sector and for the local authorities. Finance companies have grown strongly in recent years. Security brokers/stockbrokers have also gained market share in the equities market and the money markets.

Table A14.2 Sector ownership 1983 to 1988: Swedish banking system.

| Category | Total banking sector assets Percentages | | Change |
	1983	1988	
Private	54.5	52.9	−1.6
Public	18.6	19.3	0.7
Mutual	26.9	24.9	−2.0
Foreign	-	2.9	2.9
Totals	100.0	100.0	-

Table A14.3 Top five Swedish banks, 1988.

	Units	S.E. Banken	Svenska Handelsbanken	P.K. Banken	Swedbank	Gotabanken
Rankings (by capital)						
Country		1	2	3	4	5
Europe		21	32	41	85	129
World		46	76	93	195	299
Measures						
Assets	$m	46,965	38,658	39,588	38,248	8,508
Capital	$m	3,412	2,510	2,045	867	551
Pre-tax profits	$m	257	597	228	138	106
Pre-tax profits on assets	%	0.54	1.54	0.58	0.36	1.25
Capital/assets ratio	%	7.26	6.49	5.17	2.27	6.48
Pre-tax profits per employee	$	27,225	90,413	45,728	107,060	43,336
Number of employees		9,440	6,603	4,986	1,289	2,446

Sources: *The Banker* (1989) Europe's Top 500 Banks, October, p. 113.
The Banker (1989) World's Top 1000 Banks, July, p. 135.

Appendix fifteen

Switzerland

The main function of the Swiss National Bank is (under Article 39 of the Constitution) to 'regulate the circulation of money, to facilitate money transfers and to carry out a credit and currency policy which serves the general interest of the country'. Under Article 22ff of the Banking Act 1934 (partially revised in 1971), supervision of banks is entrusted to a body called the Federal Banking Commission, which is elected by the Federal Council.

At the end of 1988 there were 630 banks and finance companies operating under the Banking Act. These institutions controlled over 4000 domestic offices and around 100 offices abroad. Table A15.1 summarizes the institutional groupings of banks for 1985 and 1988. It is interesting to note that in 1985 the total balance sheet and fiduciary accounts (off-balance-sheet) of Swiss banks were roughly four times the GNP for the year. Table A15.1 confirms the wide range of banking institutions that operate in Switzerland.

The big banks comprise five institutions – the Union Bank of Switzerland (UBS), the Swiss Bank Corporation (SBC), Crédit Suisse (CS), Swiss Volksbank (SVB) and Bank Leu. The last two belong to this group for historic reasons; the 'Big Three' (UBS, SBC and CS) form the core of the big bank sector. The big banks are universal banks and in Switzerland they have a geographical focus on Zurich. They accounted for nearly 50 per cent of total banking sector assets in 1988.

The 29 cantonal banks are a reflection of Swiss federalism. Every canton and half-canton has its own cantonal bank. Although these banks are set up under Cantonal Law, some of them do not have a Cantonal Government guarantee. The cantonal banks occupy a similar position to the savings banks in the German system, although there are several banks called savings banks under the heading of regional and savings banks in Table A15.1. The main areas of business of the cantonal banks are mortgage loans and working credit for agriculture and trade. Over time, however, most cantonal banks have evolved into full-service banks and several of them have the characteristics of big banks.

The regional and savings banks comprise a group of 217 primarily small banks which operate through more than 1000 branches. They are oriented towards domestic business. The group of 'other banks' in Table A15.1 includes a number of sub-groups with different business structures. This group is sub-divided statistically into Swiss-controlled and foreign-controlled banks. Over 75 per cent (in terms of balance-sheet totals) of this group comprise the foreign-controlled banks. The Swiss-controlled banks are divided into four sub-categories: commercial banks; stockbroking, securities trading and portfolio-management institutions; personal

Table A15.1 Swiss banking system: institutional and sector breakdown by assets.

Institutions	Balance sheet total				Sector ownership				Number of Institutions	
	Percentages		Francs billion				Francs billion			
	1983	1988	1983	1988	Private	Public	Mutual	Foreign	1983	1988
Commercial banks										
Large banks	49.3	49.9	328.7a	483.5	449.7		33.8		5	5
Cantonal banks	19.0	18.6	126.7	179.7		179.7			29	29
Regional and savings banks	8.4	8.5	55.9	82.4			82.4		216	217
Other banks	14.6	14.7	97.6b	142.1	58.3			83.8	189	205
Credit co-operatives	2.6	2.9	17.1	28.1			28.1		2	2
Branches of foreign banks	1.8	2.5	11.9	24.1				24.1	16	17
Special status banks	2.5	2.9	16.7c	27.7	9.3	9.8	8.6		136	155
Other banking institutions										
Postal cheque accounts	1.8	–	12.6	–						
Total	100.0	100.0	667.2	967.6	517.3	189.5	152.9	107.9	593	630

Source: (i) Banque National Suisse *Les banques Suisses* (1988), no. 75, Tables 1.0, 2.0, 2.1, pp. 52–7.
(ii) Revell, (1987), *Mergers and the Role of Large Banks*, Institute of European Finance Research Monographs in Banking and *Finance*, No. 2, Table 6.3, p. 202.

Notes: a Includes 308.1 bn francs private and 20.6 in mutual-sector ownership.
b Includes 29.6 bn francs private and 68.0 in foreign-sector ownership.
c Includes 5.6 bn francs private, 6.4 public and 4.7 in mutual-sector ownership.

loan, hire-purchase and consumer finance banks; and other types. At the end of 1988 the group of 'other banks' included 205 institutions, of which over 130 were foreign-controlled.

The credit co-operatives and Raiffeisenbank comprise approximately 1300 local savings and loan institutions (branch offices), operated by two associations. They are found predominantly in rural regions and concentrate on mortgage, agricultural and small business credits. Together with the foreign-controlled banks (under 'other banks'), the branches of foreign banks (17 institutions with over 30 branches in 1988) form the group of foreign banks in Switzerland. The group of 'branches of foreign banks' in Table A15.1 includes all dependent branch offices of foreign banks that conduct business in Switzerland. Each branch must keep 10 per cent of its assets in Switzerland.

The 'special status' banks include finance companies and the private banks (around 80 per cent of the 155 institutions are finance companies). The finance companies (unlike the banks) are invariably active in long-term financing. They focus on investments and issue transactions, hold participations and grant finance credits. The private banks are the oldest establishments in the Swiss financial centre and concentrate on portfolio management, securities trading and the issue and placement business (non-credit transactions). A noteworthy feature of the private banks is that the owner has personal and unlimited liability for the firm's activities. Other important financial intermediaries in Switzerland include the central mortgage bond institutions, insurance companies and mutual funds.

Table A15.2 Sector ownership 1983–8: Swiss banking system.

Category	Total banking sector assets Percentages		
	1983	1988	Change
Private	51.4	53.4	2.0
Public	21.8	19.6	−2.2
Mutual	14.7	15.8	1.1
Foreign	12.0	11.2	−0.8
Totals	100.0	100.0	−

Table A15.3 Top five Swiss banks, 1988.

	Units	Union Bank of Switzerland	Swiss Banking Corporation	Crédit Suisse	Swiss Volksbank	Zürcher Kantonal Bank
Rankings (by capital)						
Country		1	2	3	4	5
Europe		4	6	13	58	82
World		11	16	28	136	191
Measures						
Assets	$m	110,760	102,466	75,388	22,985	23,176
Capital	$m	6,715	6,055	4,785	1,318	886
Pre-tax profits	$m	728	623	523	104	55
Pre-tax profits on assets	%	0.66	0.61	0.69	0.45	0.24
Capital/assets ratio	%	6.06	5.91	6.35	5.73	3.82
Pre-tax profits per employee	$	34,879	35,646	34,739	17,444	14,706
Number of employees		20,872	17,477	15,055	5,962	3,740

Sources: The Banker (1989) Europe's Top 500 Banks, October, p. 113.
The Banker (1989) World's Top 1000 Banks, July, p. 134.

Appendix sixteen

United Kingdom

The Bank of England is the central bank of the United Kingdom. The supervision of institutions undertaking deposit-taking business in the United Kingdom (with the exception of the building societies, National Savings Bank, local authorities and insurance companies) is undertaken by the Bank of England in accordance with powers conferred on it by the Banking Acts 1979 and 1987. The latter established the central bank's Board of Banking Supervision on a statutory basis and increased the role of auditors in monitoring and reporting, although the Bank's approach to supervision is still quite flexible.

Table A16.1 provides an institutional breakdown of the UK banking system. We have included the building societies sector in the table as they are important deposit-taking institutions, although technically they are not 'authorized institutions' and are not supervised by the Bank of England. Building societies have their own regulatory body, the Building Societies Association.

At the end of 1988, 276 UK and 305 foreign bank branches and subsidiaries reported on a monthly basis to the Bank of England. By far the most important domestic group are the retail banks, which accounted for over 50 per cent of total bank sterling deposits and 24.4 per cent of total banking sector assets at the end of 1988. The retail banks have been known traditionally as the clearing banks because they deal with the majority of the country's cheque and credit clearing.

Six London and Scottish clearing bank groups dominate this sector: Barclays, Lloyds, Midland, National Westminster, Royal Bank of Scotland and Bank of Scotland. The first four, the 'Big Four', have extensive branch networks throughout England and Wales, whereas the branch network of the other two is predominantly in Scotland. Girobank (state-controlled until early 1990 but currently being sold to a building society) was established in 1968 to offer money transmission services through post offices. The Trustee Savings Bank (officially listed in September 1986) and the Co-operative Bank are also members of the centralized clearing system in London. Recent deregulation of the British payments systems, following the Child Report (1984), took effective responsibility for payments and clearings away from the Committee of London and Scottish Bankers and vested it in a new body, APACS (the Association for Payment Clearing Services).

The Big Four London clearing banks (LCBs) offer a wide range of banking products and services to the general public, and dominate the money transmission facilities within the United Kingdom. Their subsidiary companies concentrate on offering specialized services and facilities, many with a bias towards the requirements of their parents' larger corporate domestic and overseas customers. The LCBs also

Table A16.1 UK banking system: institutional and sector breakdown by assets.

Institutions	Balance sheet total				Sector ownership				Number of Institutions	
	Percentages		Sterling billion		Sterling billion					
	1983	1988	1983	1988	Private	Public	Mutual	Foreign	1983	1988
Commercial banks										
Retail (clearing banks)	24.8	24.4	182.7	283.0	283.0				14	17
Girobank	0.1	0.2	0.9	1.9		1.9			1	1
Co-operative Bank	0.1	0.2	1.0	2.2			2.2		1	1
Other British Banks	7.5	6.4	55.5	74.2	74.2				328	305
Foreign banks	52.6	53.3	389.0	617.5				617.5	250	316
Discount markets	0.9	1.0	7.0	11.5	11.5				10	8
Other banking institutions										
Trustee Savings banks[a]	1.3	–	9.6	–					1	–
Building Societies[b]	11.9	13.8	87.2	160.1			160.1		167	134
National Savings bank	0.8	0.7	6.2	9.2		9.2			1	1
Total	100.0	100.0	739.1	1159.6	368.7	11.1	162.3	617.5	773	784

Sources: (i) *Bank of England Quarterly Bulletin*, May 1989, Tables 3.2, 3.4–3.8.
(ii) Committee of London and Scottish Bankers, *Abstract of Banking Statistics*, May 1989, Table 5.21, 5.41, 5.61, pp. 39–43.
(iii) Revell (1987), *Mergers and the Role of Large Banks*, Institute of European Finance Monographs in Banking and Finance, No. 2, Table 5.1, p. 127.

Notes: a The TSB became a public limited company in September 1986.
b Figures for the end of 1987.

dominate the retail and corporate lending markets in the United Kingdom.

The 16 accepting houses (not shown in Table A16.1), all members of the Accepting Houses Committee, form the 'top echelon' of the merchant banking sector. These banks have a special relationship with the central banking authorities, and their sterling acceptances are eligible for rediscount at the Bank of England. In addition to acceptance credits, these banks also provide a wide range of corporate finance and investment-management services. They are heavily involved in the new issues of securities and mergers and acquisitions business, and they have investment subsidiaries that manage mutual funds (unit trusts), investment trusts and large securities portfolios for private as well as institutional investors. Accepting houses and related companies provide a wide range of other services that include leasing, insurance broking, export finance, bullion dealing and the provision of venture capital. There are many other merchant banks which perform the same functions as the accepting houses, but they do not have the same 'special' relationship with the Bank of England. The major non-accepting house merchant banks are subsidiaries of other banks (for example, County NatWest and Barclays De Zoete Wedd) as well as various British overseas banks.

The Bank of England classification 'other British banks' is a 'catch-all' category, which 'comprises all other UK-registered institutions and certain institutions in the Channel Islands and the Isle of Man, which are either independent companies, or controlled by UK companies or by individuals'. By December 1988 there were 305 banks (including subsidiaries) in this group, ranging from British overseas banks, finance houses, trust companies, leasing firms and merchant banks to investment companies. Table A16.1 shows that these banks accounted for 6.4 per cent of total banking sector assets in December 1988.

Foreign banks held nearly 54 per cent of the UK banking system's total assets but only 28 per cent of total sterling deposits (excluding building society deposits) at the end of 1988. They have tended to concentrate on commercial lending, trade finance and trading on the money markets. The US, Japanese and European banks are very active in the UK capital markets, and they offer a range of services similar to those of the UK merchant banks. Japanese banks' share of total banking sector assets increased from around 16 to over 23 per cent between 1983 and 1988, whereas the corresponding figures for the US banks were 13.9 and 8.9 per cent respectively. Japanese banks' assets in the UK now exceed those of the clearing banks. There is also a range of financial institutions known as consortium banks. These are banks owned by other banks, in which no individual institution has a shareholding of more than 50 per cent, and in which at least one shareholder is based overseas. Consortium banks are mainly involved in the provision of foreign currency term lending, predominantly to overseas borrowers. These banks are also involved in syndicated loans and international bond-issuing business.

The other deposit-taking institutions sector is dominated by the building societies. At the beginning of 1988 there were 134 building societies, with total assets exceeding £160 billion, operating in the United Kingdom. The building societies accounted for over 40 per cent of the total UK sterling deposits held by UK residents, compared with 38 per cent for the London and Scottish clearing banks. In fact, building societies have had a larger share of the market since 1975. Traditionally, this group has obtained funds from consumers through share and deposit balances, and used

282

these mainly for financing home purchases. In terms of total deposits, the two largest UK building societies would rank amongst the world's largest 100 banks. The 1986 Building Societies Act extended the traditional role of the building societies, and they are now able to offer a wider range of banking, investment, insurance and non-financial products.

Various government savings institutions also participate in the financial system. The National Savings Bank and Girobank offer their services through the Post Office. The Girobank offers deposits and cash withdrawal facilities primarily for retail customers.

The 8 discount house members of the London Discount Market Association (LDMA), together with two firms of discount brokers and the money trading departments of five banks, comprise the London discount market. The main operation of the discount house is to discount and hold bills with funds borrowed at call from the banks: these bills can then be rediscounted with the banks or central bank. In general, the discount houses act as a buffer between the central banks and the banking system as a whole. It is through the discount houses that the central bank operates as a lender of last resort. Most of the discount houses' funds are obtained through the short-term money markets, predominantly money at call and short notice from the banks.

Table A16.2 Sector ownership 1983–8: United Kingdom banking system.

| Category | Total banking sector assets Percentages | | |
	1983	1988	Change
Private	33.2	31.8	− 1.4
Public	1.0	1.0	0.0
Mutual	13.2	14.0	0.8
Foreign	52.6	53.3	0.7
Totals	100.0	100.0	–

Table A16.3 Top five UK banks, 1988.

Measures	Units	National Westminster Bank	Barclays Bank	Lloyds Bank	Midland Bank	Trustee Savings Bank Group
Rankings (by capital)						
Country		1	2	3	4	5
Europe		1	2	7	9	22
World		1	2	18	21	47
Measures						
Assets	$m	178,505	189,368	93,800	100,849	40,078
Capital	$m	10,907	10,545	5,867	5,499	3,364
Pre-tax profits	$m	2,546	2,517	1,723	1,254	748
Pre-tax profits on assets	%	1.43	1.33	1.84	1.24	1.87
Capital/assets ratio	%	6.11	5.57	6.25	5.45	8.39
Pre-tax profits per employee	$	22,937	21,257	22,973	21,221	17,707
Number of employees		111,000	118,410	75,000	59,093	42,243

Sources: *The Banker* (1989) Europe's Top 500 Banks, October, p. 114.
The Banker (1989) World's Top 1000 Banks, July, p.137.

Appendix seventeen

West Germany

The Deutsche Bundesbank is the central bank of the Federal Republic. There are 11 states (*Länder*) of the federation and each one has its own central bank (Landeszentralbank) and these act as branches of the Deutsche Bundesbank. The Federal Banking Supervisory Office (FBSO) deals with the supervision of banks in line with the provisions of the 1961 Banking Act as amended in 1984. The Banking Act also provides for co-operation between the FSBO and the Bundesbank in the area of banking supervision.

Table A17.1 shows the balance-sheet totals of German banking institutions. These can be classified into two main categories; multi-purpose banks and specialist banks. Multi-purpose banks are full-service institutions, providing all kinds of commercial banking activities and all sorts of business typical of investment dealers, brokerage houses, investment funds and trust companies. Although the multi-purpose or universal banks dominate the German financial system there are also a variety of specialist banks which provide specific functions.

The multi-purpose banks include the commercial banks, savings banks, central giro institutions, regional institutions of credit co-operatives and the co-operative banks. Their combined share of the banking volume of business increased from 72.4 per cent in 1983 to 76.9 per cent in 1988. Commercial banks account for nearly one-third of multi-purpose bank business. This group represents Germany's three largest banks – Deutsche Bank AG, Dresdner Bank AG and Commerzbank AG – together with their Berlin subsidiaries (the big banks in Table A17.1), 164 regional and other commercial banks, 58 branches of foreign banks and 89 private banks. The big banks dominate the commercial bank sector. Typically they all provide a universal banking service. Their operations range from traditional deposit-taking and lending business, trade finance, loan syndication, equity participations, to all types of securities business.

The single, most important type of institution rivalling the commercial banks is the savings banks. These are mainly municipal or district banks operating in specific geographical areas. Their market share increased from 20.6 to 21.4 per cent of total volume of business between 1983 and 1988. In Germany various laws exist governing the operations of savings banks and these are aimed to encourage savings and giro transactions, to provide credit for low- and middle-income households and to serve the financial requirements of local communities. A large proportion of their assets and liabilities are held in the form of mortgage credit and savings deposits. The central giro institutions act as the central organizations of the savings banks.

The 12 central giro institutions (Landesbanken Girozentrale) act as the central

Table A17.1 West German banking system: institutional and sector breakdown by assets.

Institutions	Balance sheet total				Sector ownership Deutschmark billion				Number of Institutions	
	Percentages		Deutschmark billion		Private	Public	Mutual	Foreign		
	1983	1988	1983	1988					1983	1988
Commercial banks										
Big banks	7.7	8.8	236.2	354.0	354.0				6	6
Regional banks & other commercial banks	9.4	11.3	287.5e	455.1	455.1				87	164
Branches of foreign banks	2.1	1.8	64.6	73.1				73.1	58	58
Private bankers	1.3	1.5	39.6	59.9	59.9				70	89
Sub-total	20.5	23.4	627.9	942.1	869.0			73.1	221	317
Other banking institutions										
Central giro institutions	15.3	15.4	470.8	622.8		622.8			12	12
Savings banks	20.6	21.4	633.2	864.0		864.0			592	585
Central institutions of credit co-ops	4.1	4.5	126.9	181.5			181.5		9	6
Credit co-operatives	11.9	12.2	364.8	491.6			491.6		3753	3361
Mortgage banks	13.4	13.8	411.2f	544.8	357.5	197.3			7	38
Instalment sales financing insts.	1.1	na.	34.7	na.					93	–
Banks with special functions	6.4	6.6	197.3g	265.8	66.4	199.4			8	16
Postal giro & postal savings bank offices	1.5	1.5	46.5	61.4		61.4			15	15
Sub-total	74.4	75.4	2285.4	3041.9	423.9	1944.9	673.1		4489	4033
All banking groups	94.9	98.8	2913.3	3984.0	1292.9	1944.9	673.1	73.1	4710	4350
Building & loan associations	5.1	1.2	155.4	50.5		50.5			38	40
Total	100.0	100.0	3068.7	4034.5	1292.9	1995.4	673.1	73.1	4748	4390

Table A17.1 *(cont.)*

Source: *Monthly Report of the Deutsche Bundesbank* (1989), vol. 41, No. 3, Table III.13.

Notes: a   For regional and other commercial banks Revell estimated the foreign sector ownership from 1981 figures given in the journal *Börsenzeistung* (26 February, 1983), p. 11.

b   The foreign bank category does not include those that are categorized under 'regional banks and other commercial banks'. Foreign banks probably account for around 150 DM billion of total volume of business.

c   Savings banks are considered as public institutions in Germany due to the powerful influence held over them by the local *Länder* governments.

d   For banks with special functions, Revell's 1983 split between private and public sectors is estimated: 'on the basis of knowledgeable advice it has been assumed that 75 per cent of the total volume of business of that sector is attributable to the public sector'.

e   Includes 51.0 attributable to foreign sector ownership, the balance is privately owned.

f   Of the 411.2 DM billion, 155.6 is allocated to the public sector and 255.6 to private ownership.

g   In 1983 DM billion was private and 148.0 was public sector.

organizations of the savings banks. They hold the liquid reserves of the savings banks and act as clearing houses for transaction purposes. They also act as the state banks for the respective federal states. These institutions undertake all types of commercial banking activities and compete with the larger commercial banks. Funds are raised predominantly through bond issues and to a lesser extent through the wholesale money markets.

The regional institutions of credit co-operatives (Zentralbanken) act as clearing houses to the co-operative banks, enabling them to provide a universal banking service to their customers. The regional Zentralbanken and their central organization, the Deutsche Genossenschaftsbank, compete with the commercial banks and central giro institutions for universal banking business. The co-operative banks or credit associations, as they are sometimes known, were originally founded to provide banking facilities to their members. They now provide a universal banking service to various sectors, such as the craft industry, mining, agriculture and also to individual members.

There are also a range of specialist institutions. Mortgage banks (*Real Kreditinstitute* and *Hypothekebanken*) provide long-term housing finance and offer credit to public authorities. They raise their funds mainly through mortgage bond and 'communal' bond issues. Their main competitors for housing finance are the savings and commercial banks. Instalment credit institutions (*Teilzahlungsbanken*) offer a range of instalment credit facilities to individuals and businesses. Some of these institutions are owned by domestic or foreign banks as well as major retailing firms. Banks with special functions are either private or public banks that operate in clearly defined areas, such as export finance or bill discounting. The Postal giro and postal savings banks are institutions of the Federal Post Office. They accept deposits but offer no loans, apart from small overdrafts, which can be arranged. Foreign banks also fall into the 'specialist' category as most of their business is dominated by foreign currency and interbank transactions. Other specialist institutions which accept deposits and/or extend credit include the buildings and loan associations (*Bausparkassen*) which provide credit exclusively for housing finance, investment companies (which undertake trust business) and insurance companies (which extend mortgage finance).

Table A17.2 Sector ownership 1983–8: West German banking system

Category	Total banking sector assets Percentages		Change
	1983	1988	
Private	31.1	32.0	0.9
Public	49.1	49.5	0.4
Mutual	16.0	16.7	0.7
Foreign	3.8	1.8	−2.0
Totals	100.0	100.0	-

Table A17.3 Top five West German, 1988.

Measures	Units	Deutsche Bank	Dresdner Bank	Commerzbank	Westdeutsche Landesbank	Bayerische Vereinsbank
Rankings (by capital)						
Country		1	2	3	4	5
Europe		5	16	26	30	35
World		13	34	56	70	81
Measures						
Assets	$m	170,808	129,733	101,331	96,147	91,224
Capital	$m	6,460	4,284	3,133	2,568	2,280
Pre-tax profits	$m	1,816	621	418	178	384
Pre-tax profits on assets	%	1.06	0.48	0.41	0.19	0.42
Capital/assets ratio	%	3.78	3.30	3.09	2.67	2.50
Pre-tax profits per employee	$	33,157	16,337	15,300	23,636	25,972
Number of employees		54,769	38,012	27,320	7,531	14,785

Sources: *The Banker* (1989) Europe's Top 500 Banks, October, p. 103.
The Banker (1989) World's Top 1000 Banks, July, p. 114.

Glossary

AIBD	Association of International Bond Dealers
AIM	Amsterdam inter-professional market
ALM	Asset and liability management
AMEX	American Express
ASAS	Amsterdam Security Account System
ASE	Amsterdam Stock Exchange
ATM	Automated teller machine
AXMI	Amex Major Market Index
BAI	Bank Administration Institute
BIS	Bank for International Settlements
BP	British Petroleum
BPFI	BP Finance International
BZW	Barclays de Zoete Wedd
C&I	Commercial and industrial (loans)
CAC	Compagnie des Agents de Change
CAC	Continuous Assisted Trading
CAP	Capital
CATS	Continuous Automated Trading System
CCB	Contingent commitment banking
CCC	Competition and Credit Control
CCF	Common claims funds
CD	Certificate of deposit
CGER	Caisse Gènèrale d'Epargne et de Retraite
CGT	Capital gains tax
CIBL	Citicorp Investment Bank
CIF	Customer information file
CMA	Cash management account
CMO	Collateralized mortgage obligation
CONSOB	Commissione Nazionale per le Società e la Borsa
CP	Commercial paper
CRH	Caisse de Refinancement Hypothécaire
CSFB	Credit Suisse First Boston
DTB	Deutsche Terminbörse
EBATRS	Electronic balance and transaction reporting systems
EC	European Community
ECP	Euro-commercial paper
ECU	European currency unit
EDI	Electronic data interchange
EEC	European Economic Community (= EC)
EFT	Electronic funds transfer

290

EFTPOS	Electronic funds transfer at the point of sale
ERM	Exchange rate mechanism
EMS	European Monetary System
EMU	European Monetary Union
EOE	European Options Exchange
ERISA	Employment Retirement Income Security Act (US)
ESCB	European System of Central Banks
FCP	Fonds Communs de Placement
FDIC	Federal Deposit Insurance Corporation
FHA	Federal Housing Administration
FHLMC	Federal Home Loan Mortgage Association
FMS	First Mortgage Securities
FRN	Floating rate note
FSF	Financial Services Firm
FSI	Financial services industry
FSM	Financial services supermarket
FTA	Financiële Termijnmarkt Amsterdam
GATT	General Agreement on Tariffs and Trade
GDP	Gross domestic product
GEC	General Electric Corporation
GEM	Gross earnings margin
GEMM	Gilt-edged market maker
GFSM	Global financial supermarket
GNMA	Government National Mortgage Association
GNP	Gross national product
H-INDEX	Herfindahl (index)
HIFS	Household information files
HMC	Household Mortgage Corporation
HOBS	Home and office banking system
HNWI	High net-worth individual
IBCA	IBCA Banking Analysis Ltd
IBF	International banking facility
IBIS	Inter-Banken Informations-System
ICC	Industrial and commercial company
IDB	Inter-dealer broker
IEF	Institute of European Finance
IET	Interest Equalization Tax (US)
IFSC	International Financial Services Centre (Dublin)
IMF	International Monetary Fund
IRS	Istituto la Ricerca Sociale
ISE	International Stock Exchange of the United Kingdom and the Republic of Ireland
IT	Information technology
LBO	Leveraged buy-out
LDC	Less developed country
LIBOR	London Inter Bank Offered Rate
LIFFE	London International Financial Futures Exchange
LTOM	London Traded Options Market
M&A	Mergers and acquisitions
MATIF	Marché à Terme d'Instruments Financiers
MBB	Mortgage-backed bond
MBI	Management buy-in

MBO	Management buy-out
MBS	Mortgage-backed security
MFC	Mortgage Funding Corporation
MMF	Money market fund
MNC	Multinational corporation
MOF	Multi-option facility
MONEF	Marché des Options Négociables et Financières
MSB	Messagerie sécurisée entreprise – banque
MTFS	Medium-Term Financial Strategy
MTN	Medium-term note
NASDAQ	National Association of Securities Dealers Automated Quotations
NATO	North Atlantic Treaty Organization
NFSM	Niche financial supermarket
NHLC	National Home Loans Corporation
NIC	Newly industrialized country
NIF	Note issuance facility
NINT	Net interest income
NIV	Note-issuing vehicle
NYSE	New York Stock Exchange
OATS	Obligations Assimilables du Trésor
OBS	Off-balance sheet
OCP	Office des Cheques Postaux
OECD	Organization for Economic Co-operation and Development
OM	Options Marknad Fondkommission (Stockholm)
OPEC	Organization of Petroleum-Exporting Countries
OTC	Over-the-counter
PBT	Profit before tax
PER	Price earnings ratio
PSBR	Public sector borrowing requirement
PTP	Pre-tax profit
PTT	Post and Telecommunications Authority
PV	Present value
RAC	Ray averages cost
RAROC	Risk-adjusted return on capital
ROA	Return on assets
ROC	Return on capital
ROX	Return on exposure
RUF	Revolving Underwriting Facility
SAX	Stockholm Automated Exchange
SBC	Swiss Bank Corporation
SBU	Strategic business unit
SCP	Structure-conduct-performance
SEAQ	Stock Exchange Automated Quotation System
SEC	Securities and Exchange Commission
SEMB	Stock Exchange money broker
SIB	Securities and Investment Board
SICAV	Sociétés d'Investissement à Capital Variable
SOFE	Swedish Options and Futures Exchange
SOFFEX	Swiss Options and Financial Futures Exchange
SRO	Self-regulatory organization
SWIFT	Society for Worldwide Interbank Financial Telecommunication
T-BOND	Treasury bond

GLOSSARY

T&E	Travel and entertainment (cards)
TLC	Transferable loan-certificate
TLF	Transferable loan facility
TLI	Transferable loan instrument
TMC	The Mortgage Corporation
TPC	Transferable participation certificate
TSB	Trustee Savings Bank
UBS	Union Bank of Switzerland
UCITS	Undertakings on Collective Investment in Transferable Securities (the European for unit trusts)
USM	Unlisted Securities Market
VA	Veterans Association (mortgage loans)
VB	Volume of business
VCFR	Voluntary Credit Foreign Restraint Programme
WACC	Weighted average cost of capital

Index

Accepting Houses Committee 185, 282
advisory services, of investment banks 196
alliances 213
all-purpose banking 5
Amsterdam 129, 148
  as financial centre 156–7
Andorra 162
asset management 67, 68, 75
Austria, banking system and institutions
  222–5
automated teller machine networks (ATMs)
  93, 95, 97, 102, 104–5

balance sheet structures 64–8
  changes 68–71
  of large commercial banks 71–3
  of savings banks 73
bank accounts 93
  overdraft facilities 118
  see also chequing accounts
bank assets
  in Austria 222–3
  in relation to GDP 32
  of world banking system 37, 135
  risk-assets ratio approach 57–8
  see also asset management
bank capital ratios 79
bank collapse 18, 129, 141
Bank for International Settlements 18
  capital adequacy ratios 57
  Cross Report 140
banking systems 1-2
  analysis of change 6–7
  diversity 217
  innovations 4, 49–50
  structural developments 28
  universalization 15
  see also European banking systems
banks see financial services firms
Barings 188
Barre Plan 17
Barre, R. 17
Basle Committee 18
  convergence proposals 55–8

'home country control' principle 53
Belgium 10, 16, 125
  banking system and institutions 226–9
Benedetti, entrepreneurial activities 197
'Big Bang' 147, 170, 189, 199–200
Blunden Committee 18
booking centres 14, 156
brokerage industry 199–200
Brussels, as financial centre 160
building societies 5, 249, 282–3

capital
  adequacy 78–81, 205
  adequacy regulations 3
  risk-assets ratio approach 57–8
capital flows 11–12
  liberalization 53
capital market products 2
capital markets 167
  role of banks 4
  types 168
capital raising 194–6
central bank credit facilities 47
chequing accounts 86–7, 93
  high-interest 93, 94
clearing banks 280
commercial banks 20–1, 47, 84
  competitive threats 31, 98, 99,
    194
  impact of technological developments
    102–6
  in Belgium 226
  in Denmark 230
  in Finland 235
  in France 239
  in Greece 243
  in Portugal 265
  in Spain 268
  in Sweden 272
  in West Germany 285
commercial paper markets 4, 5, 178–9
'common market' 16
  see also European Community
commodities markets 148

competition 2, 4, 36–7, 204, 205
  in corporate banking 31, 116, 119–23, 124
  in retail banking market 5, 30–1, 85,
    98–102, 107
concentration, in individual banking systems
  34, 273
conglomeration movement 31, 34, 190
consortium banks 283
consumer credit 95–7, 102
Continuous Assisted Trading 153
convergence movements 55–8
  within Europe 58–9
Cooke Committee 18
co-operative banks 20, 222, 237, 241, 258
Copenhagen, as financial centre 157–8
'core' banks 19, 32, 33
corporate banking 4, 110, 126
  competitive trends 31, 116, 119–22
  corporate treasury function 5, 194
  effects of securitization 122–3
  historical background 110–13
  impact of technological developments
    124–6
  products and services 117–19
  relations with industry 114–17
  structural changes 114
corporate financing 110–12
  in Europe 113–14, 118–19
corporate sector, assets and liabilities
  11
costs reduction, and technological
  innovation 2
credit, in monetary policy 43–4, 46
credit cards 91, 95–7
credit controls 46
credit co-operatives 5, 20, 35
credit flows 4
  cross-border bank 14
credit institutions
  in Italy 253
  in Luxembourg 256
  in Portugal 265
  supervision 59
credit intermediation 5
credit system, in Italy 251
Cross Report on financial innovation and
  risk 140
customers
  needs 4, 86–9, 93, 98
  pricing packages 93
  unitization of consumer banking 95
Cyprus 162

debt, growth 11
deficit sectors 11
Delors, J. 51
Delors Report 51–2

Denmark 10, 17
  banking system and institutions 230–4
deregulation policies 2, 3, 133, 192, 195
Deutsche Bank, 1992 strategy 14
Deutsche Terminbörse 150, 151
disposable income 11, 12
Dublin, as financial centre 162

economic factors, effects on European
  banking 9–16
economic growth 10, 12
economic policies, market-based 14–16
economies of scale
  and financial centres 145
  and financial supermarkets 216–18
economies of scope 217–18
equity markets 170, 173–4
  see also Euroequity
Eire see Republic of Ireland
'electronic banking' 124–6, 150, 153, 159
electronic funds transfer 95, 97, 102, 105–6
  EC code of conduct 105
employment
  in European banks 37
  in financial services sector 12–13
  in insurance sector 13
equity to assets ratios 79–80
Eurobonds 2, 3, 130, 174, 192
  top lead managers 205–6
Euro-commercial paper 5
Eurocredit 130, 139
Eurocurrency 3, 130, 131
  centres 139
  market growth 139
Euroequity 174–6, 178
Euromarket 189
  globalization of 195–6
Euronotes 67, 73, 117, 123, 131
European banking markets 85
  concentration 34
  non-EC 33, 163
  structural characteristics 32–4
  structure 29–30
European banking systems
  changes in 3–5, 24–5, 39, 218–19
  comparisons with Japanese system 23–4
  comparisons with United States of
    America 24
  competitive trends 30–1, 36–7
  convergence 53–8
  corporate products and services 118–19
  electronic cash management 124–5
  financial conglomerates 140, 190, 191
  historical context 7, 19–20, 130
  internationalization 38
  legal frameworks 30
  market characteristics 81

European banking systems *cont.*
  merchant 187–9
  merger and acquisition activity 208–13
  payment systems and services 102–4
  planning and marketing 6
  regulation and supervision 18, 23, 53–8
  sector ownership 21–2
  strategic management 204
  strategic marketing 207–8
  structural differences 20–3
  structural trends 37–9
  see also individual countries
European Commission
  banking directives 53–4, 58–9
  electronic payments systems code of
    conduct 105
  investment directives 59–60
  mutual definition of listings directive 183
  White Paper proposals on single European
    market 52–3
European Community 10
  common market 16–17
  internal market in financial services plan
    16, 36, 52–3, 192–3, 208
European Currency Unit 17–18, 51, 52
European financial centres 143–5, 164
  implications of 1992 163–4
European Monetary Fund 16
European Monetary System 15, 16, 17, 50–1
European Monetary Union 18, 51
European Options Exchange 181, 182
European stock markets 168–70
European System of Central Banks 52
exchange-rate
  coordination 15–16
  role in monetary policy 48, 50
Exchange-Rate Mechanism 17, 50

financial centres 19, 144–5, 162–3, 164
  small 162
  see also European financial centres
financial conglomerates 140, 190, 191
financial innovation 49–50, 126, 130,
    140–1
  problems 17
financial institutions
  as competition 31, 99
  as innovators 49–50
  compartmentalization 15
  conglomerates 123, 140
  corporate lending activities 120–1
  despecialization 3
  inter-institutional links 3
  liberalization 53
  mergers 3
  monitoring 3
  non-bank 5

non-EC 59
  specialist 5, 228, 233, 239, 260, 262, 274,
    278, 282, 288
financial instruments 67, 117, 131, 141, 195
financial markets 2, 167
  coalescing of 3
  crash 1987 7, 113, 131, 140, 176, 204–5
financial revolution 1, 2–3, 4
financial services firms 7
  competitive trends 30, 36–7
  consumer needs 87, 89
  growth of off-balance sheet activities 77–8,
    81
  organizational design and strategies
    214–15
  securitization 67–8
  services 93–4
  size 214, 215–16
  types 91
Financial Services Organization 92
financial services sector 2
  competition in 31
  economic dimensions 12–14
  role of banks 7
  role of financial centres 164
  specialization 92
'financial supermarkets' 3, 60, 208, 219
  diversity 217
  global 214, 225
  niche 214
  synergy concept 218
financial systems
  bank-orientated 5, 20, 28–9, 115, 116
  market-based 5, 20, 28–9, 115, 167
Finland
  banking system and institutions 235–8
  electronic banking 125
floating rate notes 67, 73, 78
foreign banks
  in European banking system 23, 38, 122,
    133–5
  in London 147
  in Luxembourg 255, 256
  in Paris 153
  in Spain 268
  in Switzerland 278
  in United Kingdom 282
foreign currency business 138–9, 151
France 5, 10, 11, 12, 15, 16
  bank market shares 90
  banking institutions 239–40
  banking product profitability and growth
    85–6
  common payments system 125
  corporate financing 118–19
  electronic funds transfer facilities 105
  financial innovations 171

financial instruments innovations 141
investment banking 189
low capitalization 79
mutual fund industry 9, 241
secondary mortgage market 179–80
Frankfurt, as financial centre 150–2
futures and options market 148, 181–2, 193

giro institutions 5, 233, 285, 287
global banking strategies 140
globalization 1, 3, 130, 133
global localization 122
'global village' concept 1
government controls 1–2, 43
government sector, as major debtor 11
Greece 10, 11, 17, 119
banking system and institutions 243–6
gross domestic product (GDP)
growth rates 9–10
Group of Seven 16

home and office banking services (HOBS) 105
Horizon 1992 16, 18
household wealth and debt 87–9

income statement structures 64–8
of European banks 68–71
of European commercial banks 71–3
of European savings banks 73
industrial countries, cross-border bank credit flows 14
industry, links with banking system 23, 110–11, 114–17
inflation 2, 9
in-house banks 5, 194
Issuing Houses Association 185
insurance companies 5
as competition 99
housing finance 91–2
Inter-Banken-Informations-System 150
interest rates 2, 49
controls 46–7
internal market concept 16, 36, 52
international banking system 4, 37, 128, 130–1, 141
growth of 131–3, 136
historical background 128–30
innovative strategies 140–1
nationality structure 135–7
products and services 137–40
risks 140–1
supervisory re-regulation 3
international debt crisis 131
international financial system 3
capital flows 11–12

convergence movements 55
intermediation 67
International Monetary Fund 18
international monetary organizations 129
international rate differences 1
International Stock Exchange 148, 167–8, 170–1
investment, international 12
investment banking 4, 131, 185, 186–7, 188–9, 202
acquisition strategies 197–9
capital raising 194–6
cluster strategies 206–7, 218
in Greece 245
market environment 192–4
merger strategies 197
secondary market trading 199–202
strategies 190–1, 204–6
investment firms 59–60
investment portfolios, cross border 200
Italy 10, 11, 15, 16
banking institutions 21, 90, 128, 187, 251–4
corporate financing 119
stock markets 172

Japan 5, 10, 116
assets in UK 283
banking system 23–4
growth in international banking 136
international equities market 191
invasion of European banking system 122, 147, 194
joint-stock banks, in Austria 222, 224

leasing 119
lending controls 46
liability management 265–7, 75–6
liberalization policies 3, 14, 53, 59, 157
see also structural deregulation
licensing systems 30, 247
Liechtenstein 162
Lloyd's of London 148
loan associations, in Norway 262
loans securitization 180–1
London
as financial centre 143–4, 146–9, 163–4, 185, 189
clearing banks 281–3
corporate merger wave 197
financial conglomerates 140, 190, 191
London discount market 283
merchant banking 186, 188
size of international banks 132
see also International Stock Exchange
London International Financial Futures Exchange 148, 181, 182

297

London Traded Options Market 148, 181, 182
Louvre Accord 16, 50
Luxembourg 10, 16
  banking system and institutions 255–7
  as international financial centre 155–6
  employment in financial services sector 13–14
Luxembourg Monetary Institute 255

macroeconomic environment and policy 9, 12, 14, 15
Madrid, as financial centre 161–2
Malta 162
Marché à Terme d'Instruments Financiers 153, 181, 182
margin trading 174
market intervention methods 44, 46
market-orientated banking markets 28–9
market pressures, impact on banking 4
marketing
  as banking function 6
  strategic 207–8
Medici Bank, Italy 128
Medium Term Financial Strategy 47–8
merchant banks 128–9, 185–6
  historical background 187–9
mergers and acquisitions activity 196–9, 209–13
Mexico, payments deficit 131
Milan, as financial centre 160–1
Monaco 162
monetary aggregates 47, 49
monetary control systems 4, 44, 46–7
  factors influencing 48
monetary policy 47–8, 60–1
  environment 42–3
  financial innovation effects 49–50
  historical context 43–7
  indicators 43–4, 45
money market funds 3
mortgage institutions 31, 91, 245
  finance 5
mortgage securitization 179–80
multinational corporations (MNCs)
  impact on international banking 130, 133
multinational banking 2, 132
mutual sector banking institutions 22, 23, 89–91, 92, 99, 241
  decline 37

national boundaries, in banking systems 1–2, 4
nationalization programmes 38, 92, 239
Netherlands 10, 16, 125
  banking system and institutions 258–61
  bank market shares 90

monetary policies 48
stock exchange reforms 172
New York, as financial centre 144
non-bank financial institutions 5
Norway 262–4
note issuance facilities 131

off-balance sheet banking 2, 4, 76–8, 81, 140–1
OPEC 14
over the counter markets 182, 205
ownership characteristics, of top banks 34–6

Paris
  as financial centre 143–4, 152–3, 171
  financial futures market 148
payments services 4
payments systems 4
pension fund management 200–2
performance characteristics, of top banks 34
personal sector 84
  debt 11
placement power 205
planning 4, 6, 207–8, 218–19
  cluster strategies 206–7, 218
  indicators in monetary policy 44, 45
plastic cards 95–7, 107
Plaza Agreement 16, 50
political influences, on banking systems development 19–20
portfolio restrictions 46
Portugal 10, 17
  banking system and institutions 265–8
postal banking institutions 89–91, 224, 245, 260, 283
Postal Savings Bank, Japan 24
post office, as competition in banking system 124
price-to-earnings ratios 80–1
private sector banking organizations 23, 268, 272
profitability, of European banks 38
public credit institutions, in Belgium 226
public sector, as major debtor 11
public sector banking institutions 21, 23, 245, 272

Radcliffe Report 186
recession 9–10
reciprocity 4
regulatory policies 14–16, 23, 30, 52–60, 148
Republic of Ireland 10, 17
  banking system and institutions 247–50
repurchase arrangement 44
retail banking 21, 83–4, 89–92, 107, 139
  alliances 98
  competition 98–102

customer needs 4, 86–9
  globalization 139
  impact of competition 85, 107
  in United Kingdom 280–2
  products and services 93–7, 100–1
  profitability 106
  revolution 84
  technological revolution 5, 85, 102–6
retail organizations
  consumer credit cards 91, 96, 97
  financial services 99
re-regulation, supervisory 3, 4, 141
risk-assets ratio proposals 57–8
risk capital 28
risk-management 75
  of off-balance sheet activities 78, 81
  products 181–2
  techniques 3, 76
Rothschilds 188

savings 11, 12
savings banks 5, 20, 73, 74, 222, 226–8,
    230–3, 235–7, 249, 251, 268, 272,
    285
secrecy laws 202
securities markets and business 15, 59–60,
    167, 182–3
  Euroequities 174–6
  in International Stock Exchange 170
  in Japan 23
  in UK 147
  in United States of America 23
  international equities 174–5
  new issues and trading 173–4
  reforms 170–3
  undertakings on collective investment in
    transferable securities 59
securitization 67–8, 81, 131, 139, 167, 176,
    178–81
  as challenge to corporate banking 122–3
solvency ratio 58
Spain 17
  banking system and institutions 268–71
  bank mergers 33–4
  GDP growth rate 9, 10
state-controlled development banks, in
    Republic of Ireland 249
stock exchanges 167–8
  European 168–70
  reforms 170–3
  see also International Stock Exchange
Stockholm, as financial centre 158–60,
    182
structural deregulation 2, 4, 61
surplus sectors 11
swaps 1, 3, 117, 130, 133
  as major OBS component 76

Sweden
  banking system 272–5
  banking institutions market shares 90
  foreign bank entry 133–4
Switzerland 3
  as international financial centre 153–5
  banking institutions 277–80
  bank strengths 141
  stock exchange reforms 172
Swiss Options and Financial Futures
    Exchange 151, 154, 172, 181
syndicated equity issues 176
syndicated lending 2, 131, 139
synergy concept 218

'targeting' 44
  monetary aggregates 47
  of retail services 84
tax havens 162, 164
technological developments, impact on
    banking 2, 4, 5, 85, 102–6, 125–7
transactional banking 122
treasury banking 2, 4, 73, 75
  corporate 5
Treaty of Rome 16

United Kingdom 5, 11
  banking and commerce 20
  banking institutions 280–4
  banking market shares 90
  banking sector deposits 146–7
  corporate banking 126
  corporate finance 115, 116
  employment in financial services sector
    12–14
  GDP growth rate 9, 10
  high-interest chequing accounts 93, 94
  Medium Term Financial Strategy 47–8
  membership of EC 17
  public sector status 11
  secondary mortgage market 180
  securitized financial system 29
  view of Exchange-Rate Mechanism 50
  see also London
United States of America 5, 10, 12
  banking system 24, 129
  electronic banking 124
  foreign bank operation 135
  Interest Equalization Tax 130
  investment banking 186
  merger and acquisitions activity in Europe
    199
  secondary mortgage market 179, 180
  supervision of banking 23
unit trusts 167
universal banking systems 23, 28, 83, 111,
    189, 258, 272, 285–8

venture capital 4

Werner, P. 16
Werner Reports 17
West Germany 3, 5, 12, 16
  banking disasters 141
  banking institutions market share 90
  banking system 286–90
  corporate financing 115, 116

  Deutsche bank strategy 214
  dominance of Deutschmark in EMS 51
  propriety networks 125
  stock exchanges 171
  universal banking evolution 111, 189
wholesale banking 2, 5, 37
World Bank 18

Zurich 164